D1807541

The PDF Print Production Guide
Second Edition

The PDF Print Production Guide
Second Edition
By Joseph Marin and Julie Shaffer

GATF*Press*
Pittsburgh

GATF*Press*

Graphic Arts Technical Foundation
200 Deer Run Road
Sewickley, PA 15143-2600
Phone: 412/741-6860
Fax: 412/741-2311
Email: Awoodall@gatf.org
Internet: www.gain.net

Orders to:

Online: www.gain.net
Mail: PIA/GATF Orders
200 Deer Run Road
Sewickley, PA 15143
Phone (U.S. and Canada only): 800/910-GATF
Phone (other countries): 412/741-6860
Fax: 412/741-2311

GATF*Press* books are widely used by companies, associations, and schools for training, marketing,
and resale. Quantity discounts are available by contacting Peter Oresick at 800/910-GATF.

Dedication

Joseph Marin:

To my father, Daniel Marin, who shared with me all of his knowledge of the printing industry.

To my mother, Dora, for giving me the confidence I needed.

To Keri for all of her understanding and support while I was locked away in our home office writing this book.

To Julie who took my technical writing and made it interesting to read.

Julie Shaffer:

To my friends and family, for never complaining on those days when I locked myself up to write.

To Joe for being such a great partner in this writing process.

And to the designer Joe and I met at a PDF Conference last year, who 24 hours after receiving a copy of the first edition of this book, had it completely dog-eared, underlined, and highlighted. There can be no greater compliment. Thank you.

Table of Contents

Acknowledgments

We saw a need in the market for a book with a clear focus on PDF for print production and GATF*Press* gave us the opportunity to publish one. We want to thank Peter Oresick, PIA/GATF vice president and director, Technical Information, for dedicating the resources needed to produce this book. Thanks to our editor, Amy Woodall, for her expert guidance in the process of authoring our first book; she was always available when we came knocking on her office door. Special thanks to Tracey Ryan, graphic designer, for coming up with such a terrific design for the interior of the book and for the attractive cover.

Introduction

Welcome to the second edition of *The PDF Print Production Guide.* With this edition, we continue our dedication to providing a useful tool for those folks who work with PDF files in a print production environment. Since the publication of the first edition, in the spring of 2003, a lot has changed in the PDF landscape. Adobe came out with Acrobat 6 and PDF 1.5 and the number of PDF-related tools and technologies have greatly expanded. This edition has been fully updated to cover these new tools.

As with the first edition, the intention of this book is to explore problems, solutions, and techniques when using PDF in a prepress or print production environment. We've test-driven every "how-to" discussed in this book, so you can be confident that if you implement any of these techniques into your production environment, it will work. Properly created PDF files can resolve many of the problems commonly encountered with digital files created for print output. We hope that this book provides you with some insight, answers, and resources about PDF for print production that you may not have been able to find elsewhere.

CHAPTER 1

BASICS OF PDF

What Is PDF?

For someone whose only experience with PDF is having seen Adobe's television commercial, a PDF file is a very inviting-looking large white box, wrapped in

a huge red bow. These boxes appear on passing trains, in remote mountain outposts, in classrooms, in offices, and on the lap of a snoring man; in short, they are everywhere. The PDF, says the commercial, is a gift—good to both give and receive.

PDF, or the Adobe Portable Document Format, is in fact a file format intended to represent documents in a manner entirely independent of the application, hardware, and operating system used to create them. Further, a PDF is independent of any output device on which it is to be displayed or printed.

For the gift of PDF, we can thank John Warnock, co-founder of Adobe Systems, Inc. In his visionary paper *The Camelot Project,* Warnock first described

the concept of PDF. "What industries badly need is a universal way to communicate documents across a wide variety of machine configurations, operating systems and communication networks. These documents should be viewable on any display and should be printable on any modern printer. If this problem can be solved, then the fundamental way people work will change."

Warnock and a small team of Adobe computer scientists and programmers then went on to develop this universal file format, building on the foundation of Adobe's very successful page description language, PostScript. Adobe first talked publicly about its new technology, originally called IPS (Interchange Post-Script), at the 1991 Seybold Seminar in San Jose, California. Carousel was the working name for the application that would become Acrobat. Even today, if you look at the file information of some PDF files on a Macintosh using a tool like Resourcerer, you may see that the file creator is still CARO—for Carousel (Figure 1.1).

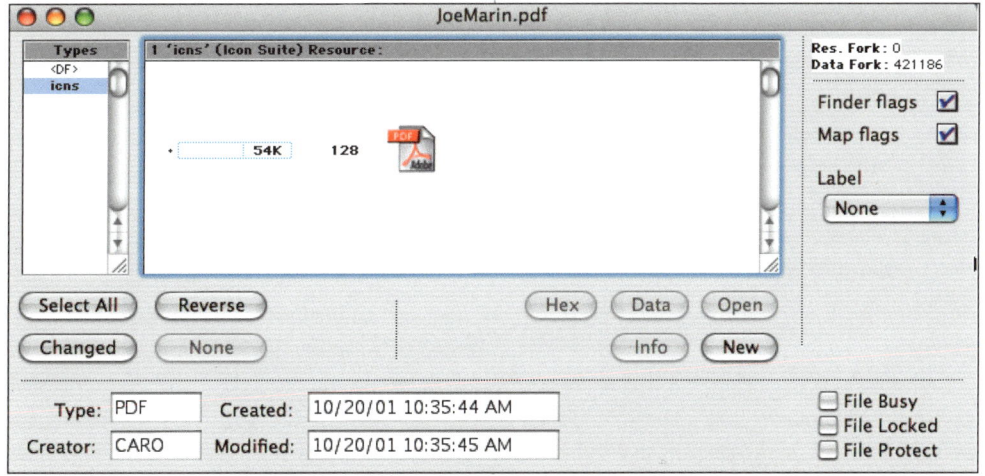

Figure 1.1. Using a tool such as Resourcerer, you can see that the file creator is still CARO—short for Carousel.

Version 1.0 of PDF was introduced at the fall Comdex show in 1992 and promptly won a "Best of Comdex" award. The first suite of tools that would allow a user to create and view PDF files, collectively called Acrobat, was released in 1993. The price of the original suite of tools was steep for the time, with the core product, Acrobat Exchange, selling for $195 and Distiller selling separately for $695. Even Acrobat Reader, that now ubiquitous free tool for viewing PDF files, originally cost $50 for a single license but could only be purchased in minimum volumes of 50 copies for $2,500!

The initial vision, at least as proposed by Adobe's marketing team, was primarily geared toward the development of the "paperless office," and PDF version 1.0 had very little use in the realm of prepress for commercial print production (all images in PDF 1.0 files were converted to the RGB color space, for example). Version 2.0 of Acrobat, and the corresponding version 1.1 of the PDF specification, released in 1994, didn't offer much more for the printing industry, but the primary PDF editing application, Exchange, was significantly enhanced, adding support for plug-ins and the ability to search PDF files. Version 2.1 was further enhanced with the ability to add sound and movies to PDF documents.

It wasn't until 1996, when Adobe released Acrobat 3.0 (and the corresponding version of the file format, PDF 1.2), that the first high-end print options were introduced. Support for CMYK color, spot colors, OPI, and halftone functions now made PDF a potential means for the exchange of digital data between content creators and commercial printers. Acrobat Exchange, with its open architecture, allowed for the development of plug-ins to further enhance PDF capabilities for the printing industry. In 1997 and 1998 vendors like Lantana and Enfocus began to develop Acrobat plug-in tools that helped make PDF a viable format in print production environments.

In 1998 Adobe developed a version of the Extreme architecture specifically for use in prepress production: Extreme for Graphic Arts and Production Printing. Adobe Extreme was actually developed for the digital printing market (IBM was an early adopter of the technology) and allowed a job to be prepared in parallel on multiple renderers, a technique necessary for fast digital printing systems to output one hundred-plus pages per minute. This architecture became the basis for the integrated PDF workflow management solutions developed by Heidelberg and Creo (in a joint venture), Scitex, and Agfa—the initial OEM (original equipment manufacturer) partners with Adobe in Extreme for prepress. Agfa's Apogee workflow and Creo's Prinergy are examples of Adobe Extreme-based PDF workflow systems.

Despite the support of graphics industry vendors, PDF did not gain rapid acceptance as a format for the submission of digital files to printers and publishers. Folks in prepress environments were finding that many of the PDF files they did receive exhibited problems, like missing fonts and low-resolution images, making them worthless for high-quality print production. PDF files began to gain a reputation among the production rank and file as being "probably bad" on sight. There were just too many ways to make a PDF file…and too many ways to make them incorrectly.

Recognizing the need for standardization in the exchange of digital data, CGATS (Committee for Graphic Arts Technologies Standards), a consortium of members representing many printing and publishing companies, began developing such a standard. In 1999 a restricted subset of PDF 1.2 called PDF/X-1 1999 became an American National Standards Institute (ANSI) standard.

Also in 1999 Adobe released Acrobat 4.0, along with the PDF 1.3 specification. The name of the "full-blown" editing application, Acrobat Exchange, was truncated simply to Acrobat, the same name used to describe the full suite of Acrobat tools—initially causing a great deal of confusion. There were a few kinks in the initial release of Acrobat 4.0, especially in the PostScript interpreter Acrobat Distiller, so version 4.05(a) was released shortly after 4.0. Despite the initial bugs, Acrobat 4 provided all of the remaining options that were needed for complete high-end print production workflows. This included things like separation information, ICC-based color, trapping information, OPI 2.0 support, bleed/trim/art box, bleed area definition, file embedding, annotations, PostScript Level 3 compatibility, and the means to define metadata. They even introduced a prepress-specific version of Acrobat, InProduction, which was essentially Acrobat 4 with several plug-ins that extended the capability of Acrobat to allow for preflight of PDF files and printing separations directly from Acrobat. However, the focus on developing PDF solutions for the graphic arts community was short-lived at Adobe, and the InProduction product was not developed beyond the initial version. It appeared that Adobe thought it best to leave support and development of printing industry-specific PDF tools to those third-party developers who had already devised some excellent Acrobat plug-ins for just that purpose.

Adobe introduced Acrobat 5.0 in 2001 along with the corresponding version of the file format, PDF 1.4. Adobe added many new options, but most were not specific to high-end print production. Notable enhancements included a transparency feature (although, at least initially, that was more of a bane than a benefit to the print production community), better printing options directly from Acrobat, enhanced color management features, and batch processing features.

Acrobat 6 Standard and Acrobat 6 Professional, along with the PDF 1.5 specification, made their debut in June 2003. With this release, Adobe remembered the graphics community once again by including some very useful tools (only available with Acrobat 6 Professional) geared toward the high-end print production market. Additions include preflight and previewing tools, and the ability to create separations. See page 10 for a detailed look at the capabilities in each version of the PDF specification.

Why PDF?

While it happened in evolutionary stages over the course of more than a decade, PDF has indeed, as John Warnock predicted, changed the way people work. As a means to disseminate information via the Internet (something which certainly did not exist as it does today when Mr. Warnock proposed his "universal way to communicate"), PDF has become ubiquitous—so much so that Adobe was willing to spend the money on a national television commercial—something unheard of for most computer software products. More than half a billion copies of the free Acrobat Reader have been downloaded from Adobe's website, and Acrobat is one of Adobe's biggest products.

Why has the Portable Document Format become so widely used? Probably because it answers so many of the needs we've had since we've begun creating and attempting to exchange digital documents. First, PDF files are platform-independent, meaning that it does not matter on which computer platform a PDF file was created—it can be viewed on any of the most common platforms in use, including Mac, Windows, and Linux. The exchange of PDF files (instead of native format files) reduce the need for an organization to purchase multiple copies of layout applications, like QuarkXPress, PageMaker, InDesign, Microsoft Office, etc., for viewing and printing graphic-rich documents. For the graphics industry, this opens the door to a much simpler approval process. Once the PDF file is created, it can be distributed to the end user(s) and viewed using a completely free application, Adobe Reader. Now the person who has to stamp that final OK on a corporate brochure, the one who doesn't have any need or desire to have layout applications on his or her computer system, can still electronically view a design file for approval (and, with full Acrobat, he or she could also literally put that stamp of approval on the file, but that's a story for a later chapter).

PDF files, being digital, are also very portable. Depending upon how the PDF file will be used, it may be compressed a little or a lot. The compact file size of PDF makes it the perfect file format for digital delivery of content via the Internet.

PDF files are self-contained. All of the elements that make up a document are built in to a PDF file.

For those of you in the prepress community, this means no more hodgepodge of files to sort through prior to final output, no more jobs coming into your shop with hundreds of different file types. Best of all, the ability to embed fonts within a PDF file minimizes the number one problem with files incoming to prepress: missing fonts.

PDF files are media- and resolution-independent. They can be repurposed for any number of uses including Internet or CD-ROM distribution, kiosk display, or on-demand and high-end print. Since PDF files are digital documents, they can be electronically delivered, virtually free of shipping costs for initial delivery of projects to service providers.

Typical print-related problems can be less likely with PDF files than with some native document files. This is especially true of PDF files created by printing from the native application to create a PostScript file and then interpreting via Adobe Distiller. Imagine a full-fledged PostScript Level 3 interpreter right on your desktop computer. That's what Acrobat Distiller is, and it comes bundled with Adobe Acrobat Standard or Professional. We will talk more about this in the next chapter, but PostScript files can be very, very large. An 8.5×11-in. page with the word *hello*

typed once results in more than one hundred pages of PostScript code. The PostScript file for a single-page ad with a couple of images and an illustration or two can run into thousands of pages of code. The deceptively simple-looking Acrobat Distiller can literally interpret such a file in seconds. Once Distiller interprets the file, it's more likely that the final output RIP will be able to handle it.

PDF files are not always created from PostScript files, however. PDF files exported from Adobe InDesign or saved from Adobe Illustrator are created directly from the native application via the Adobe PDF Library. These, while generally very good for print production, can contain things like transparent objects, which can pose some problems down the production line. More on this in Chapter 6.

Finally, when created properly, PDF files are very predictable. By predictable we mean that when you view a PDF document using one of the Acrobat applications, what you see on your computer monitor is usually what you get when you print. Some of the viewing tools in Acrobat 6, like the Overprint and Separation Preview, along with enhanced color management capabilities, make WYSIWYG (what you see is what you get) nearly a reality with PDF documents.

Meet the Family

The members of the Adobe Acrobat software family, or sometimes just their names, have changed throughout the life of the product line. Today there are several applications available under the Acrobat banner. With more than five hundred million downloads to date, the most widely used member is Adobe Reader (Figure 1.2), the free application that is the lowest common denominator of the entire PDF family. Adobe Reader (formerly Acrobat Reader) allows users to open, view, and print PDF files and not much more. That is, unless the PDF file was served up via the Internet from an Adobe® Document Server for Reader® Extensions. PDF files dished up from this

Figure 1.2. Adobe Reader is the free application used for opening, viewing, and printing PDFs.

server actually activate hidden functionality within Adobe Reader, enabling any end user to fill in, annotate, sign, save, and submit the PDF document. The functionality only exists in Reader for that particular PDF file. This is an entire server-side solution, rather expensive, and is geared primarily toward large enterprise or government organizations that want to collect information from a large audience without requiring that audience to invest in additional software. Most printers won't likely be investing in a Document Server for Reader® Extensions to allow their customers to approve PDF soft proofs with Reader!

Another product, Adobe Approval 5, is the only commercially available, low-cost alternative ($39 retail price) to a full copy of Acrobat. Approval is essentially Reader with some additional functionality enabled. Approval lets the user fill out and save forms as well as apply digital signatures and 128-bit encryption to PDF documents. Note however, that in order to fill in a form using Acrobat Approval 5.0, it must have been created as an interactive Adobe PDF form. One other "low cost per unit" Acrobat alternative is Acro-bat Elements, a Windows-only product geared toward business users. Elements enables PDF creation directly from Microsoft Office products but, here's the kicker, can only be licensed in quantities of one thousand seats or more.

Paper capture functionality is now built into Adobe Acrobat 6, but Adobe offers the standalone Acrobat Capture 3.0 for organizations that need to convert large volumes of paper data into PDF archives. Capture turns a scanner into an optical character recognition (OCR) device that converts captured paper documents into searchable PDF files. Capture is a Windows NT- or 2000-only application and at this time retails for $399.

Adobe Acrobat Messenger, also a Windows-only application, is installed on a dedicated workstation, creating a paper-to-PDF dispatch center. Messenger allows the user to convert a paper document into an Adobe PDF file, annotate it, then distribute it by fax or email.

The core applications in the Acrobat family are Acrobat Standard and Acrobat Professional 6 (Figure 1.3). Either can be enhanced by any of the hundreds

Figure 1.3. Acrobat Professional adds many prepress-specific tools not available in Acrobat Standard.

of available plug-ins that have been developed by a vast number of software vendors. In fact, Adobe tells us that, to date, there are more than 1800 developers of PDF-related products. Adobe encourages plug-in development as it vastly expands the capabilities of the core application. To make Acrobat a prepress tool, one would acquire plug-ins geared toward prepress workflows, such as Heidelberg's Supertrap or Enfocus's PitStop Professional (many of these tools are discussed in detail in Chapter 4). Other plug-ins can enhance Acrobat as a multimedia authoring tool, an enhanced catalog development tool, or a forms creation application.

The core application of the entire Acrobat family is, of course, Adobe Acrobat, now in two flavors, Acrobat Standard 6 and Acrobat Professional 6. Standard is aimed at business professionals and includes all of the features that we are familiar with from the previous version of Acrobat. Acrobat Professional contains all the features of Acrobat Standard and more, adding tools and features geared specifically for creative and prepress professionals. A very short list of the many features included with Acrobat Standard and Professional include adding document security to PDFs; editing text; adding form fields, tags, and accessibility features; moving and manipulating pages within and between PDF documents; searching; exporting PDF to other formats (including PostScript); and saving PDF files. Acrobat Professional 6 includes an entire prepress production toolbox, including a preflighting tool, enhanced batch processing, a transparency flattener preview, separation preview, and the ability to create separations without using third-party plug-ins.

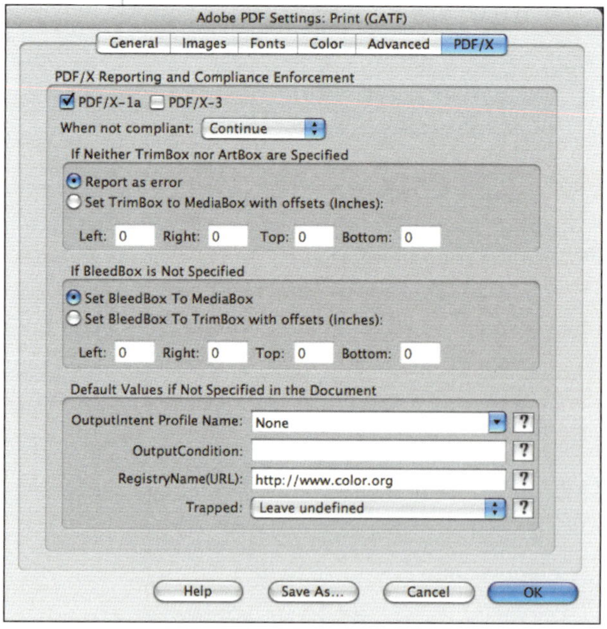

Acrobat Distiller, a full-fledged PostScript interpreter, comes bundled with the full version of both Acrobat Standard and Pro. Each Distiller application is identical with one exception: Acrobat Professional adds a PDF/X tab in the Adobe PDF Settings (formerly Job Options) dialog box (Figure 1.4). PostScript, the initial product created by the then-fledgling Adobe Systems, Inc. back in 1982, is a page description language (PDL) that is generated from just about any application that has a print function. Distiller can be customized to convert PostScript or EPS files differently, depending upon the needs of the user. By using different PDF settings, changes can be made to compression, font embedding, and color management options.

Finally, Adobe offers a subscription-based online service for the creation of PDF files called Create Adobe PDF Online (Figure 1.5). For $99 per year, or $9.99 per month, subscribers can upload files in a variety of formats to the Create Adobe PDF Online server, designate basic job option and security settings, and, after processing, receive back a PDF file. Supported file formats include most Adobe formats, Microsoft Office products, Corel WordPerfect Office products, AutoCAD, text and many image formats, and Adobe PostScript formats. Decidedly missing from the list is QuarkXPress, still the layout application of choice for many design professionals. But never fear, Quark documents can be saved in either PostScript or EPS format, then sent to Create Adobe PDF Online.

Figure 1.4. Adobe PDF Settings in Distiller.

This is a great tool to create usable PDF files, if, for example, you are a service provider and receive a file in a format for which you do not have the native application to open it. Adobe offers a temporary free subscription for the Create Adobe PDF Online service, providing conversion for five files before the account expires. So go sign up and check it out.

PDF Structure

One of the reasons that PDF is such a great format for print production files is that it can describe professional-quality graphics and typography. PDF is based on the same device-independent graphic imaging model as PostScript. This Adobe imaging model is a very simple view of two-dimensional graphics, where graphic objects, like text (glyphs), vector art, or images are essentially "painted" on a page. PostScript files can be easily converted to PDF, then back to PostScript again for imaging.

PDF files can be created directly by applications, like Adobe InDesign, or indirectly from conversion from other file imaging models or file formats, like PostScript. Since PDF files intended for print production are often made by creating a PostScript file and then interpreting that file with a tool like Acrobat Distiller, a brief discussion of the PostScript language might be helpful at this point.

In the early 1980s, John Warnock and Charles Geschke worked together at Xerox's Palo Alto Research Center (PARC) developing a page description language (PDL) called Interpress. Xerox would not release the product, so in 1982 Warnock and Geschke formed Adobe Systems, Inc., intent on developing a means to improve communication between personal computers and printers. The team succeeded in developing what they eventually called PostScript, a page description language that describes all graphics, colors, and fonts in programming code. They developed a relationship with Apple Computers to incorporate their new PDL with Apple's new laser

Figure 1.5. Using Adobe's Create PDF Online resource, you can upload files and convert them to PDF for a nominal fee.

printer technology. In 1984 Apple was Adobe's primary customer, and the following year Adobe PostScript was bundled with the Apple LaserWriter. This truly marked the birth of desktop publishing.

Desktop publishing refers to the creation of documents by arranging text, illustrations, and images within a page layout software application. In order to print a file, this software converts the native application document into PostScript code with the assistance of a PostScript driver (Figure 1.6). The resulting PostScript data is printed through a network to the output device's raster image processor (RIP) for further processing. PostScript is necessary in desktop publishing because files are constructed from many sources, and PostScript is the common language needed to universally print digital files.

Any output device that is PostScript compatible, that is, capable of accepting PostScript data, requires two components: a raster image processor (RIP)

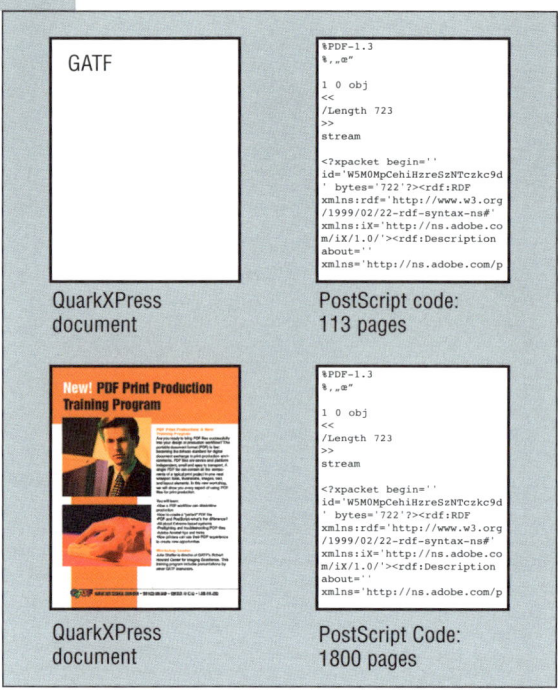

Figure 1.6. The native application document (left) and resulting PostScript code (right).

and a marking engine. A RIP is an application that converts PostScript code into a one-bit pixel file.

PostScript data is rasterized (or RIPed) differently based on the resolution of the target output device. PostScript data intended for imagesetters or platesetters is prepared at a high resolution (typically 2400–3600 dpi, but some systems image at more than 10,000 dpi). PostScript data intended for laser printers is prepared at a lower resolution (300–600 dpi).

The RIP sends these machine pixels to the marking engine (imagesetter, platesetter, laser printer) as a large picture composed of on and off commands, or spots, for imaging.

The RIPing Process

In order to get a better understanding of how Acrobat Distiller works, a discussion on the details of how a RIP processes PostScript data is in order first. When a PostScript file is received at the RIP, there are

Figure 1.7. The RIPing process consists of interpretation (top), rasterization (middle), then screening (bottom).

three distinct processes that occur: interpretation, rasterization, and screening.

PostScript files contain a series of commands that instructs the RIP to render (or draw) objects into shapes. These objects are rendered in the interpretation process into vector graphics (scanned or bitmap images are already in pixel format). In order for the file to be imaged by the marking engine, these vector shapes must be converted into pixels. This is called *rasterization*. Finally, the raster image is screened into halftone (or stochastic) dots for the output device (Figure 1.7).

Acrobat Distiller actually completes the first stage of the RIPing process: PostScript interpretation. A PDF file created by Distiller is a compressed, interpreted PostScript file (Figure 1.8). There are no Illustrator EPS files "placed" in PDF files as there are in native desktop publication application documents. There are no Photoshop TIFF images or any other application-specific type of digital file. Once converted to PDF, all of the elements in the original "page" are boiled down to three things: path (vector) objects, image (raster) objects, and text objects. PDF files can contain much more, but for print production purposes, a PDF file that describes a graphic page is made up of these three types of objects. And these objects are "generic" in the sense that a Photoshop TIFF placed in a layout application will become simply a raster object in a PDF file created from the layout. So don't look for specific file types in PDF files—they don't exist as such anymore once a file has been converted into PDF.

PostScript page description
↓
Acrobat Distiller
↓
PDF
↓
Acrobat

Figure 1.8.

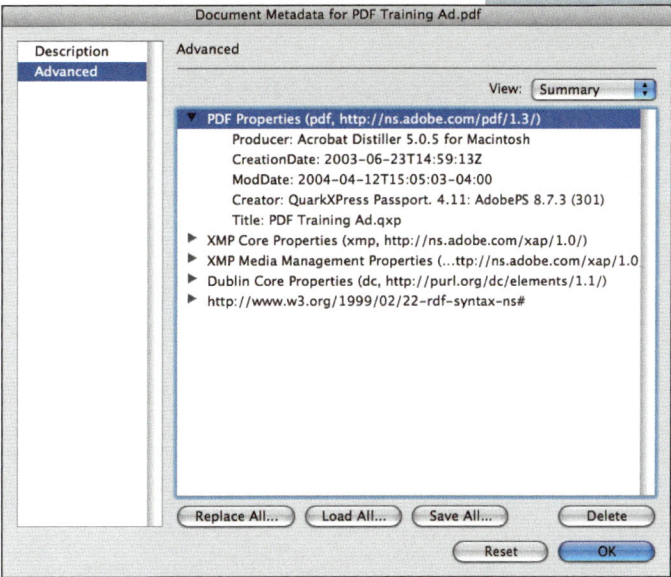

Figure 1.9. Document metadata contained in a PDF can include information such as the producer, creation date, and original file creator.

The relationship between PDF and PostScript is one reason a PDF file is considered so reliable for print production purposes: if a PostScript file (created from a page layout) cannot be interpreted, it will not likely print either! This is why a lot of folks in prepress environments use Acrobat Distiller as a kind of output preflighting tool. They might print a PostScript file from a complicated document, say one with a lot of illustration vector objects, and then use a PostScript interpreter like Distiller to create a PDF file. If the process is successful, they know that the data could be interpreted by a PostScript interpreter. Once interpreted, it is a much surer bet that the file will print, especially to another PostScript printing device.

PDF goes well beyond just describing the contents of a page, of course. A PDF file can also contain many objects in addition to those that can come from a PostScript file, including document metadata (Figure 1.9), or information about the file; job tickets; interactive hyperlinks; sounds; movies; and forms data. In fact, PDF files can act as a container to hold any type of digital file via file attachments (Figure 1.10). Fonts, layout application files, JavaScripts,

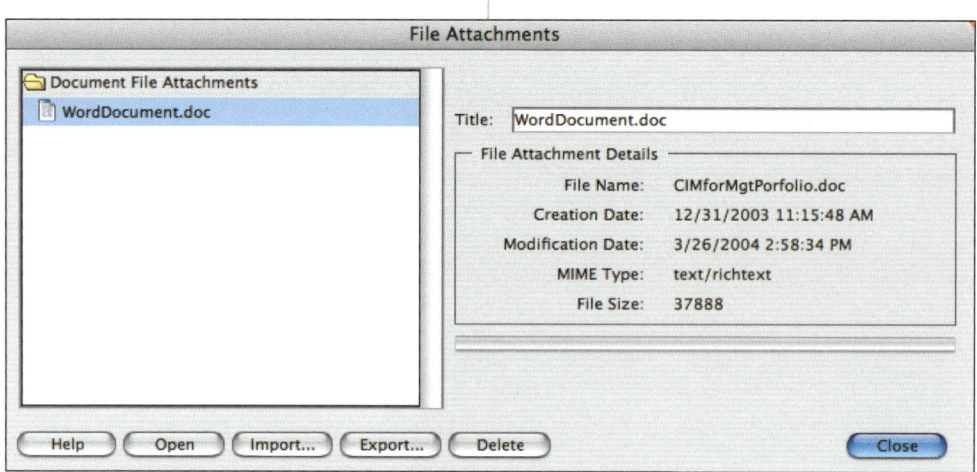

File Attachments

Document File Attachments

WordDocument.doc

Title: WordDocument.doc

File Attachment Details

File Name:	CIMforMgtPorfolio.doc
Creation Date:	12/31/2003 11:15:48 AM
Modification Date:	3/26/2004 2:58:34 PM
MIME Type:	text/richtext
File Size:	37888

Help   Open   Import...   Export...   Delete   Close

Figure 1.10. PDF files can contain file attachments, such as a Microsoft Word document.

PDF VERSION 1.2 FEATURES	PDF VERSION 1.3 FEATURES	PDF VERSION 1.4 FEATURES	PDF VERSION 1.5 FEATURES
• CMYK color space (originally RGB only!) • Spot color support • PS Level 2 patterns • OPI 1.3 support • Device-dependent parameters • Halftone information • Transfer function • Black generation • UCR • Overprint • Stroke adjustment	• Separation information • ICC-based color • Trapping information through job ticketing! • OPI 2.0 support • Bleed/trim/art box • Ability to define bleeds • Embedded files • Annotations • PostScript Level 3 compatible • Means to define metadata (info about the PDF file)	• Transparency • Compression of 1-bit images • Version key for updates • Allows incremental updates • PrinterMark annotations • Added Viewer preferences • Referenced PDF • One PDF can reference another • Better color management function • New annotation methods • Markup & Squiggly lines • Glyph width override • More consistent appearance between print and screen text • 128-bit encryption • Better storage of metadata • XML • Tagged PDF • Logical structuring: headline, body, captions, etc. • Text reflow; spell checking • Conversion of PDF to HTML and RTF (text to MS Word)	• Better compression • Selectively view and hide content • JPEG 2000 compression • Layered PDF • Additional encryption capabilities • Tagged PDF enhancements • Digital signature enhancements

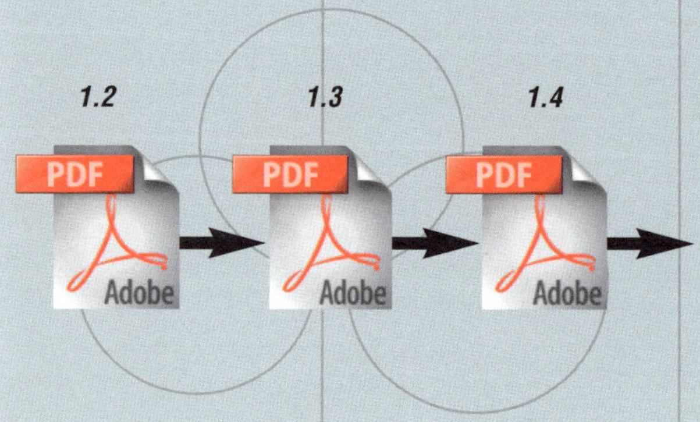

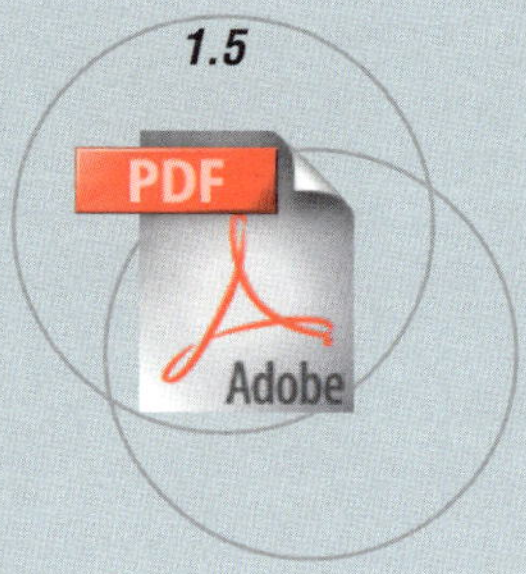

1.2 PDF Adobe → *1.3* PDF Adobe → *1.4* PDF Adobe → *1.5* PDF Adobe

Figure 1.11. A features comparison of the different PDF versions.

even entire applications can be put inside of a PDF document, although they aren't compressed and could make for very large PDF files.

PDF Versions

Just as manufacturers continue to release new versions of software offering added functionality, the PDF file format has also gone through major revisions since it was first introduced in 1991. Each newly released version of the Acrobat application came with a corresponding new version of the PDF file format. So with Acrobat 3.0 came PDF version 1.2, Acrobat 4 supported PDF version 1.3, Acrobat 5 supports PDF version 1.4, and Acrobat 6 supports version 1.5. With each new PDF version comes new features and support (Figure 1.11). Note, however, that Acrobat products have always been backward compatible with previous versions of the specification. In fact, you can still view a PDF 1.0 file via Acrobat 6.0. However, any file created from Distiller 6 in the PDF 1.5 version can only be opened in Acrobat 6 or Reader 6. Previous versions of Acrobat do not support and are unable to open a PDF 1.5 file.

Capabilities that make PDF a worthy print production format came with the introduction of PDF version 1.3. One of those is support of the PostScript 3 DeviceN Operator. The DeviceN Operator allows for the use of several different colors in a single element, such as duotones and spot-to-spot colored vignettes. Also, digital proofers that support more than the standard four-color output (such as six-color or hi-fi inkjet proofers) can take advantage of the DeviceN Operator to produce a wider gamut of colors.

Another feature added to PDF version 1.3 was support for smooth shading. Prior to the release of PostScript Level 3 and Acrobat 4.0, a PDF would contain a blend similar to that in the original application. Blends in QuarkXPress or PageMaker, for example, are created by a multitude of lines or boxes that were offset slightly with slightly different colors. What appears on output is a blend created by up to 256 overlapping boxes (Figure 1.12). The problem with this was that, in many cases, the gradient couldn't be smoothly defined with these boxes, and

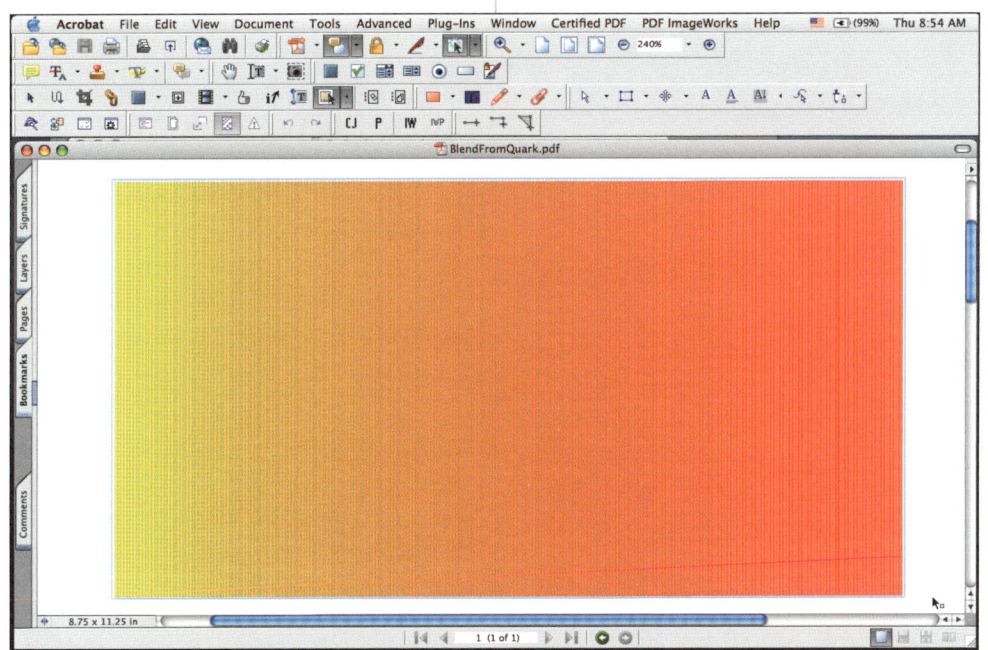

Figure 1.12. This blend, part of a PDF file, is made up of many individual objects and could result in banding.

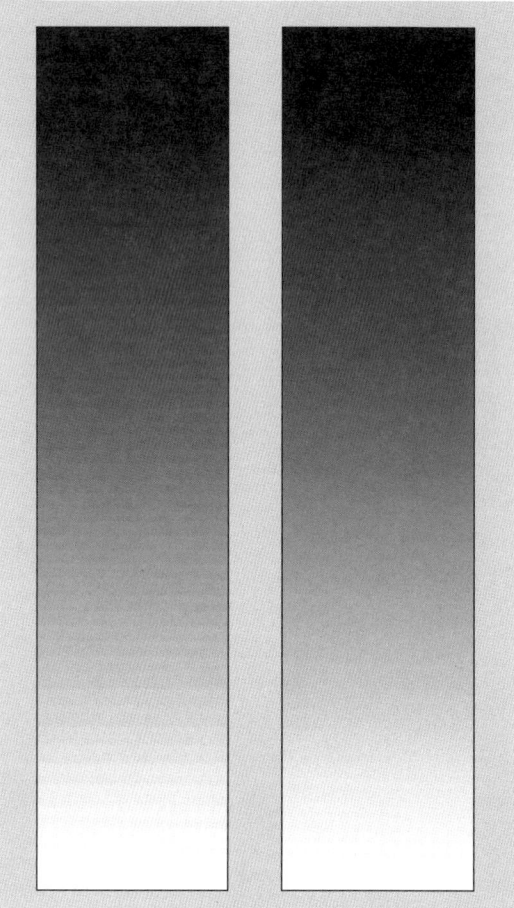

Figure 1.13. A gradient without smooth shading (left) and a gradient with smooth shading applied (right).

you could actually see the steps between them, resulting in what we call "banding."

The ability to improve these blends made in the originating application is accomplished through a PostScript 3 operator called "smooth shading" (Figure 1.13). This operator, when invoked, scans PostScript files and looks for blends. These blends are then replaced with superior PostScript Level 3 smooth shading, a mathematical algorithm that supports thousands of gray levels, not just 256. With the boxes removed, the banding disappears as well.

New to PDF version 1.4 was support for transfer functions. A transfer curve is used to retain information in an image file that can be used to compensate for the print characteristics of an output device. For example, compensating for dot gain on a printing press can be accomplished by using a transfer curve saved with an image from Photoshop.

PDF version 1.4 also supports transparency. The PDF 1.3 models renders objects (text, images, etc.) opaquely onto a page. The objects on the page are in a stack, where the stacking order is defined by the order in which the objects are specified from bottom to top. The color at any point on the page is defined by the color of the top object. However, under the PDF 1.4 transparency model, all of the objects can potentially contribute to the color on a page.

Illustrator 9 and above, Photoshop 6.0 and above, and all versions of InDesign all include support for transparency. Transparency is the result of interaction of different colored objects.

Print requires that these objects are separated before they can be output. Most PostScript RIPs don't support transparency, and any file containing transparency must be resolved, or flattened, before it can be output successfully. Saving an Adobe Illustrator file with transparent objects in the EPS (Encapsulated PostScript) format and placing it into another layout application for output is one means of flattening transparency. Both Illustrator and InDesign CS provide a transparency flattening tool for PDF files saved or exported as version 1.3 (which did not support transparency). Some newer RIPs also contain a means to detect and automatically flatten transparent objects in PDF files.

PDF version 1.5 adds a number of features relevant to print production, some of which are not quite ready for prime time in the print shop. One such feature is support for JPEG2000 compression. JPEG2000 is an ISO standard compression format, using a wavelet-based method for image compression. Like the Zip format, it offers lossless compression, and Adobe touts it as the way to create a single

PDF file that can be made small enough to display on the Web but can also contain enough high-resolution image data that it can be used for print production as well. The problem is that PDF files containing JPEG2000-compressed images can only be displayed in Acrobat 6 viewers. Worse for print production is that many RIPs, even those that can accept PDF files, cannot handle PDF files with JPEG2000 images.

Layers can now be a part of a PDF 1.5 file created from Adobe Illustrator CS, InDesign CS, or several CAD applications. This could be a boon for packaging projects as dielines, varnishes, and other information that is often stored on separate layers in Illustrator can now carry through into PDF files. The down side, again, is that PDF files containing layers may not be handled properly by many output devices on the market. We'll cover some examples of the problems that may be encountered when working with layered PDF files intended for print output in Chapter 6.

Other new features of PDF version 1.5 include an enhanced DeviceN color space which supports thirty-two spot colors (only eight were supported in PDF version 1.4) and additional options for PDF encryption and digital signatures (Figure 1.14).

PDF and Standards: PDF/X

Initially, the concept of PDF/X was intended to facilitate the complete exchange of reliable digital data, particularly in a publications advertising workflow. Complete exchange means the file can be relied upon to be correct without further technical discussion or involvement.

PDF/X is not yet another file format—a PDF/X file is a PDF file. More specifically, however, it is a restricted subset of the PDF format. What's a "restricted subset"? Well, PDF files can contain lots of elements that have nothing to do with printing, like sounds, movies, and scripts. They can also contain a lot of elements that could result in incorrect output, like RGB images, missing bleeds, or fonts that are not embedded. PDF/X limits or restricts the inclusion of data that can compromise the integrity of the printed output from a PDF file. Think of it as a PDF file for print that contains what's needed to print correctly and without the excess baggage of non-print-specific elements. In addition, the PDF/X specification defines how a prepress production tool will render the PDF/X file. For example, the fonts embedded within the PDF/X file must be used when it is output rather than any similar fonts which might be resident on the RIP.

Content in a PDF/X file is limited according to four "conditions":

- Content that is *required:* a conforming PDF/X file must contain this key or object.

- Content that is *prohibited:* a conforming PDF/X file cannot contain this key or object.

Version of PDF	Native transparency	Transfer functions	Support for Acrobat layers	JPEG2000 compression	RC4 security	DeviceN color space support
1.3	No. Artwork that interacts with transparency is flattened	Preserve or remove	No	No	40-bit	8 colors
1.4	Yes. Transparency is preserved	Preserve, remove, or apply	No	No	128-bit	8 colors
1.5	Yes. Transparency is preserved	Preserve, remove, or apply	Yes. Top-level layers become Acrobat layers	Yes	128-bit	32 colors

Figure 1.14.

- Content that is *restricted:* where and how certain keys or objects are used is limited by pre-established rules.
- Content that is *recommended:* it's suggested that the conforming PDF/X file contain this key or object, but it does not have to.

Here are a few examples of PDF/X limitations. In order to be a PDF/X-1a-conforming file, a PDF file cannot contain a movie, as it has no place in print manufacturing, so movies are *prohibited.* Annotations, like notes, are allowed, because they do have value in print production workflows for the purpose of document approval. However, most forms of annotations will print, so if they have been placed inside of the live area of a page, they could result in faulty output. Annotations are allowed in the PDF/X specification, but only outside of the bleed area of the document; in other words, they are an example of *restricted* content. Specific general information (key-value pairs) like the title, creator, and producer of the file is important to print production workflows, so they are *required* in PDF/X documents.

Who "created" PDF/X? The Digital Distribution of Advertising for Publications (DDAP) and Newspaper Association of America (NAA), seeing the emerging Portable Document Format as a viable means to digitally deliver advertising to publications, first requested a prepress-specific standard for PDF.

The Committee for Graphic Arts Technologies Standards (CGATS) originally developed the PDF/X standard (DDAP and NAA are voting members of CGATS). The first PDF/X standard was ratified by CGATS and ANSI in 1999. Adobe is an active member of DDAP, CGATS, and ANSI and so has participated in the development of the PDF/X standard through this involvement, but PDF/X is not, as some people erroneously believe, another Adobe product. It is a completely non-proprietary accredited standard for the exchange of digital data.

As with any other application or file format, PDF/X is ever evolving. The first format, PDF/X-1, officially called ANSI PDF/X-1:1999, is based on PDF

1.2. By the time it was ratified, Adobe had released Acrobat 4, so PDF 1.3 was available in the marketplace. In a sense, it was outdated before it had a chance to be of much practical use. The International Standards Organization (ISO) expanded the ANSI standard in a project originally called ISO 15930. The committee decided that there was a need for several types of PDF/X files based on different production workflow environments. ISO ratified a version of PDF/X in 2001, officially called ISO 15930-1:2001. This replaced the old ANSI PDF/X-1:1999 and was based on PDF 1.3. PDF/X-1a:2001 was intended for the blind exchange of digital data primarily for ad distribution. Originally, there were two conformance levels: PDF/X-1:2001 and PDF/X-1a:2001. The difference between them was small. PDF/X-1a:2001 prohibits the use of encryption as well as OPI objects; otherwise, the two were identical. For all intents and purposes, PDF/X-1 is dead and only PDF/X-1a is being implemented today.

In order for a PDF file to conform to the PDF/X-1a specification, it must meet certain criteria. All fonts must be embedded and legally embeddable. Images must be encoded as CMYK, DeviceGray, DeviceN, or spot color spaces. No RGB or Lab color is allowed. The trapping key must be set to "on" (true) or "off" (false). The file must contain correct media box and trim box or art box definitions. The trim box or art box cannot exceed the media box array. The media box is established by the paper size defined when a file is printed to an output device from a layout application. Think of it as "virtual paper." The media box must be of sufficient size to encompass the trim size of a document (and should be large enough to accommodate bleed and outside objects like crop marks as well).

PDF/X-3, originally called ISO 15930-3, was originally ratified by ISO in 2002 and is very similar to PDF/X-1 except that it allows device-independent, or "three-color," color spaces, like RGB or Lab. While PDF/X-1a is geared entirely to CMYK-based print production workflows, PDF/X-3 can be used for workflows in which alternate color spaces are important, such as for photographic output or fully color-managed environments where ICC profiles are applied to images or other color elements based on a particular output intent.

PDF/X-2 is based upon the PDF/X-3 specification but allows for the "partial exchange" of data. Partial exchange means that some of the data required for the successful output of the file can reside at the output provider's site, not necessarily within the PDF/X file itself, including such things as fonts or image files. This is very different from the "blind exchange" of PDF/X-1a in that it requires some sort of communication between the sender and receiver of the file. It is intended for OPI-like workflows, in which the print provider may keep high-resolution copies of images, while the content-creators work with low-resolution proxies of those images. When the PDF/X2 files arrive at the print shop, the high-resolution images can be swapped for the low-resolution images.

The entire PDF/X family was updated in 2003 and is now based on PDF 1.4. It's important to refer to PDF/X standards by the full name, which includes the year of ratification. This helps differentiate old from new versions. Here's an overview of the current lineup:

PDF/X-1a:2003 (ISO 15930-4:2003)

PDF/X-1a: 2003 is the current conformance level of the PDF/X-1a standard and has been updated to include these new technologies:

- Transparency—while transparency is part of the PDF 1.4 specification, partial transparency in PDF/X-1a is prohibited. If transparency is used to create content, it must be flattened before converting the file to PDF/X-1a:2003.

- JBIG2 compression—JBIG2 is a standard for bi-level image compression and very effective for things like copydot scans. It is prohibited in PDF/X-1a:2003 apparently because of difficulty obtaining licenses to the intellectual property from the JBIG2 standardization group.

- Encryption—remains prohibited. PDF/X-1 (without the "a") has been eliminated.

PDF/X-2:2003 (ISO 15930-5:2003)

PDF/X-2:2003 is the new conformance level of the internationally accredited PDF/X-2 standard. It is considered a superset of PDF/X-3:2002 because it allows for the use of device-independent color spaces like Lab and RGB based on ICC profiles, but the exchange of that data is not blind. This version of the PDF/X family was only first ratified in 2002 and has been little used in production. It's expected to be used on OPI workflow scenarios.

PDF/X-3:2003 (ISO 15930-6:2003)

PDF/X-3:2003 is the current conformance level of the PDF/X-3 standard. PDF/X-3 allows for the use of device-independent color spaces such as Lab and those based on ICC profiles as well as CMYK. Like PDF/X-1a: 2003, it has been updated to include these new technologies:

- Transparency—while transparency is part of the PDF 1.4 specification, partial transparency in PDF/X-1a is prohibited. If transparency is used to create content, it must be flattened before converting the file to PDF/X-3:2003.

- JBIG2 compression—JBIG2 is a standard for bi-level image compression and very effective for things like copydot scans. It is prohibited in PDF/X-3:2003 apparently because of difficulty obtaining licenses to the intellectual property from the JBIG2 standardization group.

- Encryption—remains prohibited.

Interested in looking at the actual minutes of the meetings where industry experts hammer out these standards? The minutes of the CGATS SC6 Task Force 1 (PDF/X) are posted online on the NPES website. NPES (The Association for Suppliers of Printing, Publishing and Converting Technologies), a trade association, is the secretariat of the group. Visit www.npes.org and navigate to the Standards Workroom. The actual published ISO standard is

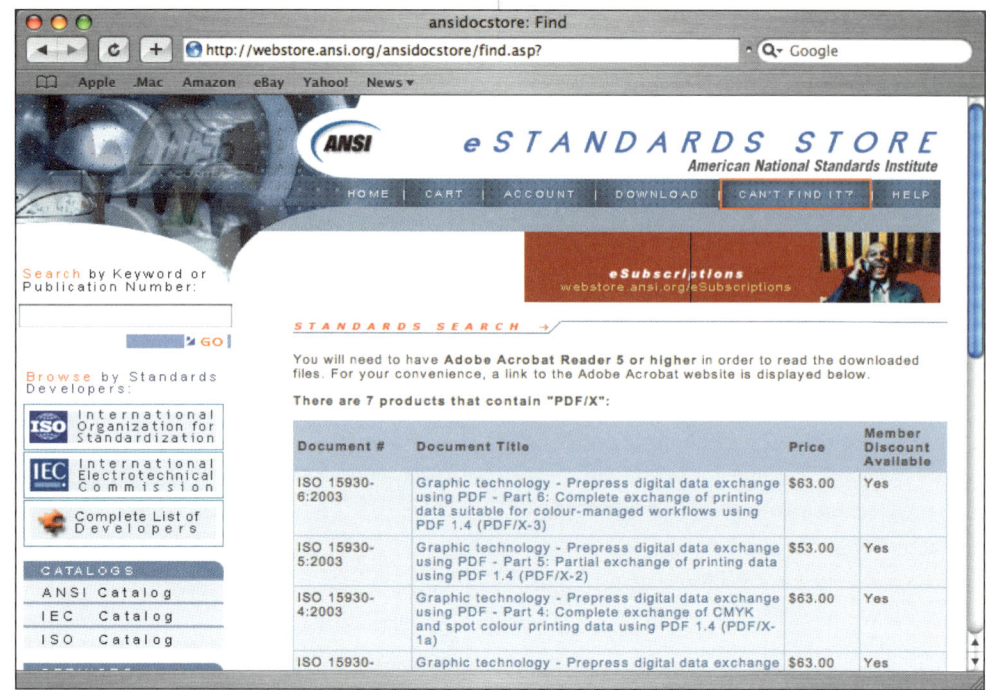

Figure 1.15. The actual ISO standard for PDF/X can be purchased from ANSI (www.ansi.org).

not freely distributed but must be purchased. It is available directly from the ISO Central Secretariat (www.iso.org) or, in the U.S., from ANSI (www. ansi.org). The cost is $63.00 for the PDF/X-1a or 3:2000 or $53 for PDF/X-2:2003 (Figure 1.15).

While supplying a PDF/X-1a- or X-3-compliant file will eliminate many of the common errors associated with the delivery of digital data for print production, the standard does not cover all of them. For example, the specification does not address image resolution in any way, so a fully compliant PDF/X file could contain pixelized, low-resolution image data. Also, each publication or printer can have other specific requirements covering, in addition to resolution, things like page size, maximum density, and printing condition requirements, such as SWOP. Recognizing the need for a second tier of file checking, a number of industry vendors have adopted the term "PDF/X Plus" for their method of identifying both the PDF/X standard and some set of additional production-specific file requirements.

The standard-bearer for PDF/X Plus is an organization called The Ghent PDF Workgroup. Founded in 2002, the Ghent Workgroup is an international assembly of industry associations whose goal is to develop and maintain a set of vendor-independent PDF/X Plus specifications for the graphic arts community. Every member of the Ghent PDF Workgroup has had experience with defining specifications for PDF files exchanged for print production processes. The product of this group's efforts is a full set of Acrobat Distiller job options and Enfocus PitStop Preflight Profiles. These tools, used properly, will result in optimal PDF/X-compliant files for specific print production processes, including magazine, newspaper, and commercial sheetfed and web printing. These files are free and can be downloaded from the Ghent PDF Workgroup's main website: www.ghentpdfworkgroup.org.

A big part of the PDF/X initiative is the fact that, in addition to creating PDF files that are optimal for print production, it is equally important that the prepress workflow system can process those files appropriately. There are dozens of workflow systems in use today and each of them can be set up to handle files differently. The same system from the same manufacturer can be set up to handle files differently in different environments. Each system renders, proofs, and images supplied PDF/X files, and they should be tested to see that they interpret them correctly.

To address this need the Altona Test Suite was developed by a consortium of European organizations including ECI (European Color Initiative), bvdm, FOGRA, and UGRA. The Altona Test Suite was initially targeted at digital proofing systems and was used in 2002 and 2003 at the Digital Proofing Shootouts organized by bvdm and ECI. In 2003, the Altona Test Suite was used to test proofing devices for the "digital proofing shootout" of the IPA in Chicago. But the Altona Suite can be used to evaluate Post-Script and PDF RIPs as well and was used for testing workflow systems in Seybold's 2003 PDF Workflow Shootout.

The Altona Test Suite consists of three DIN A3-size (tabloid) PDF pages. The first page, called Altona Measure, contains the ECI 2002 characterization chart and several other color patches. The Altona Visual (Figure 1.16) test page consists of numerous graphic and image elements that can be used to judge the reproduction of the page in terms of color fidelity and imaging. The Altona Technical (Figure 1.17) page looks at overprint simulation and handling of all font types allowed in the PDF 1.3 or PDF/X standard. Warning: The Technical page takes a very long time to display in Acrobat, so don't open it unless you've willing to wait quite a while for it to fully display!

The Altona Test Suite version 1.1 is free and available for download from the European Color Initiative website www.eci.org. A full kit including the Altona Test Suite and ICC profiles on CD along with reference prints of each file printed on different paper and under a variety of printing conditions is also available at www.altonatestsuite.com. This is not free,

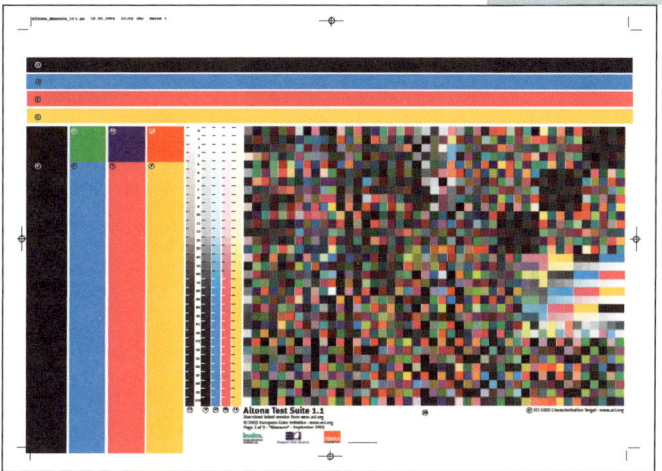

Figure 1.16. Part of the Altona Test Suite, the Altona Visual test page is used to judge color reproduction and fidelity.

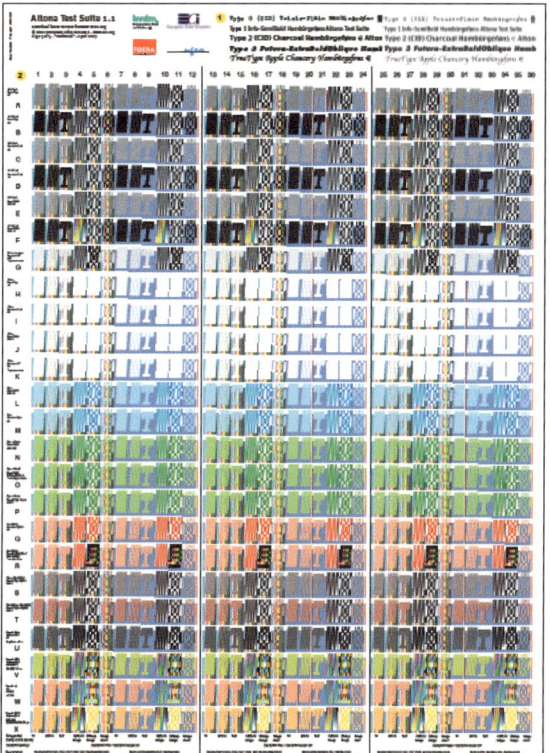

Figure 1.17. The Altona Technical page tests for over-printing capabilities and font handling.

Figure 1.18. One of the test "patches" in The Kensington Suite, a set of test files that can help identify common output problems with PDF/X files.

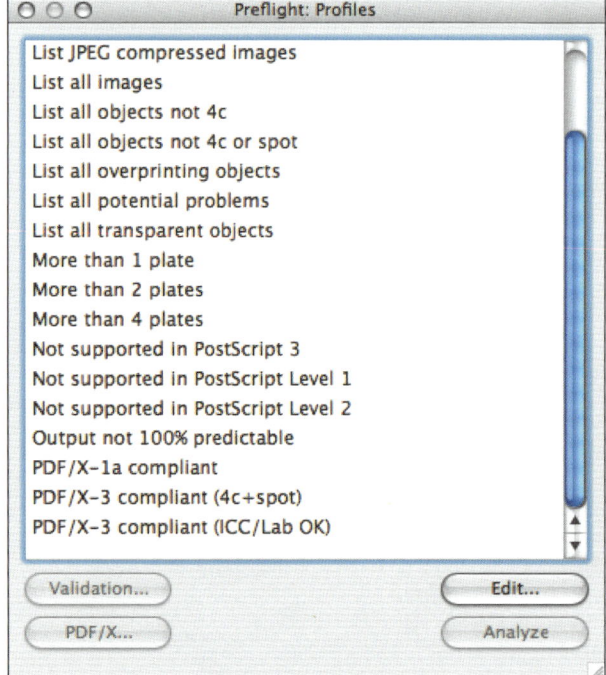

Figure 1.19. Using the Acrobat Professional's Preflight tool, a PDF file can be tagged as PDF/X compliant.

and the price is offered in euros (EUR 480,00). FOGRA, ECI, or UGRA members get a better price.

The DDAP organization developed their own set of tools called The Kensington Suite. The Kensington Suite is a collection of several dozen test patches specifically designed to identify common production workflow issues that may be encountered when working with PDF/X-1a:2001 files. Specifically, the suite tests for characterized printing condition, separation and DeviceN color spaces, font embedding, font support, overprinting, smooth shading, and pattern fills. The test files are a series of PDF/X:1-a:2001-compliant files, each 4×5 inches in size. The person doing the testing can gang these "patches" in the most efficient way for their output device. Each patch is a test for one specific potentially problematic issue. For instance, the patch shown in Figure 1.18 was created to test all occurrences of trapping in a six-color job (CMYK, PMS 354 CVC, and P1495). Complete documentation is part of the tool set. The Kensington Suite is freely downloadable from www.pdf-x.com.

Which flavor of PDF/X is the best one to use? Well, it would depend upon the needs of the sender and receiver. In the United States, it will likely be PDF/X-1a, at least until more companies begin to really use full color management in their workflows. In Europe, where more companies have already adopted color-managed workflows, PDF/X-3 is the standard format of choice. With PDF/X-1a, 2, or 3:2003, a file is based on PDF 1.4, so the prepress provider must make sure all components in their workflow can handle those PDF files. It shouldn't be much of a problem because transparency has to have been resolved in the 2003 version of the PDF/X specification, and JBIG2 compression is not allowed. Also, it will take some time before applications can write the 2003 version of the PDF specification, so we likely won't see these in the workflow until the next round of upgrades to desktop publishing applications.

How does one create a PDF/X file? Prior to Acrobat 6 Professional, creating a PDF/X-compliant file required a third-party plug-in for Acrobat.

Distiller in Acrobat Professional adds a PDF/X tab in the Adobe PDF Settings dialog box. Now, PDF/X files can be created directly in Distiller simply by selecting the PDF/X tab and choosing a compliance option (either PDF/X-1a or PDF/X-3). We'll go over what the options mean in Chapter 2. Acrobat 6 Professional also contains a method to tag PDF files as PDF/X-1a:2001 or PDF/X-3:2002 compliant through the Preflight tool (Figure 1.19). This tool will tag the file as PDF/X-compliant only if the objects in the file meet the requirements of the specification; if not, it will fail. Acrobat Professional does not offer any way to repair a file in order to make it compliant.

Other third-party tools do, however. One of the first dedicated tools developed to both verify and create PDF/X-compliant files was Apago PDF/X Checkup, by Apago, Inc., and it remains one of the simplest to use. The core tool is an Acrobat plug-in that can be set up to verify whether a PDF file is PDF/X-compliant and will even check for some additional items that are part of a PDF/X Plus check (Figure 1.20). If the file fails, the plug-in offers the option to attempt to "fix" the file in order to bring it into compliance. It can easily fix things like the trapping key, setting it to "false" instead of the default "unknown." It cannot, however, fix major issues with PDF/X-1a:2001 compliance, such as converting detected RGB images to CMYK or finding and embedding fonts into the file. When the PDF/X Plus option is used, it can also flag those problems. When PDF files are successfully "fixed" they can be saved as PDF/X-1-compliant files; on a Macintosh, this can also include a special icon that indicates at a glance that the file has been processed using Checkup and is likely PDF/X-compliant (Figure 1.21).

Enfocus PitStop Pro, another Acrobat plug-in, lets the user not only check for and tag files with PDF/X:1a:2001 or PDF/X-3:2001 compliance but also edit nonconforming files so that they meet the requirements. For example, a PitStop Profile can be made for PDF/X-1a:2001 that checks for RGB images in a file and, if it detects them, automatically converts them to CMYK using a pre-selected ICC profile if

Figure 1.20. Apago PDF/X Checkup users can set up the plug-in to check for potential problems not covered by the PDF/X specification.

Figure 1.21. Verifying a compliant PDF/X file will give you a smile.

desired. Enfocus offers a number of profiles already set up to check for PDF/X compliance (check their website www.enfocus.com), but most do not include automatic editing. Users can, however, easily build a

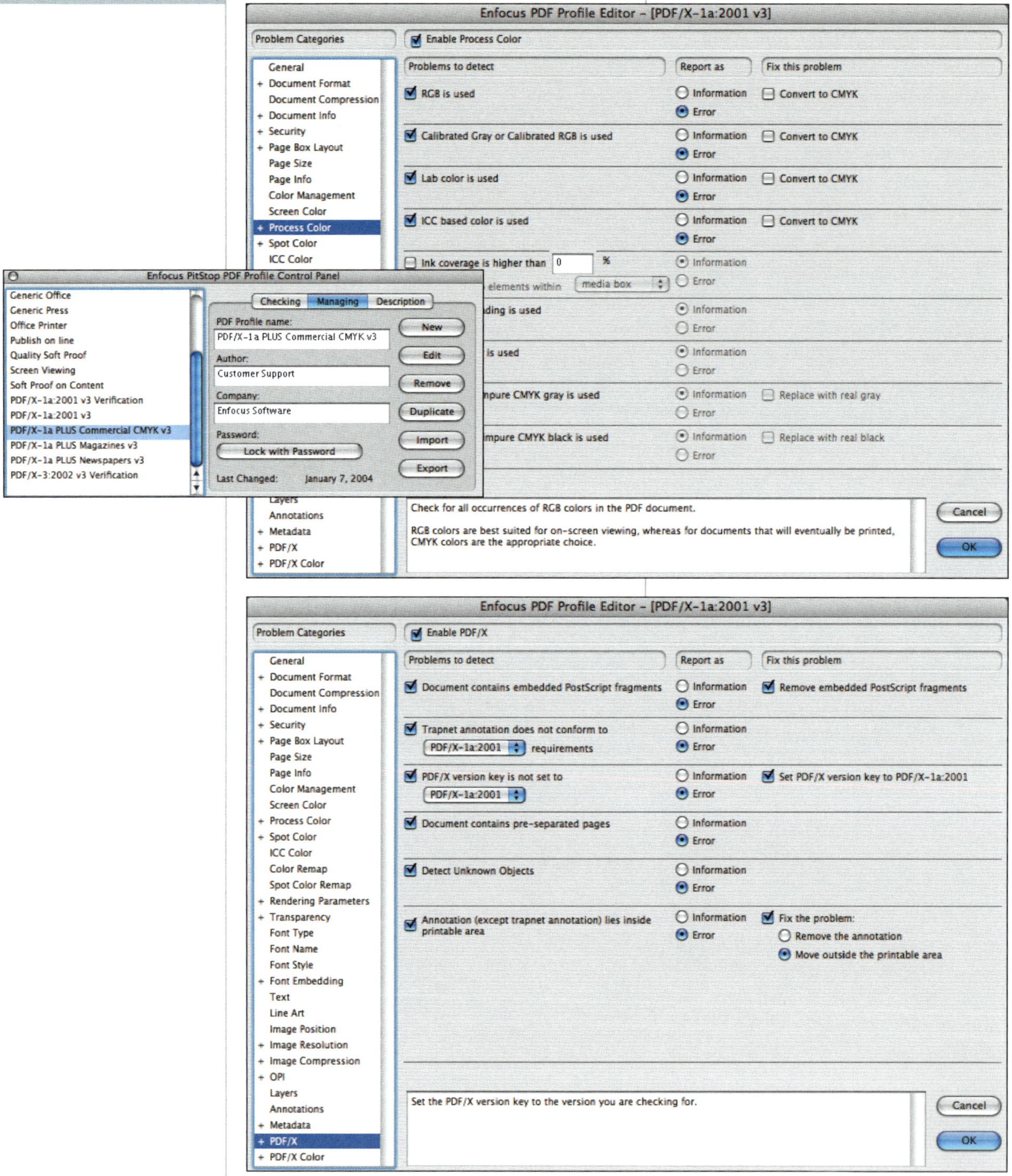

Figure 1.22. PDF files can be verified and tagged as PDF/X compliant using Enfocus PitStop Professional. The preflight check can also contain automatic fixes, to convert RGB images to CMYK for example, that will transform an otherwise non-compliant original PDF file into a viable PDF/X file.

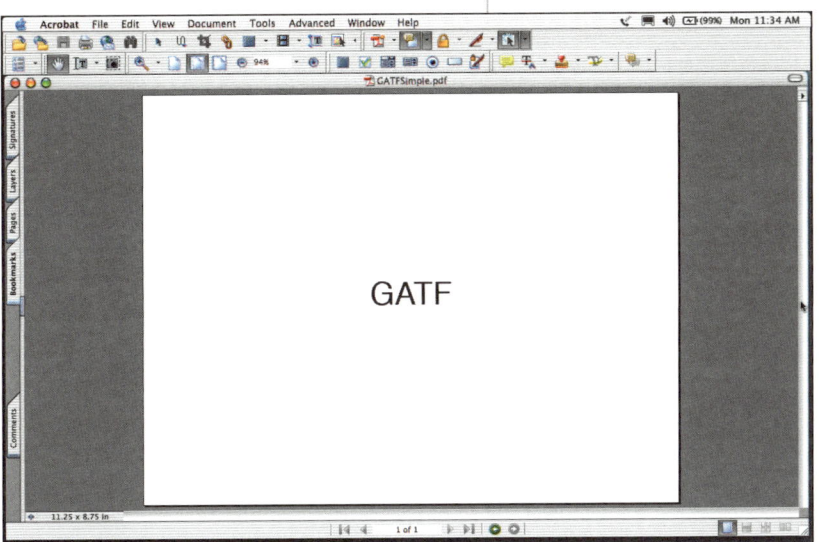

Figure 1.23. This figure shows a simple PDF file (top) and its structure (right).

```
%PDF-1.5                    Header
1 0 obj
<<
/Type /Page
/Parent 5 0 R
/Resources 3 0 R
/Contents 2 0 R
>>
endobj
2 0 obj
<<
/Length 51
>>
stream
BT
/F1 24 Tf
1 0 0 1 260 330 Tm
(GATF)Tj
ET
endstream
endobj
3 0 obj
<<
/ProcSet[/PDF/Text]
/Font <</F1 4 0 R >>
>>
Endobj                      Body
4 0 obj
<<
/Type /Font
/Subtype /Type1
/Name /F1
/BaseFont/Helvetica
>>
endobj
5 0 obj
<<
/Type /Pages
/Kids [ 1 0 R ]
/Count 1
/MediaBox
[ 0 0 612 446 ]
>>
endobj
6 0 obj
<<
/Type /Catalog
/Pages 5 0 R
>>
endobj
trailer
<<
/Root 6 0 R
>>
xref              Cross-reference table
0 7
0000000000 65535 f
0000000009 00000 n
0000000103 00000 n
0000000204 00000 n
0000000275 00000 n
0000000361 00000 n
0000000452 00000 n
trailer
<<
/Size 7
>>                          Trailer
startxref
532
%%EOF
```

new profile by duplicating an existing one to include automatic fixes (Figure 1.22).

The list of applications that can create, save, or process PDF/X-compliant files is long and ever growing. DDAP keeps track of what they call "PDF Implementors," vendors who offer PDF/X-compliant products. A chart detailing all of these organizations along with their products is available from the www.pdf-x.com website.

A New Standard: PDF/A

ISO is currently hashing out a new standard, dubbed PDF/A. The PDF/A (the "A" is for archive) format, initiated by NPES and the Association for Information and Image Management, International (AIIM International), is aimed at creating a standard way to archive documents electronically to ensure preservation of content over an extended period of time.

The United States federal government is very interested in this initiative because of its ability to reduce paper storage and costs associated with the manual retrieval and shipment of paper documents. The PDF/A format may contain a mixture of text, raster images, and vector graphics. The initial version is to emulate static paper with the added need to include annotations, digital signatures, approvals, etc. In the future, the standard will eventually include the storage of audio and video within the PDF/A file.

Look Inside a PDF File

If you are lucky, you will not have to spend much time examining PDF files with a text editor, but we thought it might be worthwhile to show you what a PDF file looks like "under the hood" (Figure 1.23).

A PDF file is composed of four parts: the header, a body area, a cross-reference table, and a trailer. The header specifies the version of the PDF file (1.2, 1.3, 1.4, 1.5). The body area contains the sequence of objects contained in the file. The cross-reference table is a list that indicates where each object can be found. The trailer tells RIPs and other applications where to find the cross-reference table.

CHAPTER 2
PDF CREATION

Creating PDF for Print Production

Because PDF is an open file format specification, anyone with the skills to do so can develop tools to create, manipulate, or view PDF files. Adobe estimates that, to date, there are more than 1,200 companies offering PDF-based solutions. A search on the Planet-pdf website (www.planetpdf.com), a terrific resource for all things PDF, turns up a list of nearly 300 tools on the market for PDF creation alone. Macophiles note: Only 36 of these run on the Mac platform. In fact, according to a financial report from Adobe in 2003, Acrobat products are sold to Windows-platform users three-to-one over Mac users. Since Mac is the primary platform of choice in the graphic communications community, and since most PDF-creation tools don't run on that platform, we can surmise that many of them are not intended to create PDF files for graphics/print production.

So, while it is pretty easy to create a PDF document using any one of the ever-growing number of tools available to do so, it is not so simple to make a "good" PDF file for print production. The creator has to know the answer to such questions as:

- In which PDF version should I save this file?
- How far can I safely compress images?
- Should I subset the fonts?
- Should I flatten transparency?
- Do I need to tag the images for color management?
- How do I know that the final PDF document will contain everything I intended?

Outside of the dedicated high-end PDF prepress workflow systems, there are two primary methods to ensure that you are making a good print-quality PDF document. The first is to make a quality PostScript file and then create the PDF file using a PostScript interpreter such as Adobe Acrobat Distiller. The second is to create a PDF using the Export To (or Save As) PDF function found in applications such as Adobe InDesign or Illustrator. We call this making "print-perfect" PDF files, and in this chapter we will show you just how this is done.

Creating PDF via PostScript

Making PDF files from PostScript data does not necessarily mean printing a physical PostScript file to disk and then submitting it to a PostScript interpreter, like Distiller—although it can. We consider exporting a PDF file from QuarkXPress 6.x as "creating PDF from PostScript" because that is what is happening behind the scenes; Quark licensed Global Graphics Jaws PDF Interpreter, and any time you export to PDF from Quark, you are actually creating a PostScript file and submitting it to the Jaws interpreter, which in turn creates a PDF file.

Saving a file from Microsoft Word using the PDFMaker (when you click on the PDF icon on the Word toolbar, you are using PDFMaker) is a way to create a PDF file from PostScript. Printing to the Adobe PDF printer from any application is also a way of making a PDF file from PostScript data. And printing a "name.ps" file from an application and manually submitting that file to Acrobat Distiller is the most obvious way of creating PDF from PostScript.

It is important to have all the right tools available and set up properly in order to successfully create PDF files for print. On both Macintosh and Windows this means setting up the Adobe PDF printer. For Windows users this also means setting up the

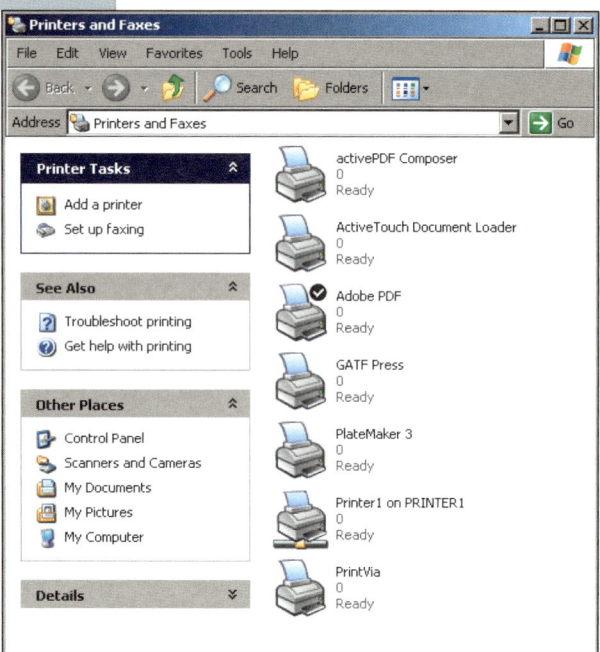

Figure 2.1. To make Adobe PDF the default printer under Windows, simply right-click the icon and choose "Set As Default."

Figure 2.2. Control many basic options, like how TrueType fonts will be handled, from the Properties menu suite.

Adobe PostScript (AdobePS) printer driver. As Mac users know, the way printing is handled under Mac OS X has changed dramatically from the way it was done in earlier versions of the Mac OS. The AdobePS driver is no longer needed when printing from a Mac running OS X. In the first edition of *The PDF Print Production Guide,* we talked about how to set up the Adobe PostScript driver and the Distiller PPD files for Mac users running OS 9. Since Acrobat 6 only runs under Mac OS X, we will limit the discussion in this edition to setting up the Adobe PDF printer on OS X only (prepress people, most tools have been ported to Mac OS X; it really is time to move on!)

The Adobe PDF printer will install on the computer system, whether Mac or Windows, when Acrobat 6 is installed. Adobe PDF is a virtual printer, meaning that it creates a digital file on the computer's hard drive instead of printing to a physical output device. By installing the Adobe PDF printer, a printer description file (PPD) is created as well. On Mac OS X these are automatically placed into the appropriate library folders. PPDs are important for any output device because they define device-specific information, such as resolution, screen ruling, colors, printer resident fonts, and media formats. Since PDF files are resolution-, device-, and media-independent, PPDs for specific output devices (such as Epson, Hewlett-Packard, and Xerox) should not be used when creating PostScript for PDF. This is especially important where fonts are concerned. Fonts defined in printer-specific PPDs tell the application that a particular font is already at the RIP, so the application does not have to include that font's data in the PostScript file. If this PostScript file is then used to create a PDF file, the font data will not be available for inclusion in the PDF file and substitution may occur! The Adobe PDF printer should always be used to create device-independent PostScript for PDF creation (unless you are using a proprietary PDF workflow such as Agfa Apogee or Creo Prinergy, which supply their own custom PPDs).

On the Windows platform, Acrobat configures the Adobe PDF printer to use the Adobe PostScript printer driver (AdobePS). If you need to install Adobe PS, but don't have access to the Acrobat installer CD, Adobe offers PostScript printer drivers and PPD files on their website http://www.adobe.com/products/printerdrivers/main.html.

For Windows users, some customization to the Adobe PDF printer is recommended. First, set up the Adobe PDF printer to be the default printer for the computer system. This is particularly important to help avoid text reflow problems from Microsoft Word (more on that in the "In the Trenches" chapter). To set up the Adobe PDF printer as the default printer, navigate to the Printers and Faxes settings window. Right-click the Adobe PDF icon and choose Set As Default from the pop-up menu (Figure 2.1). In Windows XP, the Set As Default option won't be available if the Adobe PDF printer is already set up as the default printer.

Once that's been done, right-click the Adobe PDF printer icon again and select *Properties* from the pop-up menu (Figure 2.2). You can control a number of basic options from the Properties menu suite. For example, you can establish whether TrueType fonts used in layout applications will be included in PDF files as TrueType or converted to Type 1 by default. The location of each of the settings differs depending on the flavor of the Windows OS you are using. Under Windows XP, you will find the font setting by clicking on the General tab, then Printing Preferences, then the Layout tab, and finally, the Advanced option. If you click the plus sign next to PostScript Options, you will see the TrueType Font Download option. If you want TrueType fonts to not be converted to Type 1 in your PDF files, choose *Native TrueType* from the pop-up menu.

Under the Device Settings tab, set *Convert Gray Text to PostScript Gray*. This will prevent the dreaded "RGB black type" problem that is often inherent in PDF files created from Microsoft Office application files. Fortunately, this is the default setting for the Adobe PDF printer. If you're still using the Distiller printer, you will have to set this manually (Figure 2.3).

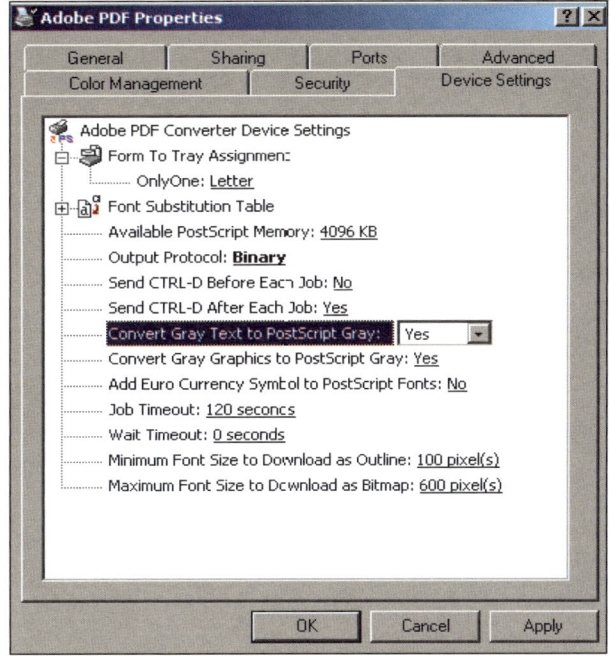

Figure 2.3. Select "Convert Gray Text to PostScript Gray" to prevent black text in Microsoft Office products from being converted to RGB.

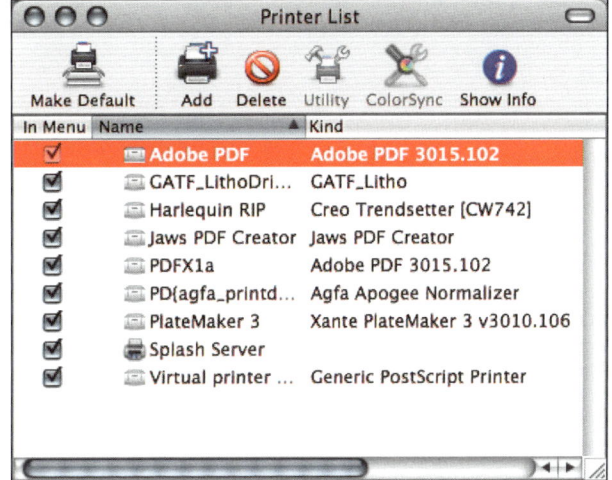

Figure 2.4. The Adobe PDF printer as it appears in the Mac OS X Printer List.

Mac users do not have to do any further setup to the Adobe PDF printer (nor can they). However, it is not difficult to accidentally delete the Adobe PDF printer from the Print Center (Figure 2.4). If that happens, there are a couple of ways to get it back.

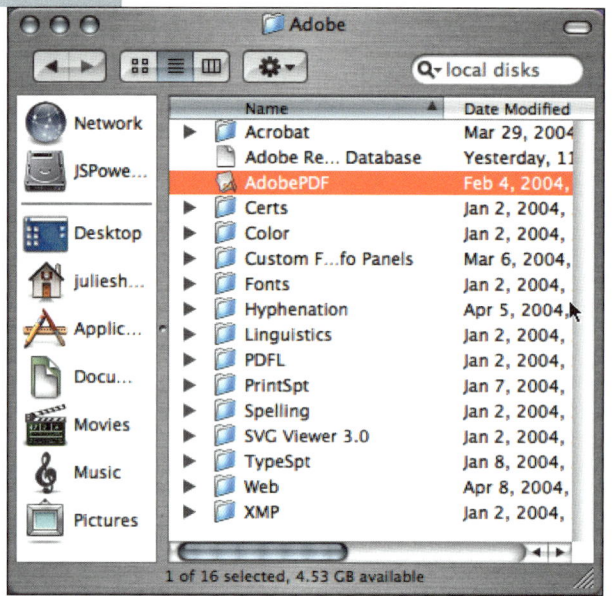

Figure 2.5. The Adobe PDF printer resides in the *Library/Application Support/Adobe* folder.

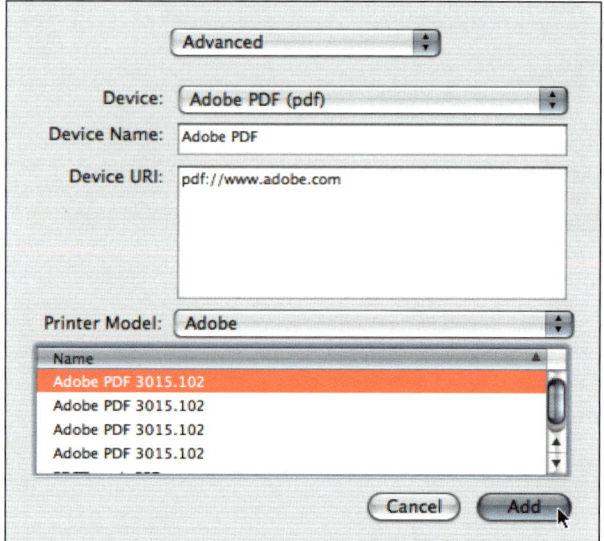

Figure 2.6. Use these settings to rebuild the Adobe PDF printer under Mac OS X (10.3.3).

Force Acrobat to repair the Adobe PDF printer:

1. Make sure Acrobat and the Print Center are not running.

2. Navigate to the Library/Application Support/ Adobe folder and delete the AdobePDF file (Figure 2.5).

3. Launch Acrobat and enter the administrator name and password when prompted. This is where Acrobat repairs the Adobe PDF printer.

4. Start the Print Center, and verify that the Adobe PDF printer has been added to the Printer List.

If for some reason this doesn't work, or if you'd rather try the more challenging approach, you can also add the Adobe PDF printer to the Printer List manually (Figure 2.6). Here's how:

1. Start the Printer Setup Utility (found in the Applications/Utilities folder).

2. Hold down the Option key, then click *Add* in the Printer List dialog box.

3. Select *Advanced* from the top (Printer Connection) pop-up menu.

4. Choose *Adobe PDF* (pdf) from the Device menu.

5. Type **Adobe PDF** in the Device Name text box.

6. Type **pdf://www.adobe.com** in the Device URL text box.

7. Choose *Adobe* from the Printer Model menu.

8. Click *Add,* and the new printer will show up on the Printer List.

Mac users can also create a generic virtual Post-Script printer that can be used to create PostScript files when one does not have access to the Adobe PDF printer. PostScript files created with a virtual Post-Script printer can be sent to another computer for interpreting. To create a virtual printer under Mac OS X, follow these steps (Figure 2.7).

1. Open the Print Center and choose *Add Printer* from the Printers menu.

2. Select *IP Printing* from the top (Printer Connection) pop-up menu.

3. Choose *LPD/LDR* from the Printer Type menu.

4. Type **localhost** in the Printer Address field.

5. Type a name, without spaces, in the Queue Name field. This will be the name of the printer as it shows up in the print dialog box.

6. Select *Adobe* from the Printer Model pop-up menu.

7. Click *Add,* and the new virtual printer will show up on the Printer List (Figure 2.8).

Before PDF: File Preparation and Preflight

Even with a PDF workflow, print projects are still created using desktop publishing software such as QuarkXPress and InDesign (and unfortunately, also non-DTP applications, like Microsoft Word). All the basic rules of good design and desktop publishing must be used when creating these documents. A poorly constructed QuarkXPress or InDesign document will create a PDF file that is of little value. That is why it is still necessary to perform preliminary preflighting of the native application file before PDF files are created.

There are dedicated preflighting tools that can preflight projects after they are completed, like the venerable Markzware FlightCheck Professional, but also tools designed to help designers avoid problems before a project is finished. These tools are plug-ins for desktop publishing applications and enable the designer to check for problems during the creation phase.

One such tool is GLUON QC, an on-the-fly quality control XTension for QuarkXPress. GLUON produces many applications, extensions, and plug-ins to enhance publishing applications (www.gluon.com). QC checks for all of the comment elements you'd expect from a preflight tool: color usage, font usage, missing elements, and so forth. What makes this product unique is that it also checks for things that a proofreader would look for, like alignment of page objects and a slew of common text errors, like missing end quotes and extra spaces between words (Figure 2.9).

Here are some specific items to check for before creating a PDF file from a native layout application:

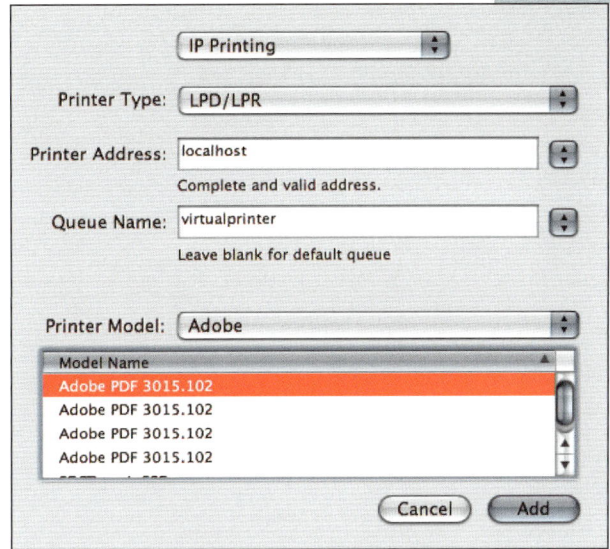

Figure 2.7. Use these settings to add a virtual printer to the list.

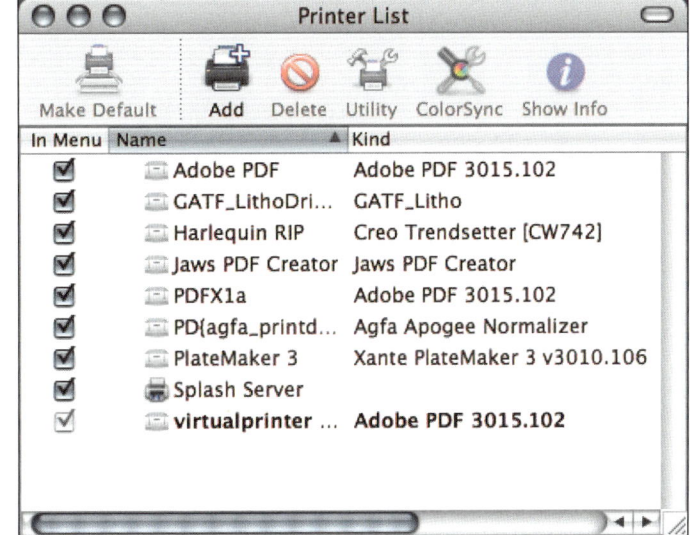

Figure 2.8. Once created, a virtual printer shows up on the Printer List and can be used like any other printing device.

Figure 2.9. Gluon QC, a Quark XTension, works like a virtual proofreader, checking for many potential problems during the design phase.

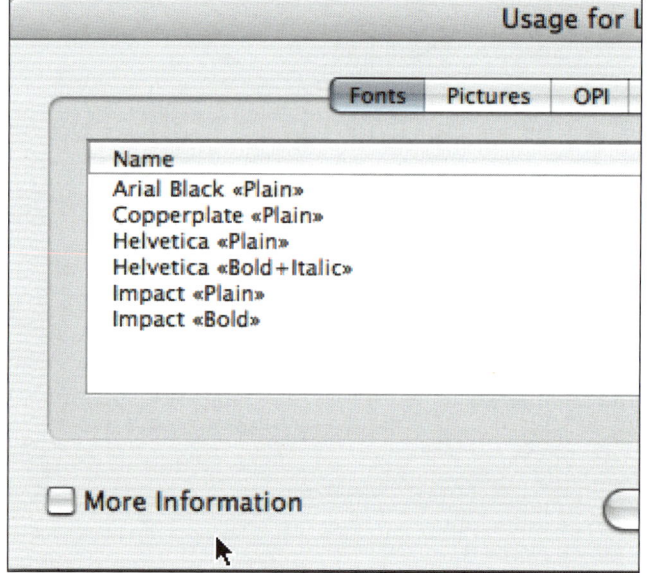

Figure 2.10. QuarkXPress users can spot menu-styled (artificial) text by viewing the Fonts tab under the Usage menu. Only <<Plain>> is OK.

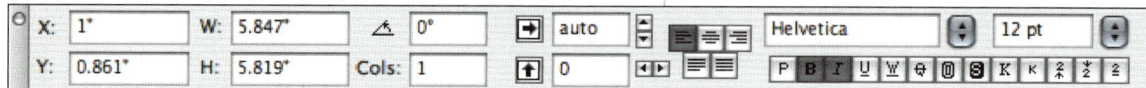

- The document should contain no RGB images or RGB colors if it is intended to print in four-color (CMYK) process. Depending upon the output device printed to, these could be separated to CMYK, but in a manner that doesn't meet the designer's expectations. They could also come out only on the black plate. Neither outcome is desirable.

- If a file contains duotone images (two-color), make sure the colors have been specified accurately in the image application and in the layout application (typically black and a spot color).

- Only the colors intended to print should be part of the color palette. If a process color is named something like "logo blue," make sure that color is set to be a process build and not a spot color in the application's color palette.

- See that there are not more spot colors on the palette than are required in the project. Make sure any spot color used is referenced by the same name everywhere it is used. If it is used in an illustration, make sure it is called the same thing there as it is in the layout application. If a color is referenced by more than one name, you can end up with too many printing plates on the output end.

- Ensure all links to placed graphics, images, and text elements are unbroken.

- Do all graphic elements, like boxes, filled with color abut properly? Windows and boxes that don't touch will leave a small paper gap and will not trap properly.

- Make sure all fonts used in the layout or in a placed graphic are available and open via the font management system on the computer. Some fonts cannot be embedded into other files, like PDF or EPS. Check the license to ensure font embedding is not restricted for the fonts used.

- Check type and make sure that no artificial, or menu-styled, fonts are used (Figure 2.10).

- Unless it is part of a design technique, use only high-resolution image data (two pixels per halftone dot; 300 dpi is a benchmark good effective resolution for high-end printing).

- The media-size specification in the page setup must be large enough to accommodate the full page size plus any bleed objects or printer's marks used. This is usually 0.25 inch on each side, or increase the media size to 0.5 inch more than the final trim size in both height and width.

- The layout should be set up to the correct color mode (typically CMYK or RGB).

- Make sure no page elements are set to overprint erroneously. A very light color will effectively disappear if set to overprint a very dark color.

- Are DCS images used in the layout? Depending on the applications, they may not result in high-resolution output in the final PDF files.

- Is transparency used in the layout? If so, a decision must be made as to how to handle it (leave it as transparent or flatten it at the PDF creation stage).

More detailed information on image compression, font usage, and color management follow in the "Setting Up Acrobat Distiller" section. The information is relevant even for PDF files that are saved or exported directly from an application, More, like how to work with DCS images and transparency, are covered in Chapter 6: In the Trenches.

Creating the PostScript File

Creating PostScript to submit to Distiller or another PostScript interpreter varies slightly from one application to another. Even though the print dialog boxes in various desktop publishing applications look different, the basic concepts of PostScript creation remain the same. Here is a generic list of what to do in order to print PostScript from a layout application.

1. Make sure all of the fonts used within the document are loaded and available to the application. We recommend loading fonts through a font management program such as Adobe ATM Deluxe or Extensis Suitcase.

2. Open the document in the application with which it was created.

3. Perform a preflight check, either manually using the checklist noted above or with a preflight application.

4. Access the print dialog box.

5. Select a printer or printer description (PPD). For PDF creation, this should always be the Adobe PDF printer or the Acrobat Distiller printer.

6. Select the media (paper) size. Make this large enough to accommodate any bleed area and printer's marks required. This is usually 0.25 to 0.5 inches larger than the trim size of the page.

7. Set scaling as 100% unless you truly wish to output the file at another size.

8. Set the output color space. For print, this is typically composite CMYK, although some applications, like QuarkXPress 6, offer other options, like DeviceN. DeviceN is a good option if your file contains colorized TIFF images or spot-to-spot blends.

9. Set resolution to an appropriate level for the target output device. (2400 dpi is typical for high-end output.) Line screen is generally established on output, not in the PDF file.

10. Under Mac OS 9, users could set the PostScript level to 1, 2, or 3. We recommended PostScript 3 with Binary encoding. When printing to a PostScript file under Mac OS X, there is no longer an

```
%!PS-Adobe-3.0
%RBINumCopies: 1
%%Pages: (atend)
%APL_DSC_Encoding: UTF8
%%Title: (Microsoft Word - Chap2 PDF Creation_chng.doc)
%%Creator: (Word: cgpdftops CUPS filter)
%%CreationDate: (Saturday, April 17 2004 17:22:08 EDT)
%%For: (Julie Shaffer)
%%DocumentData: Clean7Bit
%%LanguageLevel: 2
%%PageOrder: Ascend
%%EndComments
userdict/dscInfo 5 dict dup begin
/Title(Microsoft Word - Chap2 PDF Creation_chng.doc)def
/Creator(Word: cgpdftops CUPS filter)def
/CreationDate(Saturday, April 17 2004 17:22:08 EDT)def
```

Figure 2.11. The header information in a PostScript file indicates the PostScript level used for the file.

option to set the PostScript level. Mac Help tells us that PostScript files printed from Mac OS X will be set to PostScript Level 2 with ASCII encoding (Figure 2.11).

11. When you access the Adobe PDF printer from a Windows application, make sure you go to the Adobe PDF Printing Preferences dialog box and click the Adobe PDF Setting tab. Deselect the Do not send fonts to Adobe PDF setting.

12. Give the PostScript file a name that makes sense, usually the same name as the original document with a .ps extension. The PDF file will be given the same name with a .pdf extension and is saved into the same directory that holds the PostScript file.

Setting Up Acrobat Distiller

As we discussed in Chapter 1, Acrobat Distiller is a type of PostScript engine. Distiller interprets PostScript code and converts it into the PDF file format. Distiller contains many powerful options that can be changed based on what the user wants in the final PDF file. While there are many different options for creating PDF files, our focus will be on creating PDF files for prepress or print production use. In prepress workflows, a PDF file may have to be created for on-screen viewing purposes (for client or internal soft proofing), for printing to digital presses, or for output

to film or computer-to-plate devices for high-end printing on commercial presses. In this section, we're going to take a very detailed look at how to set up Distiller to accommodate each of these needs. And while we focus on Distiller, please note that many of the concepts we discuss, particularly fonts, image compression, and color, apply to any method of PDF creation.

The Distiller main interface (Figure 2.12) consists of Adobe PDF Settings (called Job Options prior to Distiller version 6) list along with Acrobat version compatibility. The status window shows any special plug-ins in use (such as the Creo Distiller Assistant files) and the progress of the PostScript interpreter as a PDF file is created. Also shown is the Distiller version and the version of PostScript interpreter on which it is based.

Distiller 6.0 is set up by default to create PDF files for six uses: Smallest File Size, Standard, High Quality, Press Quality, PDFX1a, and PDFX3. The settings are designed to balance file size with image quality. Smallest File Size is the lowest resolution and is designed for on-screen viewing only—never use it for print production. Standard is designed for viewing and outputting documents to desktop printers or digital copiers. The High Quality and Press Quality settings are the same except for two important options: (1) With Press Quality, *Auto-Rotate Pages* is set to *Off* (this is set to *Collectively By File* with High Quality) and (2) when font embedding fails, the PDF conversion process is cancelled (this is set to *Warn and Continue* with High Quality). The PDFX1a and PDFX3 settings are new to Acrobat 6 and provide a way to create PDF/X-1- and X-3-compliant files directly from Acrobat (Acrobat 5 and earlier require a third-party tool to create PDF/X-compliant files).

You can define custom PDF settings by selecting *Settings>Edit Adobe PDF Settings*. Settings created here may be saved and provided to other users. For example, if a printer requires a standard set of Adobe PDF Settings, they may be saved and sent to the user creating the PDF file. We recommend using the Press Quality settings as a base and then tweaking them as follows.

Generating PDF files intended for high-end printing on a commercial press requires an optimized set of Adobe PDF Settings. File size is less of a consideration here than maintaining adequate resolution and embedded fonts. Maintaining the integrity of the original file is the highest priority. Here is how to set up Adobe PDF Settings for "Print-Perfect" PDF files.

The General Tab

The General Adobe PDF settings (Figure 2.13) is where the version of an Acrobat file's compatibility is specified. The Acrobat version selected will dictate which version of PDF (1.2, 1.3, 1.4) is created. File resolution and a default page size are also specified here.

Compatibility. PDF files may be saved as PDF version 1.2, 1.3, or 1.4. Some PostScript Level 3 RIPs can handle PDF 1.4 or 1.5 files, but when creating PDF files for print production, one should use those options with caution. Some RIPs will have difficulty handling PDF files that contain things like transparency, layers, or JPEG200 compression. Some will reject PDF 1.4 or 1.5 files entirely. Since the PDF 1.3 specification contains just about everything needed for quality output for press, there is no reason to set

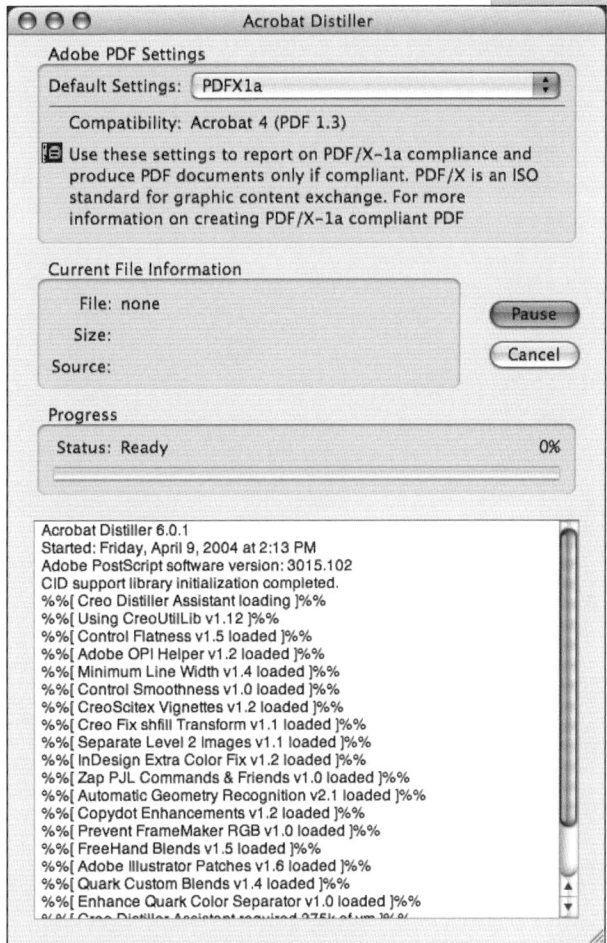

Figure 2.12. The Distiller main interface. The status window shows that the Creo Distiller Assistant plug-in is being used.

the PDF version to 1.4 (unless you wish to secure the files with 128-bit encryption). Transparency is not an issue when creating PDF files from Distiller, because PostScript does not understand transparency, so a PostScript file submitted to Distiller will not contain any transparent objects (they will have been flattened in the creation of the PostScript file). Set Compatibility to *Acrobat 4.0 (PDF 1.3)*; this will sacrifice very little but will ensure that the DeviceN color space (for duotones and spot color vignettes), smooth shading, and large formats are supported.

Object-Level Compression. Select *Off* if you want to maintain structural information such as

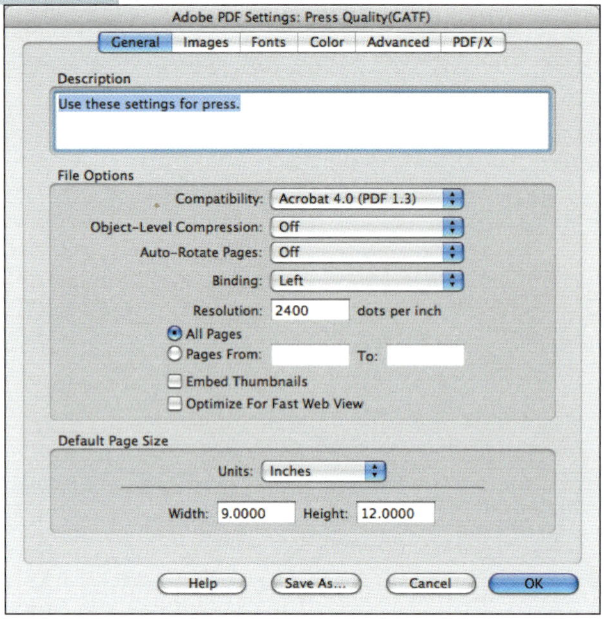

Figure 2.13. The General Adobe PDF settings is where the version of an Acrobat file's compatibility is specified.

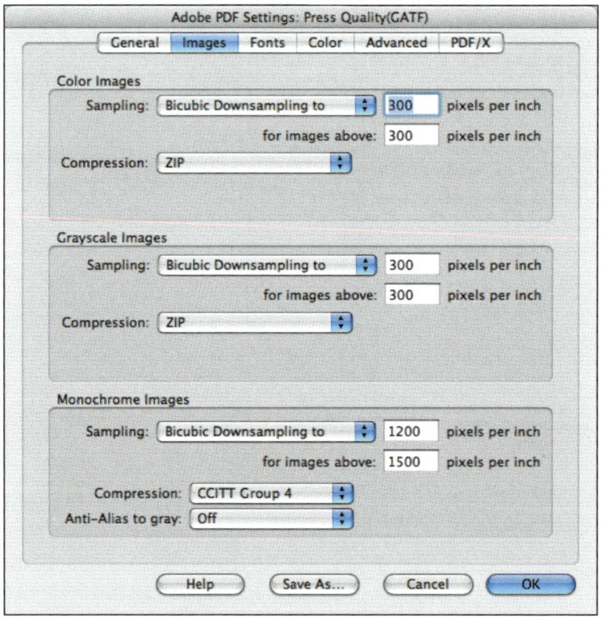

Figure 2.14. The Images tab is where users can set compression or downsampling options to reduce PDF file size. Downsampling throws out excess pixel data only if image files contain more pixels per linear inch than the user indicates here.

accessibility or tagged PDF. This data allows the end user to navigate and interact with bookmarks and other structural information using Acrobat 5.0 or later. Select *Tags Only* if you wish to compress this structural data that would make accessibility, bookmarks, etc., Acrobat 6-compatible only.

Auto-Rotate Pages. This option switches page orientation based on the way the type reads in the PDF file and doesn't need to be checked for print production purposes.

Binding. Binding is for screen-display purposes and affects how pages are viewed in the Continuous-Facing page layout and Thumbnails in the Acrobat viewer. Set Binding to Left (unless you're working with an Asian text or other language that requires right binding).

Resolution. Distiller should be set to emulate the final output device. The resolution setting can affect the number of steps in a blend or gradient. You would think that it would affect the quality of text or line art on output, but it doesn't seem to have any effect in the testing we've done. However, it's best to set resolution to match high-end output devices, which are typically 2400 or 3600 dpi.

Embed Thumbnails. This creates small previews of each page in the PDF file, which aids navigation. This setting will increase the size of the PDF file and is unnecessary for print production, so leave Embed Thumbnails unchecked.

Optimize for Fast Web View. When selected, this option will compress all text and line art. This is designed for page-at-a-time downloading from Web servers and doesn't need to be checked if the PDF file is being created for print production purposes.

Default Page Size. This specifies the page size to use only if one is not indicated in the original file. Generally, this option only applies to EPS files which contain bounding box information but not a page size. PostScript files already contain page-size information and will supersede any setting in this field. The maximum page size for PDF files is 200×200 inches (Acrobat 4 and later).

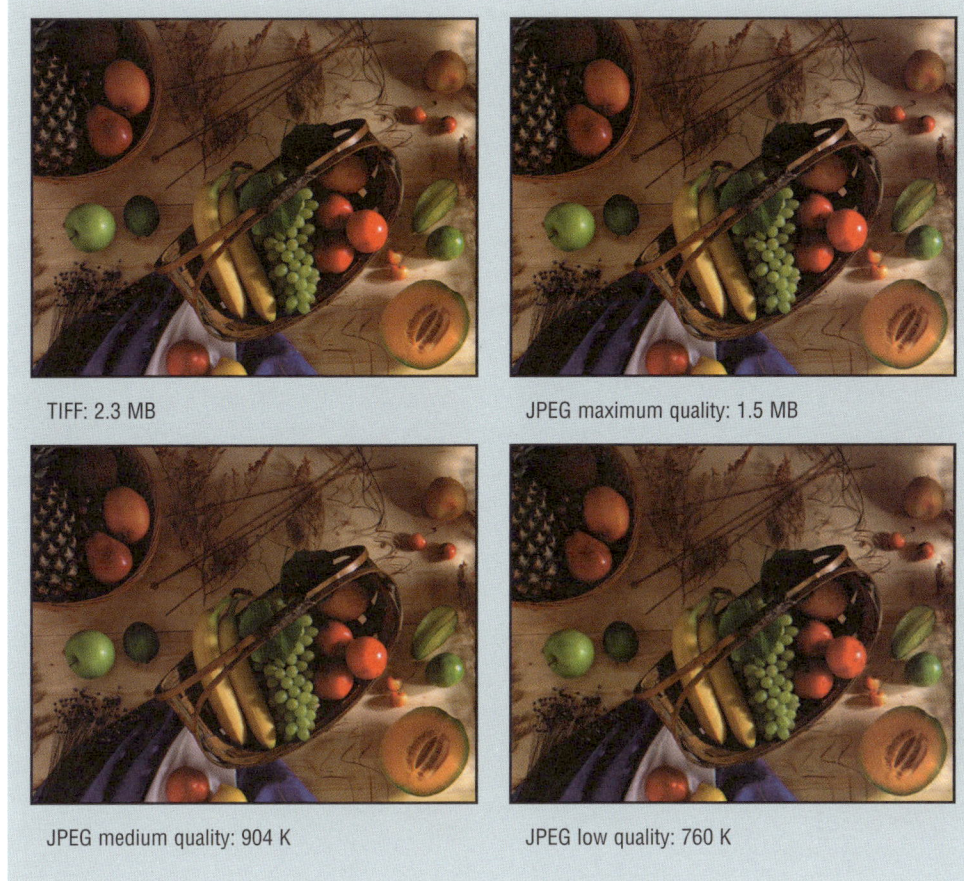

TIFF: 2.3 MB

JPEG maximum quality: 1.5 MB

JPEG medium quality: 904 K

JPEG low quality: 760 K

Figure 2.15. A TIFF file (upper left) and JPEG files showing varying levels of compression.

Compression

Distiller offers the option of compressing image and text files in PDF documents. With the right settings, compression will reduce file size without sacrificing image quality. If you absolutely wish to avoid any chance of image quality being degraded due to compression, uncheck all of the boxes under the Images tab (Figure 2.14). The drawback of this is the resulting PDF file will be much larger than if some form of compression is used. Compression can be used very safely in PDF documents with little or no image degradation. Read on.

ZIP Compression. ZIP compression works well on images that contain large areas of single colors or repeating patterns. ZIP compression is lossless (no

data will be sacrificed) if 4-bit compression is used with 4-bit images and 8-bit compression is used with 8 bit images. ZIP is lossy (data will be sacrificed) if 4-bit compression is used with 8-bit images. While it doesn't offer tremendous compression with four-color bitmap images, ZIP compression results in no loss of data, so it is a completely safe way to gain some image compression.

JPEG Compression. JPEG compression is always lossy: data will be lost when images are compressed. If files are compressed too far, the images in the PDF file will contain visual artifacts. That may sound ominous, but for many images, JPEG compression can be used with little or no noticeable image degradation. Distiller offers five levels of JPEG compression: minimum, low, medium, high, maximum. These options refer to image quality; i.e., minimum is the lowest image quality (most compression), and maximum is the highest image quality (least compression) (Figure 2.15).

JPEG2000 Compression. JPEG2000 is a new international standard for compressing image data. JPEG2000 is not meant to succeed JPEG but is an entirely new form of compression. JPEG2000 supports

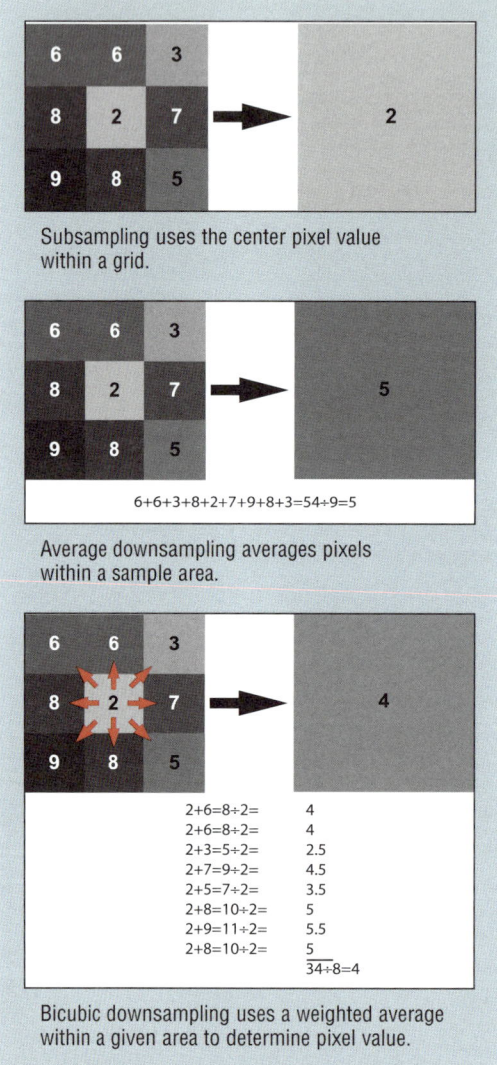

Subsampling uses the center pixel value within a grid.

6+6+3+8+2+7+9+8+3=54÷9=5

Average downsampling averages pixels within a sample area.

2+6=8÷2= 4
2+6=8÷2= 4
2+3=5÷2= 2.5
2+7=9÷2= 4.5
2+5=7÷2= 3.5
2+8=10÷2= 5
2+9=11÷2= 5.5
2+8=10÷2= 5
34÷8=4

Bicubic downsampling uses a weighted average within a given area to determine pixel value.

Figure 2.16. An illustration showing how Distiller samples pixel information.

alpha channel transparency, 16-bit color, and a lossless compression option. Distiller offers six levels of JPEG2000 compression: minimum, low, medium, high, maximum, lossless. These options refer to image quality; i.e., minimum is the lowest image quality (most compression), and lossless is the highest image quality (least compression). A problem with JPEG2000 compression is that a PDF file containing images with this compression scheme can only be displayed with an Acrobat 6 viewer; there is no backward compatibility for older versions of Acrobat. Also, many RIPs don't handle PDF files with JPEG2000 compressed images yet, so we can't recommend using this option yet.

Automatic Compression. Automatic compression enables Distiller to choose the type of compression based on image content. For images that contain sharp transitions, ZIP compression will be used. For all other types of images, JPEG or JPEG2000 compression will be applied.

Sampling. Sampling images refers to averaging and removing pixels from raster images, resulting in smaller file sizes. For example, if you've placed a 300-dpi image into a layout application but scaled it to 50% of the original size, the effective resolution of that image is now 600 dpi, far more than is needed when printing at 150-line screen. Downsampling will throw away that excess data. Distiller can only downsample images; it cannot resample up to increase resolution. Resampling images in Distiller will analyze pixels in a given area and replace those pixels with their average value. Sampling options include Average Downsampling, Subsampling, and Bicubic Downsampling (Figure 2.16).

Average Downsampling. Average downsampling averages pixels within a sample area. The average pixel value is then assigned to the entire pixel area.

Subsampling. Subsampling simply chooses the center pixel value within a sample area. The center pixel value is then assigned to the entire sample area. Subsampling is the fastest of the three methods but yields the lowest quality and should only be used for things like charts.

Bicubic Downsampling. Bicubic downsampling uses a weighted average within a given area to determine pixel value. With this type of downsampling, all pixels are compared and averaged to the center pixel. The new pixel is an average of these neighboring pixels. Bicubic downsampling takes the longest to process, but it yields the best results.

Resampling color or grayscale images requires an appropriate resolution setting (dpi) in the field adjacent to the sampling options pull-down menu. Typically, the value set in the dpi field should be twice the line screen (lpi) of the job printed. The field labeled *For Images Above* is for images that have a resolution above the assigned dpi threshold. Entering the same dpi value here as in the field just above it will further remove unneeded pixels from image files, reducing the size of the PDF file even further.

Downsampling can indeed result in color shift in some pixels of an image, and some purists say that it should not be selected when creating Adobe PDF settings for high-end print production. The informal testing we've done, however, indicates that in most cases bicubic downsampling can be used with little or no noticeable color shift at all.

For example, we created a page with three 600-dpi images (one high key, one low key, and one with flesh tones and neutrals) and then created PDF files from it using different methods of compression. We created one with no compression, one with ZIP only, one with JPEG only, one with ZIP plus bicubic downsampling (for images over 300 dpi), and one with ZIP plus average downsampling (for images over 300 dpi). We then did individual pixel readings at random within each of the images. We found, naturally, no difference in pixel values between the file with no compression and that with ZIP only. The pixels we read in the file created with ZIP plus bicubic downsampling were sometimes dead-on to the file with no compression and sometimes off by a percent or two. There was a little more variance in the file employing average downsampling and even more, as one would expect, with the file containing JPEG-compressed images.

We then printed proofs of the five PDF files and asked the attendees at some of our workshops to review the proofs and tell us if they could see any differences. These are folks who work in the graphic arts industry and are used to reviewing color. Most of them could not see a difference between any of the files; only a few could identify a color shift in the proof made from the PDF file containing the JPEG-compressed images. Everyone said they'd consider all of the proofs sellable in terms of color.

So what's the answer—to downsample or not to downsample? Well, the savings in terms of file size is really not great between ZIP compression and ZIP plus bicubic downsampling, so if you want to take no chances with any type of color shift, select ZIP compression only. However, we feel there is little quality loss in using bicubic downsampling, and ultimately excess image data will be discarded at the RIPing stage anyway, so it's OK to choose that option as well.

CCITT Group 3 and 4. CCITT compression is a general-purpose compression scheme which produces good compression for monochrome images. CCITT compresses images in horizontal rows one row at a time. This type of compression is also used by fax machines.

Run Length Compression. Run Length is a lossless compression format which is best suited for monochrome bitmap images. Images which contain large solid areas of white or black will benefit most from this compression method.

Resampling monochrome images also requires an appropriate resolution setting. Ideally, the resolution setting here should be the same as the intended output device. Keep in mind, though, that a resolution setting above 1500 dpi will significantly increase the size of the PDF file without noticeably increasing quality. We recommend selecting *CCITT Group 4* with a resolution setting of 1500 dpi.

ZIP   JPEG

CCITT   Run Length

Figure 2.17. Suitable compression choices for various art types.

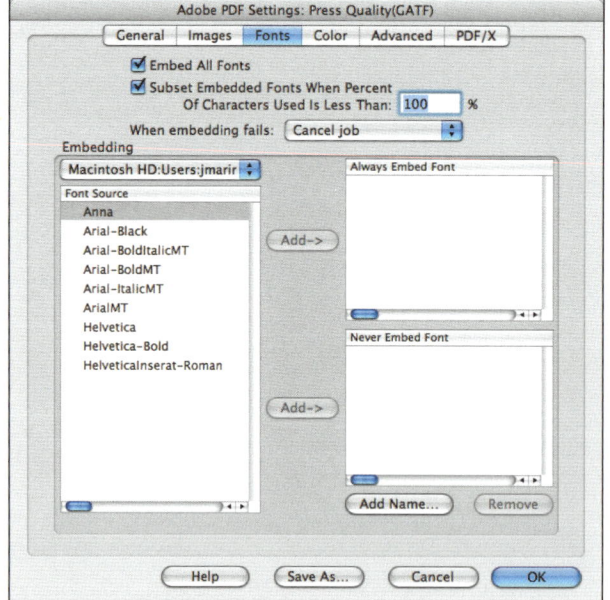

Figure 2.18. One of the most important settings in Distiller, it is critical to include all fonts in PDF files intended for print production.

Compress Text and Line Art. Compression used for text and line art is ZIP. This type of compression results in no loss of image quality and may be selected for all uses. For text compression, ZIP replaces frequently used data (such as the word *the* in a text file) with a single character. The resulting compression ratio is approximately 2:1. Text is stored in a PDF file line by line, meaning that line breaks and paragraph formatting are not honored in the PDF file. If Acrobat is used to make a small correction to a line of text, words will not overflow or rewrap to the next line. The variety of compression options and their relative art styles are shown in Figure 2.17.

Fonts

Ever since the advent of desktop publishing, survey after survey has confirmed that the number one problem with files submitted for print production is missing fonts. Unfortunately, the ability to embed fonts within PDF files has apparently not yet changed this fact. Missing fonts in a project supplied to a service provider for print production means that the job is held up in production until the needed fonts are obtained. The ability to embed fonts within a PDF file is one of the format's greatest strengths (except for fonts that cannot be embedded due to restrictions within the font itself, creators simply need to check the right box to make it happen as shown in Figure 2.18). Embedding fonts will include a compressed, encoded set of glyphs within the PDF file.

Distiller must have access to fonts in order to embed them, and it gets this access in one of two places. Distiller can access fonts that have been included in the PostScript file itself, if the creator set up the virtual printer to include them. If fonts are not contained in the PostScript file, Distiller offers another option for font embedding. Under the Settings menu, there is an option called Font Locations. In the Font Locations dialog box, Distiller can be given access to fonts in specified folders on the computer's hard drive or on another drive accessed over a network. If it finds the fonts called for in the PostScript file, it will embed them into the PDF document. If it does not, it will either use Courier or attempt substitution of the font. Acrobat creates a substitute font by referencing the Multiple Master font descriptions on the host system. The option to cancel any further processing of a PDF file if fonts are not available is an option in Distiller as well. If this is set, a PDF file will not be created if Distiller cannot embed the needed fonts into the PDF file.

When creating PDF files for print production, it is critical to check Embed All Fonts under the Fonts tab. For Type 1 fonts, this will ensure that the entire character set for each font used in the PostScript file is included with the PDF file. Each character set embedded into the PDF file will increase the size of the file by about 40K. Again, if fonts are not embedded, either because they are not available to Distiller or because the Embed All Fonts box is left unchecked, Acrobat will either use Courier or substitute a Multiple Master font when the PDF file is viewed or printed.

Substitute fonts will seldom match the original font exactly, especially for non-standard fonts such as script faces (Figure 2.19). Acrobat uses substitute fonts Adobe SerMM and Adobe SanMM for display on screen or for printing; it never embeds these substitute fonts in PDF files. Further, these substitute fonts are only used by Acrobat and cannot be used by other applications. If you've ever tried to edit a PDF file using Adobe Illustrator but found that the fonts look like alphabet soup when you open the file in that application, it could be because the fonts had not been embedded in the PDF file.

Only Type 1 (PostScript) fonts can be fully embedded into a PDF file. Multiple Master fonts, Type 3, TrueType, and CID (Asian) will always subset, even if subsetting is disabled in Distiller's Fonts options. When subsetting is selected, Distiller only includes the information required to draw the characters (glyphs) actually used in the PDF file. Since subsetting does not embed the entire font set, it can reduce the size of the PDF file. Distiller offers the ability to define a threshold for when to subset a font. The value can be set from 1% to 100%. For example, if the percentage of the font's characters used in the document is

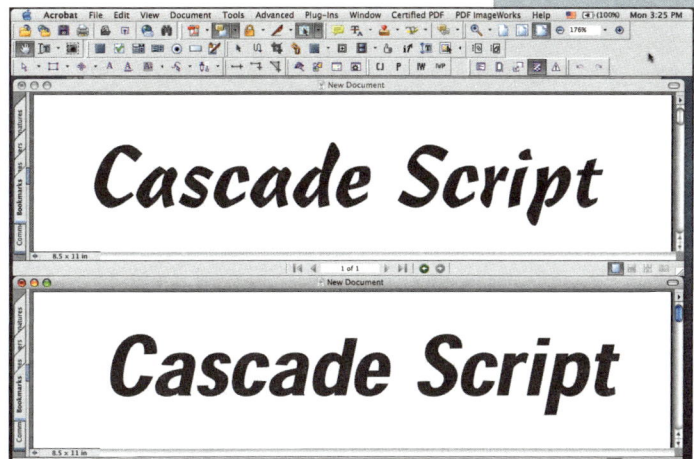

Figure 2.19. Substitute fonts will seldom match the original font exactly, especially for non-standard fonts such as script faces.

higher than the subsetting value, then the entire font set will be embedded. If the percentage of the font's characters is lower than the subsetting value, the font will be subsetted. Some fonts, especially symbols and dingbats, are always fully embedded to make sure the characters are displayed and printed properly.

When fonts are subsetted, they are renamed within the PDF file with a six-letter prefix and a plus (+) sign. For example, EOBDIA+Poetica might be the name given to a subset of the Poetica Type 1 font. If another PDF file were made from the same PostScript file using the same font, it would encode that font with a different name the second time, something like DFEBAC+Poetica. The intention of this is to ensure that the original fonts and font metrics are used and not substituted at print time by the service provider outputting those files.

Prior to Acrobat 6, users of the Enfocus PitStop Pro plug-in could access and edit fonts fully embedded in a PDF file, even if that font was not resident on the computer system they were using. Adobe effectively nipped that capability in the bud, and now any editing of text in a PDF file requires that the font be resident on the computer. Subsetting can cause some problems if PDF files will later be merged. Think about our Poetica example. Imagine a project in which many PDF pages are to be merged into a single PDF document. That merged document will contain multiple subsetted instances of the same font, resulting in things like missing characters, not to mention a larger file size.

Embedding of fonts into PDF or other file types (Flash files for Web display require embedded fonts) have become a big issue with font foundries. Font developers think of the fonts they create as software, protected by usage licensing. TrueType and OpenType fonts can contain usage restrictions set directly in the code by the font foundry or manufacturer. Fonts are increasingly sold with different levels of usage rights so that, for example, a font can contain the right to be used for viewing and printing but not for embedding into digital documents. Agfa Monotype was an early adopter of strict licensing restrictions in the fonts they sold, and for a time some Monotype faces could not be embedded into PDF files at all. A font that cannot be embedded into a PDF file at all makes it worthless for print production purposes. Recognizing this, most font manufacturers offer fonts with the basic license to use the font to view and print documents, but not to edit. Even Adobe has begun to restrict usage of Adobe fonts. Here is the current Adobe policy on font embedding: "Adobe permits embedding certain typefaces into documents for the purposes of viewing and printing only. Documents with embedded typefaces may not be edited unless those embedded typefaces are licensed to and installed on the computer doing the editing. The reason for this is that editing the file adds value to the file. For this, the customer is obtaining value from the typefaces and is therefore required to have a valid license for the typefaces."

Some font sets contain embedding restrictions that were unintentionally set and it went largely unnoticed because earlier versions of interpreters, like Acrobat Distiller 3.0, did not respect font licensing restrictions. Fonts supplied with Corel WordPerfect, for example, contained embedding restrictions that the company did not intend to impose on their clients. (Corel offered a free fix for the problem with the WordPerfect Office 2000 Symbols Fonts Update,

but a recent search found the link to the file is now dead.)

If you attempt to create a PDF file via Distiller and a restricted font has been used in the document, you will likely get this error message:

%%[ProductName: Distiller]%%
%%[Error: [font name] cannot be embedded due to licensing restrictions.]%%
%%[Error: invalidfont; OffendingCommand: (varies)]%%

What can you do if you find that you are working with a font that contains embedding restrictions? Your options are to use another font that does not contain restrictions or to contact the font manufacturer to see if the restriction can be removed, either by purchasing the rights to embed the font or through a fix like the one provided by Corel. While we cannot condone attempts to bypass font licensing restrictions, we have already mentioned that Distiller version 3 did not honor licensing restrictions. When TrueType fonts are included in the PostScript file from a Macintosh application, they are almost always converted to Type 1. When this happens with a font containing embedding restrictions, those restrictions may be removed.

When you purchase a font, you really purchase the right to use it based on a licensing agreement. It's very important that you read the agreement and know what it says before you purchase any font, especially OpenType or TrueType fonts, to see if embedding is allowed. If it isn't, that font is of no value for PDF file creation—so don't buy it! A good online resource for fonts from just about every manufacturer can be found at www.fonthaus.com, where a phone number is provided for potential font buyers to call and discuss licensing issues prior to buying.

A last word on the Fonts tab of Distiller. Make sure you set the *When embedding fails* option to *Cancel job*. The other options can result in a PDF file without embedded fonts—and possible problems down the line in print production.

Color

When it comes to color, Distiller provides two basic options. You can either let color pass through unchanged or you can attach ICC profiles to manage color. The only situation in which color is actually altered using Distiller color management settings is when you select *Convert All Colors to sRGB*, something you'd not generally want to do for print production purposes. Here is a discussion of each of the settings (Figure 2.20).

Settings File. Options here include a variety of default settings from other desktop publishing applications, like Photoshop. If you are using a color-managed workflow, you can choose from a list of existing default settings here. If you are not using an ICC-based color-managed workflow, select *None* from the pull-down menu.

Color Management Policies. This is where you specify how the color will be handled in a PDF file. *Leave Color Unchanged* will leave all images in their current color spaces. *Tag Everything for Color Management* embeds an ICC profile when distilling the PostScript file and affects all color in the document. *Tag Only Images for Color Management* will embed an ICC profile only to images and will leave other color data unchanged. *Convert to sRGB* is device-dependent and is designed primarily for consistent on-screen viewing of PDF files.

Rendering Intent refers to how colors are converted from one color space to another. *Perceptual* preserves the visual accuracy of colors when converting from one space to another, but the actual color values can change. *Saturation* will make colors more saturated and can be used with business graphics such as pie charts but should never be used for high-end printing. *Relative Colorimetric* will adjust the white point of the source space to the white point of the destination space. *Absolute Colorimetric* will map out-of-gamut colors to the closest possible color of the destination gamut. With Absolute Colorimetric, the visual accuracy of colors is sacrificed to maintain the actual numeric color values. Selecting *Default*

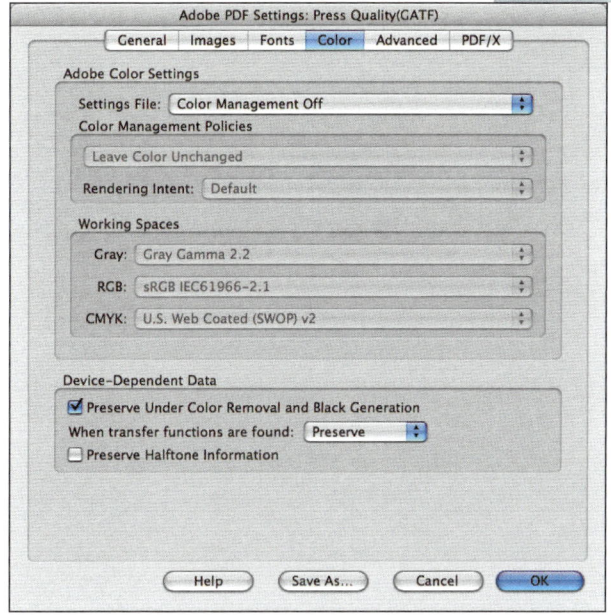

Figure 2.20. Distiller provides options to either let color pass through unchanged or to attach an ICC profile to manage color.

from the list will use the intent specified in the output device, typically Relative Colorimetric.

Working Spaces. This allows you to choose from the ICC profiles available on your system. Choosing *None* for gray, RGB, or CMYK is the same as setting *Color Management Policies* to *Leave Color Unchanged*.

Preserve Under Color Removal and Black Generation. When selected, this option will preserve the black channel in CMYK images. *Undercolor removal (UCR)* refers to how much cyan, magenta, and yellow is replaced with black in a color separation. This is done to reduce the amount of ink applied to the press sheet when the job is printed which, in turn, reduces ink drying problems. If you are not using a color-managed workflow, our tests have shown that this selection has no effect on CMYK images to which UCR or gray component replacement (GCR) has already been applied.

When Transfer Functions Are Found. A transfer function may be applied and saved to an image in Photoshop. Transfer functions can be used for special

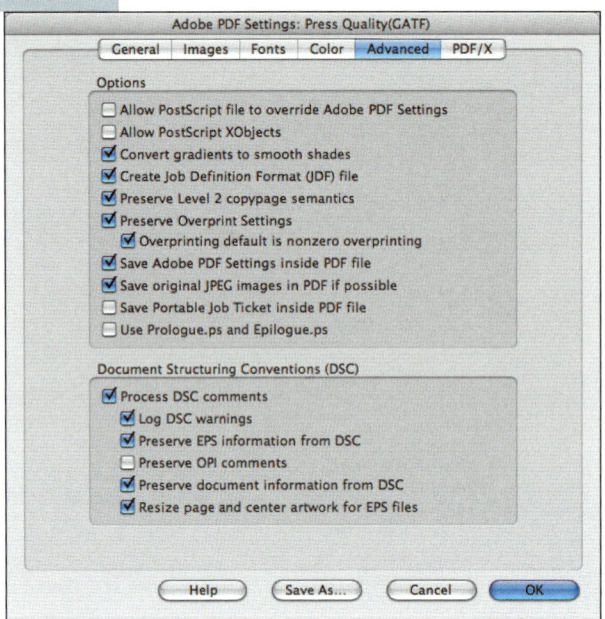

Figure 2.21. The Advanced tab contains settings for high-end printing, like ensuring overprint objects pass through into the PDF.

effects or to compensate for printing conditions, like dot gain. *Preserve* will keep the transfer functions so they can be applied when the file is output. *Remove* will strip out any transfer information applied to an image. *Apply* will not simply maintain the transfer curve but will apply it to the images in the PDF file. As a general rule, we recommend that you remove transfer functions.

Preserve Halftone Information. Halftone information, or dot shapes, line screens (lpi), and screen angles, can be saved along with an image in Photoshop. Selecting this option will preserve this information. Again, this is generally something to be set later in the production process by the output provider.

Advanced

The Advanced Adobe PDF Settings contain all of the options that are necessary for high-end printing (Figure 2.21). Controls here include the ability to include portable job ticket information, OPI information, and overprints in a PDF file. PostScript

smooth shading is also enabled in the Advanced Adobe PDF settings.

Allow PostScript File to Override Adobe PDF Settings. It is possible to set specific parameters to control things like compression or font embedding in a PostScript file, and those settings can be allowed to take precedence over the Distiller settings if this button is checked. Deselecting this will enable the Adobe PDF Settings to take precedence over settings in the PostScript file. This is for advanced users who understand PostScript coding, and, as a general rule, we suggest disabling *Allow PostScript file to override Adobe PDF Settings.*

Allow PostScript XObjects. PostScript XObjects are bits of PostScript code that, if this button is checked, can be passed into the PDF file uninterpreted (i.e., it won't be "distilled"). These are things that could be executed in specific digital printing workflows, like drawer pulls for digital print projects. PostScript XObjects are not allowed in the PDF/X specification, and some RIPs may not be able to process PDF files with PostScript XObjects included. As a general rule, leave *Allow PostScript XObjects* unchecked.

Convert Gradients to Smooth Shades. The ability to improve blends created in the originating application is accomplished through a PostScript operator called "smooth shading." When smooth shading is invoked, PostScript files are scanned for blends. These blends are then replaced with superior PostScript Level 3 smooth shading, which supports thousands of gray levels, not just 256. To avoid banding in blends created in native application files, select the *Convert gradients to smooth shades* option.

Create Job Definition Format (JDF) File. Selecting this setting will create an XML-based job ticket designed to exchange information from different applications and systems used in print production. JDF is a specification required if a printer has implemented computer-integrated manufacturing (CIM) in the production workflow. If your service provider requires, you may have to select this option, otherwise leave unchecked. This information may be used if the printer is using a CIM print workflow, but unless you know that the service provider you're sending the file to is using one, there's no need to select this option.

Preserve Level 2 Copypage Semantics. Copypage was an operator that was used primarily to test Level 2 printers. It's been replaced by the "showpage" operator in PostScript 3. Sometimes preserving copypage semantics will help if a PDF file will not print to a Level 2 device. Check with your service provider for this setting. It is typically not necessary to select this option.

Preserve Overprint Settings. When creating files from native applications such as FreeHand, Illustrator, QuarkXPress, and InDesign, the option of overprinting colors is available. This is typically done to create traps in the applications or for special effects. To preserve the overprints set in these illustrations, select this option. If you don't, all overprint settings made in the native applications will be lost in the resultant PDF file.

Overprinting Default Is Nonzero Overprinting. Applies to process colors, patterns, and smooth shades. This option should always be turned on when *Preserve Overprint Settings* is used in order to ensure proper conversion of overprints.

Save Adobe PDF Settings Inside PDF File. Selecting this option will embed the settings used in Distiller to create the PDF file. This information is very useful in the preflighting process to determine if optimum settings were used to create the PDF. This information can be accessed in Acrobat by selecting *Document>File Attachments*.

Save Original JPEG Images in PDF if Possible. Selecting this option will process JPEG-compressed images that were placed in the native application without recompressing them. When selected, Distiller will decompress JPEG images to ensure that they are not corrupt, but leave the original JPEG compression intact. This is a good option to check since it speeds up processing because JPEG files

are left in their original compression format and are not recompressed in Distiller.

Save Portable Job Ticket Inside PDF file. Think of a portable job ticket as an envelope which carries information in a PDF about the original PostScript file. Job tickets carry information such as page size, trapping information, line screen, and resolution. This information may be used in various high-end PDF workflows, but unless you know that the service provider you're sending the file to is using one, there's no need to select this option.

Use Prologue.ps and Epilogue.ps. When Acrobat 6 is installed, two files named prologue.ps and epilogue.ps are placed in the Acrobat 5.0> Distiller>Data folder (Windows) and in the Users> Shared>Adobe PDF 6.0>Data folder (Mac OS X). Think of prologue.ps and epilogue.ps as templates where code can be written to enhance PDF files. For example, prologue.ps is sent before the body of Post-Script code and can be used to add a cover page to all distilled PDF documents. Also, Distiller 4.0 does not have an option for smooth shading, but by editing the prologue.ps file, smooth shading can be invoked. The epilogue.ps file is sent at the end of the body of PostScript and can be used to resolve PostScript procedure problems.

Distiller will process the prologue.ps and epilogue.ps files only when they are placed in the proper location. If the Open command or watched folders are used to process PostScript, the files need to be located in the same folder as the Distiller application. Unless you have some specific code that you need to use when Distilling files, leave *Use Prologue.ps and Epilogue.ps* unchecked.

Process DSC Comments. Document structuring comments (DSC) contains information, or metadata, about a PDF file. Selecting this option enables Distiller to scan the PostScript or EPS file for the original creator application, creation date, file size, PDF version, page size, and security information. This data can be very useful for the service provider when preflighting the PDF file.

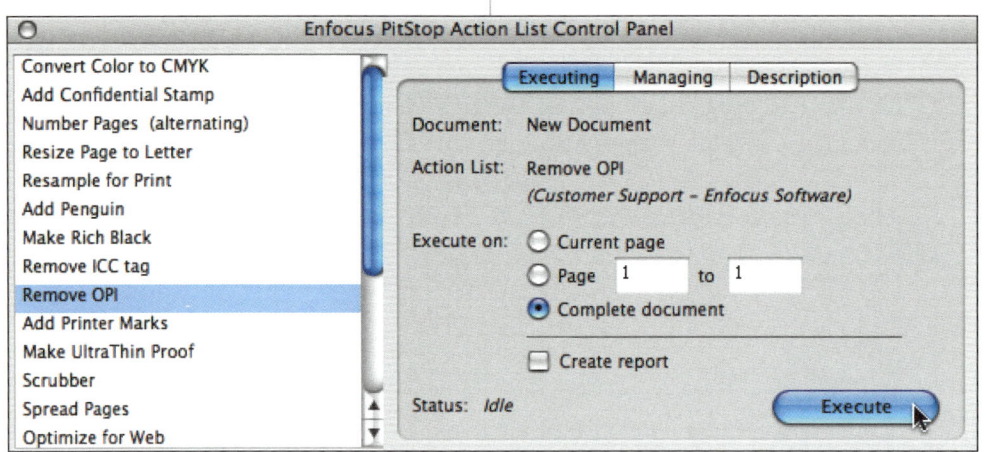

Figure 2.22. Using an Enfocus PitStop Action, OPI comments can be eliminated from a PDF file in one fell swoop.

Log DSC Warnings. Selecting this option will enable Distiller to scan for errors found in the document structuring comments. Any errors encountered will be added to a log file. This option is generally not necessary and can remain unchecked.

Preserve EPS Information from DSC. This option preserves DSC information from EPS files such as the original creator application, creation date, file size, PDF version, page size, and security information. This information is valuable during the preflighting process and can be viewed in the File>Document Properties>Summary dialog box.

Preserve OPI Comments. The Open Prepress Interface (OPI) is a system in which high-resolution color images reside on a central server to which all other workstations have access. Low-resolution images are sent out from the server and placed into the page layout document. When the document is printed, the low-resolution images in the page layout document are swapped out for the high-resolution images on the server. The advantage of this type of workflow is that low-resolution files in the page layout document minimize network traffic and speed up the printing process. OPI information is retained in a PDF as an invisible window on top of each image. This can make editing a PDF file more difficult.

If you are involved in using an OPI workflow, select this option; otherwise leave *Preserve OPI*

Comments unchecked. Images with OPI comments preserved will have a sort of bounding box placed in front of them. When you attempt to access such an image using a selection tool in Acrobat, instead of selecting the raster image file, you will select this bounding box. Drilling down to the actual image object can be a frustrating experience. OPI comments can be eliminated in PDF files in one fell swoop using a preset action available with the Enfocus PitStop Professional plug-in for Acrobat (Figure 2.22).

Preserve Document Information from DSC. Selecting this option allows processed DSC comments to be displayed for a PDF document in Acrobat's File>Document Properties... dialog box. This dialog box contains metadata (information about the PDF file), including the original creator application, creation date, file size, PDF version, page size, and security information. This information is quite valuable for preliminary preflighting of a PDF document. See Chapter 4 for a more thorough discussion of the preflighting process.

Resize Page and Center Artwork for EPS Files. EPS files do not contain page size information, rather they are defined by a bounding box. If this option is not checked, the distilled EPS file will be placed in the lower lefthand corner of the PDF file, which will be the size indicated as the default page size under the General tab in Distiller Adobe PDF

Settings. If the EPS file is larger than the page specified in the General Adobe PDF Settings, image clipping will occur. Selecting this option will resize the PDF page to accommodate the bounding box of the EPS file. This option is used only for jobs that consist of a single EPS file.

PDF/X

As discussed in Chapter 1, PDF/X files are designed to meet standards required for high-end print production (Figure 2.23). The options in this tab are used to ensure that the PostScript file being distilled meets PDF/X-1a or PDF/X-3 standards before the PDF file is created. Also, options may be selected in the PDF/X tab to make sure that PostScript file meets additional criteria.

PDF/X-1a or PDF/X-3. Select which compliance the PDF file should meet. Select the PDF/X-1a standard. For more information on these two standards, see Chapter 1.

When Not Compliant. Options here are *Continue* or *Cancel Job*. Choosing *Continue* will create the PDF along with a text file noting problems found. *Cancel Job* will create a PDF file only if all the criteria in the PDF/X tab are satisfied. If both *PDF/X-1a* and *PDF/X-3* are selected and only one set of PDF/X criteria is met (for example, PDF/X-1a only), Distiller creates the compliant file and notes the problem in the report. If you have to provide a PDF/X-compliant file, the only sensible option to select here is *Cancel Job* so you don't erroneously create a PDF file that doesn't meet the PDF/X specification.

If Neither TrimBox nor ArtBox Are Specified. The *Report as error* option will flag an error if there is no trim or art box specified in the PostScript file. This is unlikely from any file created from a desktop publishing application. The other option is to enter actual offsets via *Set TrimBox to MediaBox*. This will create a media box from the values you enter in the fields added to the Default Page Size setting under the General tab (Figure 2.24). The Default Page Size becomes the Trim Box, and the Default Page Size plus

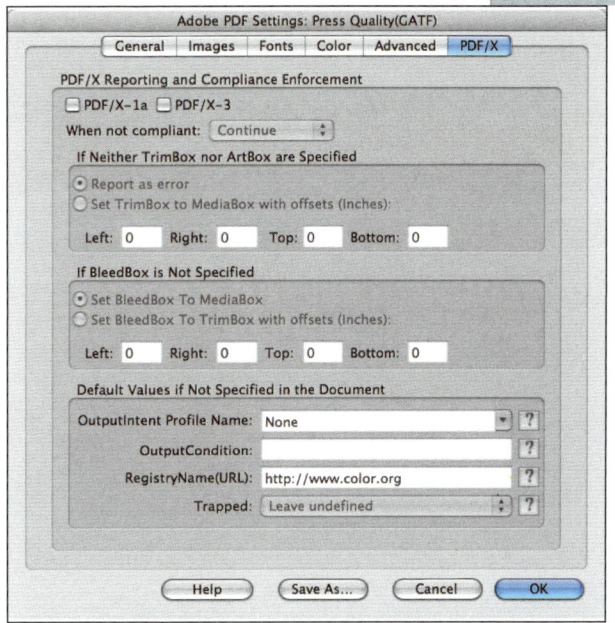

Figure 2.23. The PDF/X tab includes options to ensure that the PDF file created will meet the PDF/X-1a or PDF/X-3 standards.

offsets becomes the media box size. Select the *Set TrimBox to MediaBox* with offsets radio button.

If Bleed Box is Not Specified. You can specify Distiller to *Set BleedBox to MediaBox* which will use the media box value if the bleed box value is not specified. The other option is to *Set BleedBox to TrimBox* and specify offsets. This will create a bleed box from the values you enter in the fields added to the Default Page Size setting under the General tab. The Default Page Size becomes the Trim Box, and the Default Page Size plus offsets becomes the bleed box size. Select the *Set BleedBox to MediaBox* radio button.

Default Values if Not Specified in the Document. The OutputIntent Profile Name (required for PDF/X compliance) represents a printing condition (or profile) for which the document is prepared. If a document does not specify an output profile, Distiller will use a profile from this menu.

OutputCondition. You can describe the intended printing condition in the OutputCondition field. The description entered here (not required for

Figure 2.24. PDF page boxes consist of (A) media box, (B) bleed box, (C) trim box, and (D) art box.

compliance) is purely informational and can be useful for the service provider outputting the file.

RegistryName(URL). The RegistryName(URL) is used to indicate the Web address for more information on the registry (not required for compliance). The URL is automatically entered for ICC registry names.

Trapped. The Trapped setting indicates whether the document has been trapped. A value of *True or False* is required for PDF/X. (The default option is "unknown" and will be used if True or False is not set here.) If a document does not otherwise specify a

Trapped value, the state (True or False) specified here will be used. Selecting *Undefined* will require the document to specify the Trapped state or else fail compliance.

After all of the options have been set, the Adobe PDF Settings file must be given a unique name and then saved for future use. Adobe PDF Settings files can be shared between cross-platform users as long as they are properly named—those created on a Mac can be accessed by PC users and vice versa. They will automatically be saved into the correct folder or directory on the computer used to create the Job

Press

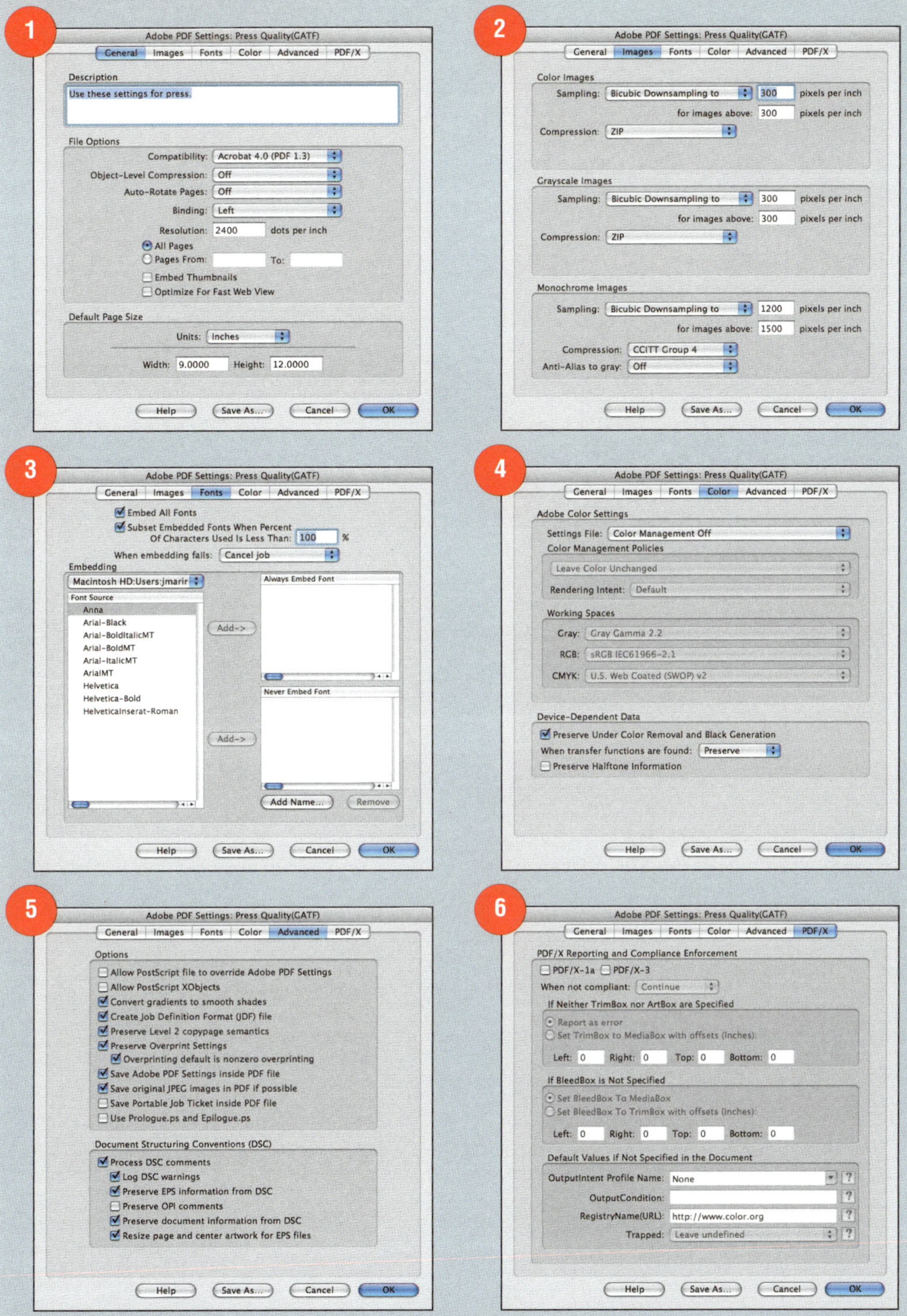

Figure 2.25. Here's a recap of Distiller Job Options settings for high-end print production output.

Digital Printing

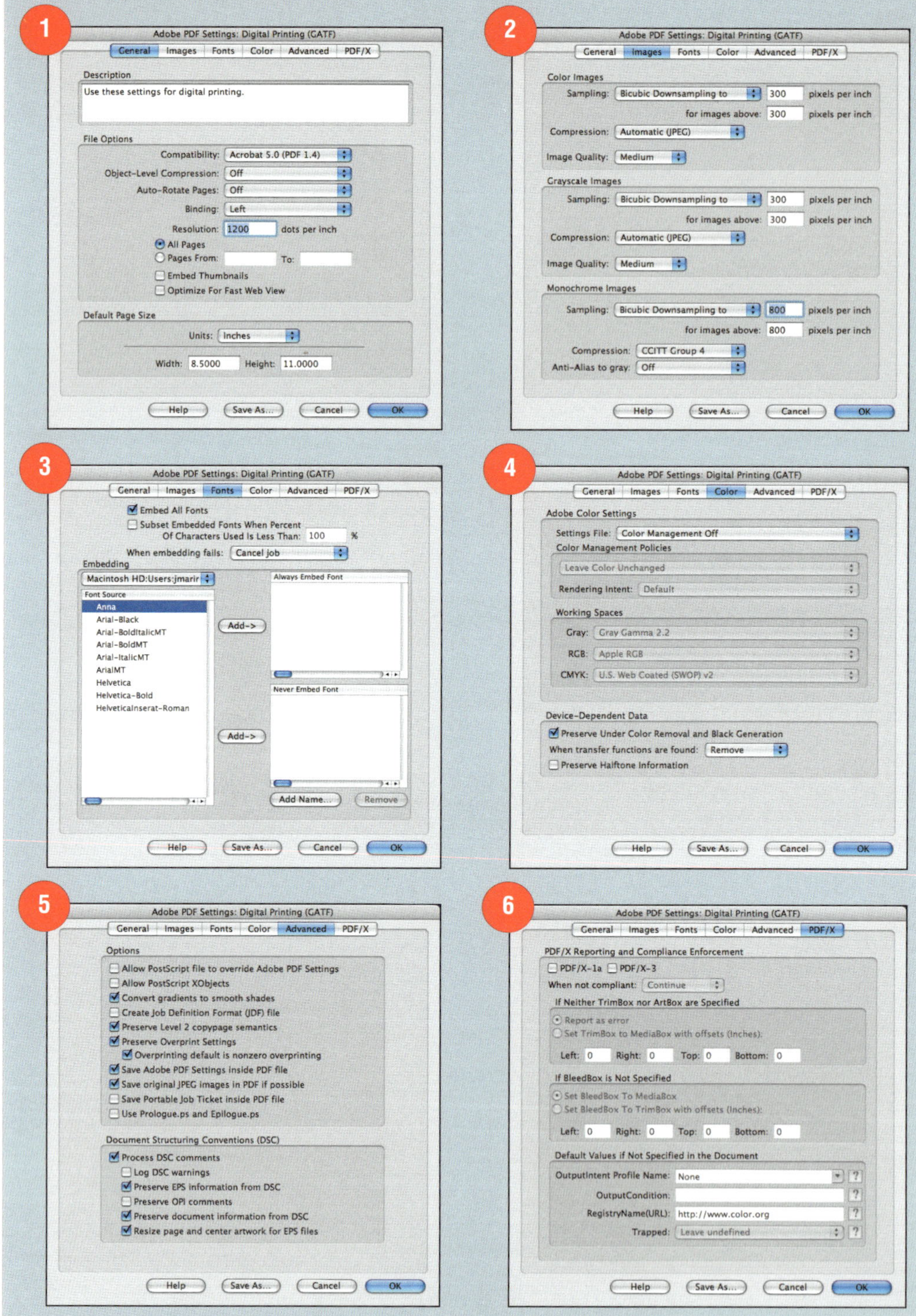

Figure 2.26. These Distiller Job Options are appropriate for digital printing.

Screen

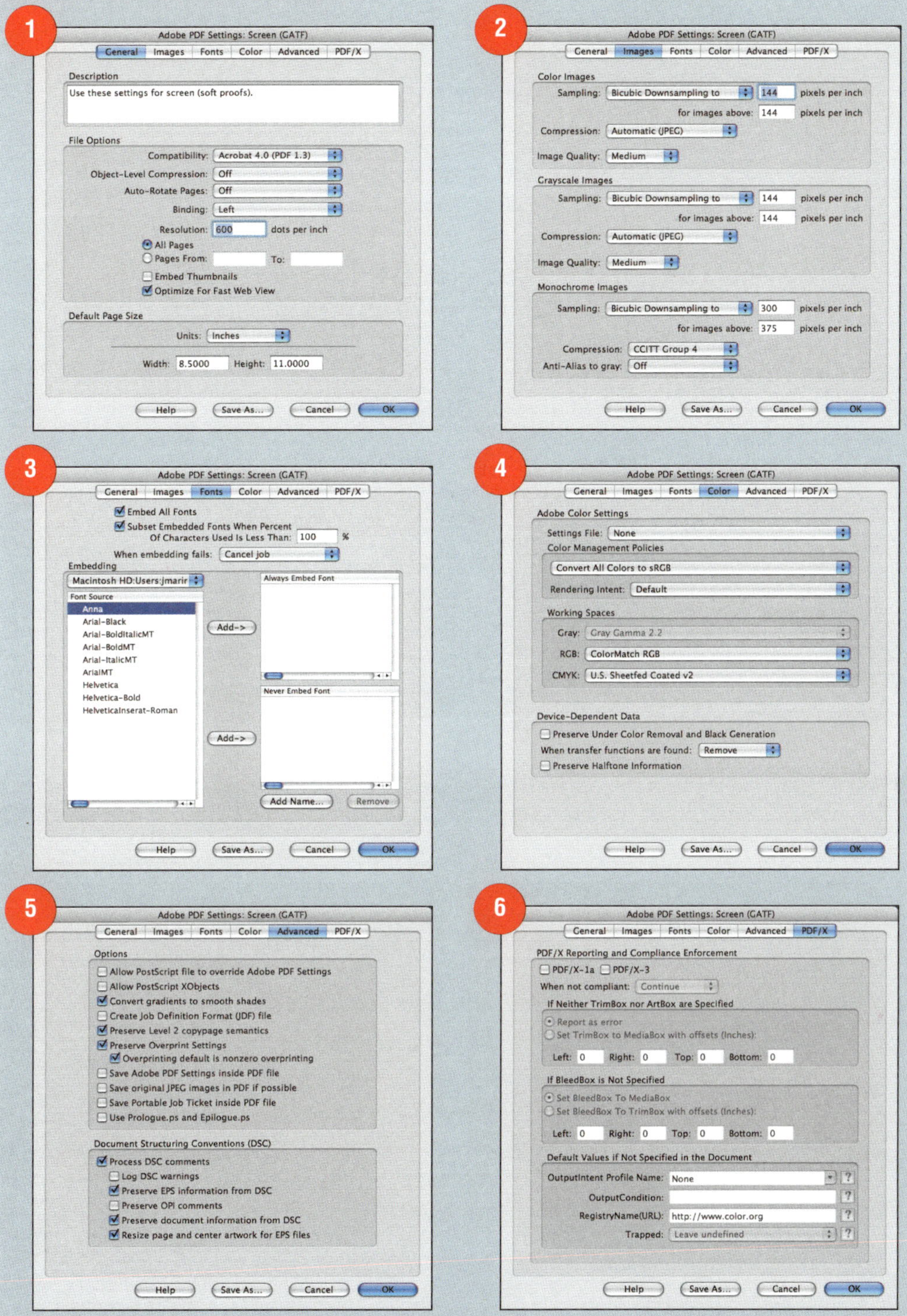

1 Adobe PDF Settings: Screen (GATF)

General | Images | Fonts | Color | Advanced | PDF/X

Description
Use these settings for screen (soft proofs).

File Options
Compatibility: Acrobat 4.0 (PDF 1.3)
Object-Level Compression: Off
Auto-Rotate Pages: Off
Binding: Left
Resolution: 600 dots per inch
● All Pages
○ Pages From: To:
☐ Embed Thumbnails
☑ Optimize For Fast Web View

Default Page Size
Units: Inches
Width: 8.5000 Height: 11.0000

Help | Save As... | Cancel | OK

2 Adobe PDF Settings: Screen (GATF)

General | Images | Fonts | Color | Advanced | PDF/X

Color Images
Sampling: Bicubic Downsampling to | 144 | pixels per inch
for images above: 144 | pixels per inch
Compression: Automatic (JPEG)
Image Quality: Medium

Grayscale Images
Sampling: Bicubic Downsampling to | 144 | pixels per inch
for images above: 144 | pixels per inch
Compression: Automatic (JPEG)
Image Quality: Medium

Monochrome Images
Sampling: Bicubic Downsampling to | 300 | pixels per inch
for images above: 375 | pixels per inch
Compression: CCITT Group 4
Anti-Alias to gray: Off

Help | Save As... | Cancel | OK

3 Adobe PDF Settings: Screen (GATF)

General | Images | Fonts | Color | Advanced | PDF/X

☑ Embed All Fonts
☑ Subset Embedded Fonts When Percent
Of Characters Used Is Less Than: 100 %
When embedding fails: Cancel job

Embedding
Macintosh HD:Users:jmarin
Font Source | Always Embed Font
Anna
Arial-Black
Arial-BoldItalicMT
Arial-BoldMT   Add->
Arial-ItalicMT
ArialMT
Helvetica
Helvetica-Bold
HelveticaInserat-Roman

Never Embed Font

Add->

Add Name... | Remove

Help | Save As... | Cancel | OK

4 Adobe PDF Settings: Screen (GATF)

General | Images | Fonts | Color | Advanced | PDF/X

Adobe Color Settings
Settings File: None
Color Management Policies
Convert All Colors to sRGB
Rendering Intent: Default

Working Spaces
Gray: Gray Gamma 2.2
RGB: ColorMatch RGB
CMYK: U.S. Sheetfed Coated v2

Device-Dependent Data
☐ Preserve Under Color Removal and Black Generation
When transfer functions are found: Remove
☐ Preserve Halftone Information

Help | Save As... | Cancel | OK

5 Adobe PDF Settings: Screen (GATF)

General | Images | Fonts | Color | Advanced | PDF/X

Options
☐ Allow PostScript file to override Adobe PDF Settings
☐ Allow PostScript XObjects
☑ Convert gradients to smooth shades
☐ Create Job Definition Format (JDF) file
☑ Preserve Level 2 copypage semantics
☑ Preserve Overprint Settings
☑ Overprinting default is nonzero overprinting
☐ Save Adobe PDF Settings inside PDF file
☐ Save original JPEG images in PDF if possible
☐ Save Portable Job Ticket inside PDF file
☐ Use Prologue.ps and Epilogue.ps

Document Structuring Conventions (DSC)
☑ Process DSC comments
☐ Log DSC warnings
☑ Preserve EPS information from DSC
☐ Preserve OPI comments
☑ Preserve document information from DSC
☑ Resize page and center artwork for EPS files

Help | Save As... | Cancel | OK

6 Adobe PDF Settings: Screen (GATF)

General | Images | Fonts | Color | Advanced | PDF/X

PDF/X Reporting and Compliance Enforcement
☐ PDF/X-1a ☐ PDF/X-3
When not compliant: Continue
If Neither TrimBox nor ArtBox are Specified
● Report as error
○ Set TrimBox to MediaBox with offsets (Inches):
Left: 0   Right: 0   Top: 0   Bottom: 0

If BleedBox is Not Specified
● Set BleedBox To MediaBox
○ Set BleedBox To TrimBox with offsets (Inches):
Left: 0   Right: 0   Top: 0   Bottom: 0

Default Values if Not Specified in the Document
OutputIntent Profile Name: None
OutputCondition:
RegistryName(URL): http://www.color.org
Trapped: Leave undefined

Help | Save As... | Cancel | OK

Figure 2.27. These Distiller Job Options are appropriate for on-screen viewing of PDF files.

Options file. Back in the Acrobat 5 days, it was critical that Distiller Job Options be saved in a certain folder in order for Distiller to see the file. With version 6, Adobe PDF Settings can be dragged and dropped over the Distiller application, which will launch with those PDF Settings open! Double-clicking a PDF Settings file will also launch Distiller. For long-term storage, however, it's important to place Adobe PDF Settings in the default folder so Distiller will access it at all times (for Windows: *Acrobat>Distiller>Settings,* for Mac OS X: *Users>Shared>Adobe PDF 6.0>Settings)*. Some compression applications allow the user to save the file to be restored to the same location on the destination computer from which it was compressed on the source computer—a great option for Windows users in particular, as long as both the source and destination computers are Wintel machines.

Creating PDF Files for Digital Printing

PDF files are also the perfect file format for digital printing devices such as laser printers, inkjet printers, and high-speed digital copiers. The settings discussed earlier which are suitable for press can serve as a good foundation (Figure 2.25). However, since digital printing devices print at a much lower resolution (typically 600 dpi) than what is required for film imagesetting or platesetting, adjustments to

these press settings are needed. The settings illustrated in Figure 2.26 are suitable for monochrome and color digital printing devices.

Creating PDF Files for Screen (Soft Proofing)

One of the major advantages of PDF is the ability to deliver documents electronically. Soft proofing PDFs can be very useful during the correction cycle of a job. Soft proofing refers to utilizing a computer monitor to represent the final printed product. PDF files can be sent to the customer via the Internet, marked up using comment tools in Acrobat, then sent back to the printer for corrections. Finally, delivery of PDF documents electronically is instantaneous (unlike using a courier service), saving time.

Adobe PDF Settings for creating PDF for soft proofing requires settings which will create a compact file (Figure 2.27). This is a balancing act, however, because file size is not the most important consideration for soft proofing. The goal is to reduce file size for faster file transfer while maintaining the document's integrity. Fonts must be included, and image resolution should be high enough to hold adequate detail when magnified on screen (Figure 2.28).

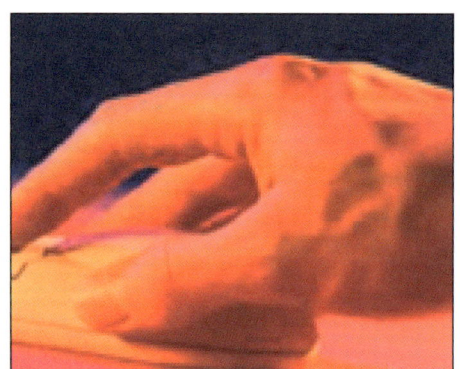 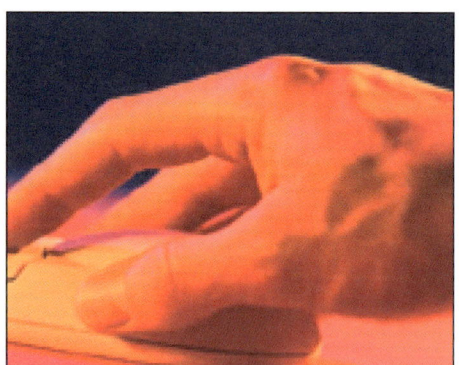

A 72-dpi image resolution enlarged to 200%.   A 144-dpi image resolution enlarged to 200%.

Figure 2.28. Typically, a resolution of 72-dpi is adequate for screen viewing. However, if the PDF must be enlarged on screen to inspect images more closely, more resolution will be required. Both PDF files above were enlarged to 200% on screen. Note the loss of image quality in the 72-dpi image (left) while the 144-dpi image (right) retains more detail.

Creating PDFs from QuarkXPress 6.0

QuarkXPress 6 contains a built-in Export to PDF function but it is still using the "PostScript to PDF" method. In version 5, Quark offered an XTension that allowed the user to export a PDF file, by printing a PostScript file (invisibly to the user) and then accessing Acrobat Distiller to create the PDF file. For version 6, Quark licensed the Global Graphics Jaws Library for PDF creation. You can set up the export layout as PDF defaults so that every time a PDF is created, you use the same options. Here's how to do it:

1. In QuarkXPress, select *QuarkXPress> Preferences.* In the Preferences dialog box, select *PDF* from the list and click the Default Options button (Figure 2.29).

2. In the Layout Info tab, you can set up defaults for Title, Subject, Author, and Creator (Figure 2.30). Information entered here will be included in the PDF file and can be viewed in the Document Properties dialog box.

3. In the Hyperlinks tab, any hyperlinks or other navigational objects created in the QuarkXPress document can be carried through to the PDF by selecting these settings (Figure 2.31). If it's necessary to carry over this information, select *Include Hyperlinks*—otherwise leave it unchecked. Creating PostScript to make a PDF (and not the Export Layout as PDF option) will drop any hyperlinks or bookmarks since these objects are not supported by PostScript.

4. The Job Options (Figure 2.32) tab is similar to the Fonts and Image tabs found in Acrobat Distiller. Here is where you will find options on how to handle fonts and images in the PDF.

- The Font Options section gives you the option to embed and subset fonts in the PDF file. As with Adobe Distiller settings, you should always choose to embed all fonts. In addition, you also have the option of subsetting fonts.

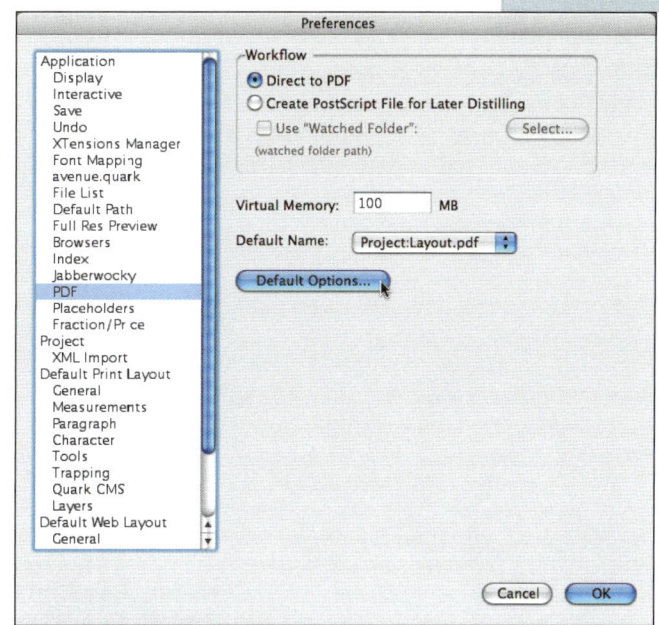

Figure 2.29. Set default options for the built-in export-to-PDF function in QuarkXPress 6.x.

Figure 2.30. The first screen of the PDF Export Options built into QuarkXPress 6. The PostScript interpreter licensed by Quark is the Global Graphics Jaws PDF Interpreter.

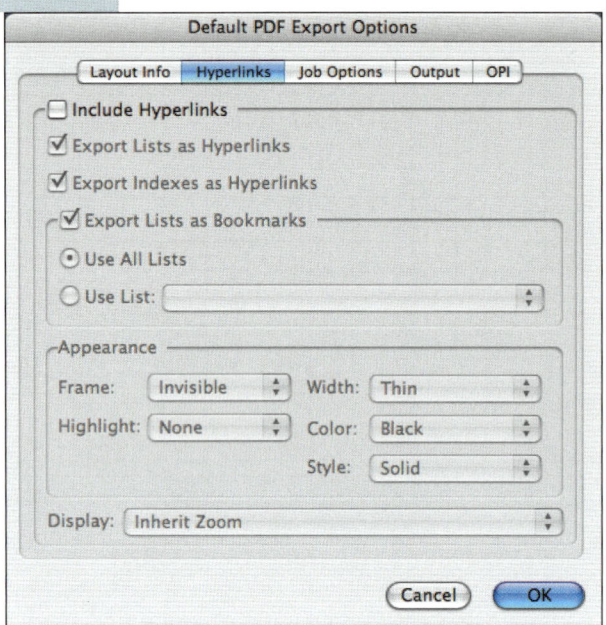

Figure 2.31. While not too important for print-ready PDF files, hyperlinks can be included in QuarkXPress-exported PDF files.

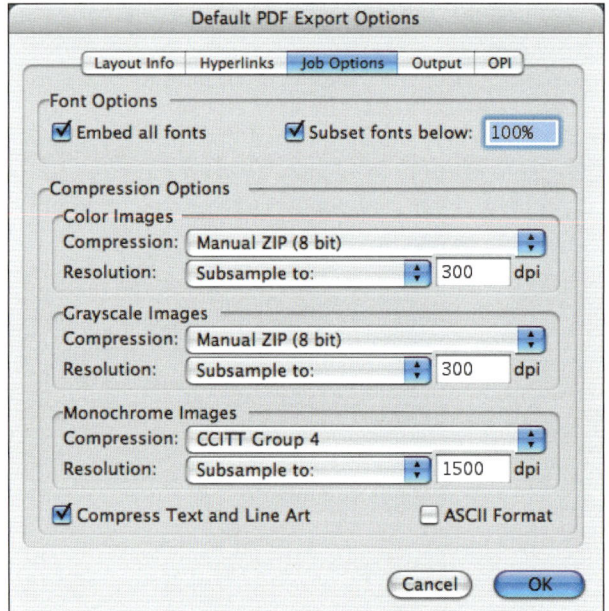

Figure 2.32. The Job Options tab offers font and compression options for PDF files exported from QuarkXPress.

• Image compression options for color and grayscale images are also found here. As with Distiller, you have the option of choosing ZIP, JPEG, or Automatic compression. But beware, if you choose JPEG High here, you'll get high compression and lowest image quality—this is different from Distiller. In Distiller, a High setting means high image quality with minimum compression. An Automatic setting with Low compression gives you a compact PDF file without sacrificing image quality.

Downsampling is handled with an option called Resolution. If you wish to invoke downsampling select either *Downsample,* which will use bicubic downsampling, or *Subsample,* which will use the "average" method of downsampling.

• The Monochrome Images compression options are similar to those found in Distiller. For most efficient compression, choose *CCITT Group 4* with a resolution setting of 1500 dpi (more than 1500 dpi can't be seen and will make the size of the PDF file significantly larger).

• *Compress Text and Line Art* should always be selected since this compression is lossless.

5. The Output tab gives you control over color output, OPI, register marks, and bleeds (Figure 2.33).

• The Print Colors pull-down menu offers six different options for color handling in the PDF file:

- Black & White—Converts all colors to solid black-and-white, not tints.

- Grayscale—Converts color to grayscale with tints.

- CMYK—Outputs spots as spot, CMYK as CMYK, but will not convert spot colors to CMYK in the PDF.

- RGB—Prints spots as spot, CMYK images as CMYK, RGB images as RGB, and CMYK screen builds as RGB.

- As Is—Outputs color in the model it is defined in (for color-managed workflows).

- DeviceN—Stores spot color info and their CMYK equivalents for output to CMYK and spot color output devices. TIFF images placed in Quark can have a color applied to them. Adding another color to the background picture box is a common way to create a "fake duotone." In Quark 5 and earlier, TIFF images colorized with a spot color would always convert to the process equivalent in composite PDF files (unless the user had a special XTension from Creo or Agfa to preserve spot colors). With the new DeviceN option, those XTensions are no longer needed. This is the best choice for press output. Note: We've found that if we save a PostScript file using the DeviceN color space and then attempt to interpret that PostScript file with Acrobat Distiller, the file invariably fails! Exporting the PDF directly from Quark works just fine, however and the resultant PDF file processes properly on several Adobe PostScript 3 RIPs and a Harlequin PostScript 3 RIP. Remember, DeviceN is only supported by PostScript Level 3 devices. Printing DeviceN spot colors to a Level 2 device will result in CMYK output.

- OPI (open prepress interface) can be selected if you're using an OPI workflow.

- Registration can be turned on to include register marks in the PDF.

- Bleed options are *Symmetric* and *Asymmetric*. Symmetric gives you the option of entering one bleed amount for all edges of the page, while Asymmetric allows you to define bleeds individually for each page's edge. A typical bleed amount is one-eighth inch.

6. Unnecessary OPI comments can make it difficult to edit images in PDF files down the line in production, so we recommend that you leave the OPI

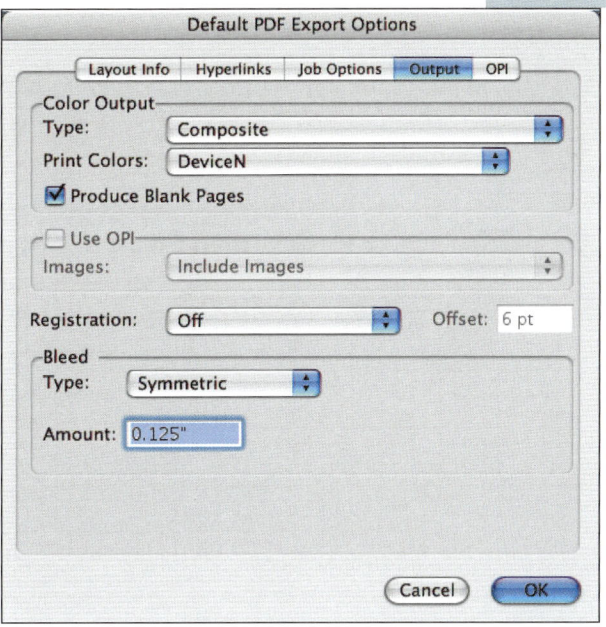

Figure 2.33. QuarkXPress 6 offers a couple of new color output options, including DeviceN, useful for files with colorized TIFFs.

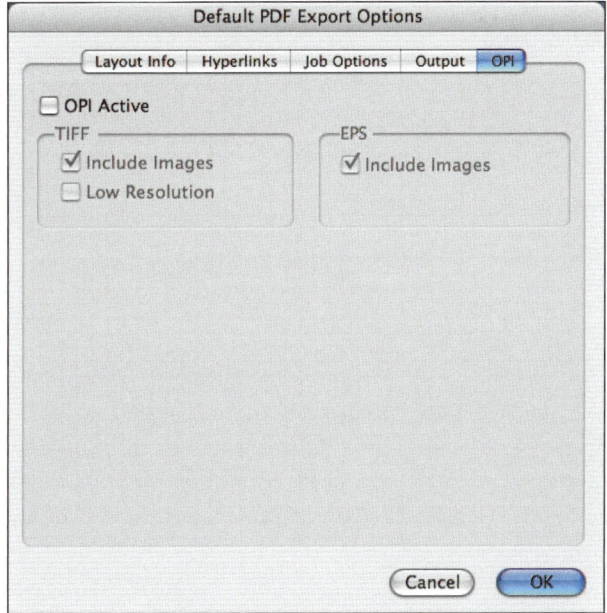

Figure 2.34. Only check "OPI Active" if working in a true picture-replacement workflow. Otherwise, deselect it, but make sure the Include Images options remain selected under both the TIFF and EPS sections.

Active box unchecked (Figure 2.34). (There is more on that in the In the Trenches chapter.) However, you must always leave *Include Images* under the TIFF and EPS sections checked so that high-resolution images are included in the PDF file.

Creating PDFs from Microsoft Office

Microsoft Word files can be converted to PDF through the PDF-Maker tool, a Word option that is available within the Word application after the installation of Adobe Acrobat. Depending on the user's platform, the PDFMaker option can appear as an icon in the Word toolbar or as a menu option. PDFMaker is really a macro that actually uses Acrobat Distiller to create a PDF file. For Mac users, the last active PDF Settings used in Distiller will be used by PDFMaker, so it is important to check Distiller settings before using this tool.

Note: AdobePDF or Distiller should be the default printer when building layouts in Word. This will help prevent text reflow that is typical when the default printer used to create a Word document is changed to an output printer. The page setup and printer settings established in Word will be used as well. Margin settings can cause page content to be moved on output from Word. We recommend a custom page setup with no margin settings for print production projects.

To create a PDF file for print from Word via PDFMaker:

1. Windows users can choose *Adobe PDF> Change Conversion Settings* to select or edit a specific Adobe PDF setting (job options) to use. Mac users must go to the Distiller application and make sure the current PDF settings are what they want to use.

2. *Choose Adobe PDF>Convert to Adobe PDF,* or click the *Convert to AdobePDF* icon on the Word toolbar, specify a filename and location for the PDF file, and then click *Save*.

PDF files will be saved into the same directory as the source document and given the same name with the .pdf extension.

PDF Direct from an Application: PDF Library

An alternative to creating PostScript and then using Distiller to create a PDF is using the export-to-PDF function found in desktop publishing applications such as Adobe InDesign and QuarkXPress 6. The difference here is that a PDF Library is used in place of Distiller to create a PDF. Most of the same settings found in Distiller are also found in the export-to-PDF function, allowing you to create Adobe PDF Settings that can be saved and used for a variety of uses. The list of what to do in order to prepare a file for export is very much the same as preparing a file to print to PostScript and then convert to PDF. One big difference is that transparency can be a part of a PDF file that has been exported from an application directly. We will specifically cover handling transparency in the In the Trenches chapter.

Note also that with any of the applications that allow direct export of PDF, users still have the option to create PostScript and submit to Distiller through the print dialog. In most cases, however, when the export option is available, it is best to take advantage of it.

Some general considerations when exporting PDF files from an application:

1. Load all of the fonts used within the document. We recommend loading fonts through a font management program such as Adobe ATM Deluxe or Extensis Suitcase.

2. Open the document in the application with which it was created.

3. Check type and make sure that that no artificial, or menu-styled, fonts are used. Make sure that the system has access to any fonts used in the document.

4. Check the links to images; ensure that they are linked, high resolution, and updated. Make sure

that spot colors are only defined for items intended to be separated as spot colors (and not process colors).

5. Export the PDF. Typically, this is found under the File menu and includes selecting Adobe PDF Settings such as image compression, font handling, and determining the correct media size to accommodate the page size, allowing for bleed area and any marks. More information on these specific settings can be found in the previous section, "Setting Up Acrobat Distiller."

Creating PDFs from Adobe InDesign CS (3.x)

You can set up presets for various types of PDF output. The settings described below are optimized for press output.

1. In InDesign, select *File>PDF Export Presets>Define*. In the PDF Export Presets dialog box, click *New* to create a new style (Figure 2.35).

2. InDesign's PDF Export Preset dialog box contains options that are very similar to those found in Acrobat Distiller (Figure 2.36). The options found under the General section include:

- Compatibility—You can choose Acrobat 6 or 5 to create a PDF 1.4 file. This will allow transparent objects to come through into the resultant PDF file. The Acrobat 4 option will require transparent objects to be flattened as it will save as a PDF 1.3 file.

- Standard—You can choose to create a PDF/X-1a- or PDF/X-3-compliant file from the pull-down menu.

- *Embed Page Thumbnails* will create thumbnails of each page and is generally not necessary for PDF for print production.

- *View PDF after Exporting* will open the PDF in a PDF viewer.

- *Optimize for Fast Web View* will allow the PDF file to be viewed more quickly in a browser when downloaded from the Internet. This setting is not necessary for print production.

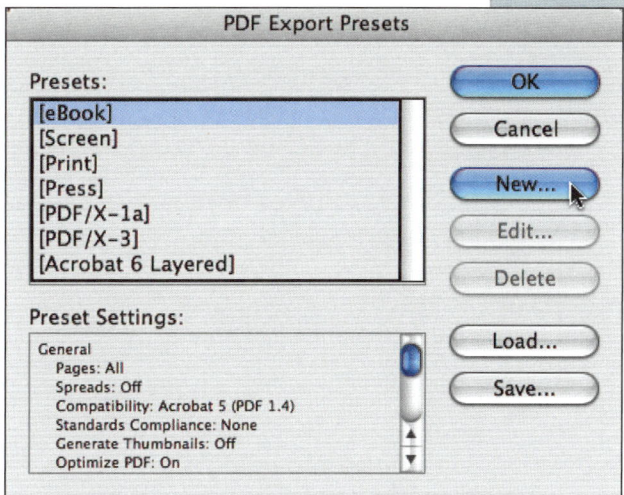

Figure 2.35. To create a new PDF Export Preset from InDesign, select *File>PDF Export Presets>Define* and click the *New* button.

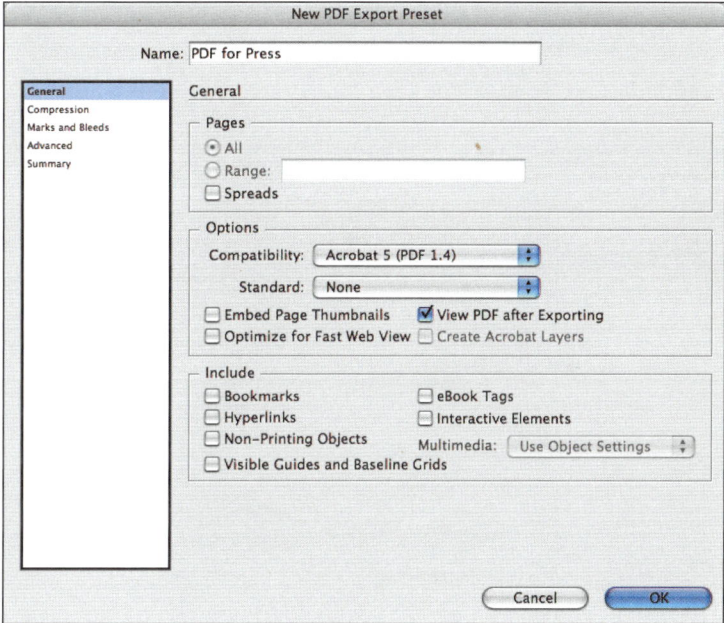

Figure 2.36. The General tab of the PDF Export window in InDesign CS.

- If there are layers in the file, they can be exported as layers into the PDF file. This can be useful for versioning or to include things like dielines in packaging projects. However, it can be a problem down the line in the print

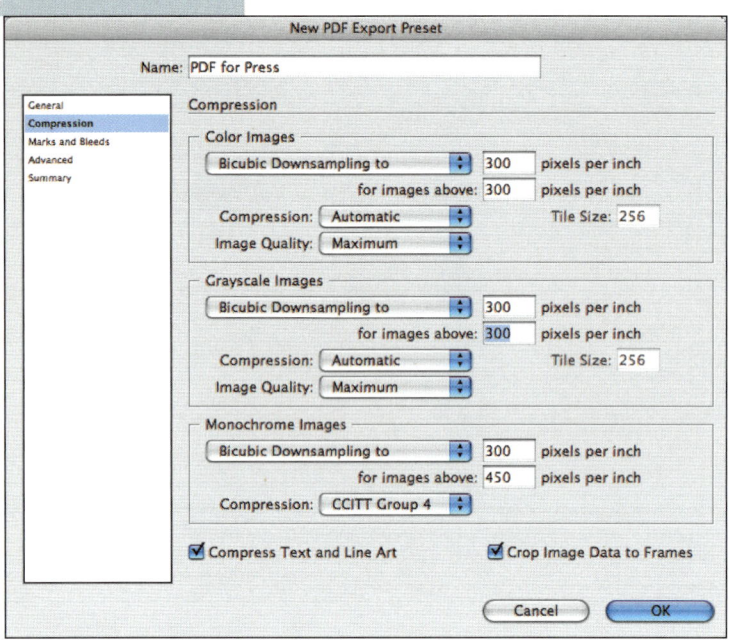

Figure 2.37. The Compression window in InDesign CS contains options that are nearly identical to those offered in Acrobat Distiller.

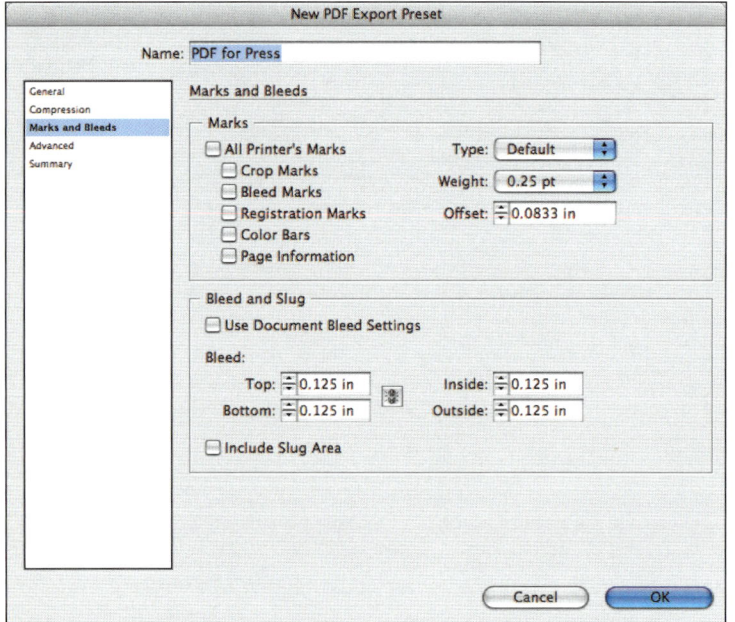

Figure 2.38. The Marks and Bleeds section gives users the option to add bleed area to the file as well as printer's marks such as crop, bleed, and register marks.

production workflow. See more in the In the Trenches section.

- eBook Tags, Hyperlinks, and Bookmarks can be included in the PDF, although they are not necessary for print production.
- Export Non-printing Objects—Individual objects set to not print will be included in the PDF.

3. Compression options are the same as those you will find in Distiller (Figure 2.37). Select *Automatic* and *Maximum Image Quality* for color and grayscale images, *CCITT Group 4* for monochrome images, and *Compress Text and Line Art*.

4. The Marks and Bleeds section allows you to add printer's marks such as crop, bleed, and register marks, if necessary (Figure 2.38). The Bleed option gives you the ability to add bleeds to the PDF file. Enter a bleed value for each edge of the page, if necessary.

5. The Advanced section contains options for color, fonts, and transparency (Figure 2.39).

- In the Color section, select *Leave Unchanged* for pass-through (non-color-managed) workflow, or choose *RGB* or *CMYK* and apply a profile for color-managed workflows.
- Fonts—Embed and subsetting options.
- Transparency Flattener—Transparency is retained in the PDF if *Acrobat 5 (PDF 1.4) Compatibility* is selected. Transparency must be flattened for Acrobat 4 (PDF 1.3) Compatibility. The way InDesign flattens transparency can be customized through Transparency Flattener Presets under the Edit menu. This will be covered in detail in the In the Trenches chapter. Briefly, a higher resolution setting will try to keep vector artwork vector but may not work for complex artwork. A lower resolution setting will convert vector artwork to raster, resulting in lower quality.

7. Click *OK*. Now the presets are available for creating PDFs.

Creating PDFs in Photoshop and FreeHand

The Save As PDF settings from Adobe Illustrator CS are very similar to the export options from InDesign. PDF from Photoshop files, however, are quite different. In general, even though text can be set in Photoshop, PDF from Photoshop will result in image files. These are typically not optimal for print production, especially if they contain text, as the text will be sampled to the output resolution and will not be editable as text later.

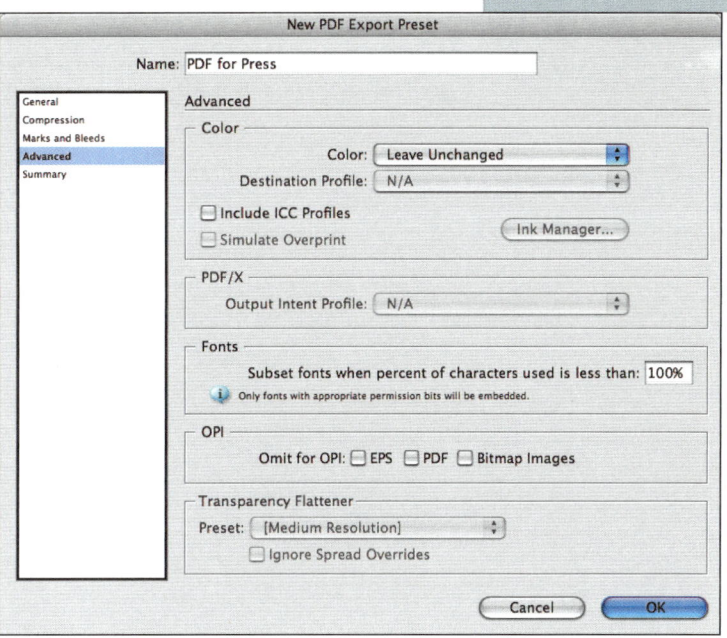

Figure 2.39. The Advanced tab offers options for color management and OPI comments. Notice that there is no option to *not* embed fonts; fonts will always be embedded, only subsetting is an option.

Macromedia FreeHand MX also includes a direct PDF export option, but with very few controls over output. One can compress images, but the method (JPEG, ZIP) is not user definable. Color options include CMYK, RGB, or both. Spot colors are converted to either CMYK or RGB. PDF files can be exported from FreeHand MX only as PDF 1.3 or lower, so transparency is not an option. Finally, there is a simple checkbox to embed fonts, but no option for subsetting (Figure 2.40).

For print production purposes, it's better to create PDF files from FreeHand documents by creating PostScript first through the print option and then submitting this to a PostScript interpreter. Spot colors will come through as expected in a PDF file created from PostScript. The same is true of overprinting objects; in an exported PDF overprinting is ignored, but using the PostScript-to-PDF method, such objects appear as expected in a PDF file.

FreeHand MX can open a PDF file, but this will do things to most files that we can only classify as dreadful. First, FreeHand doesn't recognize embedded fonts in a PDF file. When you open a PDF file in FreeHand, all fonts will have to be viewed using fonts resident on the local system! Spot colors will be converted not to the process equivalent, but to black! Blend objects (not gradients but PostScript 3 gradient

Figure 2.40. Macromedia FreeHand includes a direct PDF export option but with very few controls over output.

mesh fills) are converted to 10% black fills. Need we say more? You want to avoid opening PDF files in FreeHand MX if you care at all about maintaining any semblance of the original.

CHAPTER 3
PDF AND MAC OS X

When we published the first edition of *The PDF Print Production Guide,* most print and publishing pros had not yet made the leap to Mac OS X. Prepress folks tend to stick to what works and are loathe to make a move to a new application or operating system unless it is proven and promises to improve production in some way. A number of key prepress production tools, like the popular imposition application, Creo Preps, were not OS X native applications. And of course the biggest reason to avoid making the move to Mac OS X was that QuarkXPress, still the most-commonly used desktop publishing application, would only run in Classic mode (Mac OS 9.x).

Today, all of that has changed. QuarkXPress 6.1 is now a native OS X application, and many of the prepress/production-specific tools have been ported or rewritten entirely for Mac OS X. Unless you're in a situation in which a necessary component of your workflow is not OS X compatible, there is no reason not to make the move to OS X. Many of you have already done so. We offer this chapter not as a complete guide to Mac OS X for creatives—there are any number of books or files on the Internet where you can get such information in great detail. Rather, we have gleaned some of the key issues we think creative professionals should be aware of when working with OS X, including working with fonts, printing, and creating PDF files.

Apple's current operating system (Figure 3.1) is version 10.3.x (also known as Panther). Quartz, Panther's composite windowing system, is actually based on PDF version 1.4. Because of this, there are tools built into OS X that allow a user to both create and display PDF files without any additional software. This statement probably sends off an alarm in the

Figure 3.1. Splash screen for Mac OS X (Panther).

head of any prepress production professional! Can we really create PDF files now in Mac OS X without benefit of Acrobat or any other application? The answer is yes. Will those files be valid for print publishing? Based on our research, the answer to that is *probably not.*

Before we get into the specifics of PDF creation under Panther, let's review some of the general issues of concern regarding Mac OS X and creative production, starting with fonts.

Fonts in OS X

Under Mac OS 9, most of us were quite comfortable working with our fonts. For some users, simply putting fonts in the Font folder of the System folder was font management enough: they all showed up in the font selection window of every application. Most professional desktop publishers, however, required more in terms of font management and invested in one of a handful of tools like Extensis Suitcase, ATM Deluxe, or Alsoft Masterjuggler. We typically used ATM Lite to render fonts to the screen. In short, for most users, fonts worked and worked pretty well.

Then we made the move to OS X, and suddenly font folders seem to be just everywhere! Actually, there are five places on a system where the OS will see fonts (some applications bring their own package of fonts to the Mac OS X party and plant them in the location of their choice).

System Font Folder. Fonts necessary for the system to run are automatically installed along with the OS installation in the System Library Fonts

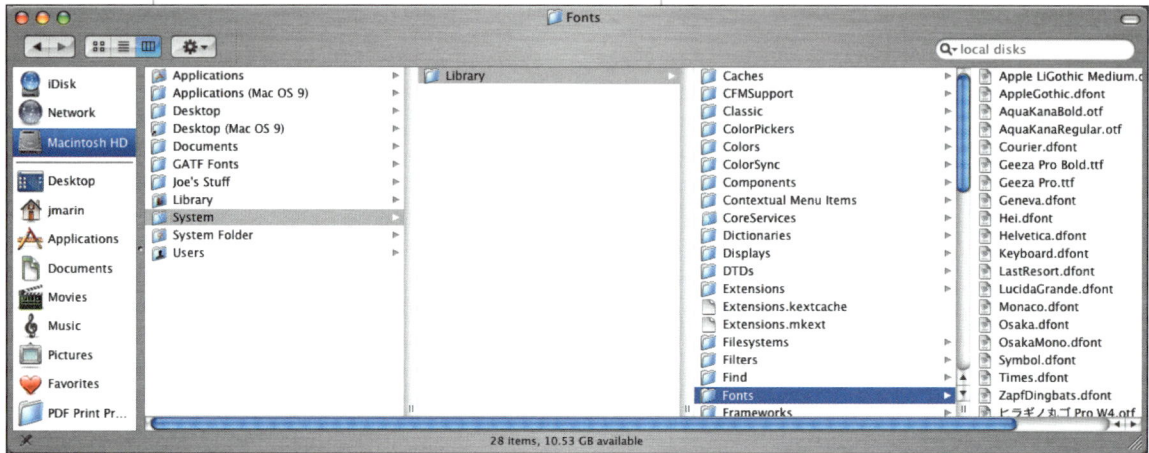

Figure 3.2. Fonts required by the Mac operating system are located in the System Library Fonts directory. Don't touch them!

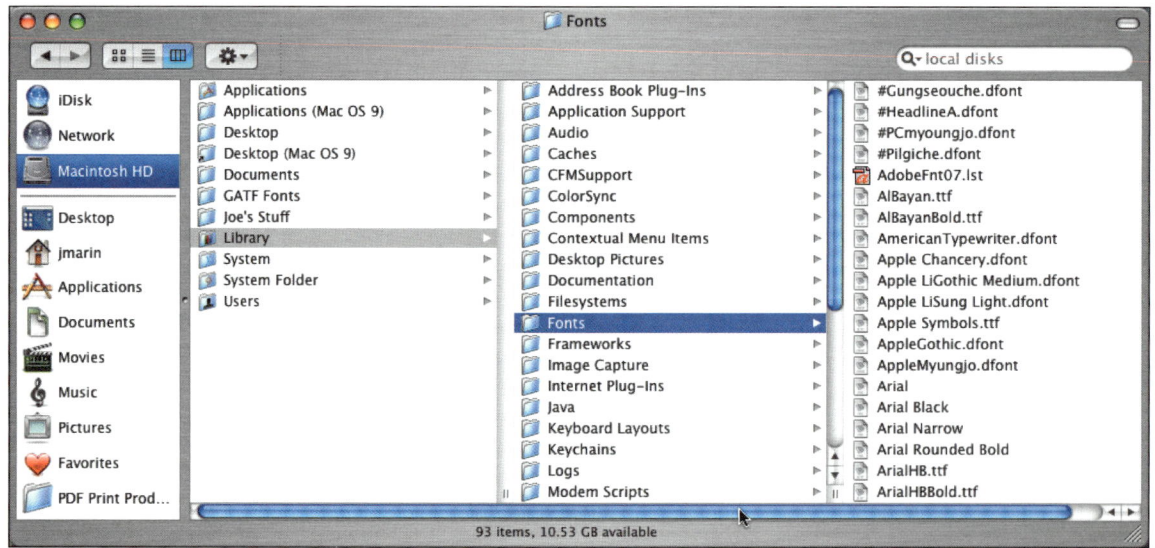

Figure 3.3. Other fonts, including those installed with the Mac OS, are stored in the */Library/Fonts* directory.

directory */System/Library/Fonts* (Figure 3.2). Know they are there, but never attempt to remove or add fonts to this folder. For example, if you were to remove the font LucidaGrande.dfont from this folder, you'd find that you would subsequently be unable to launch your system at all!

Computer Font Folder. Also with the OS installation comes the gift of many new fonts located in the */Library/Fonts* directory (Figure 3.3). Here we see fonts like the Warnock Pro series, which we may never want to actually use, and most of them can be removed without crippling the system. Be aware, however, that some applications, including Safari, do indeed make use of these fonts.

User Font Folder. Fonts may also be found in individual users folders *~/Library/Fonts* (Figure 3.4). The fonts installed in this folder will only be available to a particular user, and Classic fonts cannot be located here. Use this with discretion on computers that are used by multiple users with different login accounts but who have to work on common projects.

Network Fonts Folder. If a system is set up as a server, you may have this directory on the system */Network/Library/Fonts/*. Fonts in this directory can

be shared among all users on a local area network. This folder is typically only used on a network file server managed by a network administrator.

System Folder Fonts. Classic applications (applications that are not yet OS X-compatible) still require that you have Mac OS 9 installed along with OS X on your Mac. OS X can access fonts installed in your Mac OS 9 System Fonts folder */System Folder/Fonts/)*. These fonts are available to any application opened in OS X. Mac OS 9 applications, however, cannot access fonts on OS X.

It is almost certain that a system will have the same font in more than one directory. The Mac OS will resolve duplicates based on a defined "order of precedence" for the standard fonts folders (meaning those we just listed). The order of precedence (from highest to lowest) is this:

1. User Fonts folder
2. Local Fonts folder
3. Network Fonts folder
4. System Fonts folder
5. Classic Fonts folder

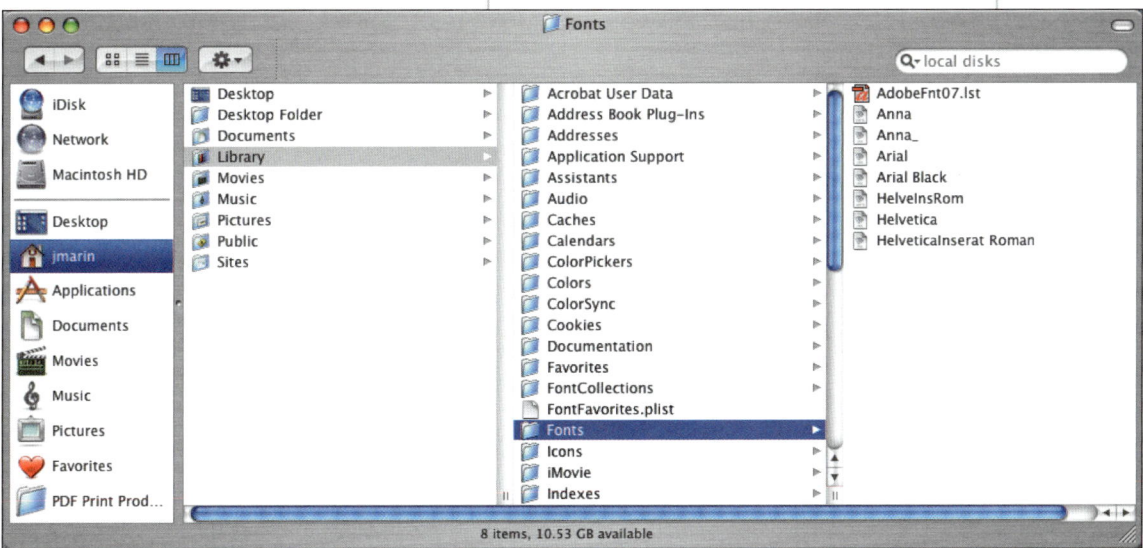

Figure 3.4. Fonts installed in individual user folders are only available to a particular user, and Classic fonts cannot be located here.

What about managing the myriad fonts often used in print production environments? Font management under OS X is still a critical issue. With Panther, Apple supplied a brand new font management tool called Font Book. For a casual user with a small number of fonts to manage, this tool might do the trick. But for the average publishing professional, a third-party font management application for Mac OS X may be a better bet. There are a number of them on the market, all of which receive both glowingly positive or bashingly negative reviews, depending upon who you ask. We have been using Extensis Suitcase X1 (11.0.2) with good results. Also available is DiamondSoft Font Reserve and Insider Software Font Agent Pro.

One tool we no longer need in OS X is Adobe Type Manager. Font rendering for smooth on-screen type is built into the operating system.

Mac OS X also introduced a new font type to the mix, the data fork suitcase (.dfont). You will see these in the System Library Font directory. Here's a brief overview of data fork fonts and all of the font types that work under OS X 10.3.

- Data-fork (.dfont) suitcases. A data fork font suitcase contains the resources associated with a Macintosh font, including 'FOND' and 'NFNT' resources, but the information is stored in a data fork rather than a resource fork. (This format is not the same as the format used for a data fork TrueType font seen in the Windows OS.)

- Macintosh TrueType font suitcase

- Windows TrueType (.ttf/.ttc) outline/bitmap fonts

- PostScript OpenType Roman outline/bitmap fonts

- PostScript OpenType CID Chinese, Japanese, Korean, and Vietnamese outline/bitmap fonts

- PostScript Type 1 outline font with Macintosh bitmap font suitcases (LWFN)

- Macintosh PostScript Type 1-enabled font suitcases ('sfnt')

- Macintosh PostScript Type 1 CID-enabled font suitcases ('sfnt'/CID)

- Multiple Master PostScript fonts. As there is no support for Adobe Type Manager under OS X, and since ATM was used to create new instances of Multiple Master fonts, only already-created MM fonts can be accessed by Mac OS X. There are two types available—LWFN and 'sfnt'.

Printing in Mac OS X

Probably the first thing that surprises a new Mac OS X user (other than the Aqua interface) is that the Chooser is gone. Under OS X Jaguar, print management was handled in the Print Center. Sounded like a nice name, but Apple chose to change it again in OS X Panther. The user accesses printers through the Printer Setup Utility located in the Application/ Utilities directory. The Printer Setup Utility is also accessible through System Preferences, from the Hardware section, under *Print & Fax* (Figure 3.5). When you access the Printer Setup Utility, you are presented with a window titled "Printer List" (it's identified as Printer Setup Utility in the header, however; a tad confusing), and this is where you can add, remove, and otherwise manage printers available to

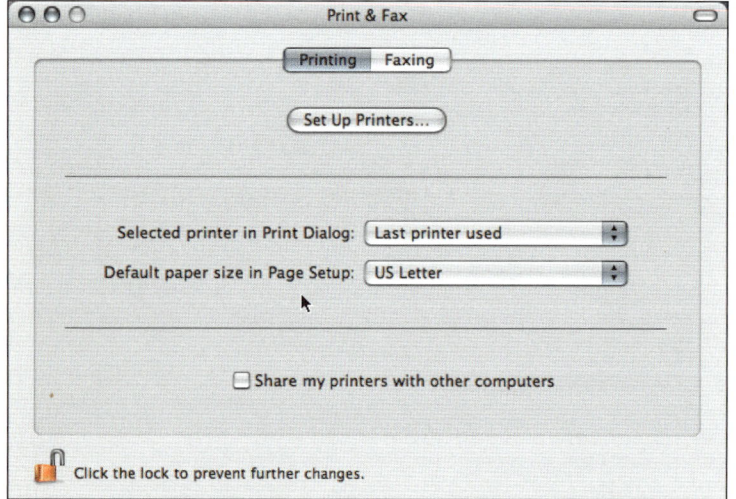

Figure 3.5. The Print & Fax option of System Preferences is one way to access the Printer Setup Utility.

your system. You can also manage individual print jobs for each output device through the Printer List window. There is no need to go to the Printer List before printing a project, and there is no equivalent to the AdobePS or LaserWriter PostScript printer driver that we used in earlier versions of the Mac OS under Panther. To print, one has only to select the output device directly from the Print window of each application (much like it is done in Windows) (Figure 3.6).

With Adobe Acrobat 6.0, the virtual printer Distiller has been replaced by a virtual printer called Adobe PDF. This printer is installed along with the Adobe Acrobat application. Adobe has always made printer drivers and Printer Description Files (PPDs) available for anyone to download from their website. Such is not the case with the Adobe PDF printer for Mac, there is no installer for this printer outside of the Acrobat installation CD. If the Adobe PDF printer gets deleted from the Printer List, it's relatively easy to get it back by following these steps.

Adding Adobe PDF to the Printer List if deleted:

1. Launch Printer Setup Utility.

2. Hold down the Option key and click the Add button in the Printer List Window.

3. Select *Advanced* from the Printer connection drop-down menu.

4. In the Device Field, select *Adobe PDF (pdf)*.

5. For Device Name, type **Adobe PDF 6.** For Device URI, type **pdf://www.adobe.com.**

6. For Printer Model, select *Adobe*.

7. Click *OK*. The Adobe PDF printer will show up in the Printer List.

Installing PPD Files in OS X

While the Mac OS X installs many common PostScript printers, the odds are you may have several that are not on the list. You can manually add PPD files (including those used under OS 9) by placing them in */System/Library/Printers/PPDs/Contents/Resources/en.lproj/*. By default, this directory is locked down, and in order to add PPD files to it, you

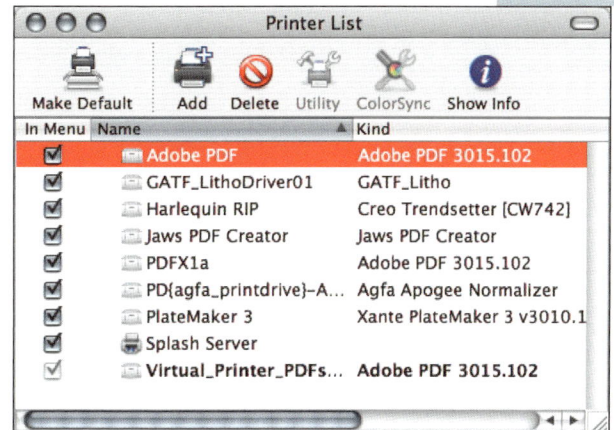

Figure 3.6. The Adobe PDF virtual printer as it appears in the Printer List.

have to change its permissions. To do so, follow these steps (Figure 3.7).

1. Select the */System/Library/Printers/PPDs/Contents/Resources/en.lproj/* directory through a Finder window. *En.lproj* is for English-language systems; if you're working in another language, choose the appropriate directory from those residing in Resources.

2. From the File menu, select *Get Info* (Command+I).

3. Click the triangle next to Ownership & Permissions to disclose its contents.

4. Note that the directory is "owned" by the system (root) account.

5. Click the padlock icon to the right of the permissions menu option.

6. You'll be asked to authenticate yourself with your user name and password.

7. Change the Owner pop-up menu to your own account name. You can now access the directory.

8. Copy the PPD(s) to the folder.

9. Change the Owner pop-up menu back to *System*.

10. Click the padlock once again to prevent further changes.

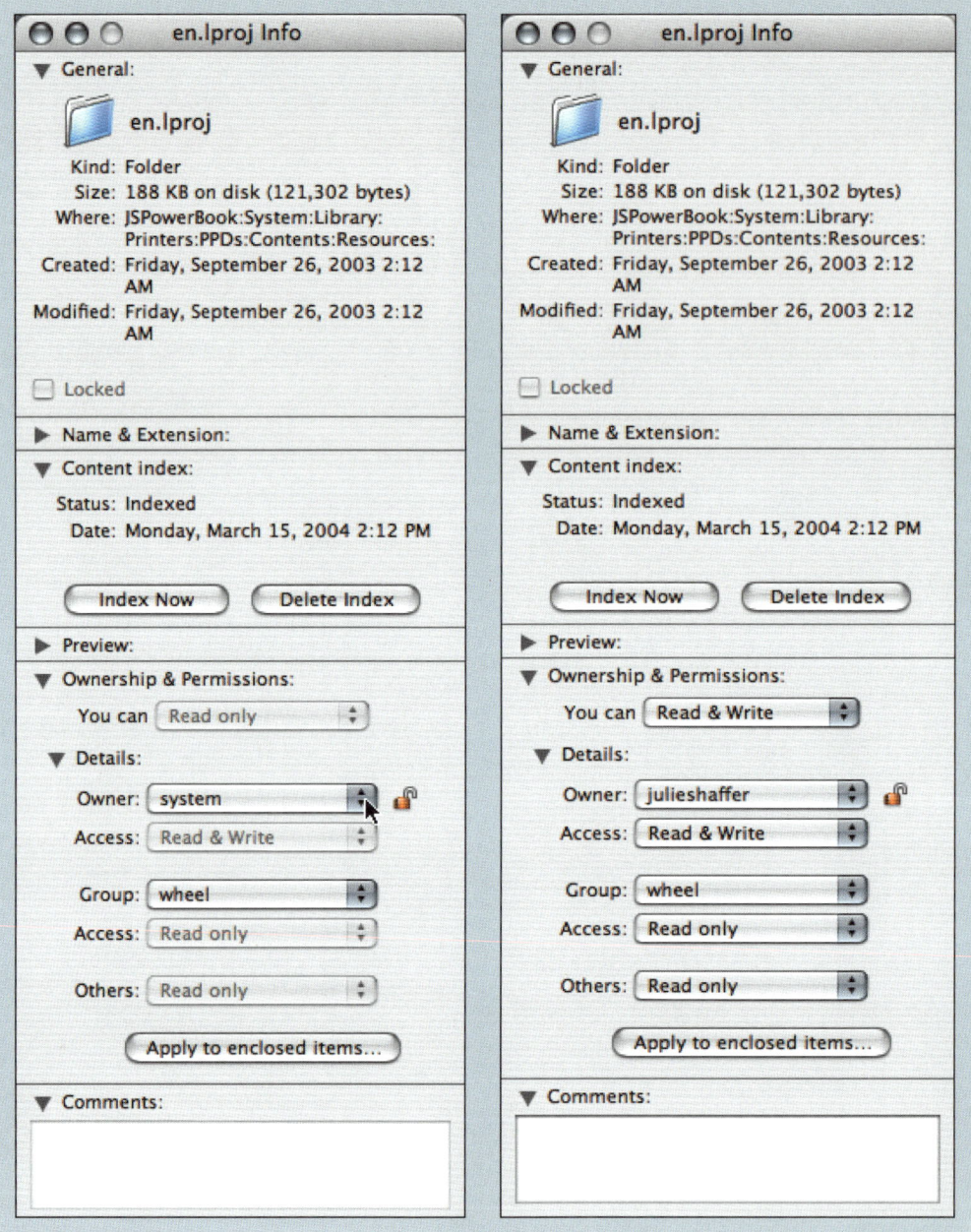

Figure 3.7. To make your old PPD files available to applications in OS X, they must be added to the En.lproj directory in the System folder. (En.lproj is for English-language systems; if you're working in another language, choose the appropriate directory from those residing in Resources.) By default, this directory is locked down, so to add PPD files to it, you have to change its permissions.

Select the /System/Library/Printers/PPDs/Contents/Resources/en.lproj/ directory and select "Get Info" from the File menu (Command + I). The screen capture, above left, shows the original owner of the directory as the system. Change this to your identity, as shown in the righthand image, and give yourself read and write access to the directory. Once the directory is unlocked, simply copy your PPD files into it.

Creating a Virtual Printer

Some applications in Mac OS X now have PDF export functions, eliminating the need to generate PostScript prior to PDF creation. However, you may still have the need to create a generic PostScript file from an application; that is very difficult to do if you do not have access to a printer of any kind. A virtual printer allows you to generate a PostScript file even when you don't have a printer connected to your computer or your computer is not connected to a network. Once the virtual printer is created, it can be selected as a printer from an OS X native application and used to generate a PostScript file to disk.

To create a virtual printer, follow these steps.

1. Open the Printer Setup Utility.

2. Select *Add Printer...* from the Printers menu.

3. In the Printer List dialog box, select *IP Printing* from the pull-down menu, then select *LPD/LPR* from the Printer Type Menu.

4. In the Printer Address field, type in the word **localhost.** This says that the printer is resident on the local computer.

5. In the Queue Name field, give your virtual printer a name. This will show up like a printer in the print dialog of any application.

6. In the Printer Model pull-down menu, you can select from a number of well-known output device names, or select *Generic* to divorce the PostScript file from any device. When the PostScript file is to be used to create a PDF, you should select Adobe as the printer model.

7. Click the Add button. The printer will show up in the Printer List (Figures 3.8a, 3.8b).

Saving a Document as PostScript

To save a document as PostScript, the Print dialog box is used. Before a document can be saved as PostScript, a virtual PostScript printer must be added to the Printer List, as described in the previous directions. Unlike printing from Mac OS 9.x, we no longer have control over the PostScript level used or font inclusion in the PostScript file. According to

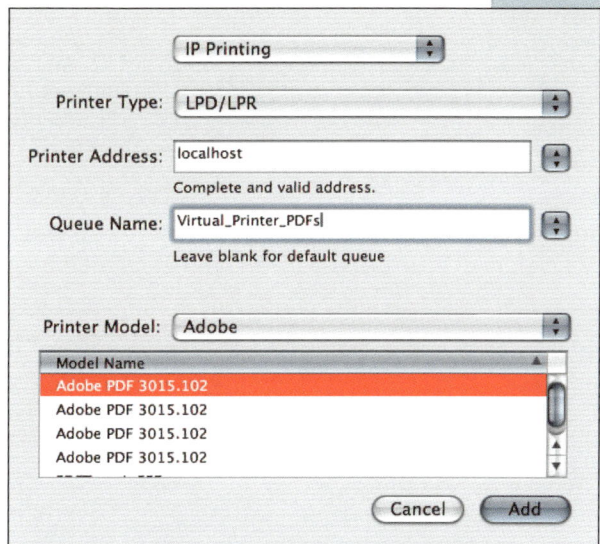

Figure 3.8a. To create a virtual printer, select Add Printer from the Printer Setup Utility and fill the option in as shown above.

Figure 3.8b. A virtual printer as it appears in the Printer List.

Apple documentation, PostScript files are saved as PostScript Level 2 in ASCII format. All fonts are included in the PostScript file except for the standard thirteen fonts. All fonts are subsetted when saving a document as PostScript.

To save a document as a PostScript file, follow these steps.

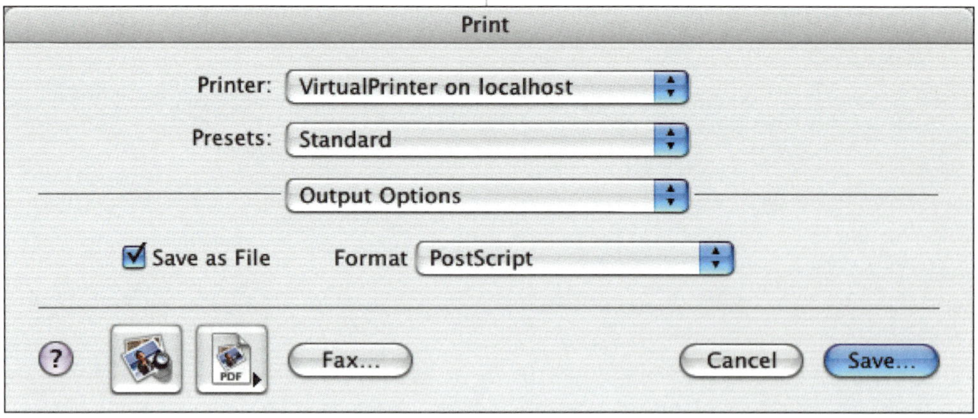

Figure 3.9. Settings under the Mac OS X printer window to print a generic PostScript file using a virtual printer.

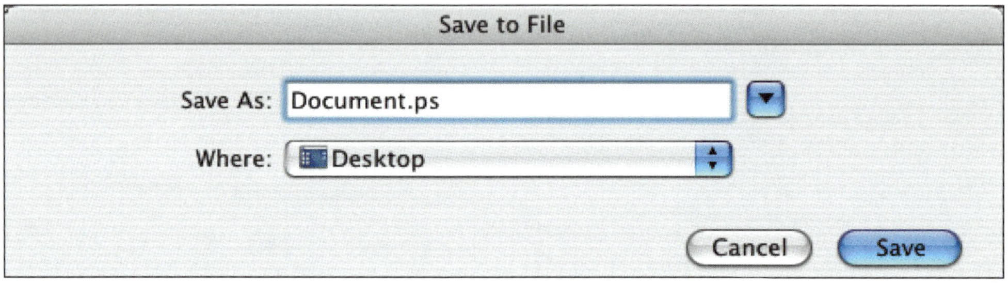

Figure 3.10. In the Save to File dialog box, give the PostScript file a name and save it to disk.

1. Select *Print* from the File menu.

2. In the Print dialog box, choose a virtual or network printer from the Printer list.

3. Choose *Output Options* from the pull-down menu.

4. Select *Save File As* and choose *PostScript* from the pull-down menu (Figure 3.9).

5. Click the *Save* button.

6. In the Save to File dialog box, give the Post-Script file a name and save it to disk (Figure 3.10).

This file can be submitted to a PostScript interpreter, like Acrobat Distiller or Global Graphics Jaws PDF Creator and converted into a PDF file. You may have noticed that PDF was another option in the Output Options menu. Why take the extra step of creating a PostScript file and then submitting it to Distiller? Why not just save a PDF directly using this method?

In fact, why not save the PDF using the button at the bottom of every print screen that says "Save As PDF"?

That pill-shaped button is like the little bottle with the tag "Drink me" that Alice encounters in Wonderland. It's tempting to do what it says, but should you? Just as Alice shrunk to ten inches tall when she drank the potion, the PDF file you create by using the "Save As" method will likely be a little short on usefulness for print production. Apple offers what they call a PDF Workflow, which involves creating PDF files using this little button. They also offer a largely undocumented method of enhancing their PDF Workflow through creating "filters" in the Color-Sync Utility and using them in conjunction with the "Save As PDF" button. Let's take a good, hard look at the "Save As PDF" method of PDF creation to see if it's viable for quality print production.

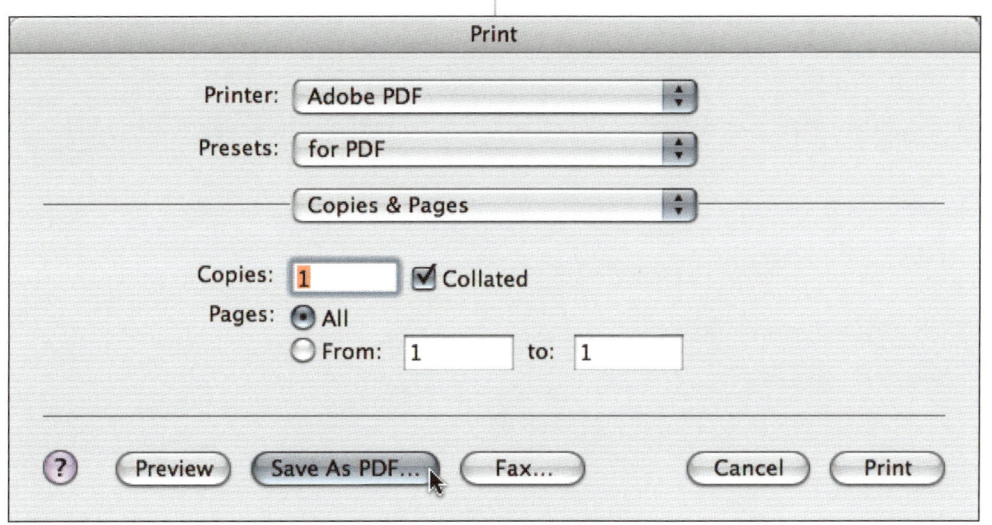

Figure 3.11. Out of the box, the "Save As PDF..." button looks like this.

Save As PDF

For PDF creation, Mac OS X offers the "Save As PDF" option (Figure 3.11). Since Word 10.2.4, a user can create a "PDF Workflow" that allows for further specification as to how a PDF file is prepared or processed.

To access the PDF Workflow button, users have to create a folder within the user's Library, named PDF Services: *~/Library/PDF Services* or */Library/PDF Services* (Figure 3.12). It is into this directory that AppleScripts or anything that is intended to be a menu pop-up for a PDF Workflow is placed.

Things that can be added here include:

• a folder or alias to a folder

• an application or alias to one

• a UNIX tool or alias to one

• an AppleScript file or alias to one

It is into this folder that we will place filters created via the ColorSync Utility. These filters can be used in combination with certain applications to enhance the OS X PDF-creation process.

Once the PDF Services folder has been properly created, the PDF Workflow button becomes visible within the Print Dialog (Figure 3.13).

The ColorSync Utility (installs with OS X and found in the Application/Utilities folder) is where you create filters that can be used to control some aspects of how PDF files are created. It offers the equivalent of Distiller job options for Quartz-based PDF creation. By selecting the Filters icon, the user is presented a place to create new filters. Clicking *Add* creates a new filter that you can name and then refine with the "Filter details." The Color tab allows the user to transform/convert the color of every object in a PDF file (or just images, text, graphics, or shading) to a particular space, as defined by an ICC profile available on the user's system. No conversion is an option as well (Figure 3.14). The Defaults tab (Figure 3.15) lets the user set default profiles for use when none are in the

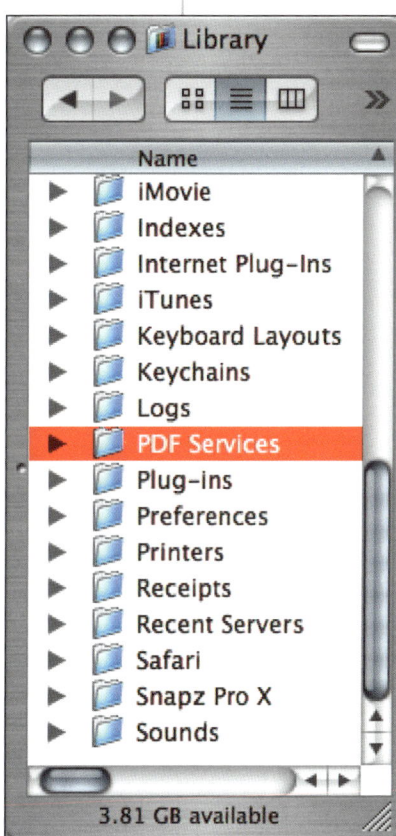

Figure 3.12. Create a PDF Services folder in the *~/Library* or */Library* directory.

Figure 3.13. Once the PDF Services directory has been created, the PDF Workflow button appears.

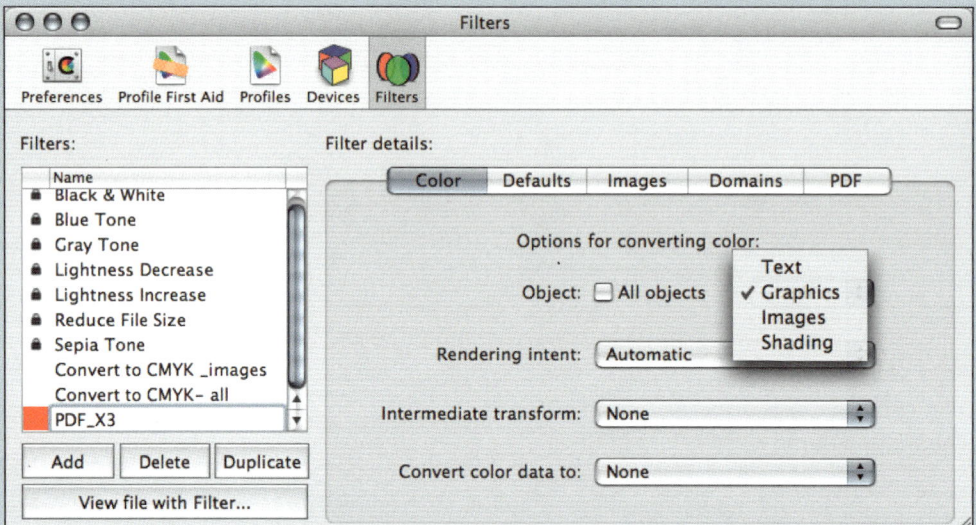

Figure 3.14. Create filters to control how Quartz-based PDF files are created in ColorSync Utilities.

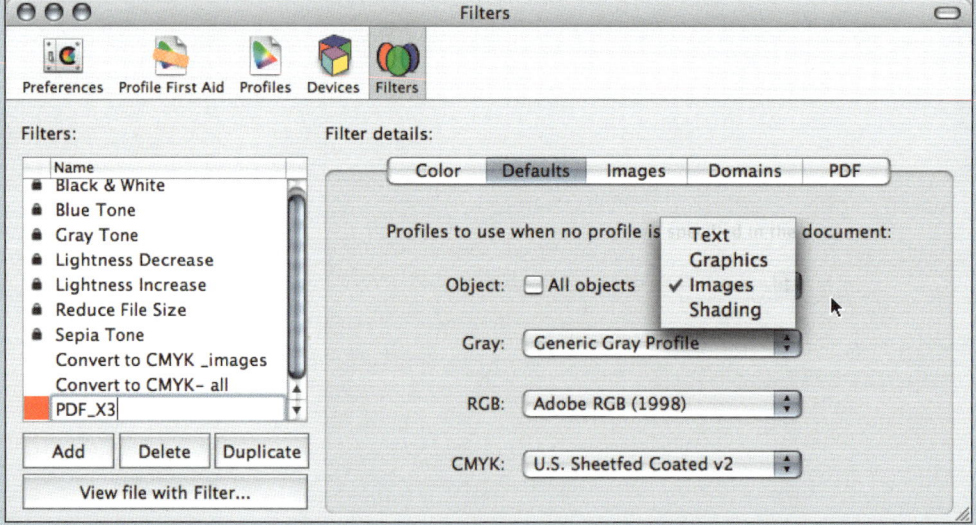

Figure 3.15. The Quartz Save As PDF filter can apply ICC profiles to graphics, images, text, and shading.

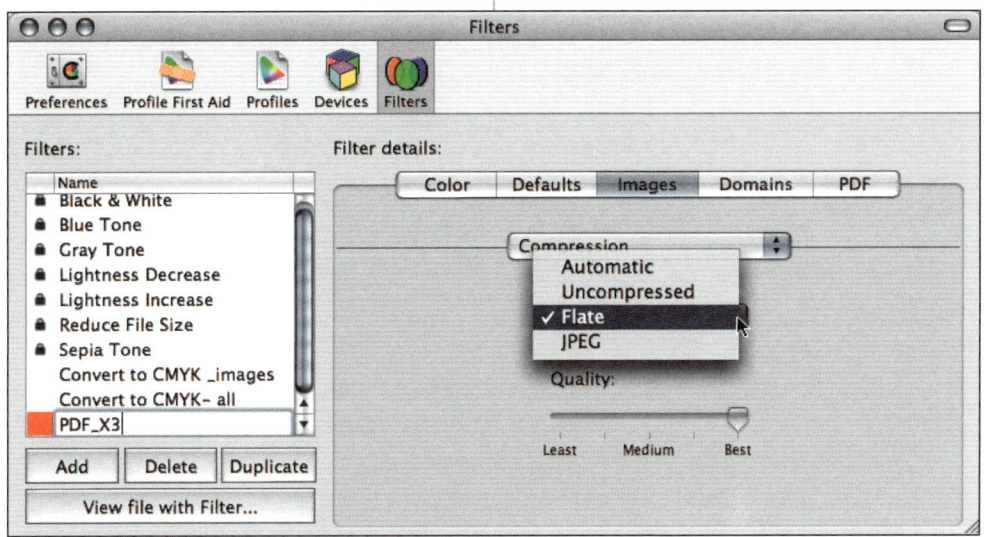

Figure 3.16. Compression can be added to images via the Quartz filter.

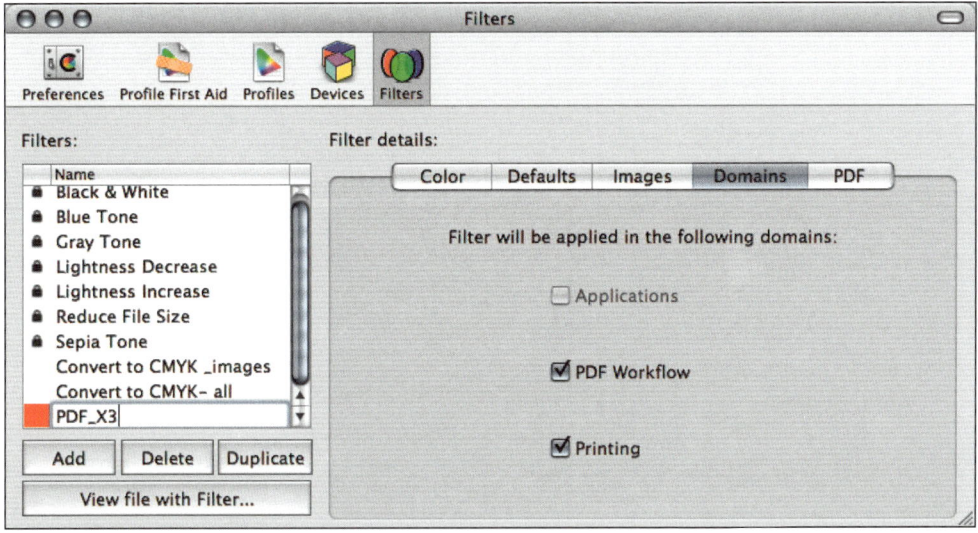

Figure 3.17. To use this Quartz filter, use domains must be indicated.

document. Images can be compressed, sampled, or convoluted. Compression options are JPEG or Flate (ZIP). Sampling offers non-Distiller-like options to downsample to a percentage (Figure 3.16). If the PDF Services folder has been placed in the user Library, the option to check *PDF Workflow* will be available under Domains. This has to be checked or the filter won't show up under *Save As PDF* (Figure 3.17).

The PDF tab allows the user to have the file tagged as a PDF/X-3, an ISO standard, and allows for RGB data to be present in a PDF file. PDF/X-1a is for CMYK-only work and more commonly used in the U.S., but it is not an option here (Figure 3.18).

There is no "save" option for filters in the Color-Sync Utility (a serious oversight on Apple's part, in

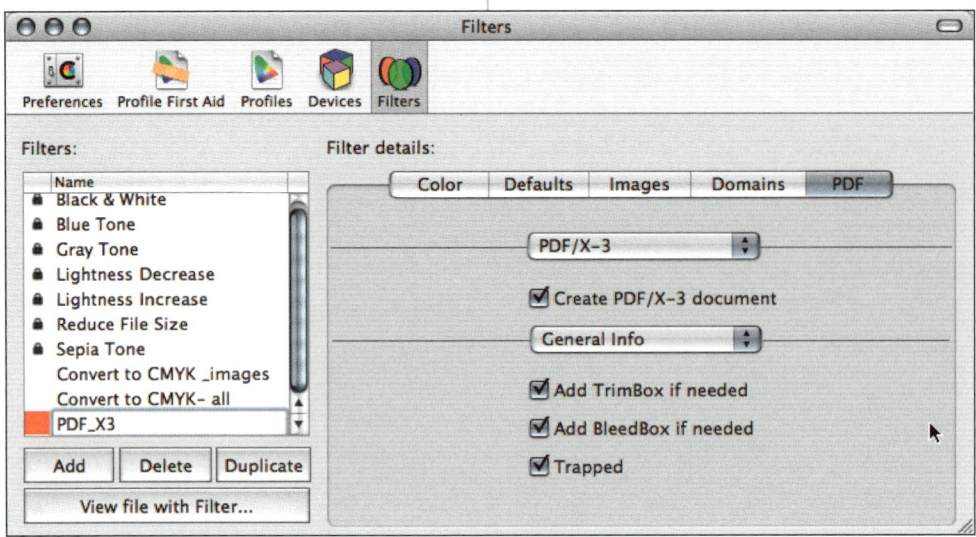

Figure 3.18. A Quartz filter can create a PDF/X-3 file (but not a PDF/X-1a file).

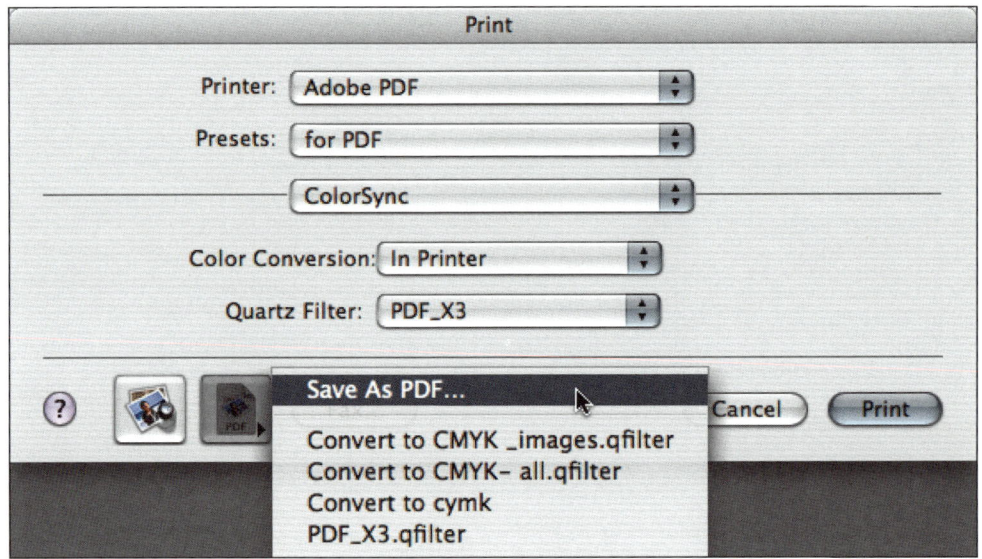

Figure 3.19. Once created, Quartz filters can be accessed through the Print dialog box.

our opinion). However, once the user has completed the selection of Filter details and quits the ColorSync Utility, the filter shows up either in the Library/Filters folder or the PDF Services folder, if one has been created. The filter must reside in the PDF Services folder in order for it to show up under the Save As PDF button in a Print dialog window.

Figure 3.19 shows the Print dialog from Microsoft Word 10.1.4 with a number of filters available. Note that above the Save As PDF option, we've selected *ColorSync* from the special options menu (this menu typically starts with the option "Copies & Pages"). The submenu Quartz Filter also shows all filters available within the PDF Library folder.

When we choose a filter from the "Quartz Filter" list and then select *Save As PDF* from the list presented in the PDF Workflow button, we will be given the option to name the PDF file and choose where to save it. This is the preferred method of working with these filters.

If we instead use the intuitive approach and select a filter from the list presented under the PDF Workflow button (why else are they there?), we are, in fact, not given the option to name and locate the resultant PDF file. One will print, however. Where does the file go? A search for "invisible" items using the OS Find option shows that the file goes to the Private folder, into the "tmp" subfolder, and is given the generic name "Print job.pdf".

For files created from MS Word, the resultant PDF file using either method is the same (but mining for the invisible file is not fun, we don't recommend this method!). This is not true from Quark—more on that later.

We created a document in Microsoft Word X for Mac (version 10.1.4) containing a number of typical design elements, including CMYK and duotone EPS images, EPS files originating in Adobe Illustrator, one containing a CMYK-outlined image, spot-colored objects, a drop shadow, overprinting objects, and outlined text. There are also a few RGB images (one can not place a CMYK TIFF into a Word document and see a preview) and a couple of objects created in Word (a smiley face and the "Wordart" illustration). Microsoft Word is not a desktop publishing application and print-destined files originating in Word often result in production problems, as any prepress professional can attest. (We will offer some tips on how to work

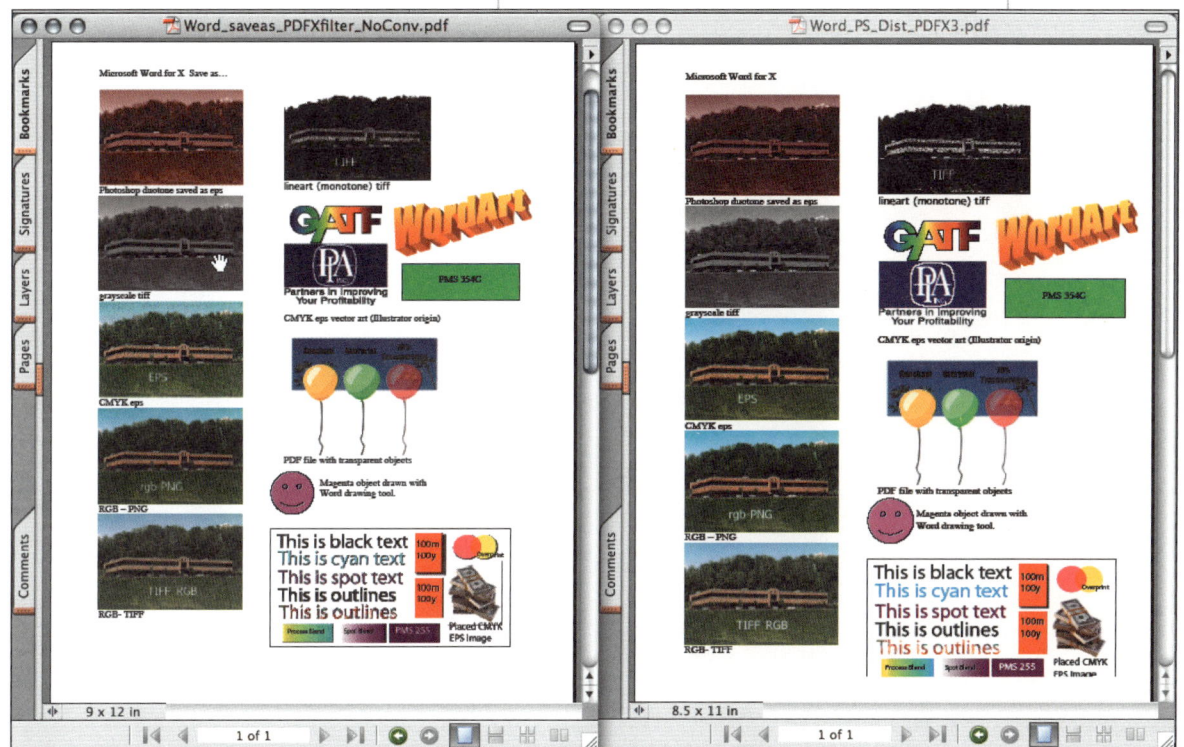

Figure 3.20. Two PDF files created from the same Microsoft Word original as viewed in Acrobat 6. The lefthand PDF file was created using the Quartz "Save As PDF" method. The righthand file was created by Distilling a PostScript file printed through Word's Print dialog.

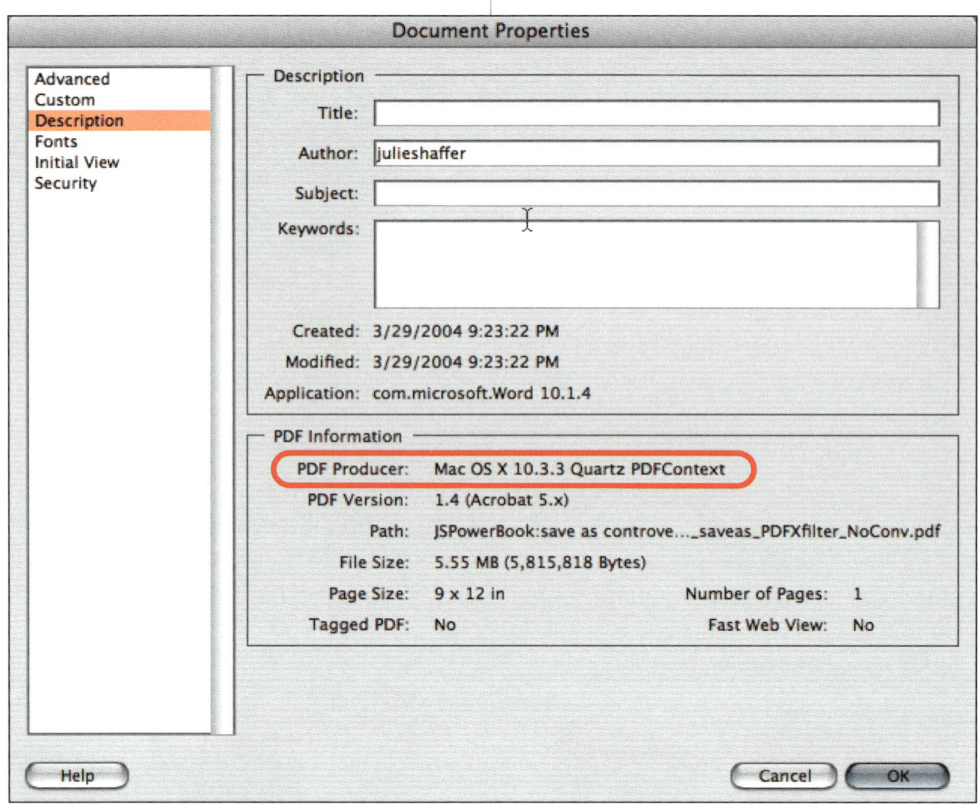

Figure 3.21. A PDF file created by using the "Save As PDF" option on a Mac OS X workstation will show the PDF Producer to be "Mac OS X 10.3.x Quartz PDF Context".

with problematic PDF files that have originated in Word in the In the Trenches section.) Right now, we're concerned with this question: Can the "Save As PDF" or Quartz Filter method make a PDF file from Microsoft Word that is as viable for print production as a PDF file created by the PostScript-to-PDF method? Let's compare.

First, we created a PDF file via the PostScript/Distiller methods. With Adobe PDF selected as the printer, we chose *Output Options,* clicked *Save As File,* and selected *PostScript* as the format. The resultant PostScript file was saved to the hard drive. Using Acrobat Distiller 6.01, the PostScript file was converted to PDF, using the default PDF/X-3 settings. The file was created successfully, meaning it was tagged as a PDF/X-3-compliant file.

Then, from the same Word file, we saved a PDF file using the "Save As PDF" method. We selected *ColorSync* in the special options area and chose the PDF/X-3 filter we'd created. Figure 3.20 shows both resultant PDF files, as viewed in Acrobat 6.01. They look pretty much the same on screen, but the differences become apparent when we do some investigation of each PDF file's actual content.

A look at Acrobat's Document Properties on the file created via the "Save As PDF," or Quartz, method shows the PDF Producer is Mac 10.3.3 Quartz PDF-Context and the PDF Version is 1.4 (Figure 3.21). Document Properties on the file created via PostScript and Acrobat Distiller shows the PDF Producer is Distiller and the PDF version is 1.3.

As we start to interrogate the files, some glaring differences become apparent. Enfocus PitStop Pro, a

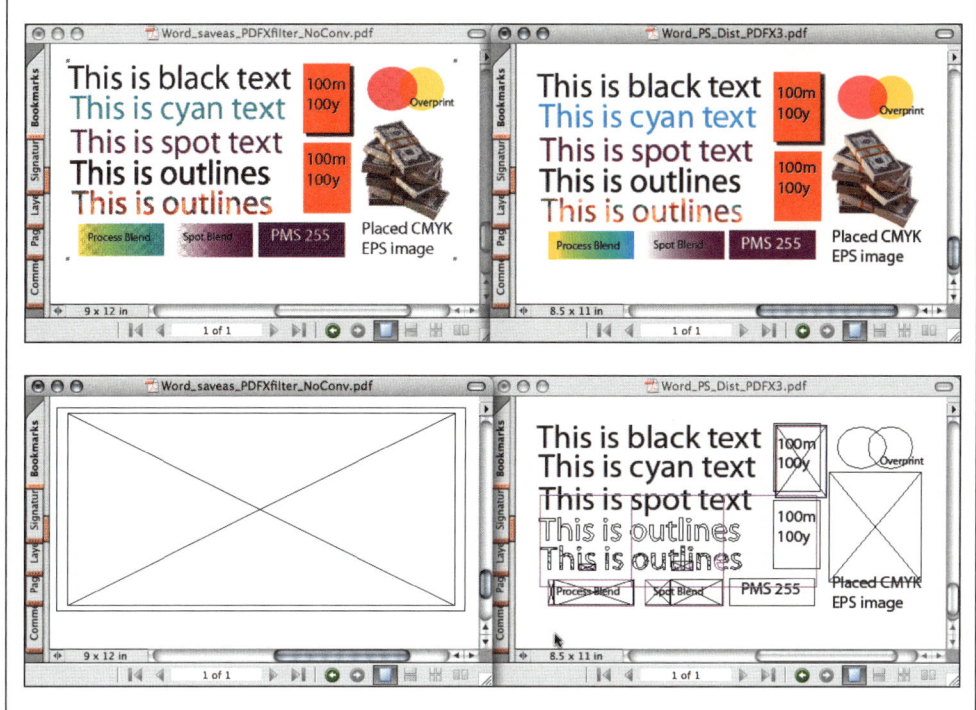

Figure 3.22. If a PDF file is created using the Quartz "Save As PDF" method, graphics that started out as EPS files in the native application will come through into the PDF file as 72-dpi bitmap images. The top image shows a graphic in a "Save As PDF" file beside the same image in a "PostScript to PDF" file. Viewed in Acrobat 6, using Enfocus PitStop wireframe mode, it's clear that the lefthand image was converted to a bitmap, while the righthand image remains in vector format.

PDF editing plug-in for Acrobat, offers a wireframe view mode that makes it easy to distinguish different types of objects in PDF files. Using it to review the portion of each file that represents what was originally a placed Illustrator EPS file in the Word document, we see that illustrations that should be vector art have been converted to bitmaps (pictures) in the "Save As PDF" file. The PDF file created via Distiller contains all elements as intended when the EPS file was created: vector art, fonts, outlines, spot-colored blends, placed bitmap art, and overprinting objects (Figure 3.22).

This tips us off that there may be a problem with EPS files in general. Sure enough, all placed EPS files are low resolution. This look suspiciously like the sort of thing the dreaded PDFWriter does for PDF creation. In fact, the reason this happens is that, using the "Save As PDF" method, the PDF file is created directly by the Quartz drawing module, the same module that is responsible for drawing 2-D images to the computer monitor. An application like Microsoft Word can only display images at 72 dpi, so EPS objects can only be included in the PDF file at 72 dpi. Image quality is determined by the capabilities of the layout application. The PDF file created via Distiller doesn't have that limitation.

The same is true of color definition. Because the same drawing routines are used for PDF creation and drawing to the screen, colors in a PDF file created via the "Save As PDF" method are typically RGB (they are tagged with an ICC profile selected when the filter was created). If none is selected, the images will come through with a Generic RGB profile. This includes text which should be black only! However, you can

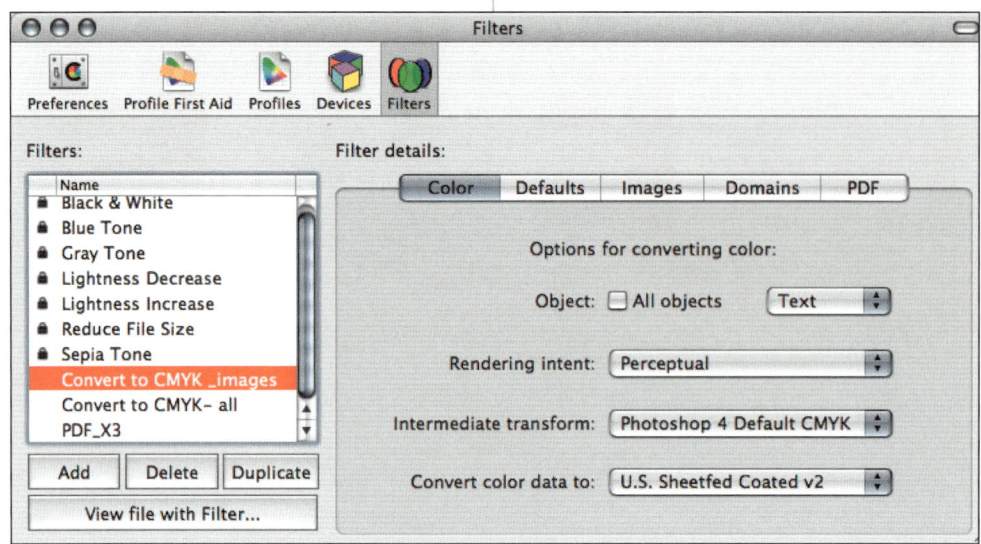

Figure 3.23. Quartz filters can be set to automatically convert all graphics to a particular color space.

create a Quartz filter to convert color to a particular color space. You have the option of converting all color objects in a file or just certain types of objects, like images, and you can convert based on a particular ICC profile (Figure 3.23). This works well if you wish to convert objects to process colors (CMYK), but doesn't work if there are spot colors involved in the file. In fact spot colors do not carry through in a Quartz-based PDF file at all, nor does the DeviceN color space (duotones, spot blends).

How about the PDF/X-3 status? You can check PDF/X compliance in several ways. The first and simplest is to look at *Custom* under *Document Properties* in Adobe Acrobat 6. A PDF-X-compliant file will show the PDF version in the Value field (Figure 3.24).

You can also check for PDF/X compliance using the Preflight option in Acrobat 6 Professional or a third-party tool, like Enfocus PitStop Pro or Apago PDF/X Checkup. For this test, the file created with Distiller passed the PDF/X-3 compliance using all of these tools. The PDF file created with the Quartz method was, however, not PDF/X-3-compliant, even though the filter we built to create the PDF file was set to make a PDF/X-3-compliant PDF file. Distiller

could have prevented the file from being created if it didn't pass; the "Save as PDF" method doesn't.

So, to recap, a PDF file created via the Quartz method from Microsoft Word results in spot colors converting to RGB, black text converting to RGB, vector and bitmap EPS files in the original layout being converted to low-resolution image objects, and all images being tagged with an ICC profile, as selected in the filter. In the case of our test, even if a filter indicates a PDF file should be made with PDF/X-3 compliance, it may not happen, but you'll be given no warning that it didn't work. Sound like a print-ready PDF file?

How about a file created in a real desktop publishing application? QuarkXPress remains a frequently used tool for producing projects intended for print, so we created a file that contained just about every type of element that a designer could throw into a Quark document. None of it will be unfamiliar to a prepress professional. Included were placed PDF files, duotones, DCS2 images, colorized TIFFs (a grayscale TIFF that has been set to another color using Quark tools with a background box set to another color), spot-colored text, Quark-drawn objects, images and placed EPS image files, blends from spot-to-spot and

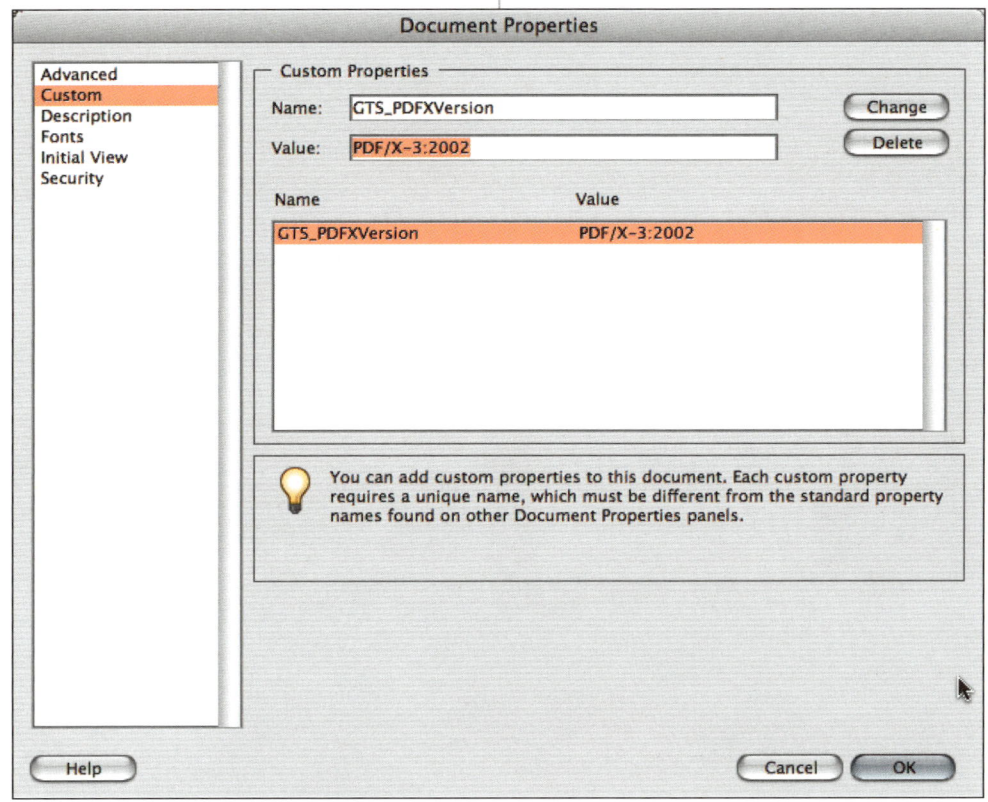

Figure 3.24. Viewing the PDF/X status of a PDF file, via the Custom window in Acrobat Document Properties.

process colors, CMYK images with and without compression, and a full-bleed background (Figure 3.25).

When we tried to create the PDF file in the same way we did with the Microsoft Word document, we could not do so. We found that from within the print dialog of QuarkXPress, or any DTP application, including all Adobe DTP products and FreeHand MX, one cannot select a Quartz filter from the ColorSync pull-down menu. This doesn't prevent the user from selecting the Save As PDF button, however. No one is warning the average user that this might create a "not-ready-for-print" PDF file, so we made one.

A look at the Document Properties for the resultant PDF file in Acrobat 6 shows the PDF Producer is Quartz just like the PDF file created from Word. Remember that the special filters built in ColorSync could not be used, so we had no control over how this

PDF file was created. When we reveal the wireframe view of the PDF file, we see that many of the images have been chopped into pieces (Figure 3.26). This file contains very little of what the creator expected: images, text, and spot colors have been converted to RGB, including the spot-colorized TIFF from the original, and nearly all objects that started as an EPS file were converted to low-resolution image objects. We compared this file to a PDF file created via the Export option built into QuarkXPress 6 (this uses Global Graphics Jaws PDF Interpreter). We selected the DeviceN color definition for our exported PDF file and found that every object came through in the resultant PDF as expected, including those spot-colorized TIFF images.

Bottom line: Avoid using "Save As PDF," even if you take the time to set up a Quartz filter to refine the process, for PDF files intended for print production.

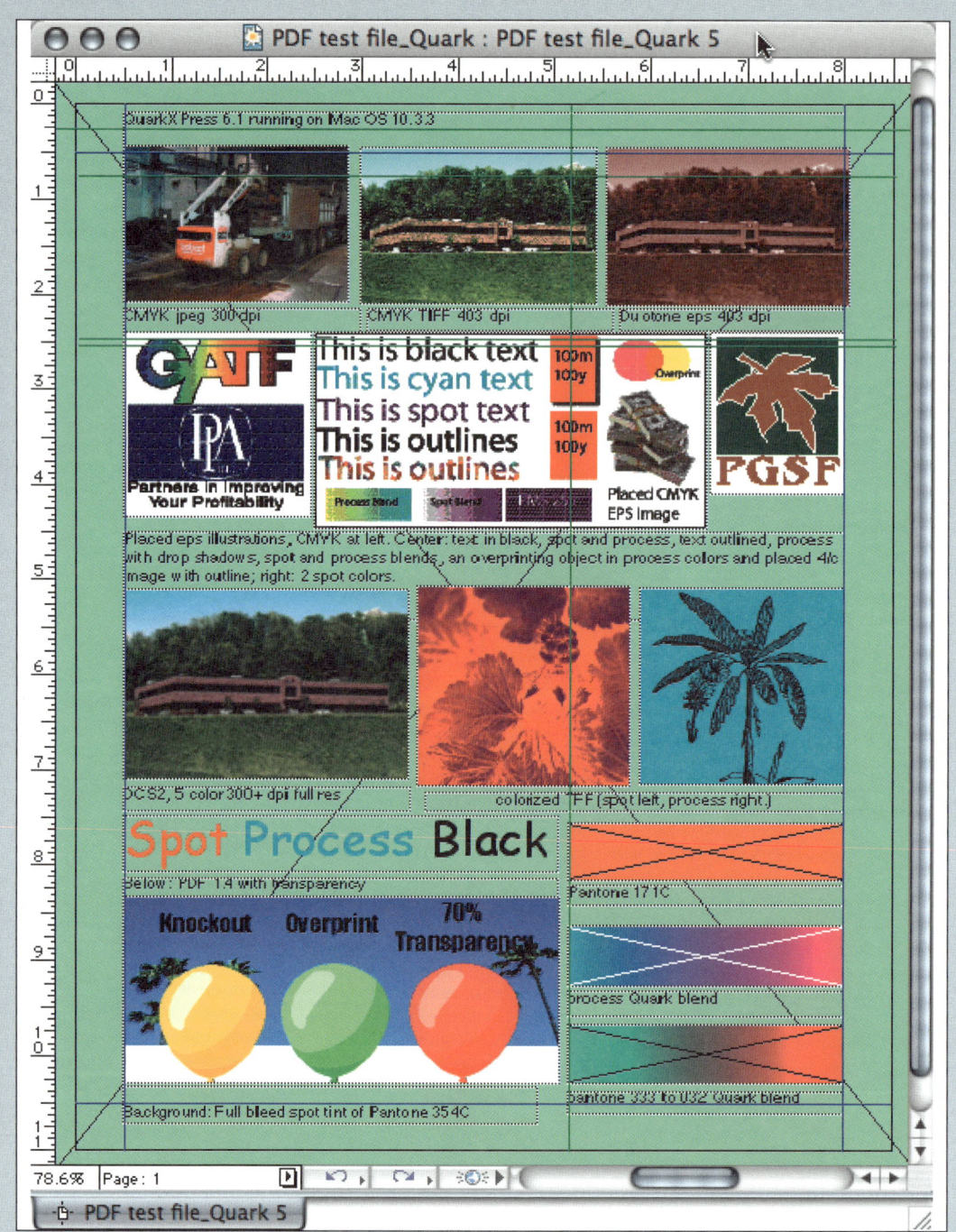

Figure 3.25. A QuarkXPress 6 document, with a sampling of all sorts of elements commonly used by designers.

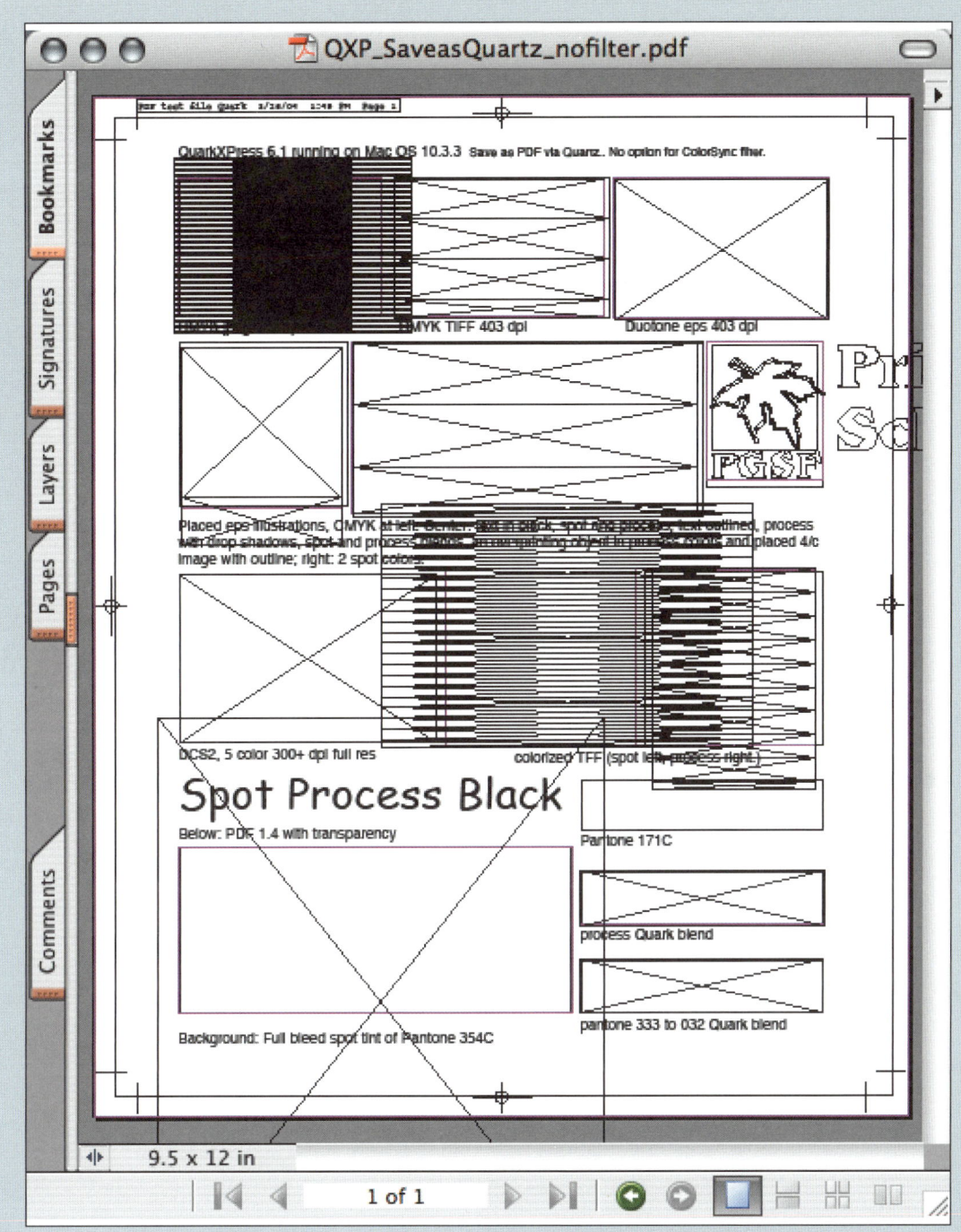

Figure 3.26. When converted to a PDF file via the "Save As PDF" button, the images are chopped up into slivers.

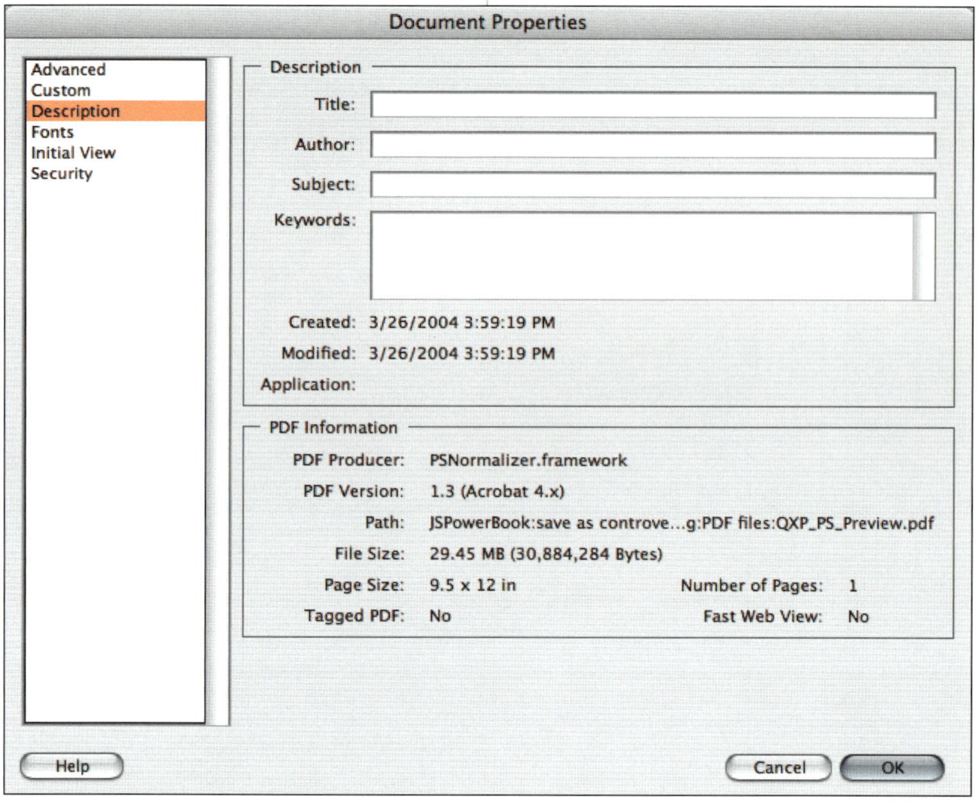

Figure 3.27. PDF files created from the Mac Preview application are created via an Adobe Normalizer.

Preview

The strangest part of this story is that Apple has licensed a version of the Adobe Normalizer for the Panther version of OS X. Adobe Normalizer is the OEM version of Distiller and is licensed for use in many high-end prepress production systems, like Agfa Apogee and Creo Prinergy. So why do we not see it being used to create PDF files via the Save As PDF button? Well, Apple only integrated the Normalizer into the Preview application. That's right, by simply double-clicking a PostScript file or drag/dropping a PostScript or EPS file onto the Preview icon, the file is converted into a PDF file for display in Preview. So Apple uses a display mechanism to create PDF files for print, but licenses a print-viable PDF interpreter from Adobe for a display application like Preview!

Preview is the default PDF viewing tool in Mac OS X. It can be very handy for a quick look at a PDF file and contains a full text-search capability (without indexing). Once Acrobat is installed in OS X, it becomes the default preview tool for PDF files on that system. To allow Preview to be the viewer of choice for a particular PDF file, you have to set it as such in the Get Info dialog box. Preview can display transparency in PDF files, but it doesn't support a number of other higher PDF functions, like annotations, overprinting, sounds, movies, alternate images, and XML tags. You really have no control over how PDF files are created by Preview, akin to setting PDF settings (job options) in Distiller. The process simply happens when a PostScript or EPS file is opened into the application.

We tested how well Preview created a PDF file from the same Quark document we used for the "Save As PDF" test. We saved a PostScript file using

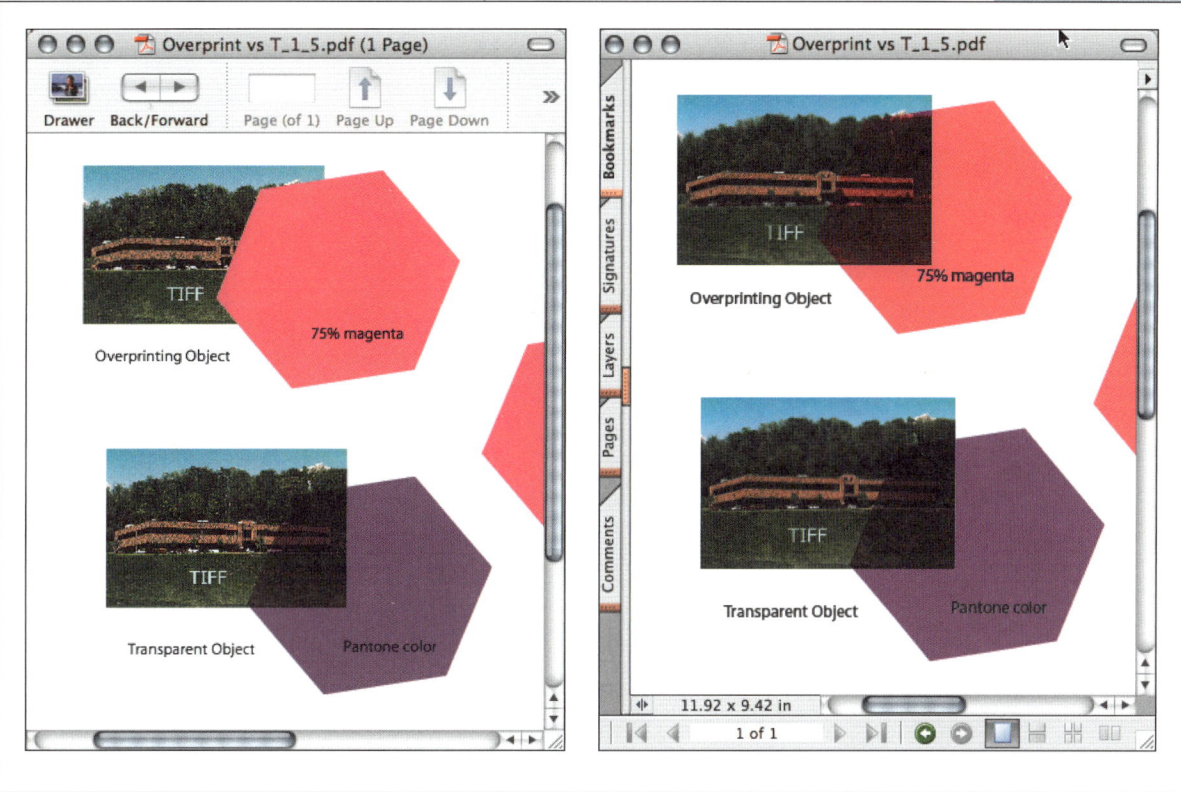

Figure 3.28. Preview cannot display overprinting objects (magenta hexagon above left). At right, the same file, viewed in Acrobat 6 Pro.

the Adobe PDF printer from Quark and dropped it onto the Preview icon. Once our new PDF file displayed in Preview, we saved it and opened it in Acrobat 6 to do some preflighting. A look at Document Properties shows that, indeed, Normalizer is the PDF creator (Figure 3.27). After the "Save As PDF"/Quartz experience we were amazed to see that we had a good PDF file for print production. While Preview could not display an overprinting object, it was defined properly in the PostScript file, so the overprint state was maintained in the PDF file and did display properly when viewed in Acrobat 6 through Overprint Preview (Figure 3.28). All objects were in the right color space, including duotones and the spot-colorized TIFF images.

Perhaps we can anticipate a future in which Apple matches the right tool with the expected output

for PDF creation. The raw pieces are there in the Mac OS X puzzle; they just have to be put together in a more workable (and sensible) fashion.

File Naming in Mac OS X

Windows users everywhere are familiar with file name extensions that consist of a dot (.) followed by several letters (usually three) that identify the type of file it is. Examples are *.doc* and *.pdf*. The Mac OS and most Mac applications have historically not required file extensions because they relate documents and applications by using the Macintosh Creator Code resource. While this is primarily true today, you may have noticed that when saving files under OS X, you're often given an option at creation to hide or display an extension. We're told that, in the future, applications may cease to support the Creator Code resource and instead rely on the filename extension

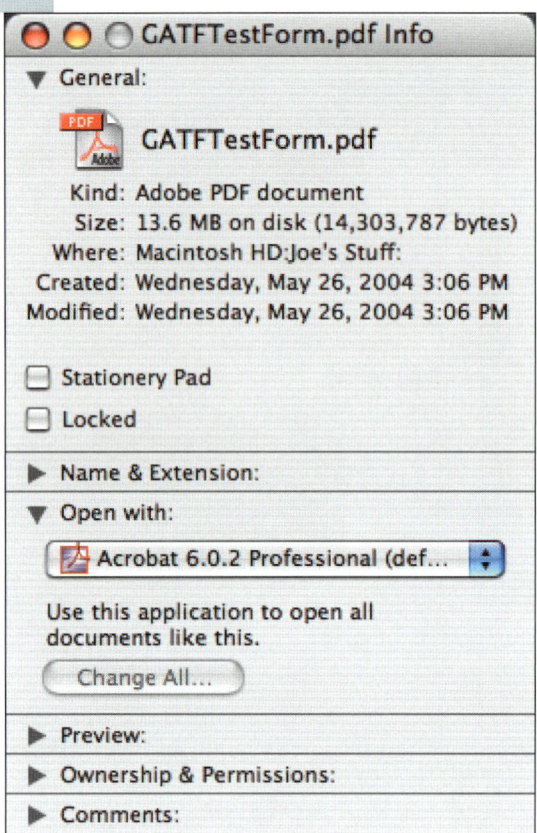

Figure 3.29. In the Info dialog box, you can specify the application that will open a PDF file.

exclusively. That's right, the Mac OS may get even more Windows-like. In preparation for this, you may want to consider using filename extensions on all of your new documents, including PDF files.

By default, filename extensions are not shown in Finder windows. To make extensions visible, choose *Preferences* from the Finder menu, navigate to the Advanced window, and click the *show all file extensions* checkbox. If you want to know what the file extensions should be for a particular file type, check out the searchable database at www.filext.com.

Linking Filenames to Applications

It's possible to have several applications that can open a particular type of file, PDF being one that can be opened by a number of applications, most particularly Preview and Acrobat. To change the application that will be used to view a particular file, using PDF as an example, do this:

1. In the Finder, select a file that has the .pdf filename extension.

2. Hit Command+I, or select *Get Info* from the Finder File pull-down menu.

3. In the Get Info window, click the *Open with* disclosure triangle.

4. In the pop-up menu, select the application that you want this file to be opened with—in this example, *Preview.*

5. If you want all files with this extension to be opened in Preview, click the *Change All* button.

6. When the confirmation dialog appears, click *Continue.*

7. Close the Get Info window.

Don't get the idea that because the bulk of this chapter has been about things for the print production professional to watch out for in Mac OS X, we don't like it. When it comes to network and print issues, Panther has it all over previous versions of the Mac OS. Remember when a Quark crash meant a system crash? Because of the way memory is handled, that sort of problem, once frequent to the creative user, is a thing of the past. With careful consideration of the potential problems, working with Mac OS X is a pleasure. We aren't looking back.

CHAPTER 4
PDF PRODUCTION TOOLS

PDF in Prepress

Before the introduction of PDF, particularly the print-production-friendly version 1.3, most print projects created with desktop publishing applications were submitted to output providers in their native file format. Some content creators supplied PostScript files to their output provider, typically those who worked in the publication industry, but for the most part, providing native files had been the norm. Until very recently, providing native files was still the norm—but now PDF is well on the way to being the primary file format submitted for print output. GATF's 2002 PDF usage study *(The PDF Era: PDF Usage in the Real World)* revealed that more than 50% of digital layout files received by the study participants were in the QuarkXPress file format, 23% in PDF format, and the balance in other native application formats or PostScript/EPS. Just a year later, Seybold Seminars and MediaLive International Research conducted their second PDF usage survey, with more than 1200 respondents from the U.S. and Europe. To the question "What 3 file types do you currently receive/submit for print output most often?" the top most-mentioned file type was PDF, followed by QuarkXPress, then Microsoft Office products and PostScript.

When native application files are provided, a large job can contain hundreds of support files, including, in addition to the base layout application native file, fonts, images, and illustrations. These files can also be in any number of file formats, adding to the confusion. Because it is quite likely that there will be missing items or some kind of problem with some of the files, they have to be checked thoroughly by the output provider. This process, called *preflighting,* is still very important, even when working with PDF files.

One of the biggest benefits of PDF is that a single file can contain all of the elements required to successfully output the job. When created properly, the PDF file will contain all of the fonts, images, and illustrations required for output. So the content creator can replace that hodgepodge of files that makes up the average print production project and submit just one file to the service provider for output. PDF files can, however, be created improperly. An overwhelming majority (88%) of the participants in GATF's PDF study stated that the biggest problem inherent in working with PDF files is that clients do not make them properly! While that number was not quite as high among participants in the 2003 Seybold survey, it was still cited as one of the top three problems in working with PDF files (Figure 4.1). Therefore, PDF files, too, must be checked to determine whether they are production-ready.

Both the designer and printer have to take a share in the responsibility of ensuring that a PDF file

	Receivers		Generators	
	US	Euro	US	Euro
More difficult to edit than native files	61%	50%	65%	51%
Not made properly	57%	70%	34%	49%
PDF different from native file	25%	24%	30%	22%
Final color doesn't match original	25%	20%	25%	21%
Version control issues	21%	18%	20%	19%
RIP and output problems	21%	34%	18%	41%
Harder to troubleshoot	20%	10%	24%	24%
Display doesn't match output	19%	16%	28%	17%
Too easy to edit	3%	8%	5%	6%
Other	7%	10%	12%	11%

Figure 4.1. The 2003 Seybold PDF Usage Survey shows top problems with PDF files.

is production-ready. The designer must be sure that all of the images have adequate resolution and all of the fonts have been embedded. They also have to make sure that pages contain adequate bleed where needed. This is a top problem with incoming PDF files, according to the PDF study, and one that is rather difficult, but not impossible, to repair with the right tools. We'll show you how in the In the Trenches chapter. The printer has to determine that the PDF files are fit for output on the designated output device. This includes determining that the PDF file was created properly and verifying that the file contains adequate bleeds, fonts, and sufficient image resolution in addition to verifying that all of the color images are in the correct color space.

Some preflighting functions, as well as very basic editing, can be performed using the standard tools available in Acrobat 6 Professional, without benefit of any third-party application or plug-in. More advanced preflighting and file editing can be accomplished with plug-ins or other third-party tools, some of which we will cover later in this chapter. As with preflighting native documents, the goal is to perform a consistent evaluation of the PDF file to ensure everything needed to successfully image the file is included.

Preflighting, Editing, and Output Using Acrobat 6 Pro Tools

Using Acrobat, one can determine basic information about a PDF file, such as how the file was created and which fonts were used. Acrobat, used in conjunction with an external image or illustration editing application, can provide additional

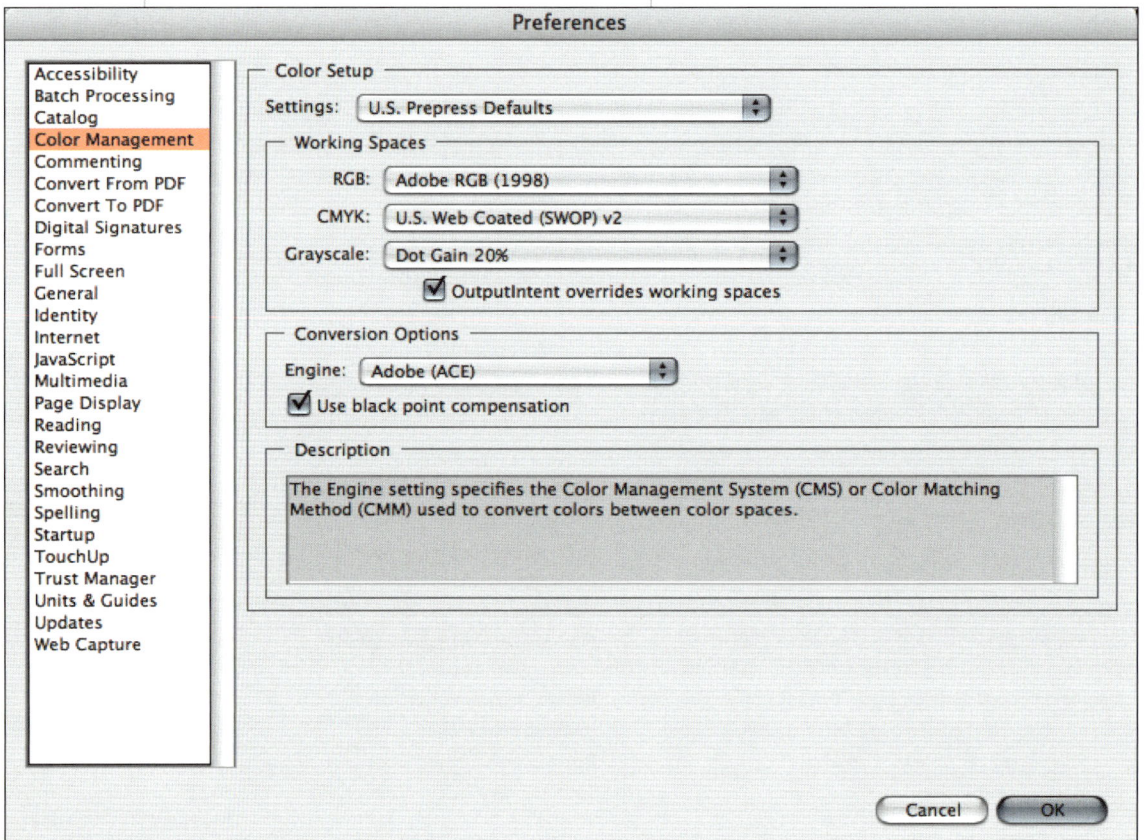

Figure 4.2. Acrobat 6 will display all untagged images with a default ICC profile, set in Color Management Preferences.

information about raster and vector objects, such as the color space of image files and their resolution. Acrobat also has the ability to create separations for film imagesetting or platesetting.

Acrobat 6 Soft Proofing

If Acrobat 6 Pro is to be a print production tool, it's important to set it up to "soft proof" PDF files so you can preview how objects will print. PDF files are typically saved in composite format, but for high-end commercial printing, the file will ultimately have to be separated to the needed printing plates. It's important to predict whether the PDF file will separate properly, and the soft proofing tools available in Acrobat 6 Pro will help do just that. Most of these tools are under the "Advanced" menu.

You can tell Acrobat 6 to display objects that have not been tagged with an ICC profile with a profile of your choice in the Color Management section of General Preferences (Figure 4.2). Note that Acrobat always honors profiles embedded in PDF files, so it only uses settings established here for untagged color. As part of Adobe's move to make color management consistent between their CS applications and Acrobat, you can choose from a list of predefined color management settings files (CSF). Several canned options are available, as well as any that have been created in Illustrator, InDesign, or Photoshop. Acrobat can use custom CSF files but provides no option to create them.

Soft Proofing conditions for Acrobat 6 Pro is set up by selecting the Advanced menu and then *Proof*

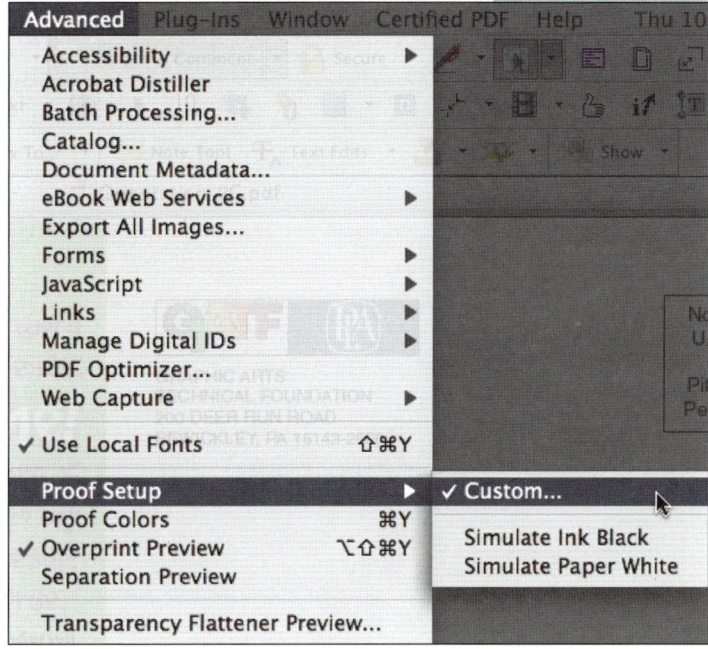

Figure 4.3. Select an ICC profile for soft proofing through the Proof Setup option.

Setup>Custom (Figure 4.3). Through Custom you can select from any ICC profile available on your system. For Windows systems, profiles must be in the System32\Spool\Drivers:Color directory for Acrobat to recognize them. For Mac OS X users, profiles must be in Macintosh HD/ColorSync/Profiles/Displays. To preview a PDF file as it will be printed, choose from an output profile that represents your final printing device. This can either be custom profiles created for the specific presses and conditions in your

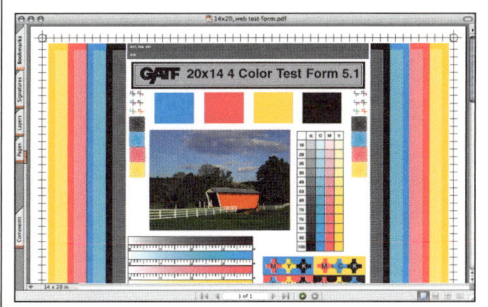
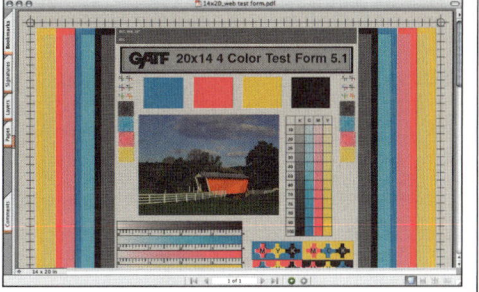

Figure 4.4. The same PDF file may not look at all the same when viewed with different Paper White conditions.

organization or canned print profiles like U.S. Sheetfed Coated v.2.

One can opt to simulate either Paper White or Ink Black. If you check Paper White, the preview will attempt to simulate what the piece will look like once printed. If the profile selected was U.S. Web Coated, for example, and you decide to simulate paper white, the white (paper) areas of the file will display as a shade of gray. See Figure 4.4 for an idea of how different a PDF file can look under different Paper White conditions. Ink Black simulation shows the dynamic range of the file's profile. A profile with high dynamic range can show good highlight and shadow detail; one with low range will show blown highlights and plugged shadows. Once Proof Setup is activated, you have to select Proof Colors from the Advanced menu to actually use the settings for preview (Figure 4.5).

Another key option under the Advanced menu is Use Local Fonts (Figure 4.6). There has been a lot of misinformation spread about this particular option, mostly by folks who claim that it is dangerous to check this option because, if you do, all fonts used in the PDF document will be replaced by same-named fonts on the local system. This is absolutely untrue: if fonts are embedded in a PDF file, the embedded font will always be used for viewing and printing (unless a RIP is specifically set up to replace fonts under certain conditions, but that's another story). When *Use Local Fonts* is selected, local fonts will be used for display and print only if the referenced font is not embedded in the PDF file. If there is no matching local font on the system and this option is not checked, then Acrobat will use the built-in Adobe Sans or Serif Multiple Master font for display and print (Figures 4.7a, 4.7b).

The Overprint Preview is another key tool that's a part of Acrobat 6 Pro and Standard (and was available in Acrobat 5 as well). It's critical to be able to preview on screen objects that are set to overprint to avoid potential errors on press. Overprinting is the technique often used to create trap areas between adjacent colors in order to prevent white paper gaps from showing up on press. Black text is typically set to

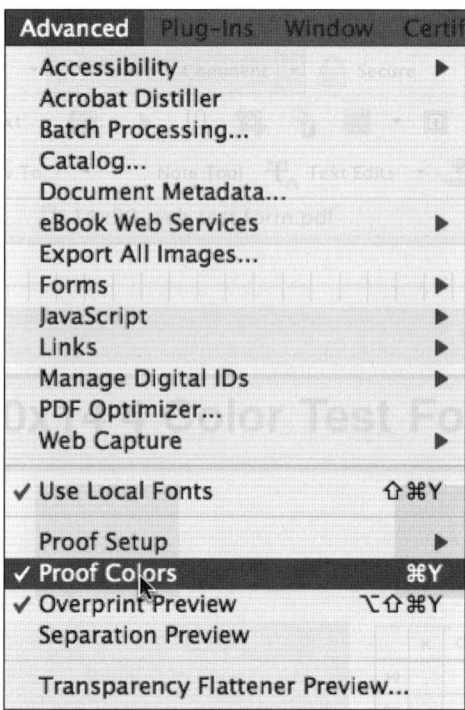

Figure 4.5. Select *Proof Colors* to view files using settings chosen under Proof Setup.

Figure 4.6. Check *Use Local Fonts* to use fonts from the local system if they are not embedded in the PDF.

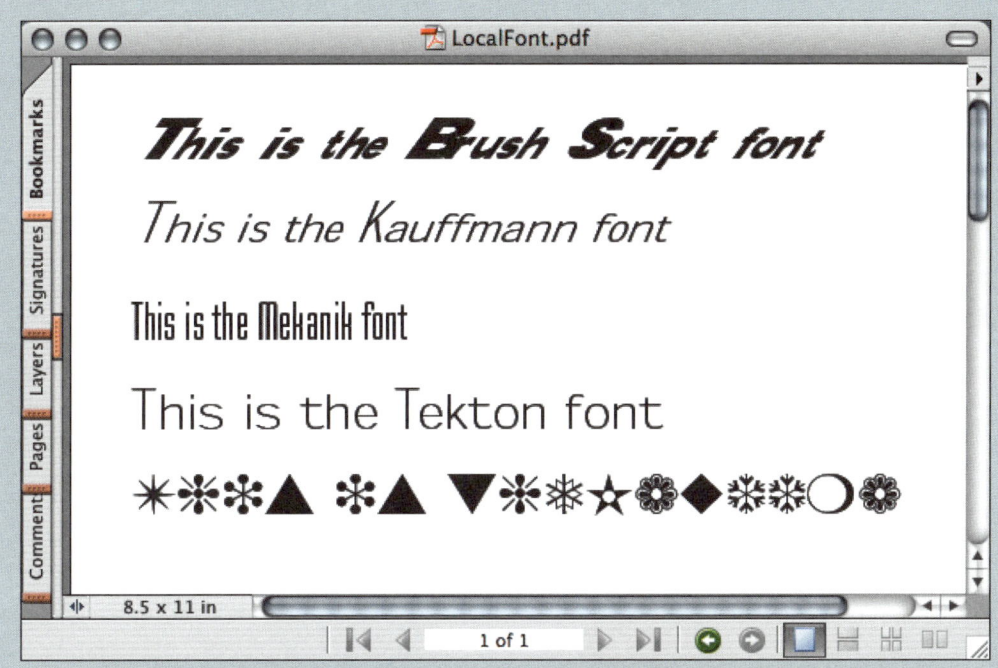

Figure 4.7a. If *Use Local Fonts* is not checked, or there are no matching fonts on the system, then Acrobat will use the built-in Adobe Sans or Serif Multiple Master font for display and print.

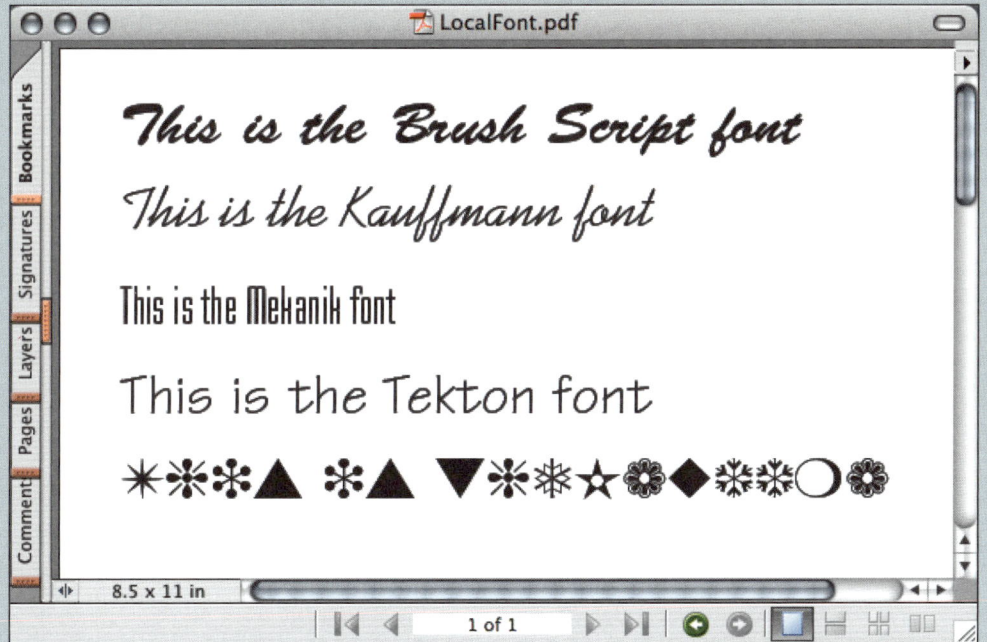

Figure 4.7b. This is how the typefaces should look, while Figure 4.7a shows how Adobe Multiple Master fonts display the text. While the text in 4.7a is readable, it certainly won't be acceptable for print production.

Figure 4.8a. With Overprint Preview deselected, who knows how these will print?

Figure 4.8b. Overprint Preview shows overprinting objects in a PDF file.

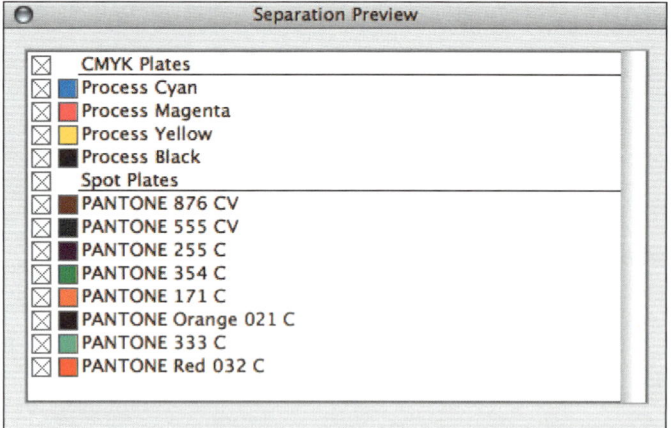

Figure 4.9. Separation Preview shows every color represented in a PDF file. Toggling these colors on and off is a great way to preflight a PDF file for things like properly set overprinting objects.

overprint for the same reason. The Overprint Preview option lets you see that overprinting has been set up properly in the PDF file. Figure 4.8a shows an illustration without overprint previewing. Figure 4.8b shows the same file with Overprint Preview selected; notice how very different they look. The objects will print as viewed with Overprint Preview selected, so if the preview shows something that isn't how the file should print, it gives you the opportunity to raise a red flag and have it repaired.

An invaluable addition to Acrobat 6 Professional for prepress production is the Separation Preview tool. Here you can see at a glance all of the colors used in a document (Figure 4.9). Colors can be toggled on or off to show where and how they are being used in a document. The Separation Preview tool is a great way to make sure black text is set to overprint by simply toggling the black channel off. If a white knockout of the text shows up when black is turned off, it hasn't been set to overprint. If the background color shows up solid, the black text has been set to overprint properly. It's also an easy way make sure the same spot color hasn't been specified multiple times with different names. Separation Preview also provides feedback on the color build of any area or object when the cursor is dragged over that area.

Finally, the last option under the Advanced menu, Transparency Preview, gives the user a tool to see just what will happen to transparent objects when they are flattened for print output (Figure 4.10). Transparency Flattener provides options similar to those you would find in Adobe Illustrator or InDesign, but it's important to note that this tool does not actually flatten transparent objects. Flattening of transparency can only be done through the Print dialog in Acrobat 6. So if you actually want to flatten transparency objects, you have got to "print" the PDF file through the print dialog. Transparency Flattener lets the user see how the entire page will look when flattened according to the options selected. It also lets you take a look at just the transparent objects, which are highlighted in red for the preview.

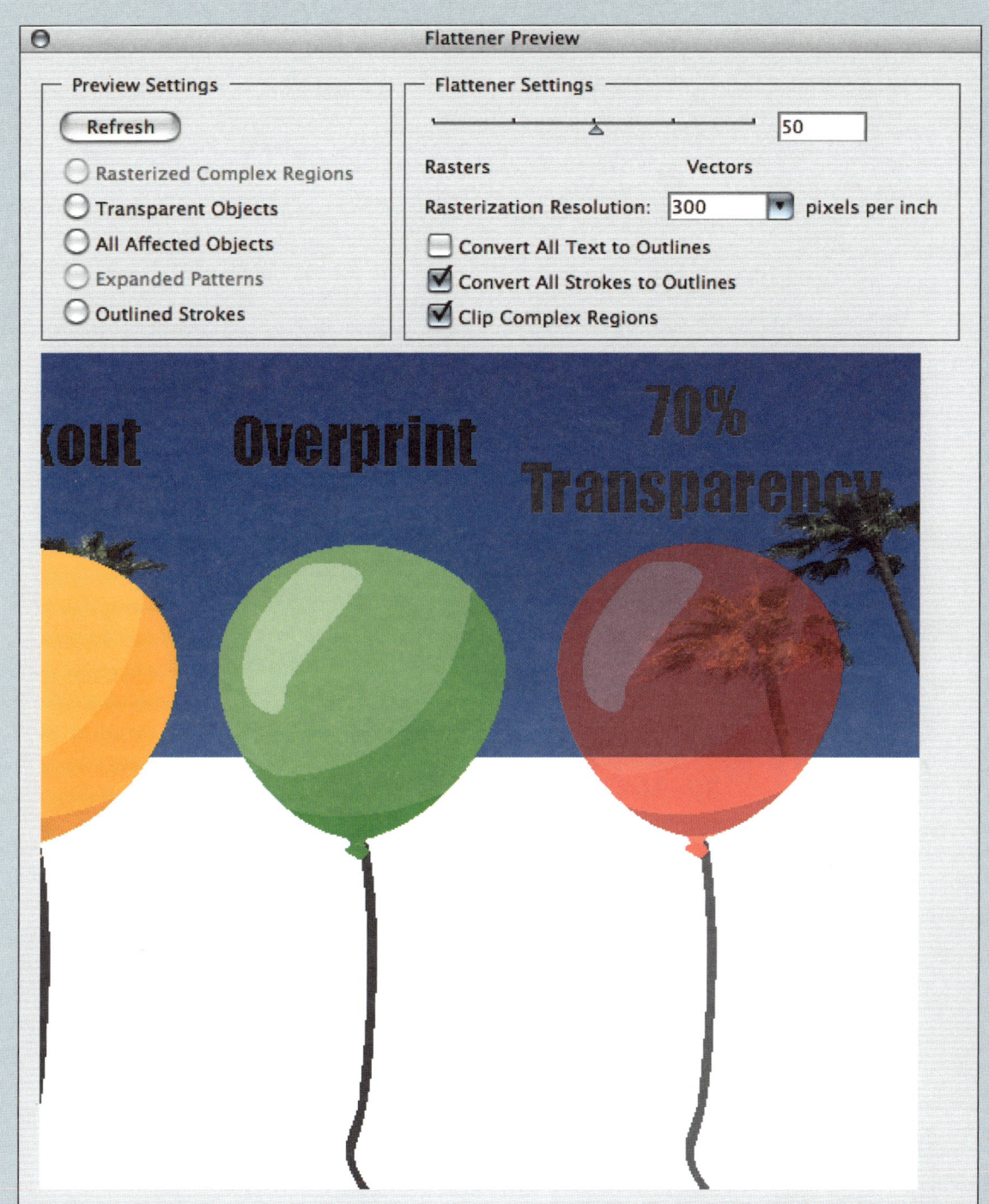

Figure 4.10. Transparency Preview gives the user a tool to see just what will happen to transparent objects when they are flattened for print output, but it is only a preview tool and cannot be used to actually flatten transparent objects.

If you were to view all the tools available in Acrobat 6, not to mention those added by plug-ins, you'd take up half of the screen with the toolbar. So we advise cutting the tools that you place in the toolbar to those essential for your production environment. At a minimum, you should have the basic and advanced editing tools on the toolbar, as well as the plug-in tools you access most frequently (Figure 4.11).

Acrobat Preflighting Tools

The first step in preflighting PDF files using the built-in Acrobat tools is to determine how the PDF was created. To do this, Select *File>Document Properties...* to activate the Document Properties dialog box. The Document Properties dialog box

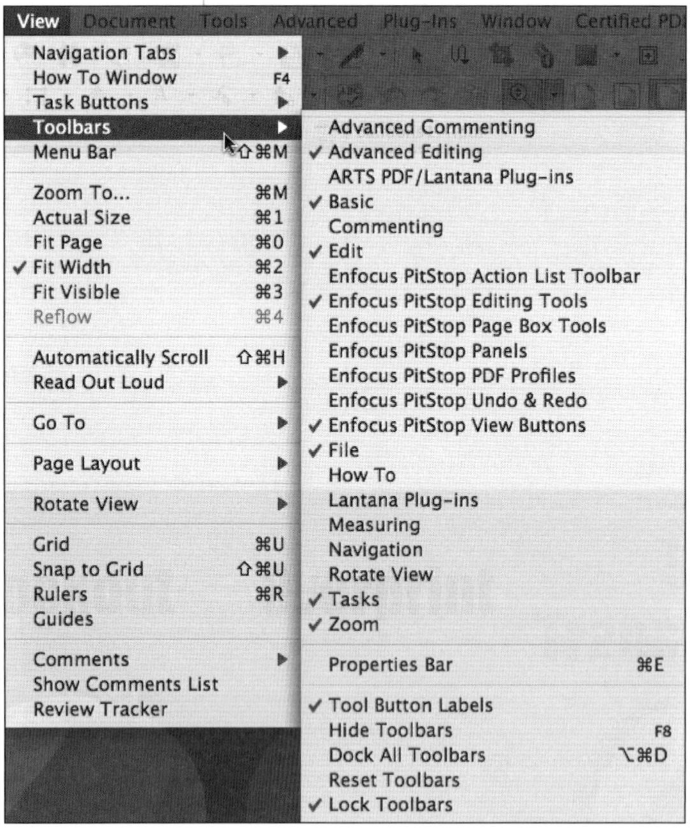

Figure 4.11. To retain precious screen real estate, display only those tools you require for your production environment in the Acrobat Toolbar.

contains the document information including Description, Fonts, Advanced, and Security.

Determining the PDF Creator. Under the Description (Figure 4.12) option within Document Properties, you can determine the creator application (such as QuarkXPress or InDesign), producer (Distiller, PDFWriter, or PDFLibrary), and PDF version (1.2, 1.3, or 1.4). The Description should always be checked first when examining a PDF file, if only to rule out that the file was created using a tool like PDFWriter. PDFWriter is a non-PostScript PDF creation tool, meaning that it uses the display method of the operating system (QuickDraw on Mac OS 9.2 or earlier or GDI on Windows) instead of PostScript to create the PDF file. This means that the high-resolution data in a placed EPS graphic, for example, would not be included in the PDF file; instead the low-resolution placeholder image used for EPS display in the layout application would be used. A PDF file created with PDFWriter will be of little value for any print production project involving anything other than perhaps black text.

Font Information. Checking font information in a PDF file is also accomplished through the Document Properties dialog box (Figure 4.13). The Fonts option displays the fonts and font types (i.e., TrueType, Type 1) used in the original document as well as the font actually used by Acrobat to display and print the PDF file (a critically important distinction). Also displayed is whether the fonts are embedded or subsetted in the PDF file. If the font is not embedded, this menu will tell you which font is being used to simulate the missing font. Acrobat will use either the Adobe Sans or Adobe Serif Multiple Master fonts, installed on the system along with Acrobat viewers, when creating a substitution for a missing font in a PDF file.

Trapping Information. The Advanced option within the Document Properties dialog box is where the Trapping setting can be found. Trapping describes whether trapping has been applied to the PDF and, unless the PDF file will be submitted to a workflow

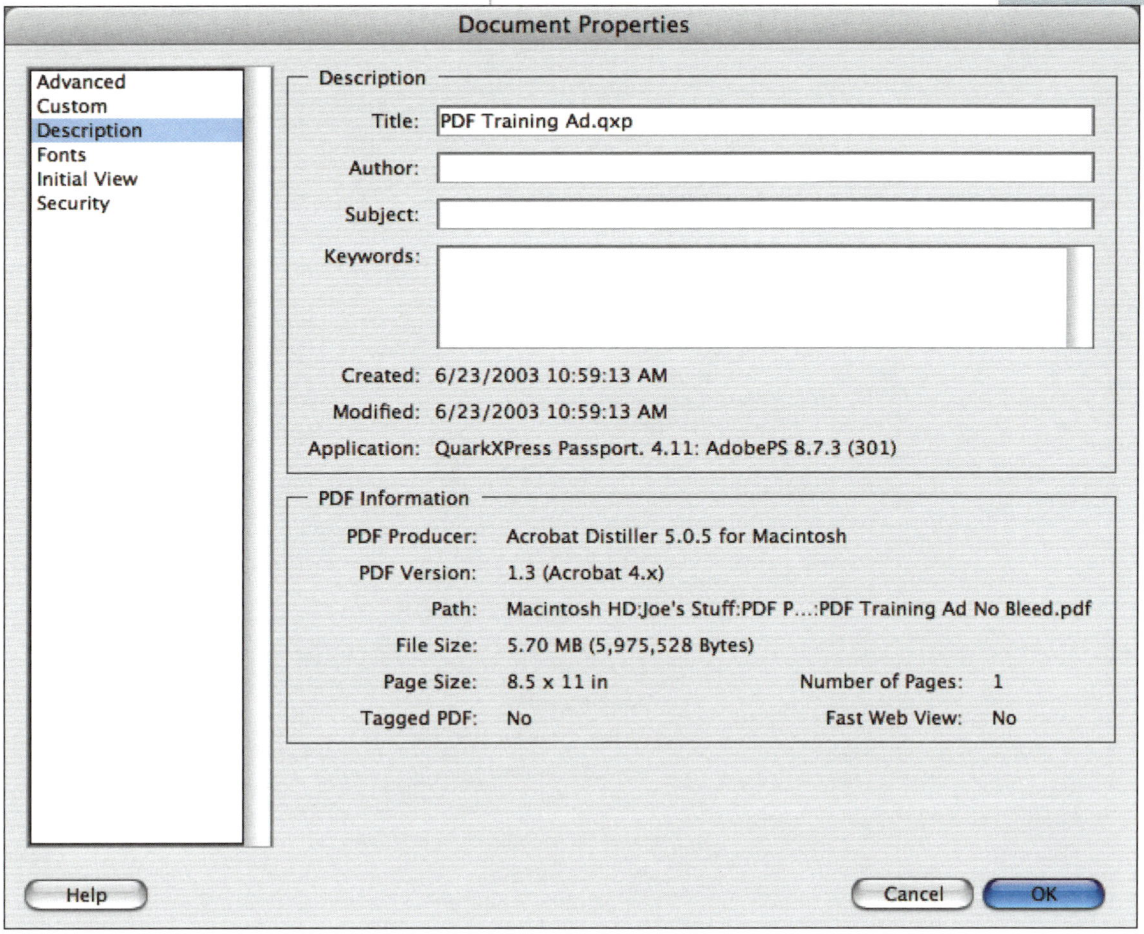

Document Properties

Advanced
Custom
Description
Fonts
Initial View
Security

┌─ Description ────────────────────────────────
│ Title: PDF Training Ad.qxp
│ Author:
│ Subject:
│ Keywords:
│
│ Created: 6/23/2003 10:59:13 AM
│ Modified: 6/23/2003 10:59:13 AM
│ Application: QuarkXPress Passport. 4.11: AdobePS 8.7.3 (301)
└──

┌─ PDF Information ────────────────────────────
│ PDF Producer: Acrobat Distiller 5.0.5 for Macintosh
│ PDF Version: 1.3 (Acrobat 4.x)
│ Path: Macintosh HD:Joe's Stuff:PDF P...:PDF Training Ad No Bleed.pdf
│ File Size: 5.70 MB (5,975,528 Bytes)
│ Page Size: 8.5 x 11 in   Number of Pages: 1
│ Tagged PDF: No   Fast Web View: No
└──

Help   Cancel   OK

Figure 4.12. A simple Acrobat preflight check includes a look at the Description option within Document Properties. You can deter-mine the creator application (such as QuarkXPress or InDesign), producer (Distiller, PDFWriter, or PDFLibrary), and PDF version.

system that can use this information, is informa-tional only. The options here are *Yes, No,* or *Unknown.*

Security. Part of PDF preflighting is to deter-mine if security has been added to the PDF. PDF files can be secured with a password to restrict printing and editing. The Security option in the Document Properties dialog will provide a summary of document restrictions. If you forget the password required to open the document, Elcomsoft (www.elcomsoft.com) offers Advanced PDF Password Recovery, password recovery software for PDF files. Simple passwords (single words only, for example) can be recovered in seconds while more complex

passwords (words with numbers and/or special characters) can take a long time to recover .

Acrobat's Preflight Feature. Acrobat's Pre-flight feature can be used to interrogate a PDF file to find out if it is a PDF suitable for high-end printing. Using this tool, Acrobat 6 Pro allows for the inspec-tion of four hundred different items within a PDF. Selecting *Document>Preflight...* will bring up the Preflight Profiles dialog box which contains a list of preset profiles that can be used to preflight a PDF. You can also create new profiles and add them to the list (Figure 4.14a, b, c).

You create your own custom profile by clicking on the Edit... button and opening the Edit Profiles

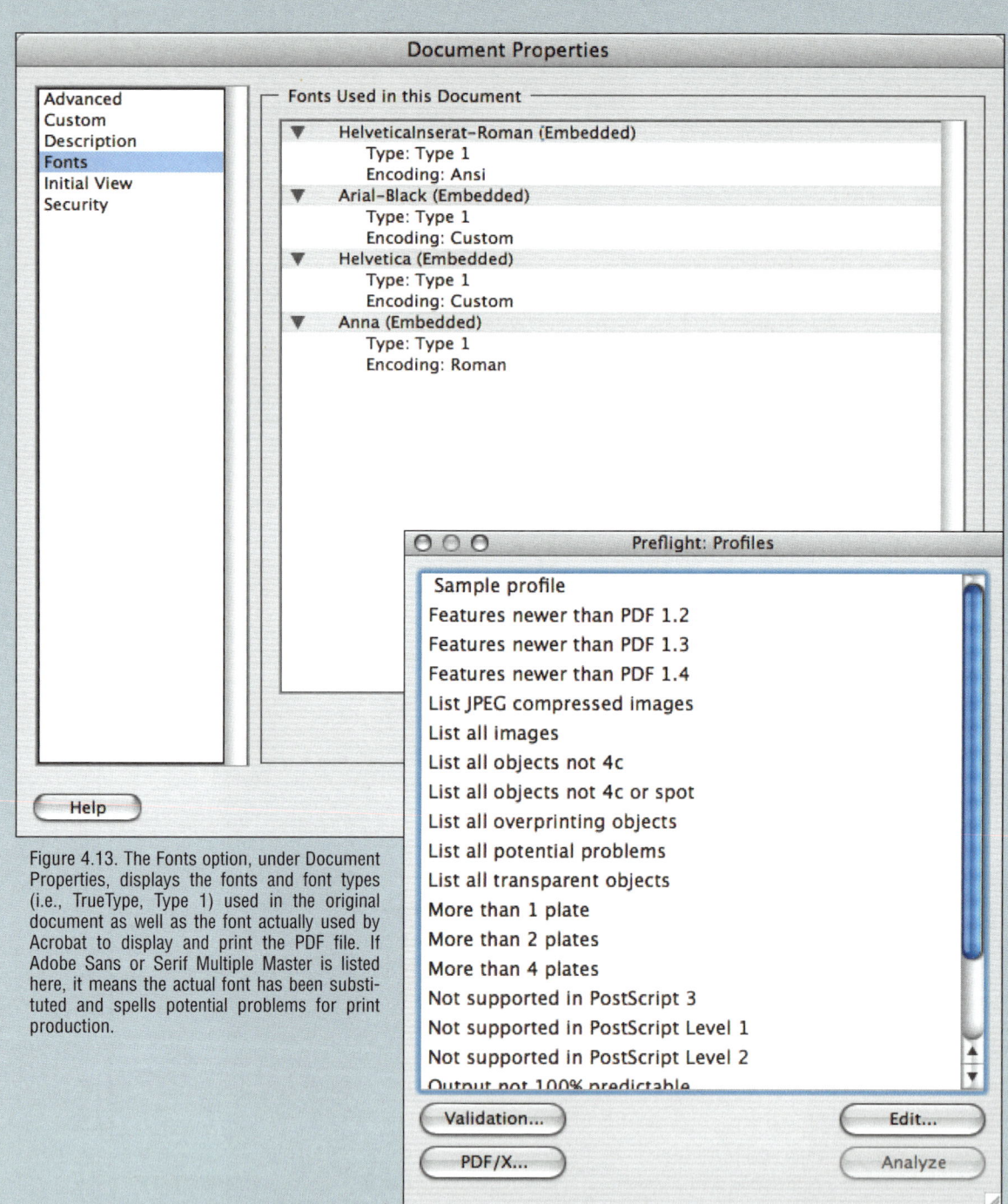

Figure 4.13. The Fonts option, under Document Properties, displays the fonts and font types (i.e., TrueType, Type 1) used in the original document as well as the font actually used by Acrobat to display and print the PDF file. If Adobe Sans or Serif Multiple Master is listed here, it means the actual font has been substituted and spells potential problems for print production.

Figure 4.14a. Preflighting is a built-in component of Acrobat 6 Professional.

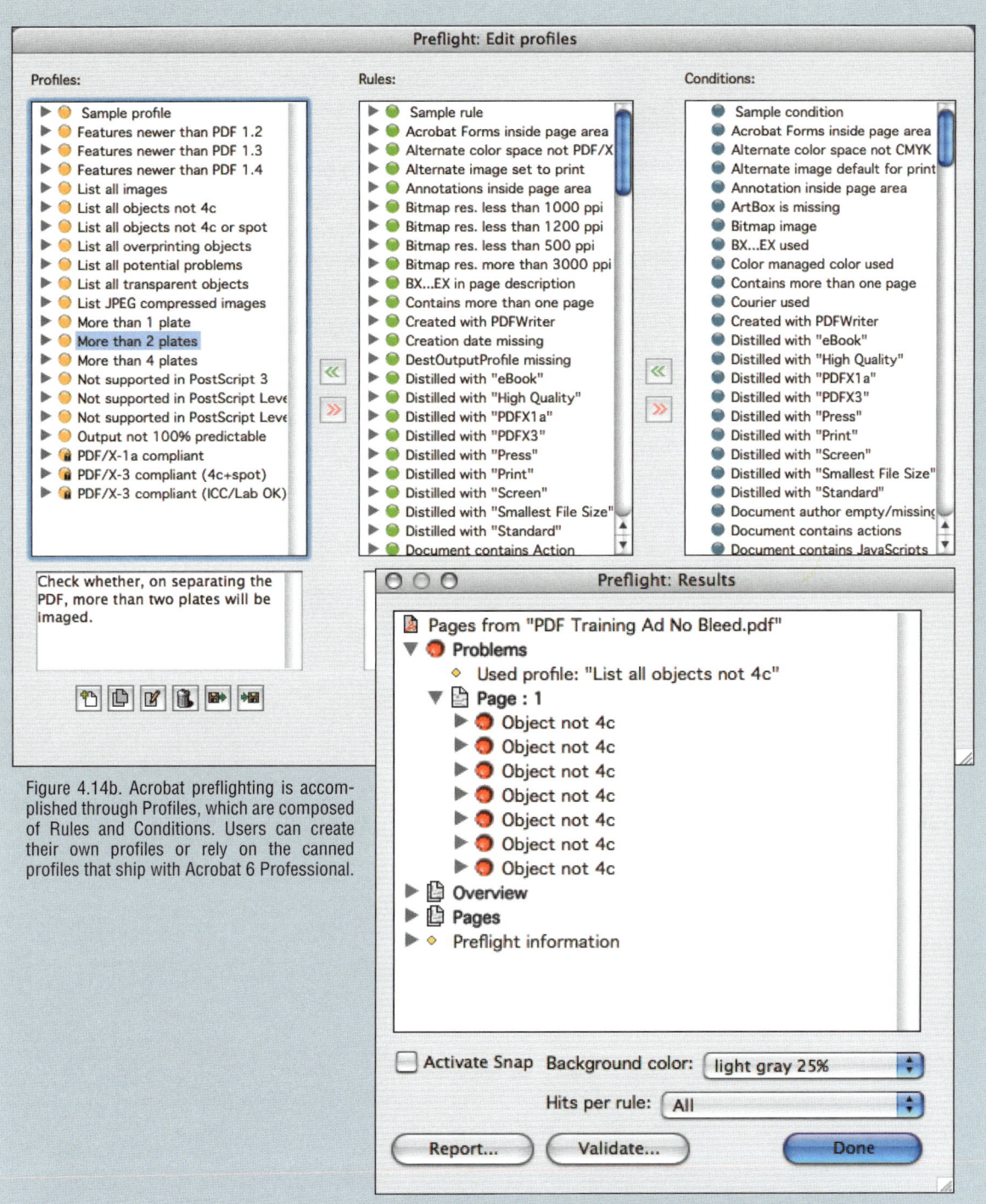

Figure 4.14b. Acrobat preflighting is accomplished through Profiles, which are composed of Rules and Conditions. Users can create their own profiles or rely on the canned profiles that ship with Acrobat 6 Professional.

Figure 4.14c. Each individual occurrence of a problem detected by a preflight check is listed and can be viewed by selecting Activate Snap.

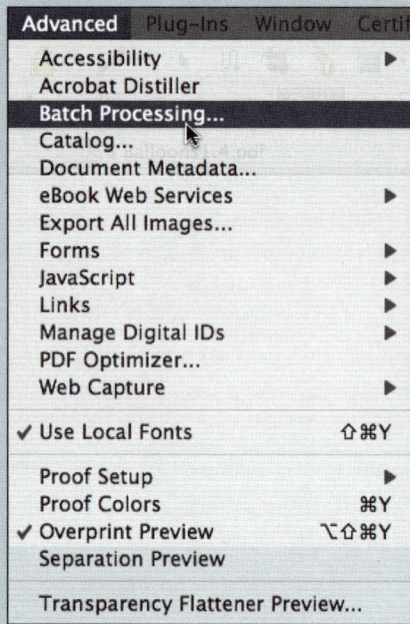

Figure 4.15. Acrobat 6 Professional offers a customizable batch processing feature.

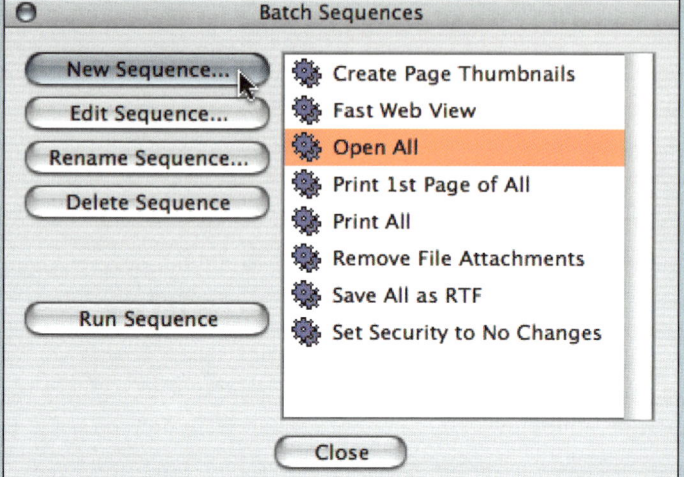

Figure 4.16. The Batch Process interface is where a user can create or edit batch sequences and actually run existing sequences.

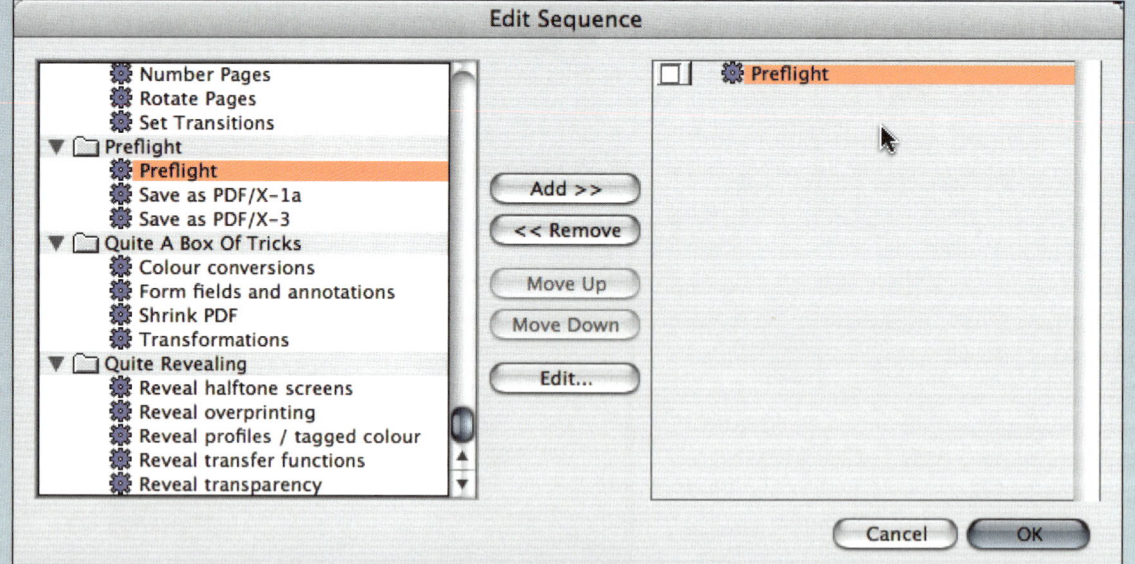

Figure 4.17. After a new sequence is intiated, the user can choose from a list of processes that can be automated. Some plug-in tools, like Quite's Quite A Box Of Tricks and Quite Revealing, make a list of functions available for batch processing.

dialog box. At first glance, the Edit Profiles dialog box looks complicated, but once you understand the hierarchy, it's actually quite simple to use. The first column contains the Profile, which is the end-use item that will be used to preflight the PDF. The second column contains the Rules, and each rule can contain one or more Conditions (third column).

This is how the hierarchy works: a Profile can contain a number of Rules and a Rule can be based on a number of Conditions. For example, a Profile can be created to check the print viability of a PDF file and include the following Conditions:

Condition #1: Font is not embedded

Condition #2: Hairline (less than 0.2 pt.)—the PDF contains hairline rules of less than 0.2 point

Condition #3: Image res. is less than 200 ppi

Condition #4: Is not CMYK—there are RGB or spot colors on the page

Condition #5: More than 4 plates for page

These five Conditions can be grouped into a single Rule that can be set to either error or report as information during the preflighting process. The Rule is then associated with a Profile where you would give it a name and description. It is this Profile that will be used to preflight the PDF.

Preflighting is one of the many tasks that can be automated with batch processing in Acrobat 6 Pro. Also under the Advanced menu, selecting the Batch Processing option brings up a window called Batch Sequences (Figure 4.15). There are a few default sequences and you have the option to create new sequences or edit existing ones. To set up a batch sequence to preflight files that are dropped into a hot folder, follow these steps:

1. Click the New Sequence… button. Enter a name for the sequence you're about to create (Figure 4.16).

2. Click the Select Commands button to choose from a list of commands available to build the Batch Sequence (Figure 4.17).

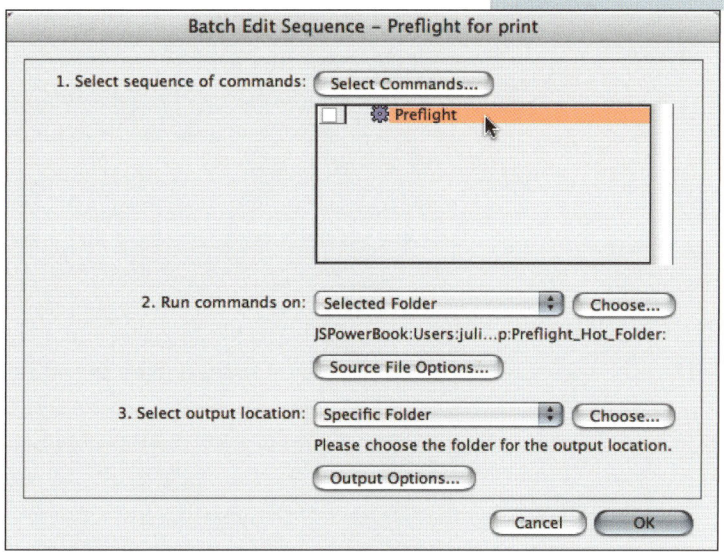

Figure 4.18. A hot folder can be set up so that the batch commands will be run on any PDF file that is dropped into that folder.

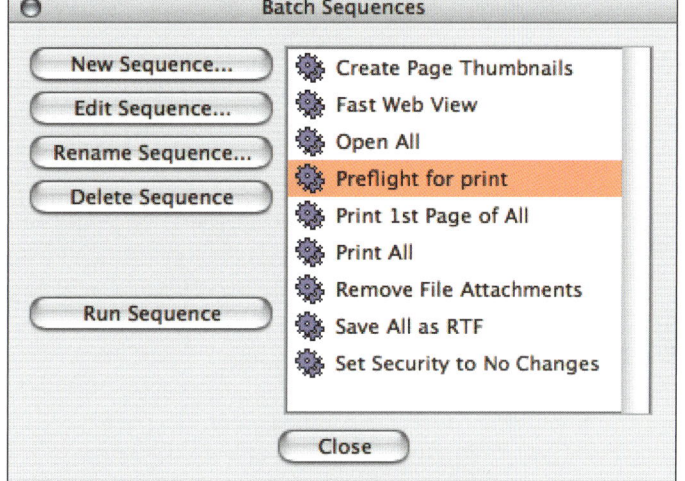

Figure 4.19. Once set, the new batch sequence is available for use.

3. Once the series of commands have been selected, set up how you would like the batch process to be run. A hot folder can be set up so that the batch commands will be run on any PDF file that is dropped into that folder (Figure 4.18).

4. A new batch sequence will show up in the list. Click the appropriate button to run it (Figure 4.19).

Acrobat Editing Tools

Editing Text. The TouchUp Text tool can be used to perform minor corrections to text in a PDF document if the font is available on the system on which the file is being viewed. In other words, although the entire set of characters for a Type 1 font used in a document can be embedded into a PDF document, those glyphs cannot be accessed for editing using the TouchUp Text tool. If you attempt to use the TouchUp Text tool to edit a PDF document on a system that does not have access to a font used in the PDF file, a warning message will be displayed reading "all or part of the selection has no available system font. You cannot add or delete text using the currently selected font" , and you will not be able to edit the font.

You can also use the TouchUp Text tool to set new text in a PDF document by holding the Option key (Mac) or Control-click (Windows) as you select the TouchUp Text tool. You'll be presented with a window to select the font you'd like to use and in which you can indicate the direction you'd like the type to flow (Figure 4.20). This is not a great way to set type more than a line or so long of text, as it doesn't recognize a line ending and wrapping text is done manually by inserting a return when you want to drop to the next line.

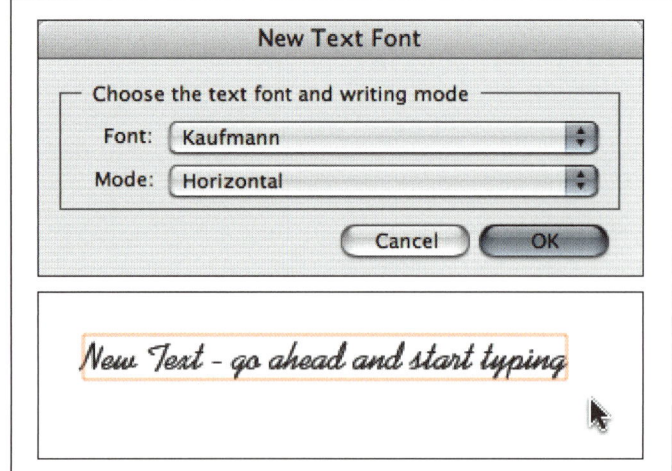

Figure 4.20. To add a new line of text to a PDF file, hold the Option key (Mac) or Control key (Windows) and select the TouchUp Text tool.

Text can also be edited using an external editing application. Text, like vector objects, can be opened into an illustration application using the TouchUp Object tool. Text can also be copied out of a PDF document onto the clipboard and then pasted into a word processing application for editing. This is done by selecting the text with the Text Select tool and copying to the clipboard using *Edit>Copy* (or Command+C on a Mac, Alt+C on Windows).

Text is encoded line by line in a PDF document, so extensive text editing, especially anything requiring the text to rewrap to the next line, cannot be accomplished. Copying a paragraph of text to the clipboard and pasting that text into Adobe Illustrator will work, for example, but no paragraph attributes will be a part of that text. Instead, the text will consist of individual lines, with no opportunity for text reflow from one line down to the next. The same is true for editing with the Text Attributes tool within Acrobat proper.

One "down 'n' dirty" way to create a new block of text in a PDF document, complete with the ability to reflow to the next line, is to use the Text Box annotation tool. Because most annotations can be allowed to print, this tool can be used to add a new block of copy to a PDF document. It can even be used to cover up existing copy that needs to be re-typeset. The Text Box tool lets the user draw out a bounding area for the text to be set. This can be drawn over an existing paragraph, then set to the color of the background, essentially allowing the user to "paste" new copy over old (Figure 4.21).

Editing Raster and Vector Objects. Raster objects (scanned or bitmap images made up of pixel data) and vector objects (illustrations made up of points and lines) can be inspected and edited in an external application, such as Adobe Photoshop, by using Acrobat's TouchUp Object tool. Before this tool can be used, you must tell Acrobat which raster and vector editing application is to be used. This is accomplished by selecting *Acrobat>Preferences...* and choosing *TouchUp* from the item list (Figure 4.22). By default, Adobe Photoshop will be used for

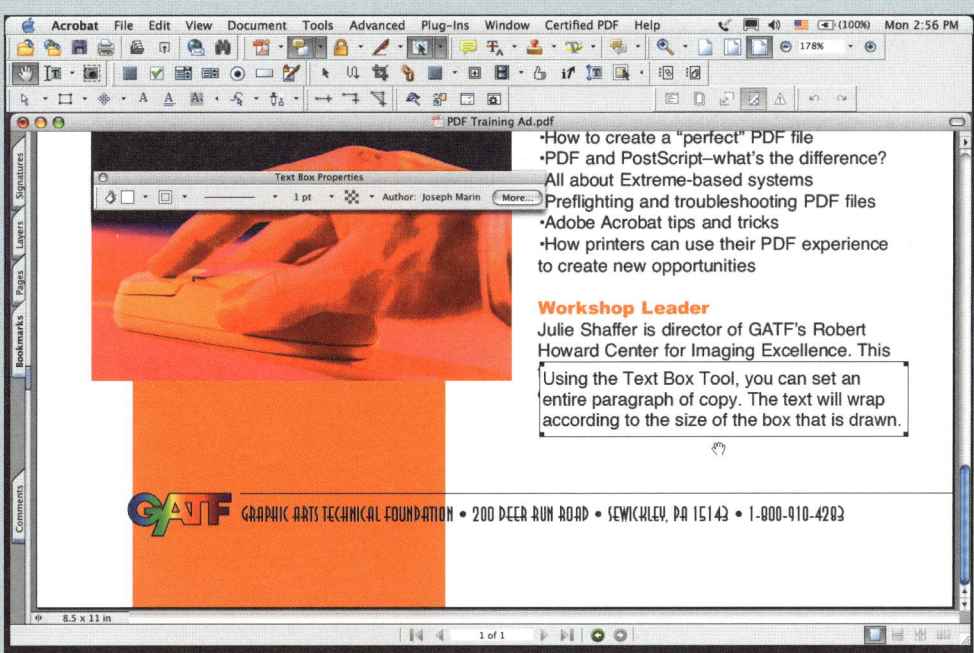

Figure 4.21. Create a new block of text, complete with paragraph wrapping, with the Text Box annotation tool.

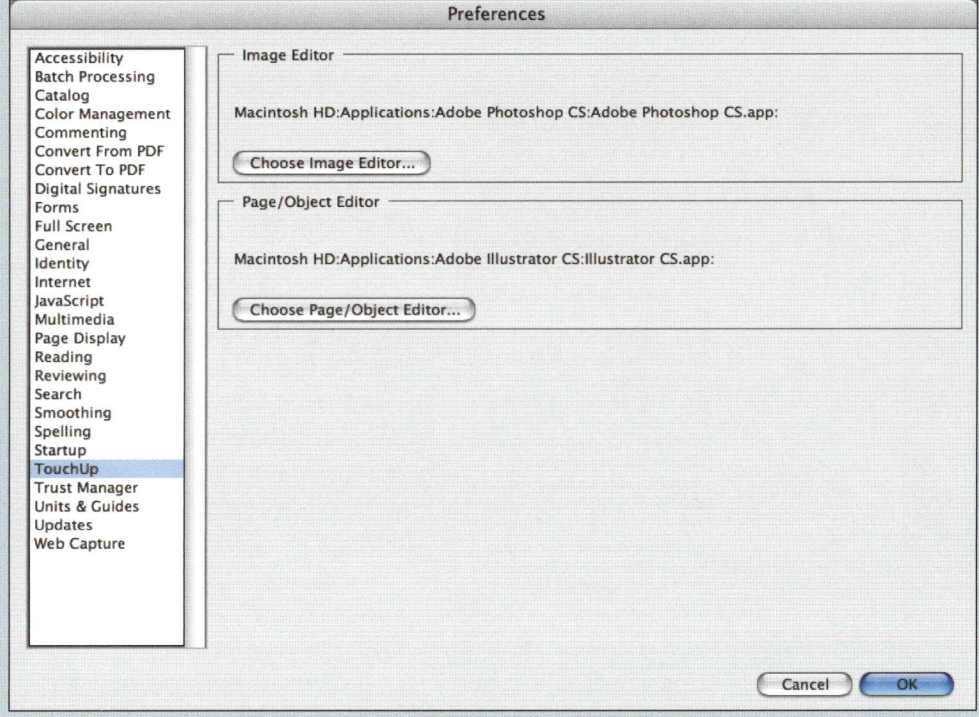

Figure 4.22. Select a default image and object editing application in TouchUp preferences.

raster image objects and Adobe Illustrator will be used for vector objects. However, other editing tools, such as Macromedia FreeHand for vector objects, can be specified as the editing tool of choice in the Preferences file.

There are two ways to open a raster or vector image file in an external editing application. You can use the context-sensitive menu by selecting the TouchUp Object tool and Control-clicking (Mac) or right-clicking (Windows) on the image and then selecting *Edit Image* from the pull-down menu (Figure 4.23). You can also Option-double-click (Mac) or Control-double-click (Windows) on an image to launch the external application. If the editing application has been set up properly (Photoshop 5.x requires a plug-in to accept images from and save images directly back into a PDF document), you will be able to do just about any editing task available within the editing application. Once edited and saved, the updated image is replaced automatically in the PDF file, providing that the file format is supported by

Acrobat PDF. (As long as you don't change the file format of the image you opened from the PDF file within Photoshop, this should not be an issue.)

When working with raster (digitally captured) images, you should consider how much image resolution is enough to adequately define them. The measure of how many pixels are in each linear inch (ppi) of a raster or bitmap image file is that image's resolution. Ideally, to achieve the optimal image quality, the resolution of an image should be twice the line screen (lpi) that will be used in the final printed piece. The mathematical equation behind this concept is called Nyquist's theorem: $lpi \times 2 \times \%$ (% being the percentage of enlargement or reduction).

For example, if a job is to be printed at 150 lpi, the resolution of the images in the file should be 300 ppi at the size that they are used in the layout application. The fixed resolution of an image is the resolution at which it was captured. So an image captured at a physical size of 2×3-in. and at a resolution of 300 dpi has a fixed resolution of 300 dpi. However, if that image was scaled to 300% in the layout file, the effective resolution of that image would be reduced to 100 pixels per linear inch, which is an insufficient resolution for high-quality output for press. The resolution of a bitmap image object in a PDF document is the effective resolution of that image file as used in the source layout application.

If you are a content creator supplying your own images in the PDF file, you may also wonder which is the optimal color space for color images: Lab, RGB, or CMYK? Converting images to CMYK involves many considerations such as the paper type (coated vs. uncoated), inks, and potential press dot gain, to name just a few. Images should not be provided in the CMYK color space unless they have been created using specific instructions provided by the printer.

Many printers want to receive PDF files with images already converted to CMYK, and this is fine, as long as they indicate how those images are to be converted from RGB (or if the images have already been converted by a prepress provider). Alternately,

Figure 4.23. Choose the TouchUp Object tool and Control- (Mac) or right-click (Windows) on the image and select *Edit Image* to use an external editor.

images can be submitted in a device-independent, ICC-based color space, giving the printer the opportunity to convert the images to CMYK for a specific printing condition. In any case, it is the printer who should ultimately determine in which color space supplied images should be saved.

It is important to mention that it is not a good idea to attempt to use Adobe Illustrator for complex editing of a PDF file unless the PDF document was originally saved directly from Illustrator. (You can verify this by viewing the creator and producer information via Document Summary in Acrobat.) You should never try to edit an entire PDF page within Illustrator, unless all else has failed and you are making a last-ditch effort to edit a file. PDF files created by other programs, such as InDesign, Photoshop, FreeHand, or even Distiller could contain objects that

Illustrator may convert (including color spaces), misinterpret, and/or entirely discard. Because of this, Illustrator should be reserved for minor vector object editing only.

Comparing Documents. Acrobat offers the ability to compare any two PDF documents to one another with the Compare tool *(Document> Compare Documents…)*. This is a great way to get an "at-a-glance" overview of what may have changed between two versions of a PDF document (Figure 4.24). The Compare Documents tool gives the user the option to set the sensitivity level of the checking mechanism such that it will check the files more thoroughly to catch subtle differences (like minor text edits) or more quickly, catching just the major changes (like global color space changes).

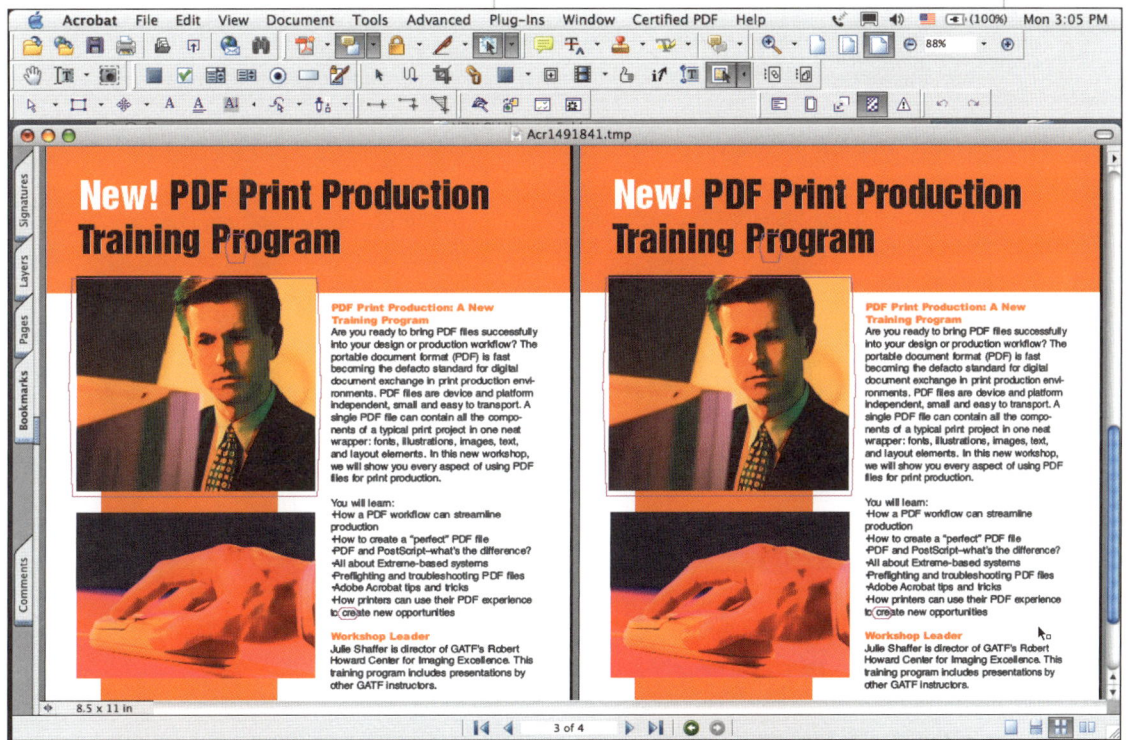

Figure 4.24. The Acrobat 6 Compare Documents option is a great way to get an "at-a-glance" overview of what may have changed between two versions of a PDF document. Objects that differ are outlined in a color set by the user.

Acrobat Output Tools

While outputting PDF in Acrobat 6 has remained relatively the same for composite printing, the real changes can be found in outputting separations. Selecting *File>Print...* and clicking the Advanced button in the Print dialog box brings up all of the controls necessary for printing separations for press (Figure 4.25).

In the Output section you will find output choices for color including Composite, Composite Gray, Separations, and In-RIP Separations. Screen ruling and output resolution can also be specified here by using one of the presets from the Screening list or by creating your own custom settings. The Plate Control list gives you the option to convert any spot colors which may be in the PDF to process color.

The Marks and Bleeds section allows you to add printer marks to the output. Options here include color bars, crop marks, bleed marks, and trim marks.

The Transparency Flattening section controls how transparent objects will be handled upon output (Figure 4.26). The Transparency Quality/Speed slider determines whether transparent object will be converted to raster data (move slider to the left) or vector data (move slider to the right). For high-end printing, the slider should be toward the Vector slide to maintain highest possible quality for press. Moving the slider to the Raster side converts all transparent objects to raster data. Depending on which objects are affected by transparency, this could result in diminished quality of the final output. For example, if text touches a transparent object, it could be considered a transparent object and rasterized when the file is flattened. If the raster resolution is set to 300 dpi, the text in that area would be output at 300 dpi. For high-quality output, text should be at least 1200 dpi. In general, the rasterization resolution can be set in the Transparency Flattener and should be set to at least twice the line screen of the final printed piece.

Finally, the PostScript Options section contains settings for things like PostScript level (2 or 3) and to emit information such as transfer functions, halftones, and undercolor removal/black generation. All of these depend upon the requirements of the output device to which you are printing.

Third-Party PDF Preflighting and Editing Solutions

Although some preflighting and editing can be done using built-in Adobe Acrobat tools, it soon becomes apparent that they are just not sufficient for all of the potential preflighting and editing needs in a print production workflow. A far more thorough way to preflight and edit a PDF document is through the use of third-party software applications. Many software developers offer plug-ins for Acrobat that are designed to allow you to perform detailed, and even automated, preflighting to and complex editing of a PDF file. What follows is an overview of some of the preflighting and editing plug-ins for Adobe Acrobat that are currently on the market.

callas software pdfInspektor (www.callassoftware.com)

callas software offers a suite of tools to enhance prepress production which includes their venerable preflighting and editing tool, pdfInspektor. pdfInspektor lists errors found in a PDF file in a separate window which can be exported as a text file. Custom preflighting profiles can be set up from a set of rules for specific jobs. More than 400 different items can be checked, including whether the PDF conforms to the PDF/X standard. If this sounds a lot like the preflight tool built into Acrobat 6, it's because they are one in the same; callas software's preflight technology was OEMed by Adobe . We'll cover callas's workflow solutions "process" in Chapter 6.

Enfocus PitStop Professional (www.enfocus.com)

PitStop Professional from Enfocus has virtually become a de facto standard plug-in for prepress and print production environments. PitStop Pro allows the user to build inspection profiles that can be used by output providers to review incoming PDF files to make sure they are print-ready. Profiles can also be distributed to content-creator to be used to preflight

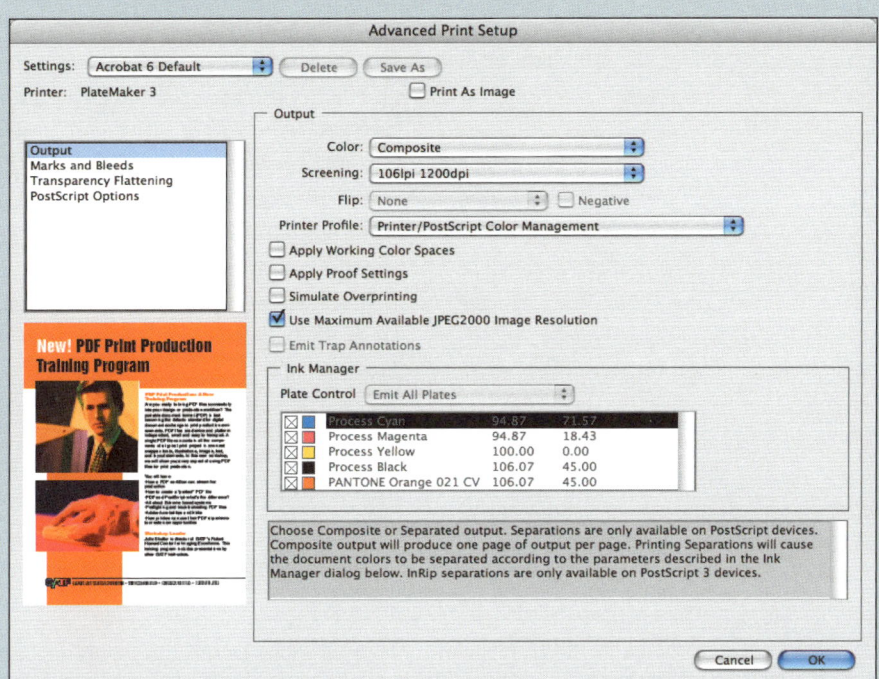

Figure 4.25. The Advanced settings in Acrobat 6 Professional allow for printing separations.

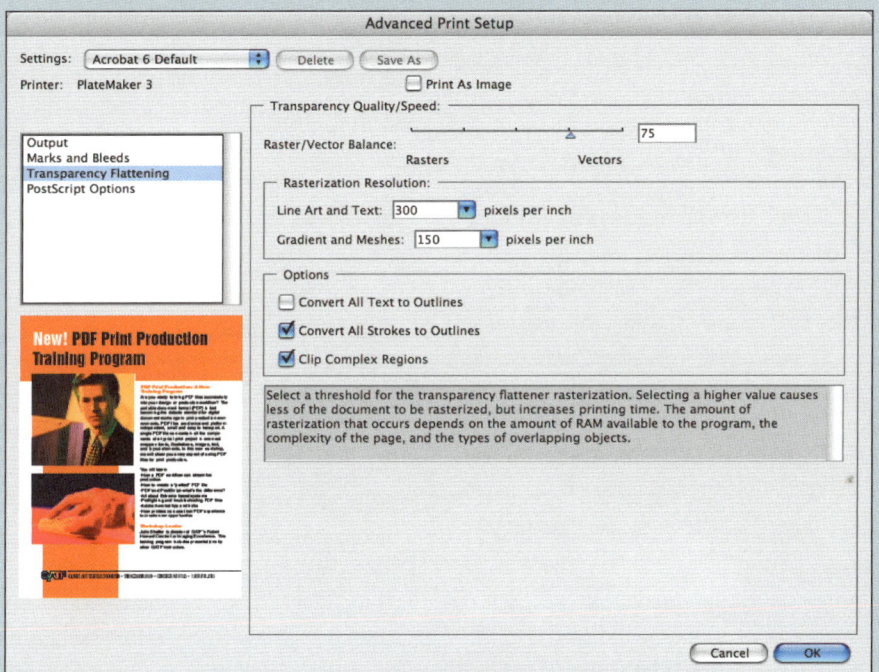

Figure 4.26. Transparent objects must be flattened prior to printing.

PDF files before sending them off to the output provider (Figure 4.27). When a PDF file is inspected, a report is generated (another PDF file) which details any potential errors and contains links to those problem areas in the original PDF document. Users can use the links to navigate through the original PDF file and review problem areas. In addition to preflighting, PitStop Professional also includes extensive file editing features. A short list of what can be done to a PDF file using PitStop tools includes repositioning text, paragraphs, or any object; embedding missing fonts; editing text (even paragraphs); modifying and specifying color spaces, including spot (PMS) colors in vector objects; and adding bleed to a document. Many of these editing features can be automatically applied during the preflighting process or saved as an Action for future use. Actions are a series of tasks that can be set up once and used to automate repetitive tasks. For example, an Action can be built to change the media box of all PDF files to which it is applied to a certain size, scale all objects on the page to fit into that page size, add crop marks, convert images to CMYK, and ensure all black text is set to overprint. We will show a number of file repair techniques using PitStop Pro in the In the Trenches chapter.

Enfocus Instant PDF
(www.enfocus.com)

Instant PDF, the PDF creation tool that is part of the Enfocus PDF Workflow Suite, has been on the market for several years, but has been entirely overhauled for the current version 3. Through Instant PDF 2.x, the product was a plug-in to Adobe Acrobat, but Instant PDF 3.0 is a standalone application. Instant PDF 2.x was used to create print-ready PDF files and could be used to initiate a "Certified PDF" workflow. A PDF file was created by printing to a custom desktop printer, using Acrobat Distiller to convert the PostScript file to PDF. The PDF file was then automatically checked against a PitStop preflighting profile, fixed if needed (and fixes were built into the profile), and, if it passed, was "certified" to have done so.

Instant PDF 3.0 is still a tool to help the content creator make error-free PDF files, but it does so through implementation of a new concept, the Enfocus PDF Queue (Figure 4.28). The idea is that PDF "receivers" (the printer or output provider) define all the settings needed to create a viable PDF file for their production process and include this information in the Enfocus PDF Queue. Instant PDF 3.0 will automatically execute this Queue on the PDF file. Specifically, the Enfocus PDF Queue can contain just about everything the content creator would need to create print-ready PDF files. Specifically, this includes:

- Acrobat Distiller PDF Settings (job options)
- Print settings for QuarkXPress 6 and Adobe InDesign CS
- An Enfocus PDF Profile for a preflight check and file fix (if fixes are part of the Profile)
- Enfocus Action Lists
- Directions on how to route the resultant PDF file (save, email, FTP) (Figure 4.29).

Instant PDF does not contain the ability to actually create PDF files; a PostScript interpreter or other means of PDF creation is still required. While an Instant PDF Queue can contain Distiller PDF settings, Instant PDF 3 is no longer tied exclusively to Distiller for PDF creation. Instant PDF includes direct integration with the PDF export capabilities of Adobe InDesign CS and QuarkXPress 6.x as well as the PDF creation method of Mac OS X.

The concept of a certified PDF workflow is core to the PitStop Suite of Tools. In a certified workflow, information about each step of the PDF creation and editing process is recorded into the PDF file (remember, PDF files can contain metadata, or information about the file, in addition to the objects and text describing a page). As such, certified PDF documents contain a record of all edits and saves, creating an audit trail or history of what was done to a PDF document. One of the greatest benefits of this workflow is that the user can "roll back" to any previously saved version of the PDF file for the sake of comparison and, if they wish, save an earlier saved version out

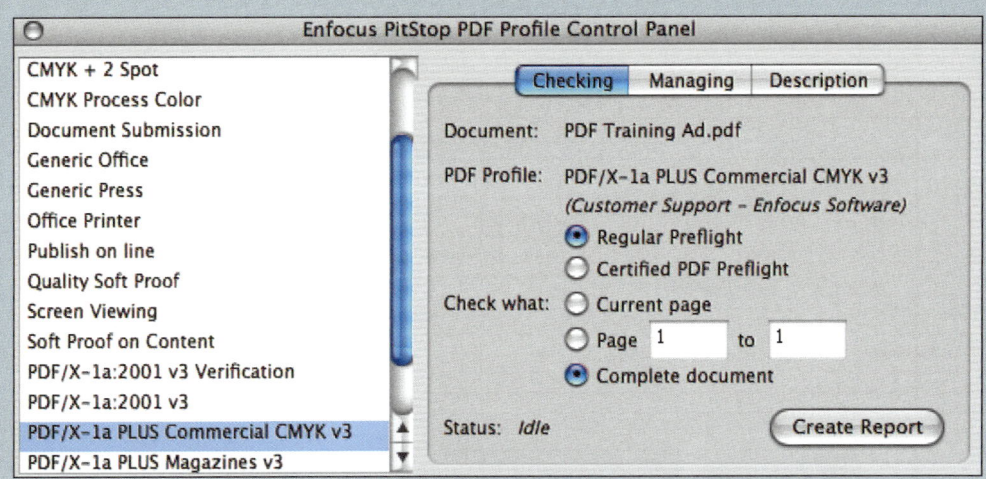

Figure 4.27. One of the key features of Enfocus PitStop Professional is the preflighting option that performs hundreds of checks and can include automatic repair of many problems once discovered.

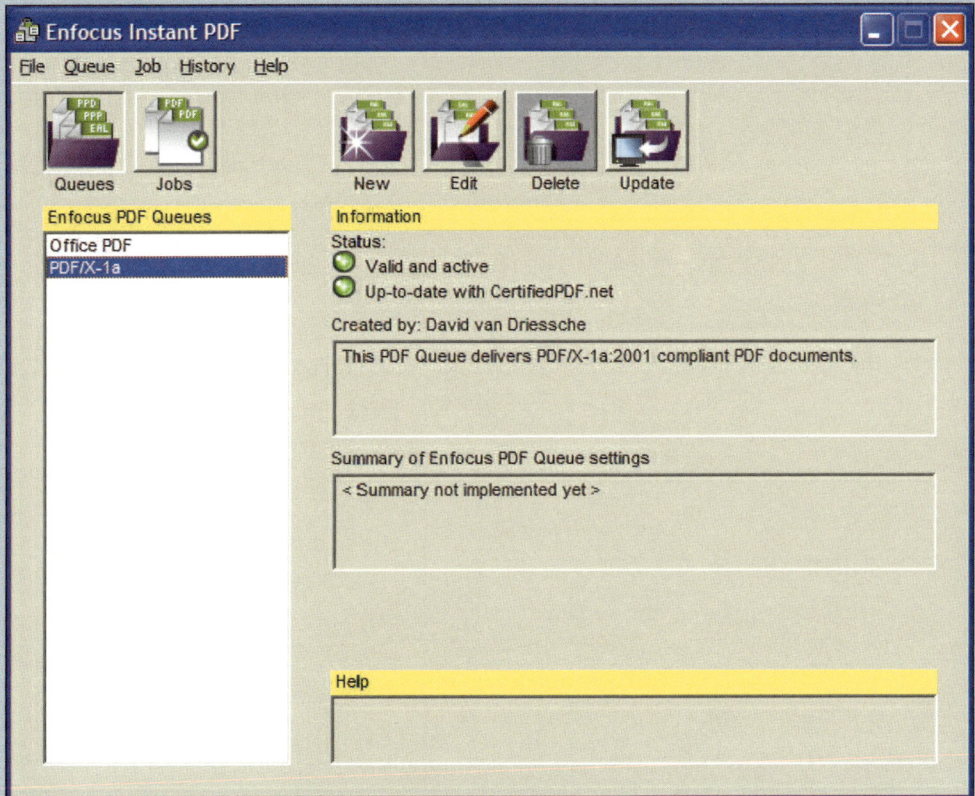

Figure 4.28. Instant PDF 3.0 is an application that helps the content creator make error-free PDF files through the implementation of the Enfocus PDF Queue.

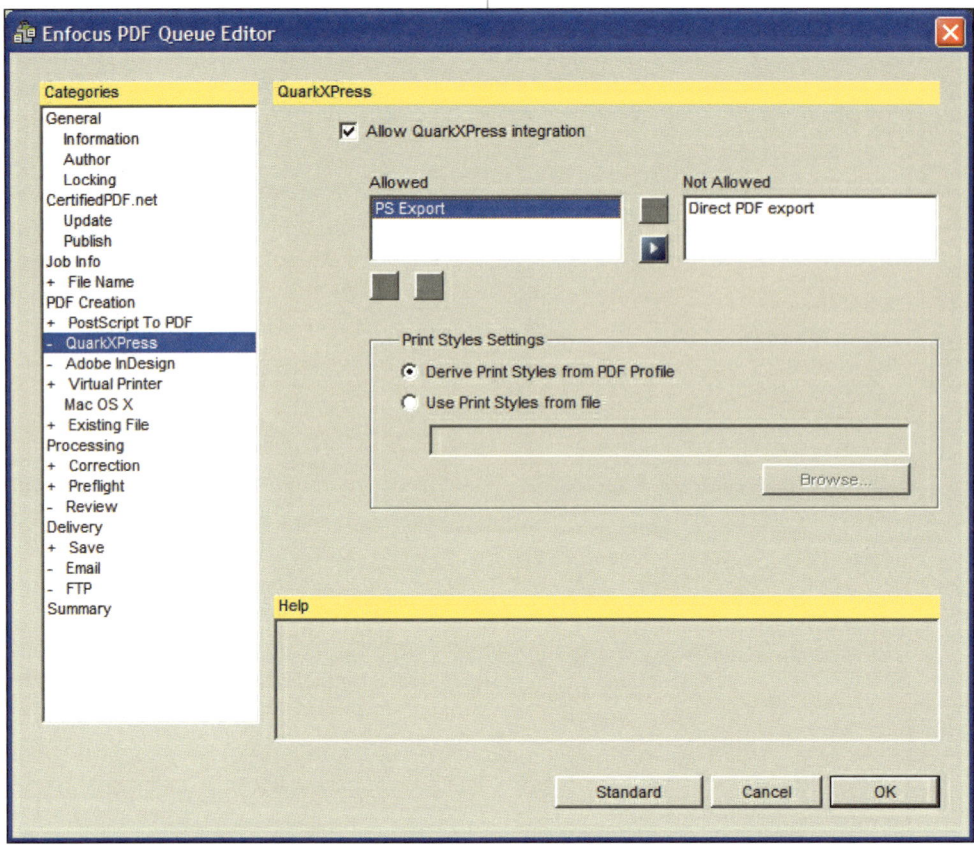

Figure 4.29. PDF "receivers" (the printer or output provider) define all the settings needed to create a viable PDF file for their production process and include this information in the Enfocus PDF Queue.

of the file to create another PDF file. Many prepress professionals have, at one time or another, been asked to "go back" to a previous version of a saved document. Unlike native documents, certified PDF files that have been saved (via the Save option, not Save As), even multiple times, still contain the original PDF file and it can be extracted using Enfocus Certified PDF tools.

Instant PDF Queues can be posted on the Enfocus-hosted website, CertifiedPDF.net (Figure 4.30). Enfocus calls CertifiedPDF.net an online communications hub between PDF creators and receivers, where receivers can make their specifications available to customers. Instant PDF 3 includes a feature to automatically post new or updated Queues to

CertifiedPDF.net and inform all "subscribers" to those Queues that a new one is available.

ARTS PDF ImageWorks (www.artspdf.com)

An alternative to editing raster images in PDF documents via an external editor is Acrobat plug-in PDF ImageWorks from ARTS PDF. Functions such as color conversion, image retouching, and resampling can be done without leaving the Acrobat application, and most of the features can be automated using PDF ImageWorks Document Tools (Figure 4.31).

Markzware FlightCheck (www.markzware.com)

FlightCheck, the desktop preflight application from Markzware, has been on the market for nearly a

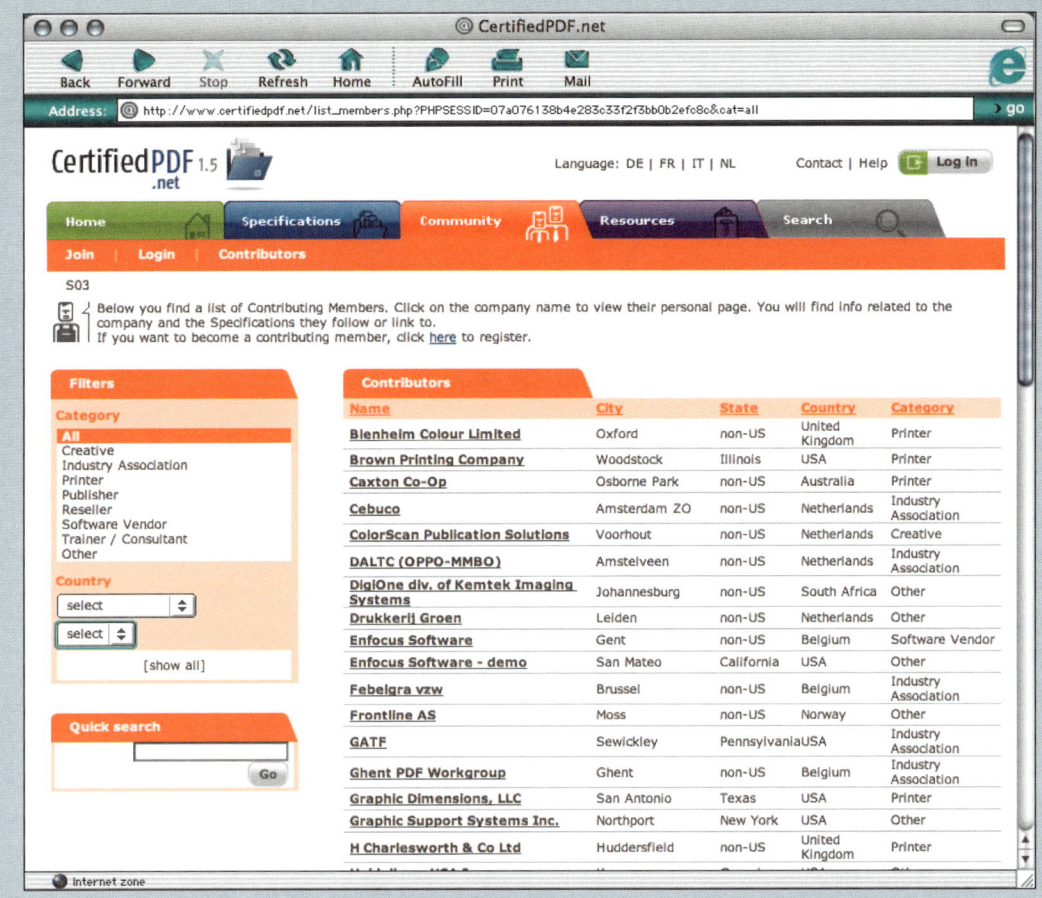

Figure 4.30. Instant PDF 3 includes a feature to automatically post new or updated Queues to CertifiedPDF.net.

Figure 4.31. Use PDF ImageWorks from ARTS PDF to convert color or to retouch or resample images without leaving the Acrobat application.

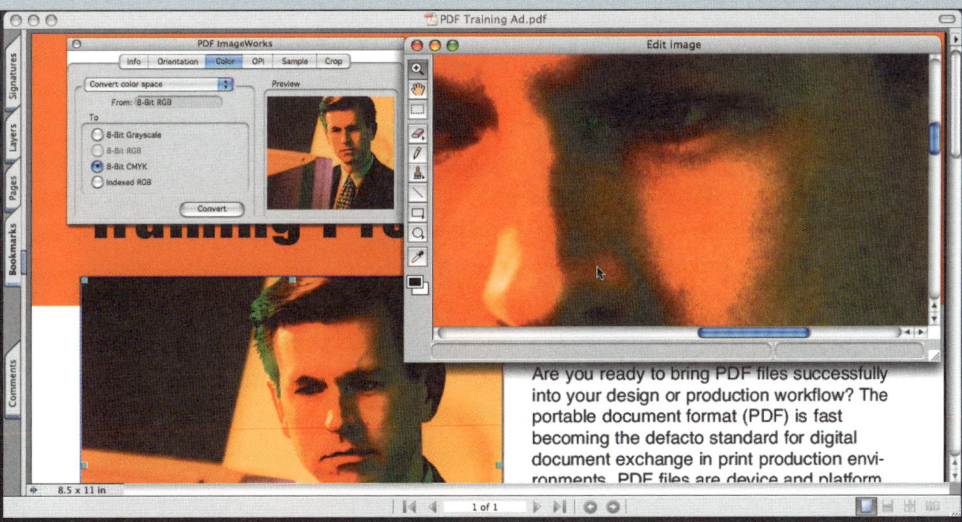

decade. Markzware has a suite of graphic production workflow tools, collectively called FlightCheck Workflow. FlightCheck is one of the few desktop applications one can use to preflight a PDF file outside of a PDF viewing tool like Acrobat. It is particularly good at examining PDF files because of the underlying technology, the MarkzONE engine, used in all of Markzware's products. MarkzONE reads all documents, from any source (InDesign, Quark, EPS, etc.) into a "standard object model" and can examine them without regard to native file formats. For PDF files, FlightCheck uses something called the Enhanced PDF Reader, where the document data is read into the Standard Object Model and then read into a second structure, the "PDF Raw Object Model." This second object model follows the Adobe PDF file format reference manual very closely and stores information about the PDF-specific building blocks—dictionaries, arrays, streams, and so forth. Using this method, the user can access virtually all of the intricate detail of the PDF file (as long as it is not encrypted) (Figure 4.32).

Quite A Box Of Tricks & Quite Revealing (www.quite.com)

QABOT and Quite Revealing are an invaluable pair of PDF preflight and repair plug-ins from U.K. software developer Quite Software. Through a single dialog box, QABOT provides an interface to "shrink" or downsample PDF files, edit colors, manipulate form field data, and "transform" documents (physical dimension size, rotation, and line thickness). We especially like to use QABOT to quickly convert RGB "black" text into true black text or convert an entire PDF file to grayscale (Figure 4.33).

Quite Revealing is a one-stop PDF preflight tool that lets the user look at very specific aspects of the PDF file, including fonts, transparency, overprinting, plates, and color profile information (Figure 4.34). For example, one can choose to preview the PDF document showing only text in a particular font or just all objects of a certain color. This is a great way to sort through a PDF file and find just those objects that may cause a problem. Quite Revealing also allows the

user to do some modification to the file, like convert colors to process, or, especially important to prepress, merge two plates (great if you have a file with what should be a single spot color specified in more than one way, i.e., PANTONE 185 C and PANTONE 185 CV).

PDF Trapping Solutions

Trapping is one of the more complicated prepress functions concerning the thin area created where two colors touch. This new area, called the trap, contains both colors so that an overlap is achieved. The width of this trap area must be greater than the average misregister of the printing press.

As sheets of paper move through a printing press, each color is applied by individual units. There are several factors which can cause misregister and/or sheet distortion: the exchange of the press sheet from gripper to gripper, humidity, moisture content in the paper, and the impact of the press impression on the paper.

Where two colors touch, how do you determine which color should be moved to create the trap? The general rule to follow is that you must modify the weaker color. What makes one color "weaker" than another is determined by comparing the density range of those colors, as shown in Figure 4.35.

Without the benefit of a desktop application that can accommodate PDF files, trapping them has to be accomplished either at the RIP, within the native application (by setting objects to overprint in an illustration application like Illustrator or FreeHand), or by setting individual objects to overprint using PitStop Professional in combination with Acrobat. Trapping options that are based on printing separations directly for an application, like those available in QuarkXPress, are not supported in a composite PDF workflow. In other words, to get "Quark traps" to come through in a PDF file created from Quark, one would have to save a separated PDF file, where each page would be made up of four pages, each of which contains the data for each color. Each of these pages would be black if viewed in a PDF preview tool and would look very much like a film positive. A much

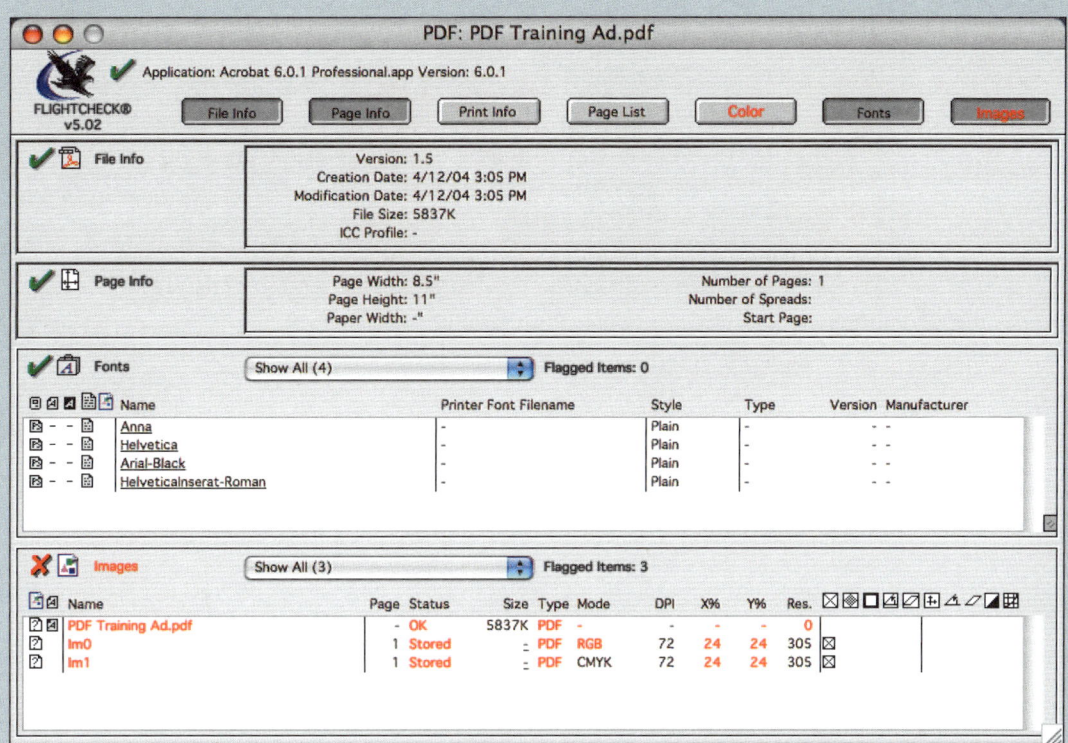

Figure 4.32. Markzware FlightCheck is one of the few desktop applications one can use to preflight a PDF file outside of a PDF viewing tool like Acrobat.

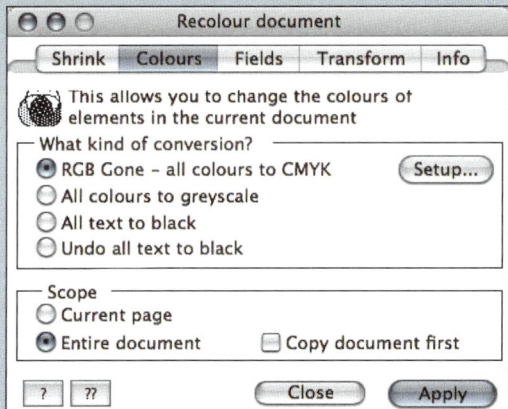

Figure 4.33. Through a single dialog box, Quite A Box Of Tricks provides an interface to downsample files, edit colors, manipulate form field data, and "transform" documents (physical dimension size, rotation, and line thickness).

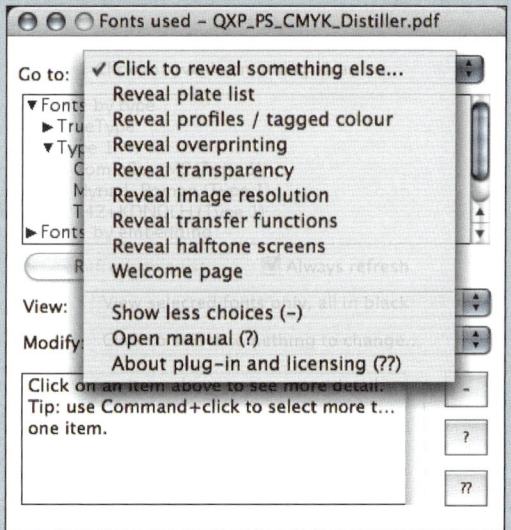

Figure 4.34. Quite Revealing lets the user look at very specific aspects of the PDF file.

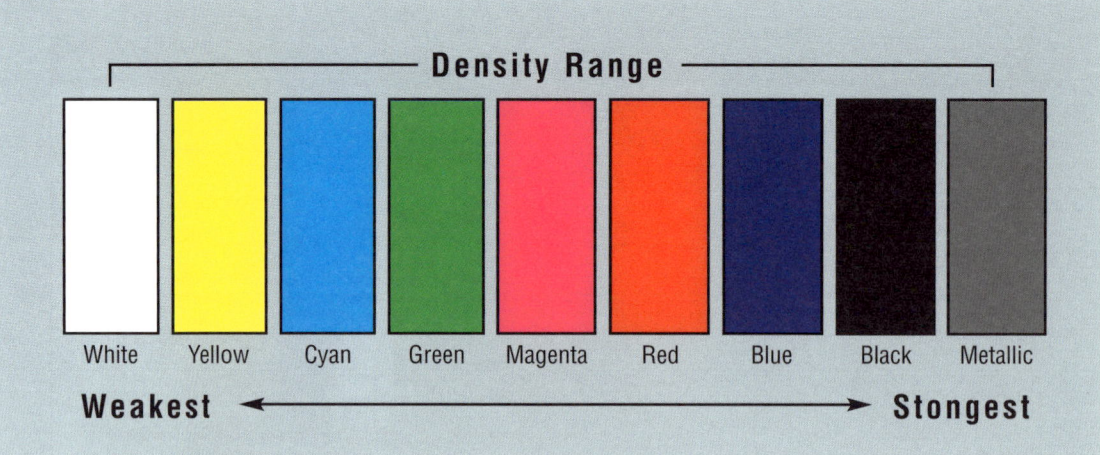

Figure 4.35. The density range of color from weakest to strongest.

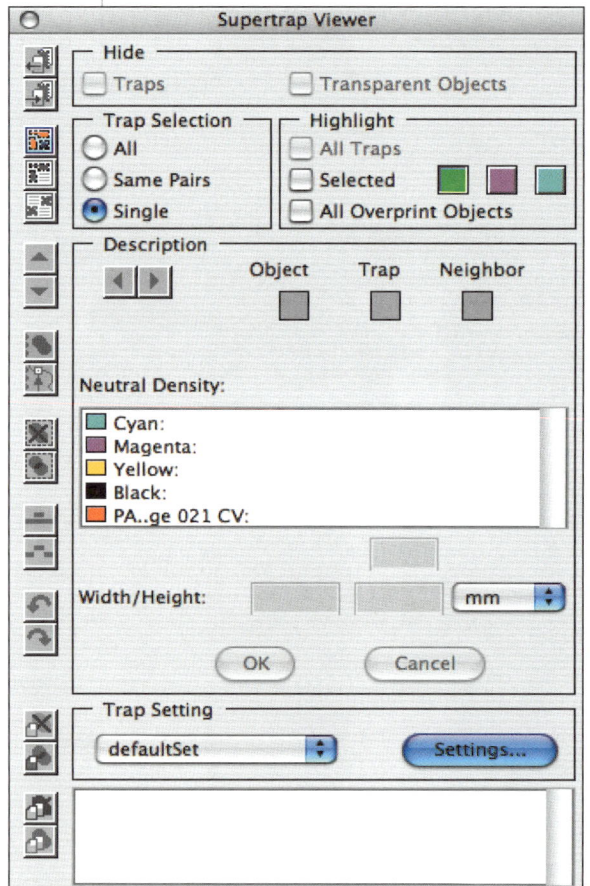

Figure 4.36. Heidelberg Supertrap is a plug-in offering quality
PDF trapping directly in Acrobat.

better method of trapping PDF files would be to use a
dedicated trapping tool, like those that follow.

Creo TrapWise
(www.creo.com)

TrapWise from Creo supports trapping of native
PDF files. TrapWise uses an Adobe PostScript Level 3
interpreter and can import, trap, and output PDF 1.3
and 1.4 files without converting to PostScript. Traps
may be viewed on screen using the trap preview
function. As of this writing, the current version of
TrapWise is 3.6 and it is not Mac OS X native.

Heidelberg Supertrap
(www.us.heidelberg.com)

Heidelberg offers the Supertrap plug-in that
allows trapping of PDF files directly in Acrobat. Traps
can be created globally or individually to allow for
modifications of the width, direction, and color. Traps
are created as separate vector objects based on the
neutral density of the adjoining vector or pixel
objects. Traps created in Supertrap can be viewed on
screen to verify widths and direction (Figure 4.36).
Heidelberg also offers a version of Supertrap
with advanced features necessary for the packaging
market.

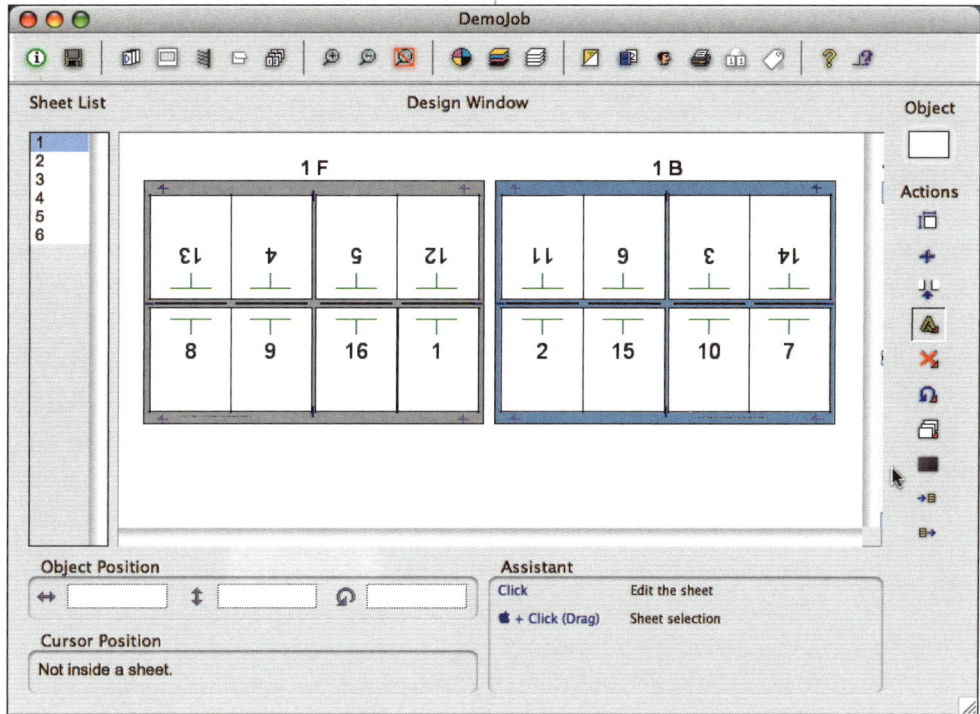

Figure 4.37. Dynagram Software's DynaStrip can import, impose, and output PDF files without any conversion to PostScript.

PDF Imposition Solutions

Imposition is the arrangement of pages for a press sheet so that when printed, folded, trimmed, and bound, everything appears in the proper sequence and orientation. Documents are created in reader's spreads, which is the page order in which the document is viewed as a finished product. For printing and binding, the document pages must be rearranged from reader's spreads to printer's spreads.

Not so long ago, imposition of PDF files was a difficult task. Most software imposition programs could not work with PDF files in their native format. PDF files would have to be converted back to PostScript before they could be imposed. Since PostScript files are much larger than PDF files, the imposition process was very memory-intensive and slow. This is not the case when imposing PDF files.

Today, most imposition software programs support native PDF files. These programs can import, impose, and output PDF files without any conversion to PostScript. Software manufacturers are offering very powerful software solutions while maintaining ease of use.

Dynagram DynaStrip
(www.dynagram.com)

Dynagram Software's DynaStrip was the first software program to offer pure PDF-in, PDF-out imposition without any conversion to PostScript. DynaStrip recognizes all colors in a PDF file, including PANTONE or other spot colors, and can remap spot colors with differing names to the same plate. The fully imposed PDF file can be viewed or edited for last-minute corrections. DynaStrip can also be used in conjunction with Creo's Prinergy, an Adobe Extreme PDF workflow system (Figure 4.37).

Quite Imposing
(www.quite.com)

Quite offers Imposing, an imposition plug-in that works within the Acrobat environment. Individual pages within a PDF file are arranged in Acrobat, and the result is a fully imposed PDF file. The process of imposing pages is unlike that of any other imposition software application. For example, individual pages first must be rotated and reordered before imposing a head-to-head layout. This software works well for fast book imposition for digital printing and offset lithography (Figure 4.38).

Creo Preps
(www.creo.com)

Although the majority of Preps users work in what Creo calls a mixed environment (PDF- or PostScript-in, PostScript- or EPS-out), Preps offers seamless PDF-in, PDF-out support. In a strictly PDF workflow, Preps does not convert PDF to PostScript during the imposition process, maintaining the predictability of the PDF file. The result is an imposed PDF file that can be opened and verified in Acrobat before outputting the job. Preps has also found its way into a variety of digital workflow solutions, including Agfa's Apogee and Creo's Prinergy PDF workflow systems.

Farrukh Imposition Publisher
(www.farrukh.co.uk)

Imposition Publisher has been on the market since 1998, but only the lastest version, 4.6, brings the ability to natively impose PDF files in all flavors of Imposition Publisher including Mac OS X, Windows, and the client/server versions. Imposition Publisher includes intelligent drivers that ensure correct information is extracted from the input PostScript or PDF files. The user doesn't need to enter the finished trim page size, for example, because this is calculated from the position of the crop marks in PostScript files or the TrimBox entry of PDF files.

Ultimate Impostrip
(www.ultimate-tech.com)

Ultimate offers Impostrip for desktop use or client/server environments and runs on Windows XP Pro or 2000 as well as Mac OS X. Impostrip promises full imposition support for CIP4 PPF and JDF and interfaces with many proprietary workflow systems. It's a truly PDF-in, PDF-out solution—files are not converted to PostScript anywhere in the process and offers a fully imposed PDF signature preview.

Other Windows-only PDF-based imposition tools include PDF Organizer Pro 2.2, from AC&C HSH Group and PDF Snake from Rennie Glen Software, LLC.

Color Separation and Output

Since Acrobat 6 Professional allows for creating and printing color separations of PDF, a third-party tool to do so is less critical than it was in the past. Acrobat 6 Standard and previous versions of Acrobat files do not natively support printing to separations. For users who do not have Acrobat 6 Pro, a possible workflow solution to this problem is to print separated PostScript from the layout application then create PDF files of the color separations for output. This contains another set of complications in that each of those PDF "pages" is made up of all "black" elements (pre-separated PDF files look like film positives). Some output devices would see each of these pages as black and output each of them on the

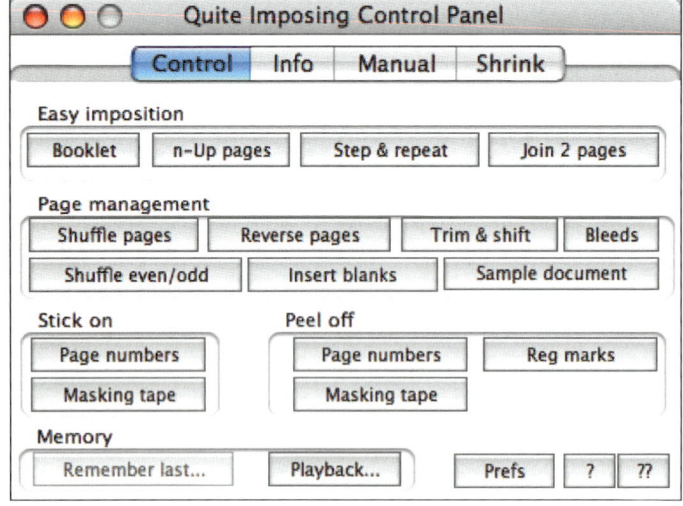

Figure 4.38. Quite Imposing is an Acrobat plug-in and lets the user impose PDF pages without leaving Acrobat.

same black screen angle—a moiré nightmare. Thankfully, there are Acrobat plug-ins such as ARTS PDF Crackerjack which allow you to color separate and print composite PDF files directly from Acrobat 6 Standard and previous versions of Acrobat.

ARTS PDF Crackerjack (www.artspdf.com)

Before Adobe included separation capabilities in Acrobat 6 Pro, Crackerjack from ARTS PDF was the de facto standard for printing PDF separations directly from Acrobat. Crackerjack can check a PDF document for non-embedded fonts before printing, with options to fix, cancel, or print. Color controls include black separation generation using undercolor removal (UCR) or gray component replacement (GCR) and use of ICC profiles to control conversion of RGB images to CMYK. Hot folder automation for PDF output is supported using the Crackerjack Pilot plug-in. Also useful is the preview function for viewing individual color separations (Figure 4.39).

In addition to PDF separation, re-merging separated files from QuarkXPress, DCS 2.0, TIFF/IT, or CopyDot scans files is an important capability in a PDF workflow. For example, QuarkXPress cannot output trapped files in a composite PostScript file—only separated PostScript will honor Quark trapping. The ability to make composite multiple files has another benefit: versioning. Versioning refers to multiple file versions for output such as different languages, different prices in ad slicks, and different indicia requirements for mailing.

Standalone Tools for PDF Manipulation

Most of the tools we've discussed in this chapter are either a part of, or a plug-in for, Adobe Acrobat. There are quite a few standalone tools intended to augment a PDF creative/production workflow. Here is a look a just a few of them.

Apago Inc. PDFmerge, PDF Enhancer, PDFshrink (www.apago.com)

Apago offers a whole line of software products for the graphics industry, some of which are OEMed by other product manufacturers. PDFmerge is a tool dedicated to the task of merging and assembling multiple documents into a single PDF on Mac OS X (Figure 4.40).

PDF Enhancer offers functionality similar to the Optimize option in Acrobat 6 Pro. With it, the user can assemble, optimize, reduce, secure, stamp, and even impose PDF files (Figure 4.41).

PDFshrink is a simple Mac OS X application for reducing the size of PDF files. With the Apago Pheon product, users can convert from TIFF/IT, Creo Brisque, CopyDot, JPEG, PNG, and TIFF formats to PDF/X-1a, PDF/X-3, EPS, DCS, JPEG, PNG, and TIFF formats either on a file-by-file basis or using Pheon's batch-processing capabilities.

Apago also offers several Acrobat plug-ins, including PDF/X Checkup, one of the first tools on the market to check for PDF/X compliance.

Impressed GmbH DCSMerger (www.impressed.de)

DCS files are images created with four or more color channels (often CMYK plus a spot "touch" plate) and saved in Photoshop DCS format. CopyDot files can be saved in DCS format at well. The problem with DCS files are that they do not work well in composite PDF workflows. DCS images placed in native layout applications can come out in composite PDF files as low-resolution images, missing spot colors, or converted into CMYK. DCSMerger is a standalone application that merges high-resolution DCS data into a single EPS file, complete with spot colors. It works either manually, as a drag-and-drop application, or in automatic batch mode and supports Photoshop-compatible DCS 1.0 and DCS 2.0 images in both single- and multiple-file formats. DCSMerger is delivered in digital form only and can

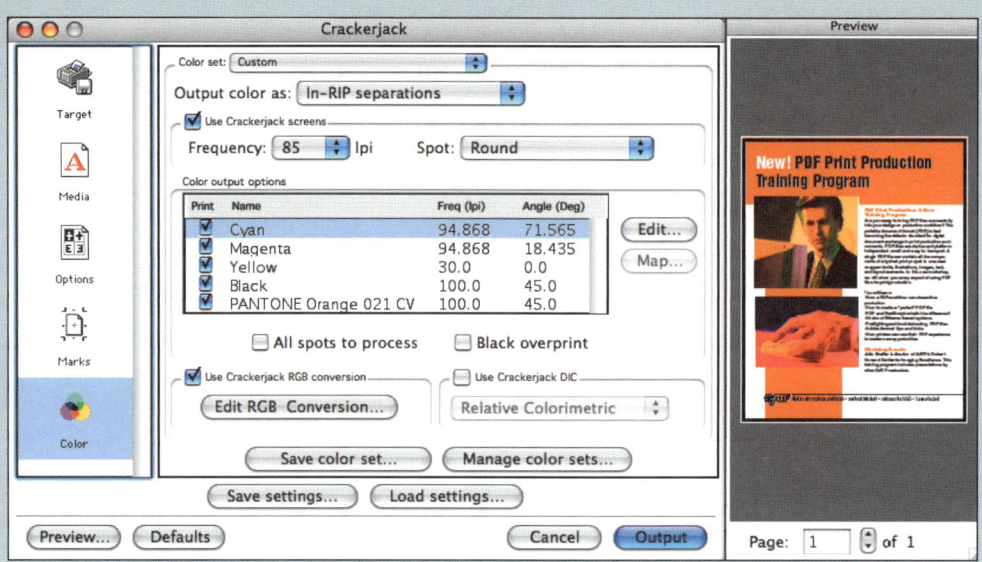

Figure 4.39. Crackerjack from ARTS PDF was the only way to print separated PDF files directly from Acrobat before version 6. Crackerjack does some things Acrobat can't, like merging two colors onto a single plate.

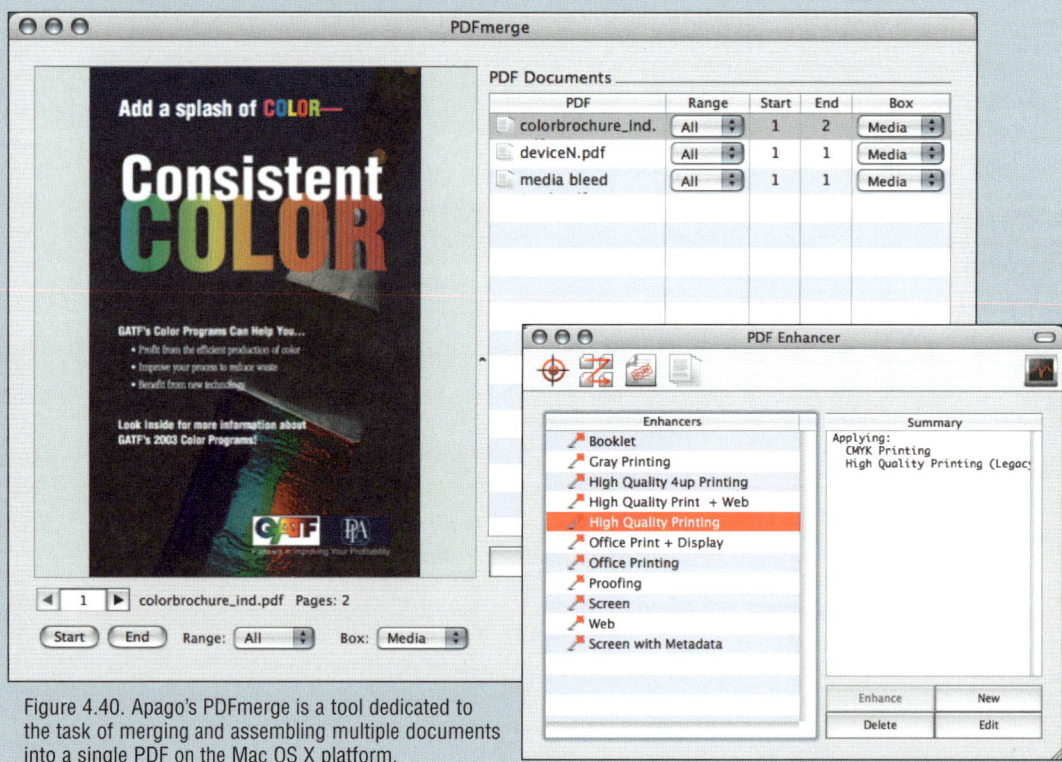

Figure 4.40. Apago's PDFmerge is a tool dedicated to the task of merging and assembling multiple documents into a single PDF on the Mac OS X platform.

Figure 4.41. Use Apago's PDF Enhancer to assemble, optimize, reduce, secure, stamp, and even impose PDF files.

be purchased directly from the Impressed website. Note: It would benefit you to bone up on your high school German to navigate the website. Although some sections contain English information, the overall site is in German.

Iceni Technology Gemini (www.iceni.com)

Iceni Technology develops software for PDF conversion and extraction. The Gemini product converts a PDF document into other formats for repurposing. PDF files can be converted with formatting intact into HTML and RTF formats, or individual objects like images and text can be extracted from the PDF file. Clipping paths and OPI names are retained when associated with images, and they can be exported in a variety of image file formats and resolutions. The product includes a standalone application and a plug-in for Adobe Acrobat (for Windows users only).

BCL Technologies BCL Drake (www.bcltechnologies.com)

BCL Drake, a Windows-only application, converts PDF files, complete with formatting, into Microsoft Word documents. Through version 5, BCL Drake was a standalone application, but version 7.1 comes with a macro so PDF files can be opened directly into Word and is offered as a plug-in for Adobe Acrobat as well. BCL Technologies also offers "Drake Workflow Server" for organizations that require conversion of large numbers of PDF files into Word documents. From our testing, BCL Drake did a pretty good job of converting files complete with graphics intact.

Mesa Dynamics Trapeze (www.mesadynamic.com)

A Mac OS X-only application, Trapeze is a drag-and-drop text-extraction utility that converts PDF files to editable RTF, ASCII, or plain text (Figure 4.42). Customization features include options for white space stripping, paragraph rewrapping, page break marking, advanced text encoding (for things like smart quotes, bullet icons, copyright and trademark symbols), RTF optimization for specific

applications like TextEdit or Microsoft Word, and support for encrypted PDF files. While Trapeze boasts a reformatting engine capable of reproducing "near facsimile of the original," it only does so for text components of PDF files.

ScanSoft PDF Converter (www.scansoft.com)

A very similar application to BCL Drake, PDF Converter is offered as a plug-in to Microsoft Word, Microsoft Outlook (you can turn PDF email attachments into Word files), Windows Explorer, and Internet Explorer. It is, as you can determine from the types of applications it plugs into, a Windows-only application.

This is just a brief overview of some of the many tools available to work more effectively with PDF files for print production. With the right suite of tools, it's possible to have a fully functional PDF prepress workflow solution without having to invest in a dedicated prepress workflow solution from a particular vendor. The advantages of the "do-it-yourself" system are that you are in control of the components and not reliant on any one vendor. This minimizes certain

Figure 4.42. Trapeze is a drag-and-drop text-extraction utility that converts PDF files to editable RTF, ASCII, or plain text.

risks—you can upgrade individual components when they become available at your own pace, and you only have to buy what you need, which can save money.

The disadvantages of a system you build yourself are that actually building the system will require much time and effort. You may have to debug errors when components from different manufacturers clash. Also, keeping up with upgrades and interactivity from a variety of applications can be time-consuming. Finally, training will not come from one vendor—you will probably have to train yourself and your coworkers.

Many of the tools we just discussed are useful within, and even packaged with in an OEM arrangement, many of the high-end print-production workflow solutions. We will take a look at a range of PDF-friendly workflow solutions in Chapter 6.

CHAPTER 5

AUTOMATING PDF

Automating PDF Creation and Editing

Workflow automation is one of the key buzz phrases in the graphic communications industry. We want to streamline our production workflow and make processes happen better, faster, and with fewer headaches. The words *PDF* and *workflow* have been said in the same breath since the first Adobe Extreme-based prepress workflow solutions hit the market back in 1998. These systems, from Agfa, Scitex, and Heidelberg, were the first to combine PDF as the system's internal working file format, with stream-lined process plans to complete prepress tasks, like trapping and imposition. Today, you'd be hard put to find a modern prepress workflow solution or RIP that does not take in and save out PDF files. PDF has become ubiquitous in the print production workflow.

There are dozens of dedicated prepress workflow solutions on the market that vary widely in price and functionality. The most expensive solutions tend to be backed with high-end databases to provide extensive file management capabilities to prepress production. Other solutions are simply RIPs with some additional functionality, like trapping. It's not possible for us to discuss each of these systems here in *The PDF Print Production Guide;* there are just too many of them, and the features each company offers change too frequently. Check out the PDF Resources section at the back of this book, and you'll find many vendors of workflow solutions listed.

We devote this chapter to showing you ways to automate the PDF creation and editing process, with tools ranging from the simplest, like Acrobat Distiller Watched Folders, to printer driver-based PDF creation tools that link the content creator to the output provider via the Internet. These are the "upstream" solutions to help ensure that PDF files are made properly before they are submitted to the final output destination.

PDF Creation: Distiller Watched Folders

Using Acrobat Distiller, you can create watched folders. A watched folder is a folder that Distiller is continually scanning for files to be converted to PDF. The great thing about this tool is that you can create multiple watched folders (on your desktop, for example) and assign each folder with a specific set of Adobe PDF Settings. For example, you can set a watched folder and assign Adobe PDF Settings optimized for Inter-net or display-only PDF files. Another watched folder might be set up to create PDF files optimized for press. Any PostScript EPS file dropped or printed into these folders will be converted to PDF using the assigned settings (Figure 5.1).

Figure 5.1.

Creating Watched Folders

When you create a watched folder, there is a hierarchy of subfolders that will be created within that folder. The watched folder will contain an In folder (this is where you would drop your PostScript file), an Out folder (this is where the created PDF resides), and the PDF settings files associated with that folder (Figure 5.2).

Watched folders can actually be more than just a folder/directory. You can assign hard-drive partitions or even dedicate an entire hard drive as a watched folder. Remember, though, there are

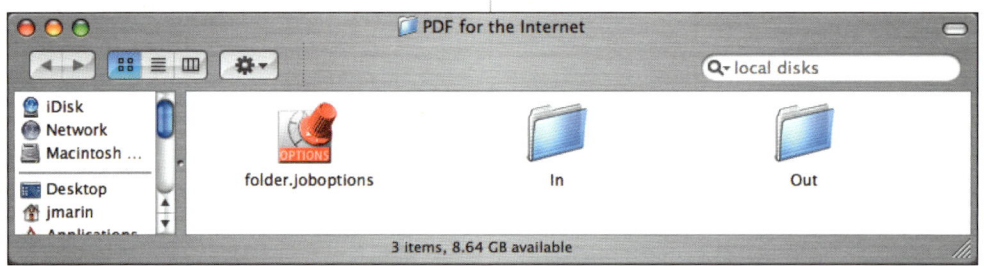

Figure 5.2. The watched folder contains an In folder, an Out folder, and the PDF settings files associated with that folder.

licensing restrictions on setting up Distiller on a networked computer in which multiple users would create PDFs (this situation would require a site license or individual purchases of Acrobat).

The Watched Folders dialog box *(Settings> Watched Folders...)* contains the following options (Figure 4.3):

Watched Folders list. This list displays all of the folders that you have set up Distiller to scan. In addition to the name of the watched folder, you also see the directory path to that folder.

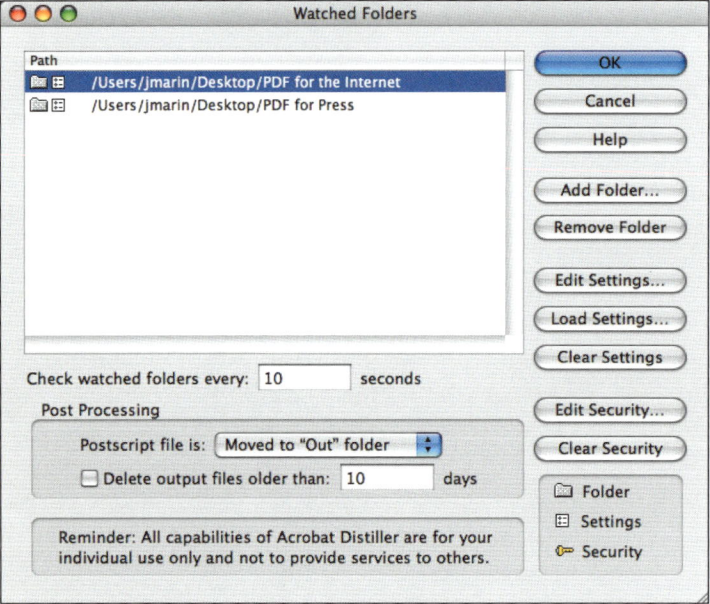

Figure 5.3. The Watched Folders dialog box is where hot folders are specified and individual settings for each folder (such as security) can be applied.

Check watched folders every [___] seconds. Set the time interval in which Distiller will scan watched folders for files.

PostScript file is. Options here are to move the PostScript file to the Out folder within the watched folder or to delete the PostScript file. If you will be using the PostScript file for other purposes, be sure to set this option to Moved to "Out" folder.

Delete output files older than [___] days. Any files kept in the Out folder will be deleted after the number of days specified in this field. If you are setting Distiller up on a network, this is a great way to automatically maintain free disk space.

To create a watched folder, follow these steps:

1. Create a folder on your computer. This will eventually become a watched folder, so it will be useful to give the folder a descriptive name (e.g., PDF for Internet, PDF for Press).

2. Launch Distiller and select *Settings>Watched Folders....*

3. In the Watched Folders dialog box, click *Add Folder.*

4. Navigate to the folder to be watched and click *Open.*

5. The selected folder along with the patch to that folder will now show up in the watched folder list. You can now decide how often Distiller should query the watched folder for a file and determine what to do with the PostScript file once it has been distilled.

6. Now you have to assign PDF settings to that watched folder. Click *Load Settings*.

7. From the Settings folder, select the Adobe PDF Settings you would like to assign to that watched folder and click *Open*.

8. You also have the option of adding security to any PDF file created through watched folders. Select *Edit Security...* to bring up the Security dialog box. Here you can require a password for opening, modifying, and/or printing the PDF file. Once you have modified the security settings, click *OK*.

9. Click *OK* to exit the Watched Folders dialog box. The folder is now ready to accept files to be converted to PDF.

PDF Creation and Error Prevention

Delivery of PDF files to print production facilities has grown significantly in the past several years. According to a survey conducted in April/May 2003 by Seybold Seminars and MediaLive International Research, the top three file formats most often received by those surveyed in the U.S. (primarily print/publishing community members) are PDF (82%), QuarkXPress (51%), and Microsoft Office (37%). The same survey reveals that 57% of those surveyed in the U.S. and 70% of the European respondents said that the biggest problem they encounter when working with PDF files is that they are not made properly. The top problems cited are missing fonts (not embedded), image resolution too low or images missing, and files in the wrong color space (RGB versus CMYK). These are the very same most common problems cited for the past twenty years!

So what can be done to improve the quality of PDF files submitted for print production? We like to remind folks that, in an all-digital workflow, incoming files should be considered another raw material in the print production process. Just as we wouldn't accept flawed paper from paper manufacturers, we should not accept flawed digital files from content creators. But since few can afford to turn work away in these highly competitive and low-margin times, simply not accepting work is not an option. What we need is a way to ensure that the files coming into our printing facility are as close as possible to ready-to-print. We need a way to "fool-proof" the process.

Since the surveys and history tell us we still cannot necessarily rely on the content-creator to do this for us, the answer is that *the print production professionals have to take control of the process.* They are, after all, the ones who know what the potential problems are, how to avoid them, and, because they so often have to, how to fix them. Combine the *expertise* of the production shop with the tools to assist in the creation of print-quality digital files and the *technology* to do it right on the client's computer, and you've got a recipe for a potential real solution to a long-standing industry problem.

We all remember the short-lived "dot-com" frenzy of a couple of years ago, when any number of Web-based print procurement systems sprouted. The idea was to leverage the ubiquity of the Internet to make print buying simple and put a link to the print shop right on the client's desktop. While the sales model didn't work for very many companies, the concept of moving certain tasks upstream into the realm of the content-creator is more than valid. What task could be more perfectly accomplished at the customer's site than ensuring that their files are ready to print—before they're sent to the printer?

There are a number of PDF creation product on the market now that can do just that. Desktop-based tools include Enfocus Instant PDF and Creo Synapse Prepare. Web-based options include systems based on two similar technologies: Adobe® PDF JobReady™ (formerly PDF Transit) from Adobe System, Inc. and Jaws® PDF Courier™ from Global Graphics Software. Note: We only discuss tools that are specifically intended to create valid PDF files for print production. There are many more tools on the market that automate PDF creation, but most of them do not focus on, or create, print via PDF files.

Creo Synapse Prepare

We discussed the Enfocus Instant PDF 3 product in Chapter 4, for details see page 98. Creo Synapse

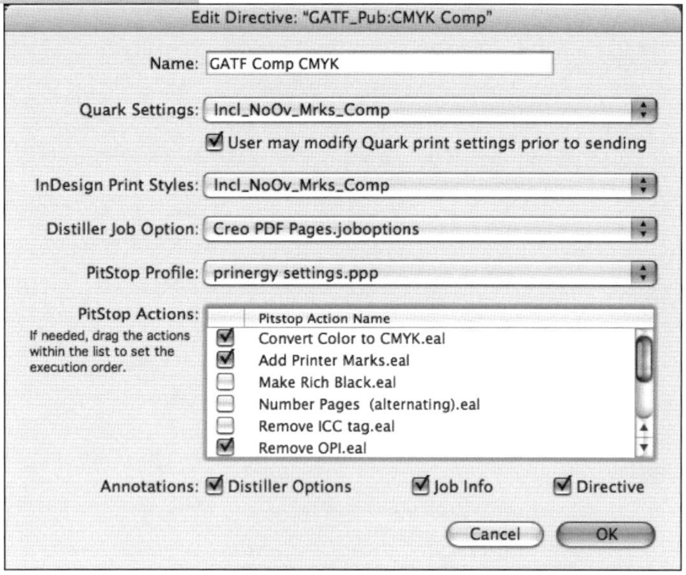

Figure 5.4. Synapse Prepare Directives can contain application-specific settings, Distiller settings, PitStop preflight profiles, and PitStop actions.

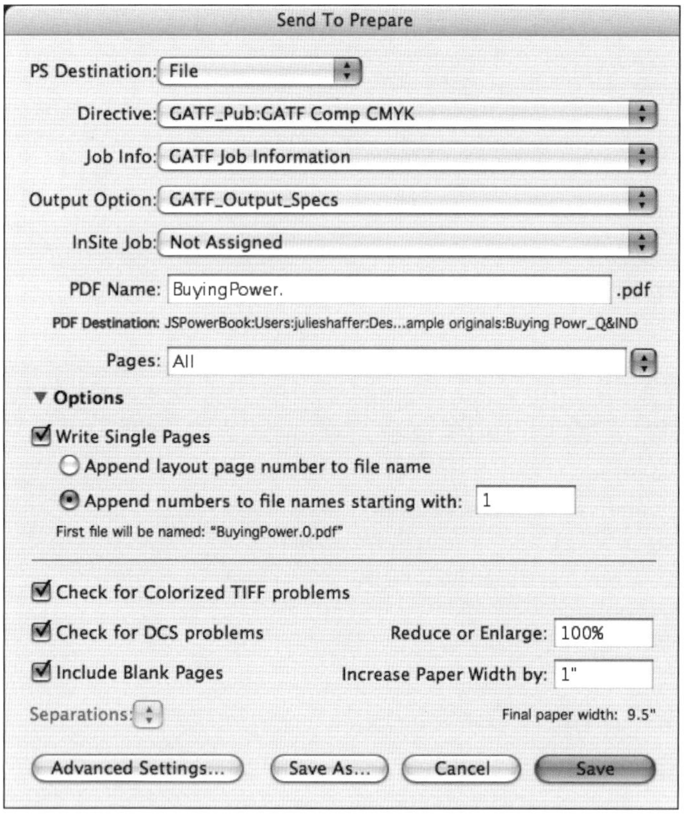

Figure 5.5. Quark users select the "Send To Prepare" option to choose a Directive and other critical settings, like checking for colorized TIFF issues.

Prepare is a similar application, one that melds PDF creation (direct from the page assembly application) with preflight and error-prevention options. Prepare can be used as a standalone product by anyone who wants to make a print-viable PDF file, but it also serves as a front-end component for the Creo Prinergy prepress production system.

The idea behind Synapse Prepare is that the content receiver (printer) builds a "Prepare Directive" and distributes this Directive to content creators. A Directive includes everything necessary to create print-ready PDF files, including the application print settings, Acrobat Distiller PDF Settings, a PitStop Preflight Profile, any number of PitStop Actions, and general job submission settings. Prepare comes with some canned Directives and more are available at Creo's website (www.creo.com), including special Directives that mirror the PDF-creation recommendations of industry groups DDAP and the Ghent Workgroup. Using the Pro version of Synapse Prepare, a content receiver can create their own Directives as well (Figure 5.4).

To create a PDF file using Directives supplied by a printer, a content creator can use the standard version of Synapse Prepare. There are a number of ways to access Prepare: directly from QuarkXPress or InDesign, by printing to a Prepare desktop printer, through a hot folder, or by dragging and dropping a PostScript file onto a Prepare applet. From QuarkXPress, for example, the user can select the Send To Prepare option from the File menu (Figure 5.5). Here, the user selects a Directive and other settings (many of which can be preset by the Directive creator to narrow the options—and chances for errors—available to the content creator). Once jobs are printed, they show up in the Synapse Prepare Queue, where they can be managed like any other print queue (Figure 5.6).

Directives can be set to automatically increase the size of the media box around a PDF file, set a bleed amount, add marks, and even add a note that gives basic information about the PDF file (Figure 5.7).

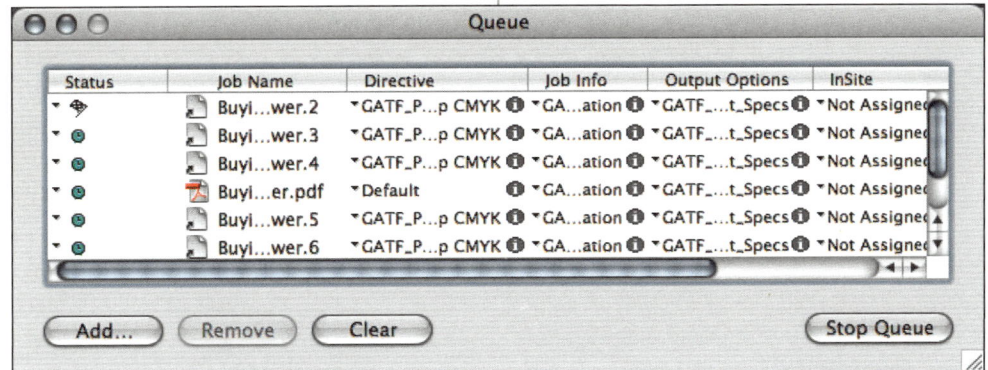

Figure 5.6. Once jobs are printed from the application via Prepare, they show up in the Synapse Prepare Queue, where they can be managed like any other print queue.

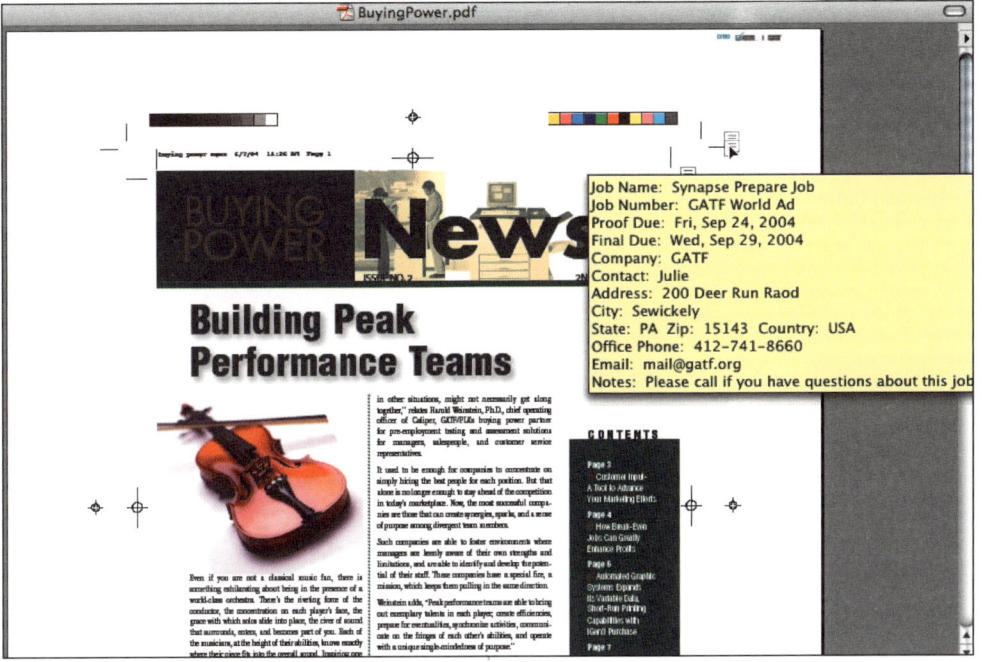

Figure 5.7. A Directive can be set to automatically increase the size of the media box around a PDF file, set a bleed amount, add marks, and even add a note that gives basic information about the PDF file.

Prepare can also be used to submit jobs directly to a Synapse InSite server for automatic processing with Creo Prinergy or Brisque prepress workflow solutions. Printers with an InSite server can even automatically update their clients' Prepare software and supplied Directives.

PDF Creation and Web-based Delivery

Adobe® PDF JobReady™ from Adobe Systems, Inc. and Jaws® PDF Courier™ from Global Graphics Software move the tasks of PDF creation and document delivery onto the desktop of anyone connected to the Internet. PDF Courier adds preflighting functionality to the mix as well.

Here's how the technology works in a nutshell: A content-creator puts together a layout in any application on either a Mac or Windows platform workstation. When the designer is ready to send the file to the output provider, he or she prints the file to a virtual printer supplied by the print service provider. That virtual printer contains the intelligence to create a PDF file built to the print provider's specification. At this point, PDF Courier-based systems include a preflight check, using Enfocus Certified PDF Preflighting technology. Depending on how the virtual driver was set up, many potential problems can be automatically corrected (including common issues, like making sure all black text is set to overprint, or all RGB images are converted to CMYK). Once the file has been checked, it is sent to the print service provider. All of this was initiated merely by a content-creator clicking *Print* right within a layout application.

While the user experience is intended to be extremely easy, neither of these technologies is a shrink-wrapped product that a printer can unwrap and start using. Both are only offered as a software

development kit (SDK) and have to be integrated by skilled engineers into a usable product. The entire online component, like browser-based job ticketing, an integral part of a print procurement/delivery system, is not a part of either SDK. Since few printers have that kind of expertise in-house, it's fallen to dedicated integrators to build complete systems around the core technologies.

In the case of Global Graphics Jaws PDF Courier, PrismaTek, Inc., the U.S. distributor of that technology, created their PrintTHAT! PDF delivery system. PDF JobReady, now available through Adobe partner Datalogics, is a core component of a number of PDF delivery systems, including Rochester Software Associates (RSA). RSA was an early adopter of the PDF Transit technology and developed two automated PDF workflow options for its WebCRD online print fulfillment/production application: SurePDF™ for client-based PDF generation and CentralPDF™ for server-based workflows.

An overview of the PrintTHAT!/PDF Courier workflow is on pages 117–121; text continues on page 122.

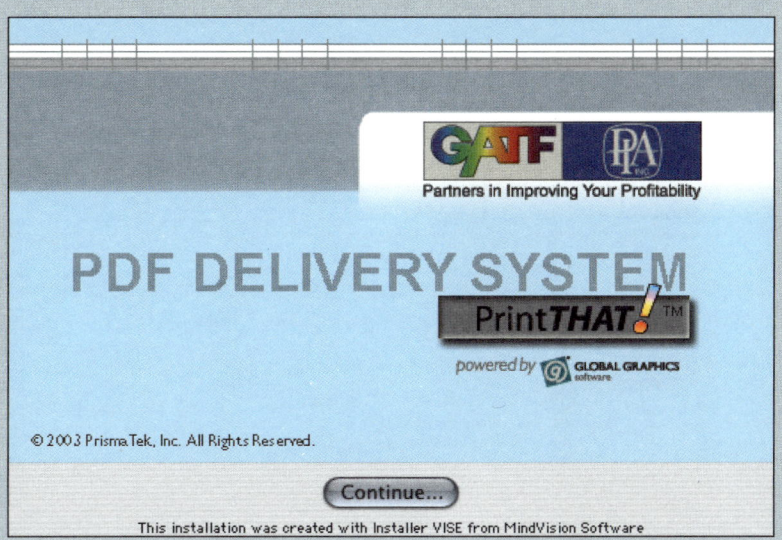

Here is a look at the PrintTHAT!/PDFCourier user experience. For this example, we are showing the interface on a Mac running OS 10.3.4. To get started, a user simply installs a print driver, provided by their printing partner. This driver includes everything needed to create a PDF file, preflight, repair, and send it to the print provider via the Internet.

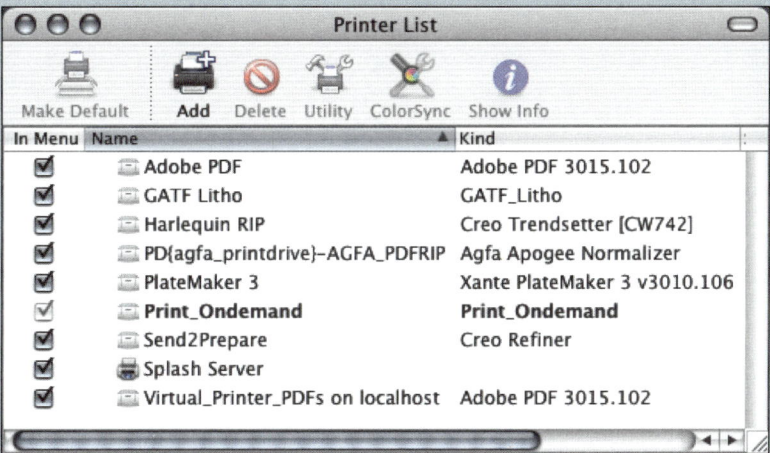

Once installed, the driver shows up as a printer on the user's computer. To initiate the process, the content-creator just has to "print" a project from the layout application to this printer.

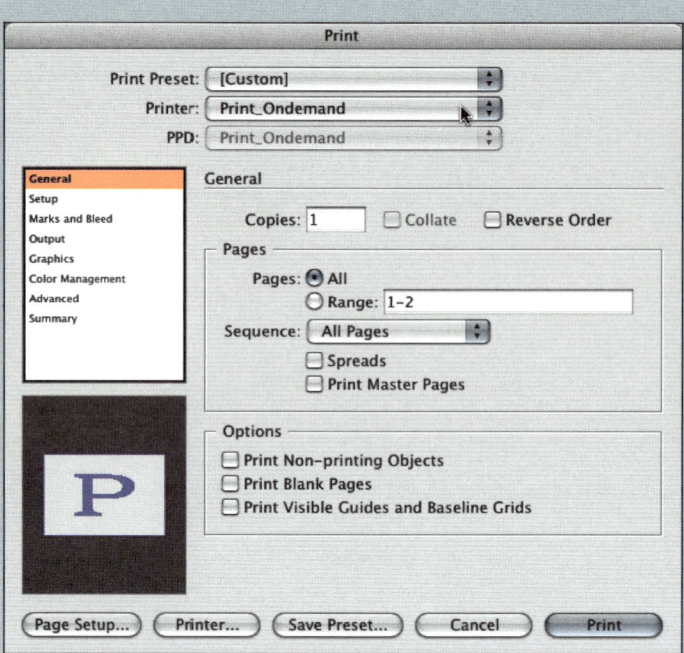

The process is initiated through any application's print window. The user selects the installed PrintTHAT! virtual printer as they would any printing device available to their computer.

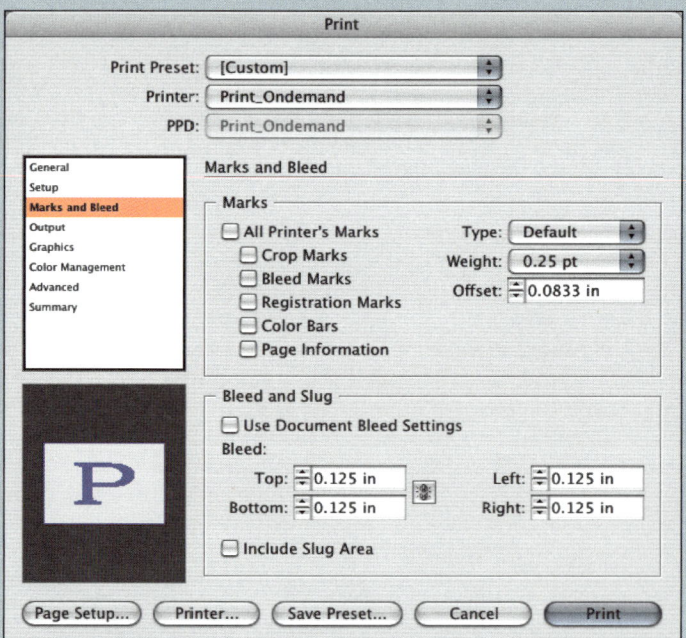

The user does have to set up the rest of the print options properly, including things link page size and bleed amount. Once this is completed, they select the Printer button.

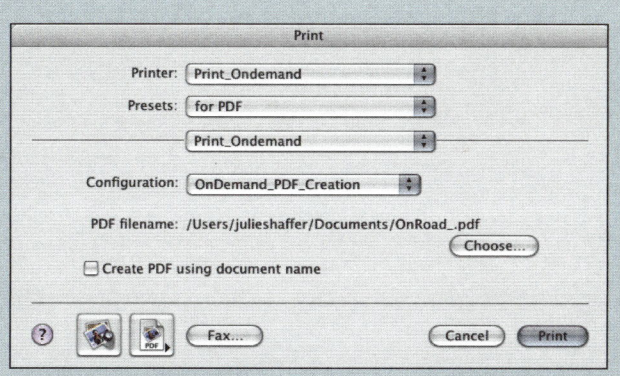

From the Printer window, the user selects the virtual printer in two places: from the printer and features pull-down menus. The Configuration option displays the Jaws PDF creation configuration the service provider built into the virtual printer. Once set, the user clicks *Print* here and in the main Print dialog box.

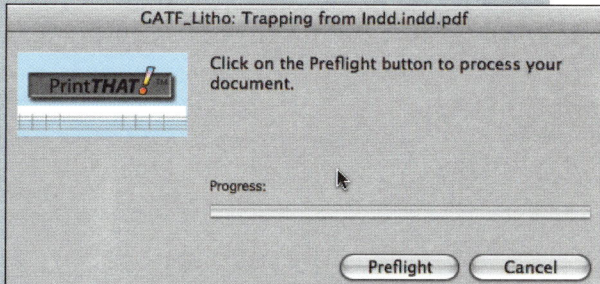

PostScript is printed and a PDF file is created based on the configuration settings. If the service provider built preflighting into the virtual printer, the user is alerted with this window. The user must click the Preflight button to initate the process.

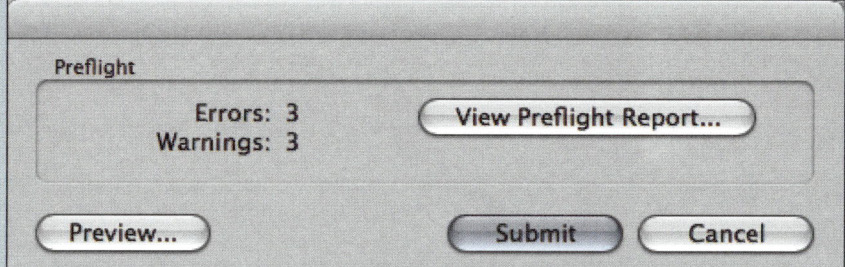

Once preflighting is complete, the user can be given the option to view the preflight report, preview the actual PDF file using a PDF viewing application of choice, and submit the job to the print provider.

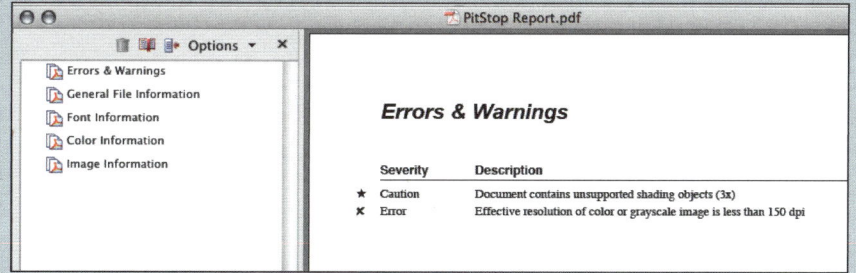

If the View Preflight Report option is selected, the user is presented a PitStop preflighting report. The user does not have to have Enfocus PitStop installed on their computer for this to work.

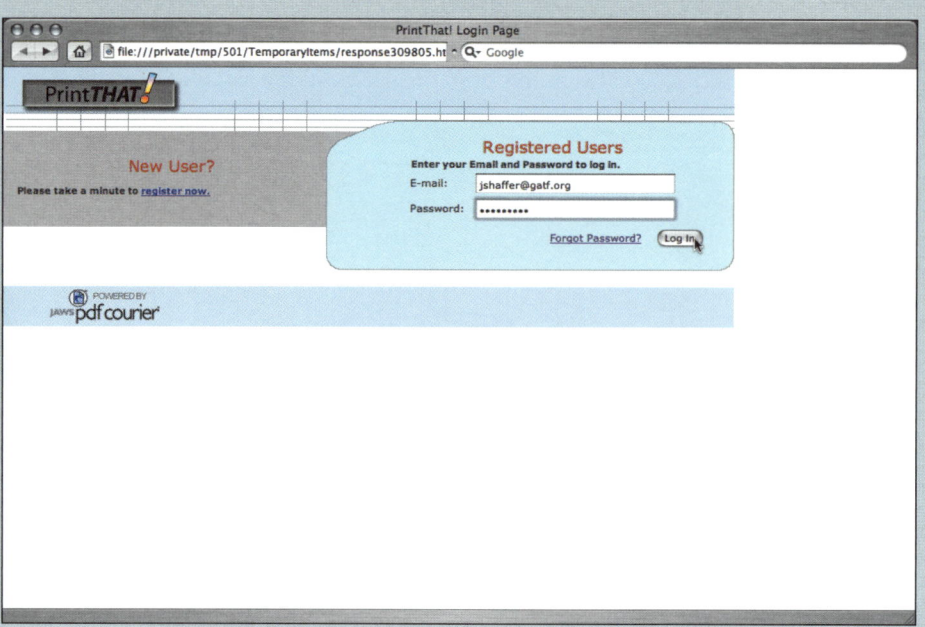

After the user selects the Submit button, their default Web browser is automatically launched and they will be taken to a registration screen. This interface can be customized at the print provider's discretion to include user and password authentication.

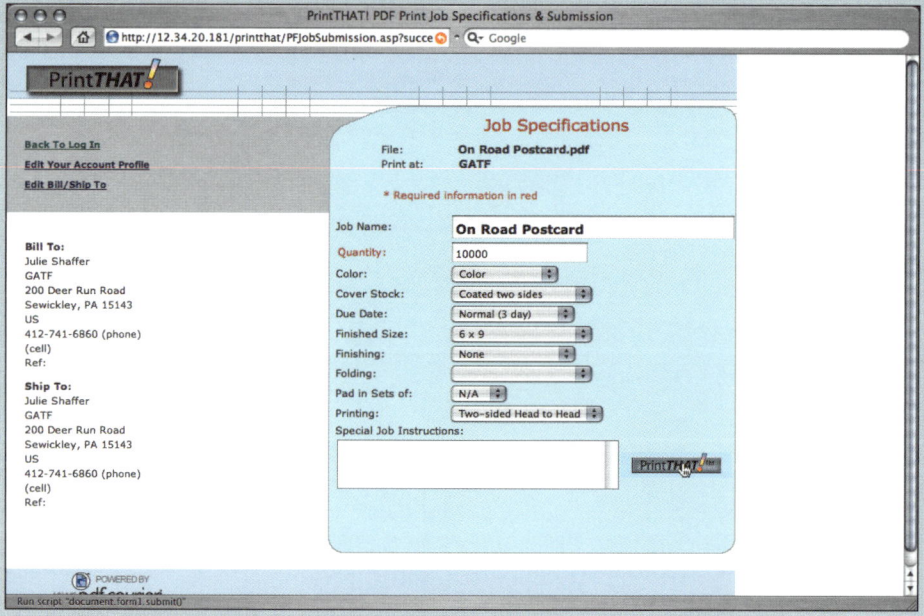

The user is then presented with a job ticket, again designed by the print provider to include as much or as little information as they require for job submission.

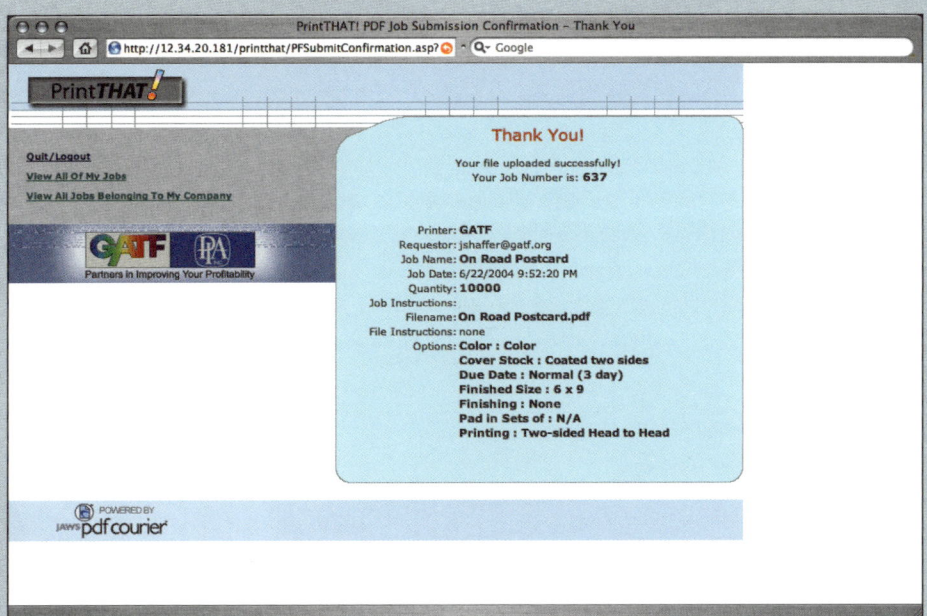

Once the ticket is filled out and the job submitted, the user is presented with an immediate confirmation on screen. They are also sent an email confirmation including this same information.

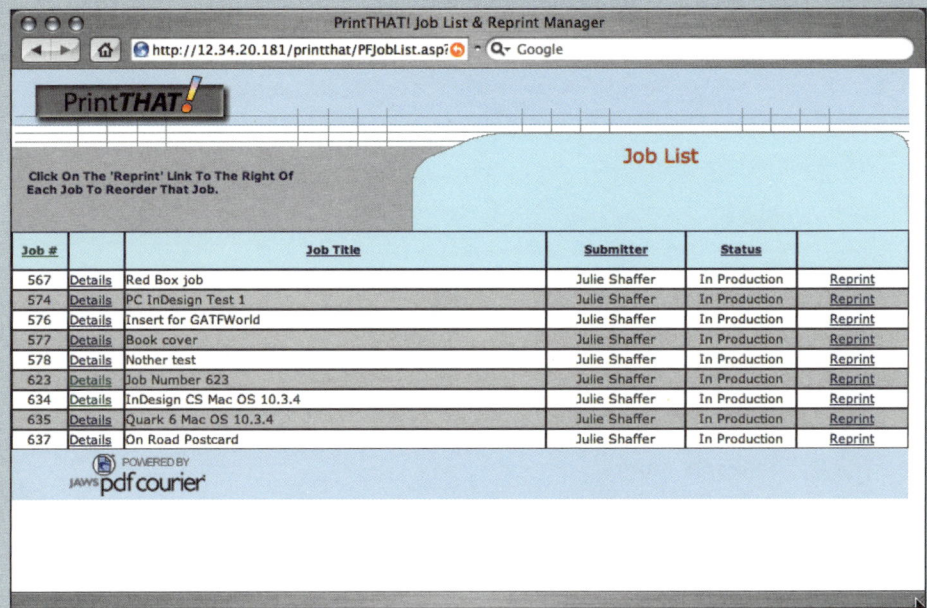

Users can review all projects resident at the service provider from this interface and even order reprints if desired.

Automating PDF Preflighting and Editing

Automating PDF workflow is not limited to just the PDF creation process. With an application such as Enfocus PitStop Server, content receivers can streamline the preflight and repair of incoming PDF files (Figure 5.8). Some of the tools you may be familiar with from the standalone version of PitStop Professional are used in the server version to diagnose and repair problems in PDF files with no manual intervention.

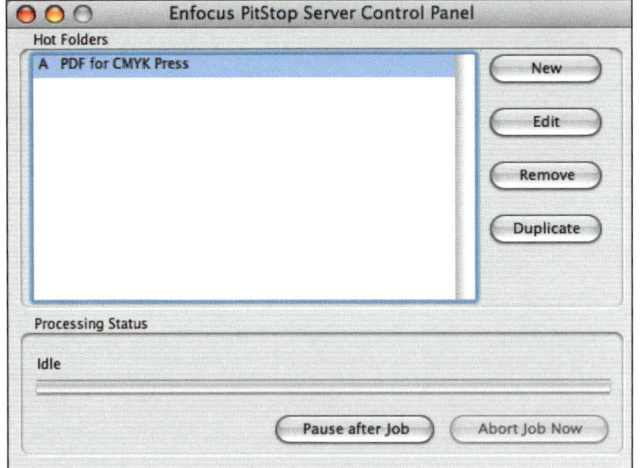

Figure 5.8. The Enfocus PitStop Server Control Panel.

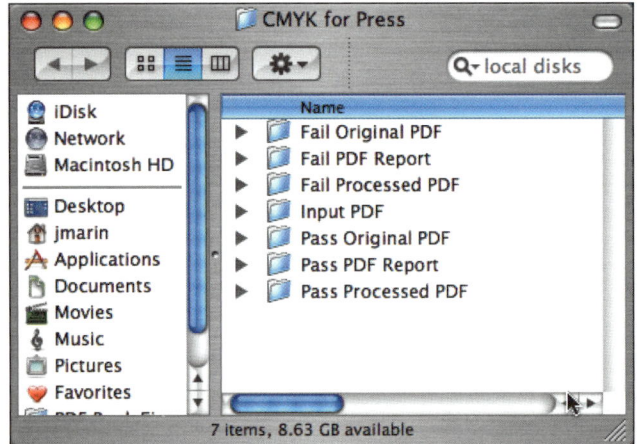

Figure 5.9. You can create a collection of subfolders within the PitStop Server hot folder. Each folder will contain specific information on how the PDF file and preflight report are handled.

PitStop Server allows you to set up a networked computer to handle the PDF preflighting and file repair process. You can set up hot folders that are customized for specific types of printed jobs. For example, you can have one hot folder designed to preflight and repair CMYK jobs only, one for CMYK plus one spot color, one for black-and-white work only, etc.

Within each hot folder you can create a collection of subfolders and assign each subfolder a specific function. The subfolders contain information such as the preflighting report and the repaired PDF file (Figure 5.9). Make sure that you use a clear naming convention when creating these folders.

Once you have set up a hot folder and a series of subfolders, the next step is to create and assign properties for that folder. Think of properties as preferences for a particular hot folder. Properties consist of action lists and preflighting profiles, folder locations, font locations, and color management. There is even a notification property where you can be alerted by email if a PDF file has passed or failed. Here is a breakdown of hot folder properties:

General. The General property contains options for both the name and a description for a hot folder (Figure 5.10).

Action Lists and PDF Profile. Action Lists can be used to edit or repair PDF files. For example, the Convert Color to CMYK action list can be assigned to a hot folder and will convert any non-CMYK objects when used (Figure 5.11). Action Lists can be created using PitStop Professional or may be downloaded from the Enfocus website (www.enfocus.com).

The PDF Profile is a collection of criteria the PDF must meet to pass the preflighting process. The PDF Profile is used both to preflight and repair problems in PDF files. Criteria that can be specified here include page sizes, bleed, font embedding, image resolution, OPI, and many others.

Folders. This is where you assign folders to which PDF preflight reports and job files will be stored (Figure 5.12). One folder is the PDF Input folder where the PDF file is to be processed, one is used retain a preflight report (pass or fail), one to retain the original PDF (pass or fail), and one to retain the repaired PDF (pass or fail).

Fonts. This is where you can specify font folders on the server. When PitStop Server preflights a PDF file and encounters a missing font, it will access the folder(s) specified here and try to replace the missing font in the PDF file (Figure 5.13).

Color Management. If you are using a color-managed workflow, you can use this property to remove or assign color management profiles to a PDF file (Figure 5.14).

Certified PDF. An Enfocus Certified PDF is a PDF file that contains information including the PDF profile, a preflight report, user and system identification, and an edit log that consists of all changes made to the PDF file per editing session. The Certified PDF concept is designed to ensure that both document creators and document receivers use up-to-date PDF specifications when creating and checking PDF files (Figure 5.15).

Notification. Here you can assign email addresses that will prompt you when a PDF file has been processed by PitStop Server. You can request an email message every time a PDF file is processed or depending on the outcome of the processing (Figure 5.16).

Once you have assigned all of the properties to a hot folder, you're ready to begin automated PDF preflighting and repair. Remember, you can create collections of hot folders to satisfy the different uses of PDF in your prepress department.

The Japanese have a concept called Poke-Yoke, which translates as "mistake-proofing." Poke-Yoke refers to devices or processes that are specifically designed to eliminate mistakes before they become a defect (the "idiot lights" in your car are an example of the concept of Poke-Yoke.) What a perfect fit for tools intended to help prevent improperly created PDF files! Think of PDF Courier, PDF JobReady, Synapse Prepare, and tools from the Enfocus PitStop Suite as examples of PDF Poke-Yoke.

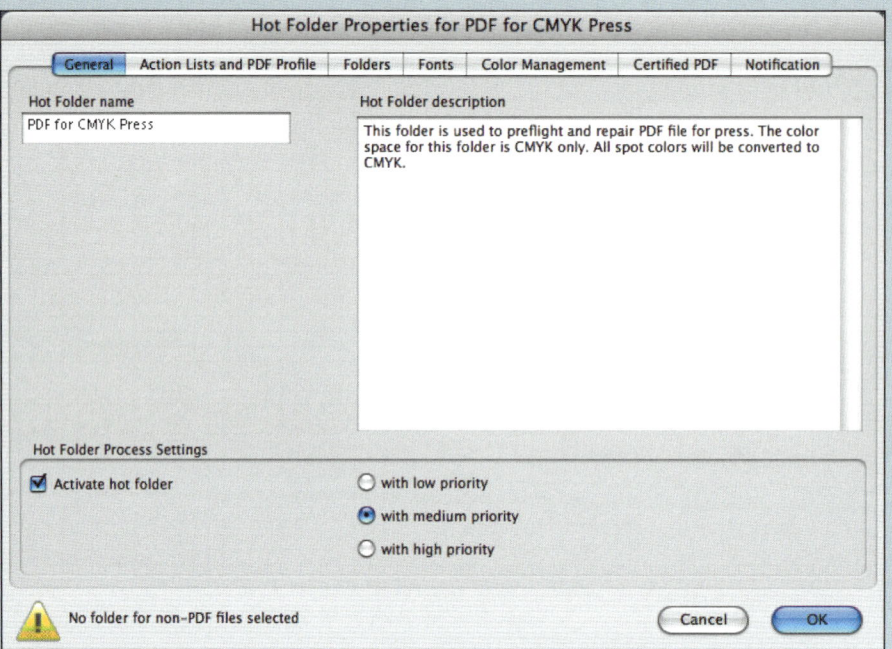

Figure 5.10. The General tab within the Hot Folder Properties dialog contains information such as the name of the assigned hot folder and a description of what it is designed to detect and repair.

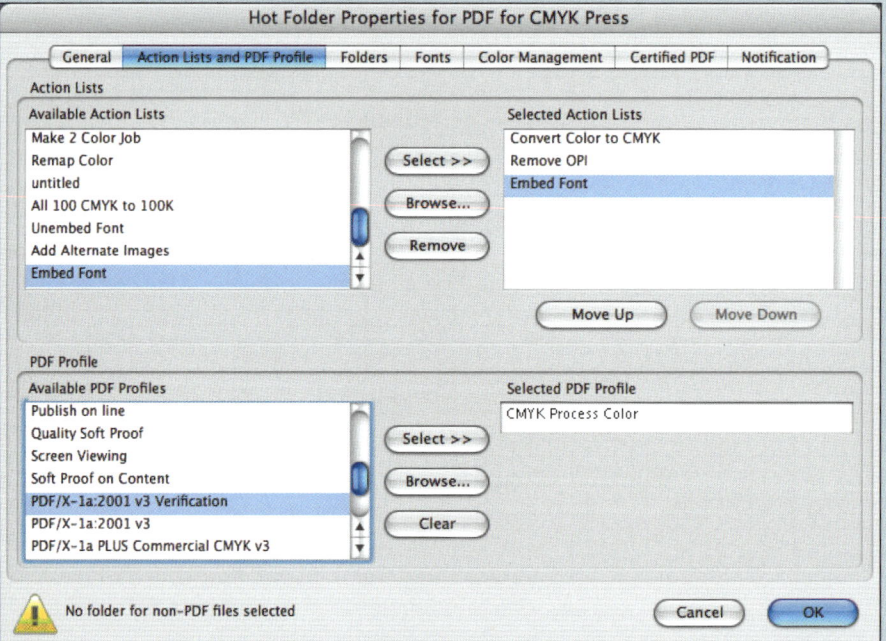

Figure 5.11. The Action Lists and PDF Profile dialog is where actions are chosen and used to repair PDFs. A PDF Profile is also assigned, which is used to detect specific problems within the PDF.

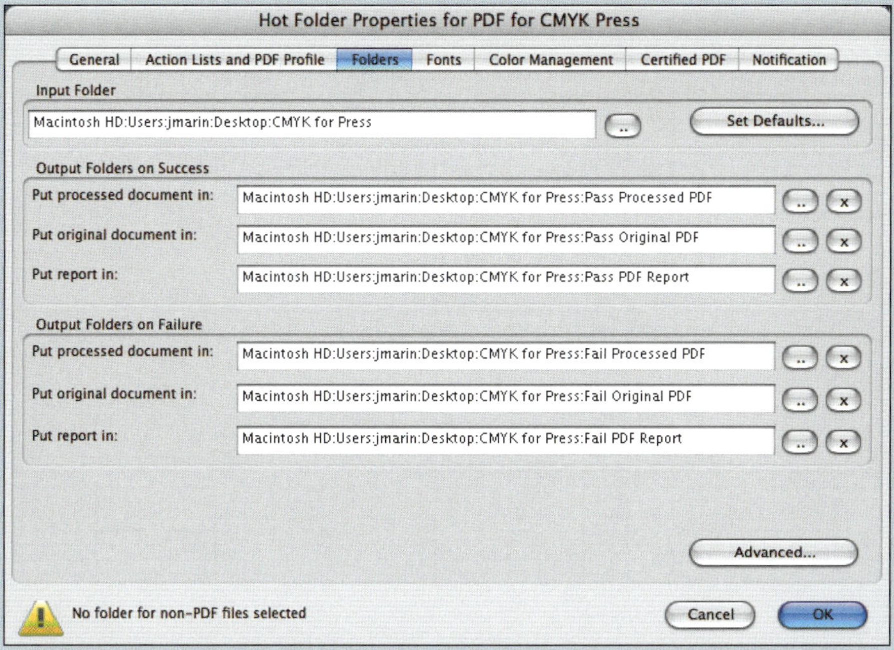

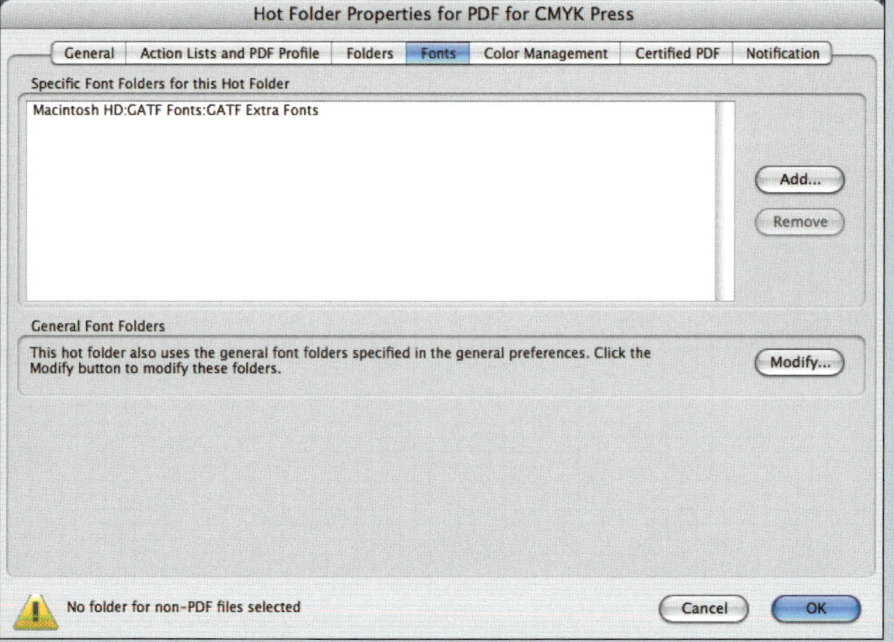

Figure 5.12. The Folders tab is where you assign locations for the preflight reports and PDF job files.

Figure 5.13. The Fonts tab is where you specify the font location(s) on your system. When a font is missing in a PDF, PitStop Server will access these folders and embed the font.

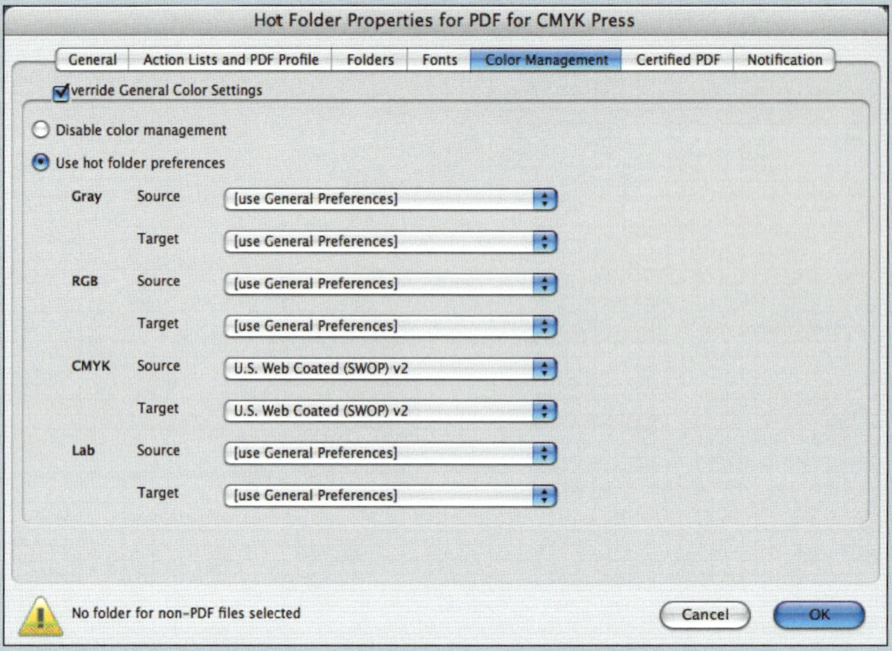

Figure 5.14. If you are using a color-managed workflow, you can assign or remove color management profiles in the Color Management tab.

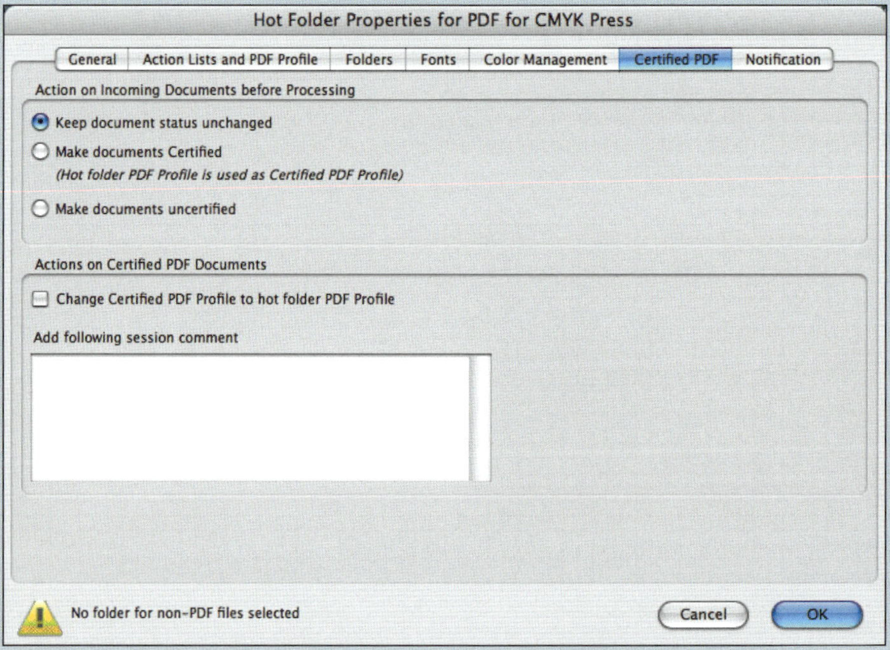

Figure 5.15. An Enfocus Certified PDF is a PDF file that contains information including the PDF profile, a preflight report, user and system identification, and an edit log that consists of all changes made to the PDF file per editing session.

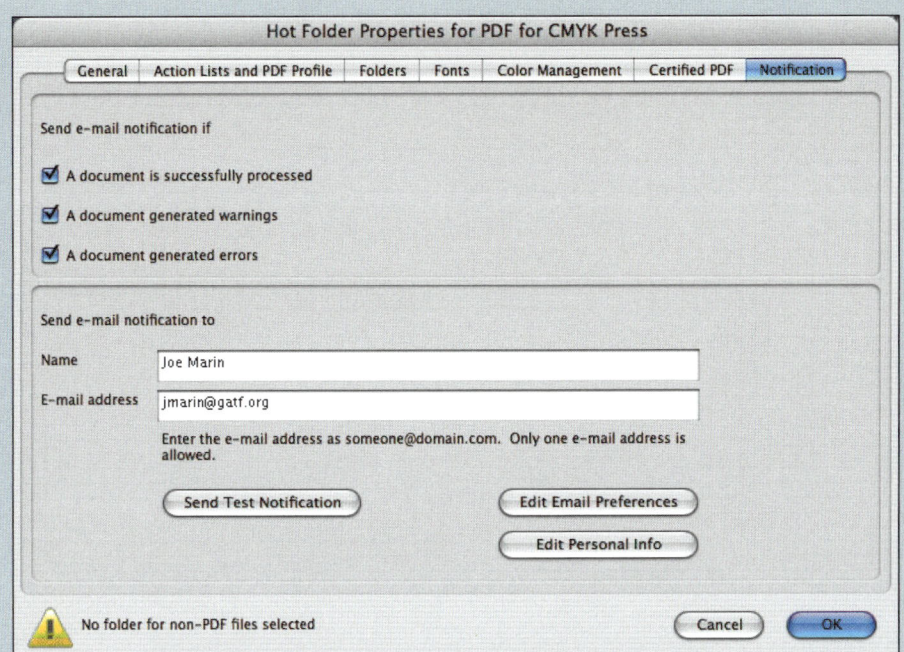

Figure 5.16. The Notification tab is where you can assign email addresses that will prompt you when a PDF file has been processed by PitStop Server.

CHAPTER 6
IN THE TRENCHES

In the Trenches: Working with PDF Files

In theory, PDF is the greatest thing to hit the print production world since, well, PostScript. It is wonderful that we can put all of the elements of a print job—fonts, images, illustration, layout, even the job ticket—into one neat package that can be compressed, digitally signed, and maybe even encrypted. The beauty of theory tends to break down in the cold trenches of reality, and nowhere is that more evident than with PDF files that come into prepress facilities for processing.

According to the Seybold Seminar's 2003 PDF Usage Survey, "content receivers" identify the top three problems with PDF files as (1) PDF files are more difficult to edit than native files, (2) PDF files are not made properly, and (3) PDF files are different from the native file. Specifically, they cite the problems of greatest concern as fonts (unembedded or subset), low-resolution images, images in the wrong color space (RGB, CMYK, etc.), and output or RIP problems. Clearly, working with client-supplied PDF files in print production is fraught with difficulty.

In our workshops and seminars, we've talked with hundreds of people in the graphic communications industry and have found that many of them are dealing with the very same problems. In this chapter, we will talk about some of the most common problems print production folks encounter with PDF files and how to get around them. We will start with details on some of the specific challenges faced by those who receive PDF files for print production—some of them brought to the party by Adobe, like transparency and layers. We will also offer some solutions to help make life in the PDF fast lane easier to navigate.

Challenges in PDF for Print Production

Transparency

Since Adobe introduced it, transparency has been a bane to the prepress production community. Like other new technologies (think TrueType font technology) transparency came to the market and was adopted by designers well before any output provider could successfully print it. PostScript does not "understand" transparency (neither does PDF 1.3 or earlier), and since just about every high-end output device converted supplied files into PostScript prior to imaging (even those that accepted PDF files directly) transparent objects caused a lot of havoc. Sometimes, when a PDF file containing transparency was RIPed, the top-most transparent object would simply knock out whatever was beneath it, thereby eliminating the transparent technique. Not a nice thing to discover on press! Other RIPs would simply reject a file containing transparent objects altogether.

While transparency has been with us since Illustrator 9, many service providers still have difficulty dealing with incoming PDF files that contain transparent objects. Transparency features of Adobe products have been evolving since its introduction, and Adobe have taken pains to make it easier to deal with in print production environments (probably in reaction to the loud screams their tech support people heard from prepress people). Today, Adobe has made transparency a seamless feature when moving Adobe-created files from one of the Creative Suite applications to another (or saved as a PDF 1.4 or 1.5), but, ultimately, when those files are printed, transparent objects have to be "flattened." Flattening merges the transparent object and whatever is under it into something a PostScript RIP can understand. Since the introduction of transparency, RIP manufacturers have slowly begun to support transparency and handle this flattening internally, but many prepress facilities do not have access to the latest equipment and have to deal with transparent files before they send them to the RIP.

We are often asked our opinion on the debate as to where PDF files with transparent objects should be flattened. We know that the official Adobe party line is "keep it live" as long as possible. In other words, if you design an illustration with transparent objects in Illustrator, you're encouraged to place that Illustrator file into InDesign with transparency intact. You can create more transparent objects in InDesign by choosing an opacity setting for an object through the transparency palette or by creating a drop shadow or adding a feather effect to an object. When you export a PDF file from that InDesign document to send to a service provider and save it as a PDF version 1.4 or 1.5 file, the transparent objects remain so in the PDF file. At this point, it is up to the service provider to flatten those transparent objects and make sure that PDF file prints the way it views on screen.

Many service providers yell "foul" to this notion and insist that their clients flatten transparent objects in PDF files before they are sent to them. This is a means of self-preservation, as the transparent objects (and objects affected by transparent objects) can look quite different in a flattened PDF file than they do

when viewed in the original layout application, often depending upon how that file was flattened. Prepress providers are very used to the "it's your fault" game, often resulting in a customer refusing to pay for all or part of a project when a printed piece does not match the original file or proof. They don't want to take the responsibility of creating a file that may not match the customer's intention—especially when any customer with the ability to create a transparent PDF file has the capability to flatten it.

We don't want to cop out on giving an opinion on this, but we can see both sides of the issue. If maintaining an editable PDF file is important, meaning one in which any object can be moved independently of any other object on the page, then transparency should be maintained until the end of the production process. Once PDF files containing transparent objects have been flattened, a previously transparent object may become a raster image (or even be broken into several raster images). The transparent object is no longer independent of what is beneath it, and they cannot be moved independent of each other.

Flattened PDF files can be much larger than their "live transparency" counterparts because some of the vector objects could have been rasterized, making them pixel-based objects with a fixed resolution. The higher the resolution of those raster objects, the bigger the file will become (Figure 6.1). These flattened PDF files can take much longer to display in Acrobat; each time you scroll or resize the page, the screen has to redraw, and this can be an agonizingly slow process, especially in a fast-paced prepress environment. Often, when flattening results in large raster image areas, these images are chopped into blocks of smaller images so that a single image is made up of perhaps dozens of pieces. These in particular take a very long time to redraw on screen. It's also very important to make sure Overprint Preview is always turned on when viewing supplied PDF files. A PDF file containing transparent objects can look ghastly when Overprint Preview is not enabled; compare the same file with overprinting enabled and

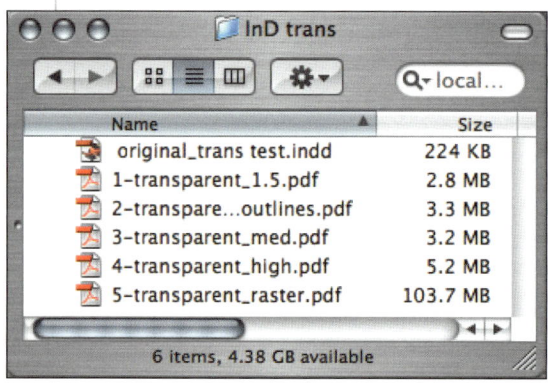

Figure 6.1. Flattened PDF files can be quite large if transparent objects have been rasterized at a high resolution.

Figure 6.2a. and 6.2b. Overprinting objects, displayed with Overprint Preview enabled, left, and disabled, right.

Figure 6.3a. and 6.3b. Flattening can result in visual artifacts that often appear as lines running through objects.

disabled in Figures 6.2a and 6.2b. The way the file looks when Overprint Preview is enabled is correct and more readily represents the way the file will print.

One of the biggest problems we've seen with flattened PDF files is that there can be nasty visual artifacts in the file, especially where raster objects meets vector objects. This can be manifested with what looks like fine lines that run right through objects, even those that don't appear to be at all related to a transparent object (Figures 6.3a, 6.3b). In some of our testing, we've found that these "lines" are the results of masks that follow the contour of new clipped objects that are the result of the flattening process (Figure 6.4). The question is whether these lines will show up on the final printed piece. In

our testing, we've found that while the artifacts show up on the display, they do not show up when output from a high-resolution imaging device. However, we have heard from other printers that they have seen these artifacts show up as actual lines on printing plates! So we wind up with a situation in which we cannot trust what we see on screen necessarily to be what we can expect on output, and that's a problem for print production.

Figure 6.4. Artifacts in a flattened PDF appear to follow the contour of masked objects.

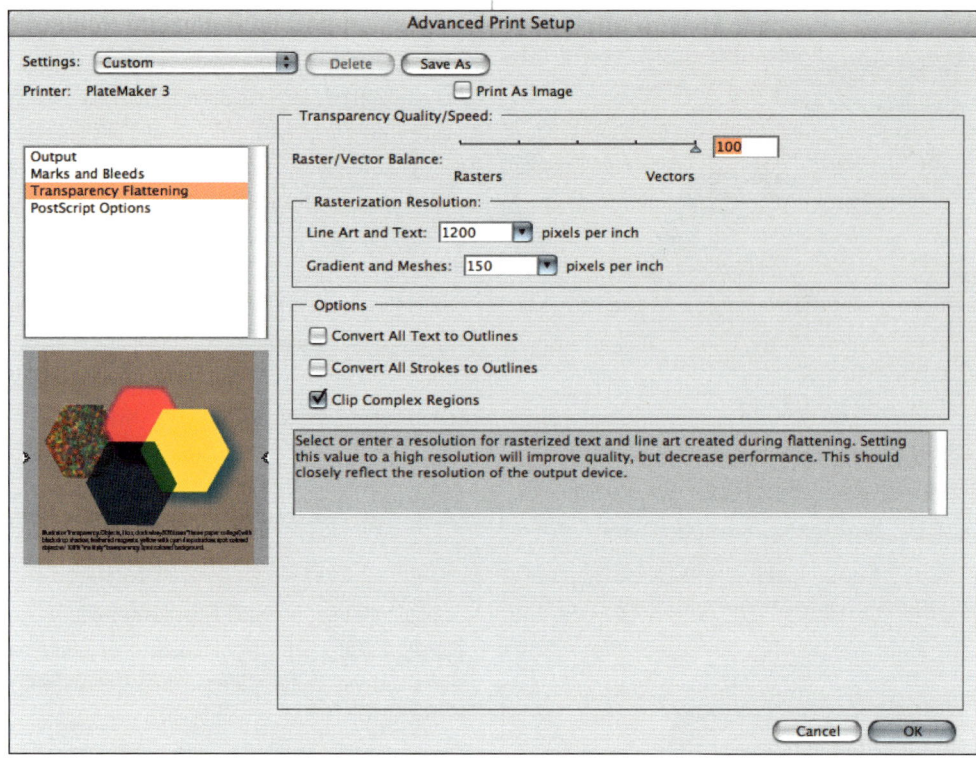

Figure 6.5. Transparency flattening options can be found in the Advanced menu of the Acrobat Print dialog.

The bottom line is this: PDF files containing transparent objects have to be flattened somewhere prior to printing. Unfortunately, while Acrobat 6 Professional has a transparency flattener preview, it is only used to predict how a flattened PDF file will print and does not offer an actual means of flattening PDF files. The only way to flatten transparent objects in Acrobat is by "printing" a new PDF file from the Print dialog. Transparency flattening is offered in the Advanced menu of the Acrobat Print dialog and contains options similar to the those in InDesign and Illustrator (Figure 6.5).

Like all of the transparency flattening options in Adobe CS products, the options from the Print dialog in Acrobat offers a Raster/Vector Balance slider with which the user determines the threshold for transparency rasterization. Pushing the slider to the right (thus setting a higher value) will allow more objects to remain in vector format, while moving it farther to the left will force more objects to be rasterized into fixed-resolution pixel-based graphics. Setting the slider all the way to the left will rasterize the entire page so that it is converted into a single large picture (virtually the same as checking the "Print as Image" option). In addition to determining what the raster/vector balance should be, the user can set the resolution of text and line art independent of, and higher than, gradients. So theoretically one can set an entire PDF file to be flattened to raster images but still maintain high-resolution pixel-based text. In addition, the user can choose to convert text and strokes to vector outlines. (In Illustrator and InDesign, these options are grayed-out if the raster/vector slider is set all the way to the left [or to a value of "0"] but nudging the slider to "1" makes these options available again.) Text that is involved in transparency (text that touches an InDesign drop shadow would fall into this category) can become rasterized to a fixed pixel resolution that may not be high enough to look clean on output. Be aware, however, that text converted to outlines can appear thicker than it did before the conversion and may not match text set to the same point size elsewhere in the document.

Which are the best settings to use? The amount of rasterization really depends on the amount of RAM available to the application, the complexity of the page, and the types of objects that are overlapping. In other words, the only way to know just what is the best setting for a particular project involves trying a few different combinations to see what results in the best product. Sorry, no cut-and-dried answers here. While the InDesign and Illustrator "High Resolution" preset option has the slider set all the way to the left, we've found that this setting can result in some of the worst visual artifacting in the resultant PDF file.

Here's the slider tradeoff: If you decide to rasterize as much of the file as possible, you'll naturally end up with a larger PDF file, containing very large raster images. The higher the resolution settings used, the bigger this file will be. Conversely, setting the slider farther to the vector side can result in more device-independent vector objects but includes more complexity in the PDF file, potentially making processing take a lot longer. There is no "best" solution that fits every PDF file.

Trapping

When it comes to trapping PDF files, prepress facilities lucky enough to have high-end prepress workflow solutions can rely on an InRIP trapping engine. In the U.S., 36% of the content receivers who responded to the 2003 Seybold PDF Survey said they rely on InRIP trapping of PDF files, 42% of European respondents said the same. Some (14–17%) used other dedicated trapping solutions (like Creo TrapWise or Heidelberg Supertrap), but an alarming 27% of U.S. respondents said they "don't try" to trap PDF files. This is to be distinguished from the 19% who replied that no traps were needed in the files they process (they might print solid color or digitally printed work). Clearly, some users simply don't have access to, or cannot afford, an InRIP or dedicated trapping solution, but they still require a way to trap PDF files.

For many years, a large number of users depended on the separation engine built into desktop publishing applications like QuarkXPress. Even today, we are surprised at how many users still are printing separations from QuarkXPress. QuarkXPress has a built-in trapping function that, while not perfect, was relied upon by many users as their sole means of file trapping (along with setting traps in the illustration program for placed EPS graphics). Trapping relationships set using Quark trapping, as many users are well aware, do not come through in composite PDF files exported or printed from Quark (although overprint and knockout setting do carry through). Overprint stroke settings in Illustrator or FreeHand, a tried-and-true method of trapping illustrations for many years, may or may not come through into a PDF file, depending upon how the PDF was created. If Distiller is used, for example, the instruction Preserve Overprint Setting must be checked under the Advanced tab. If this is deselected, overprint instructions set in Illustrator (or any application, including Quark) will be discarded in the resultant PDF file.

So how can a user create traps in PDF files without a dedicated solution? One option is to use Enfocus PitStop Pro, with which a user can select vector objects in a PDF file, apply stroke thickness and color to them, and even set them to overprint. But be warned: this technique is not for the casual PitStop user and, with very complicated files, is not at all easy to do. We have a brief overview of how to do this in the Common Problems section.

Another option is to use the trapping engine built into Adobe InDesign. Similar to the Adobe InRIP engine that is part of many high-end RIPs, any file printed from InDesign can be fully trapped. While this doesn't apply to PDF files created by using the Export option from InDesign, it works very well when an InDesign file is printed to PostScript and then

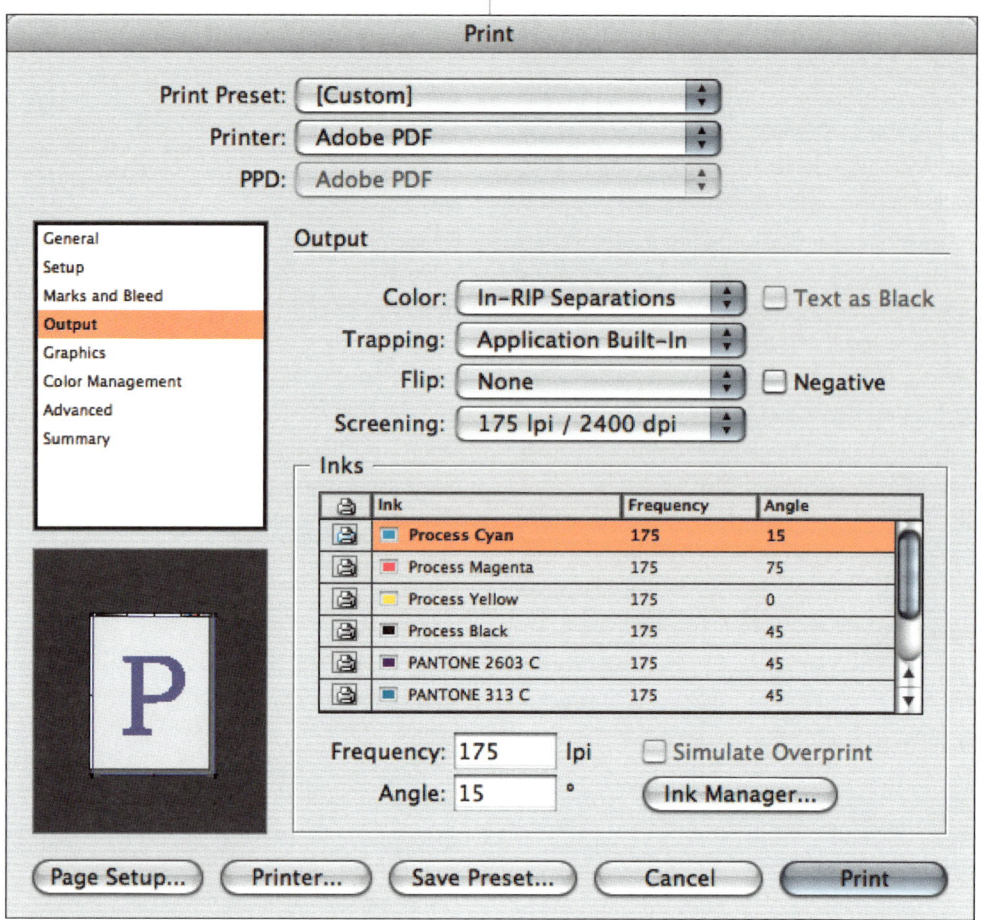

Figure 6.6. InDesign will honor trapping information in a PostScript file as long as In-RIP Separations is selected in the Output section of the Print dialog. Select *Application Built-In* in the Trapping pop-up window.

converted to PDF using Acrobat Distiller. To get Quark traps to come through into a PDF file, the Quark document has to be printed as a separated file, resulting in a PDF containing multiple "black" pages, one for each color in the document (these look a lot like film positives). Separated PDF files often pose problems for output devices, because some RIPs see each page as "black" and will output each color on the "black" angle—a moiré nightmare on press. Not so from InDesign; the built-in application trapping can be applied to PostScript output as long as the file is printed as InRIP separations (Figure 6.6). When this PostScript file is interpreted with Acrobat Distiller,

Distiller tosses out the commands to separate the file but keeps the "trapping" PostScript commands. The final PDF will be a composite trapped document. The traps can be viewed in Acrobat 5 or 6 by activating Overprint Preview and they will print appropriately.

Trapping has been part of InDesign since version 1.5. Through version 2.x, only InDesign objects, like text and graphics, could be trapped to placed images, text, or vector objects. Placed PDF or EPS objects were not handled by the InDesign trapping engine. InDesign CS has changed that, and includes a new method of printing placed native Illustrator (.ai) and PDF files that will actually trap them (placed EPS files, however, still cannot be trapped). This means that a PDF file, even one created from QuarkXPress, can be placed onto an InDesign CS page and the contents of that PDF file will be trapped in the resultant PDF file along with all of the other objects on the page. A step-by-step guide on how to set this up is included in the Common Problems section.

Layers

The PDF 1.5 specification allows for true layers in PDF files. This means that layers set in a number of applications (AutoCAD, Visio, Adobe Illustrator and InDesign) can be saved into PDF files created from those applications. Sounds like a great idea, and it does allow for some good things in PDF-based print production workflows that did not exist before. For packaging work, a die line can be a part of a PDF file but can be set on a separate layer so that it will not affect the rest of the work. Layers can also be used for versioning—so that a single PDF file can contain all versions of a document. Layered PDF files can be used in print workflows, but there are a few caveats we want you to know about so you can work with them successfully.

Let's look at a sample layered document created in Adobe Illustrator CS. Figures 6.7a, 6.7b, and 6.7c show that our sample file has three layers in the native Illustrator application. To include these layers in a PDF file, it has to be saved as an Acrobat 6 (PDF 1.5) compatibility (Figure 6.8). Only when this compatibility level is selected is the Create Acrobat Layers From Top Level Layers option available. Check it, and the layer data will be included in the resultant PDF file.

To view and edit layer data, select the Layers navigation tab at the left of the document window in Acrobat 6 Professional. Layers can be independently viewed and edited via the Options pull-down menu (Figure 6.9). Using the Layer Properties dialog options, you can change the state of a layer in terms of visibility, printability, and portability. So, for example, if you wish to print only a particular layer

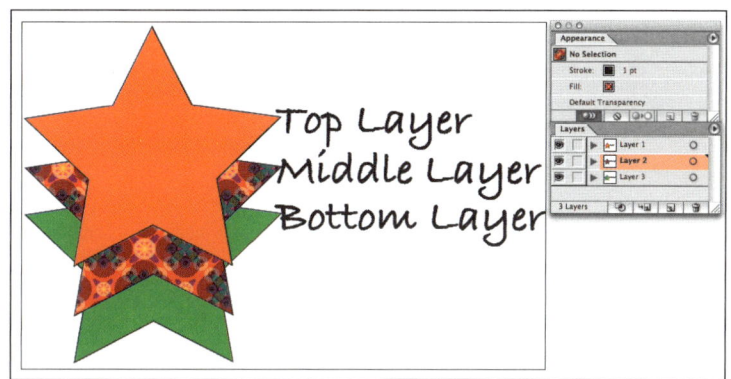

Figure 6.7a, b, c. A document containing three layers built in Adobe Illustrator CS.

of a PDF file, you can set a particular layer to print only when visible or to never print (Figure 6.10). This sounds great, but it is also one of the caveats to working with layered PDF files for print. While the layer printing status as set in the Layer Properties is honored when printing directly from the Print dialog

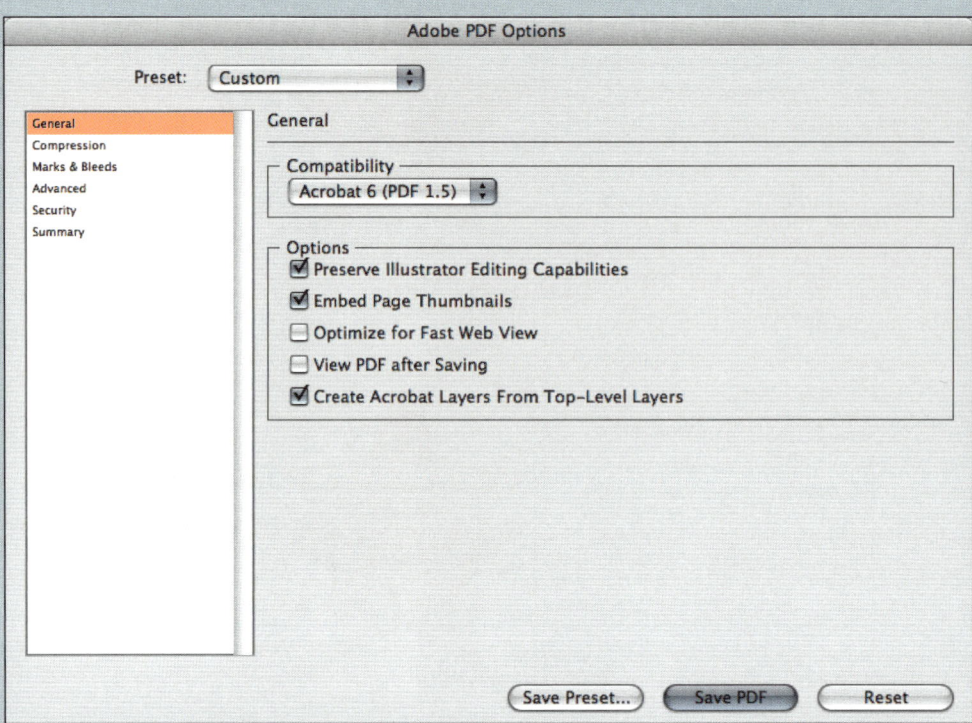

Figure 6.8. The PDF file compatibility must be set to Acrobat 6 (PDF 1.5) to preserve the layers from the Illustrator CS file.

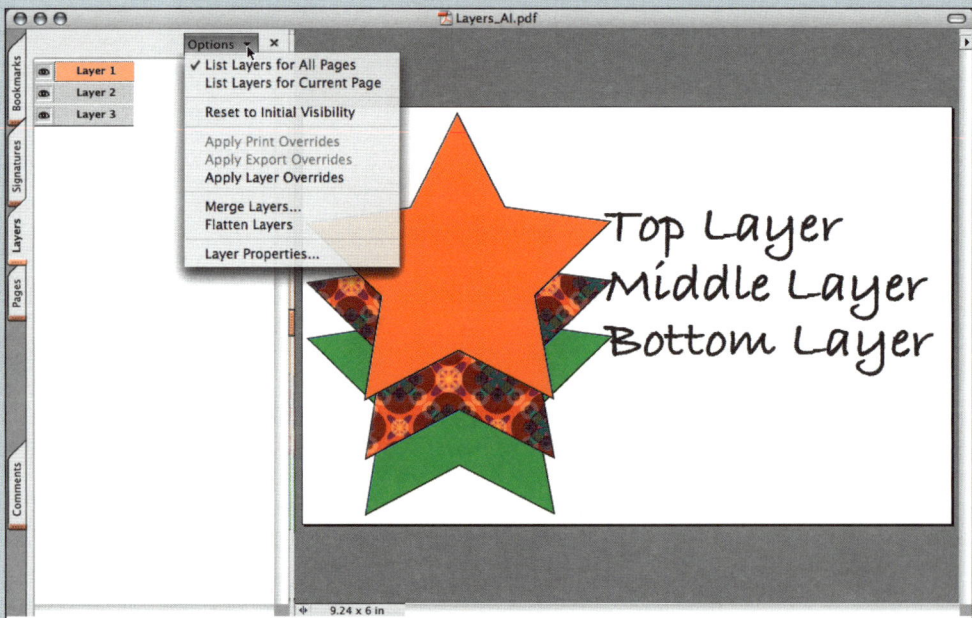

Figure 6.9. Layers can be viewed independently in Acrobat under the Options pull-down menu in the Layers tab.

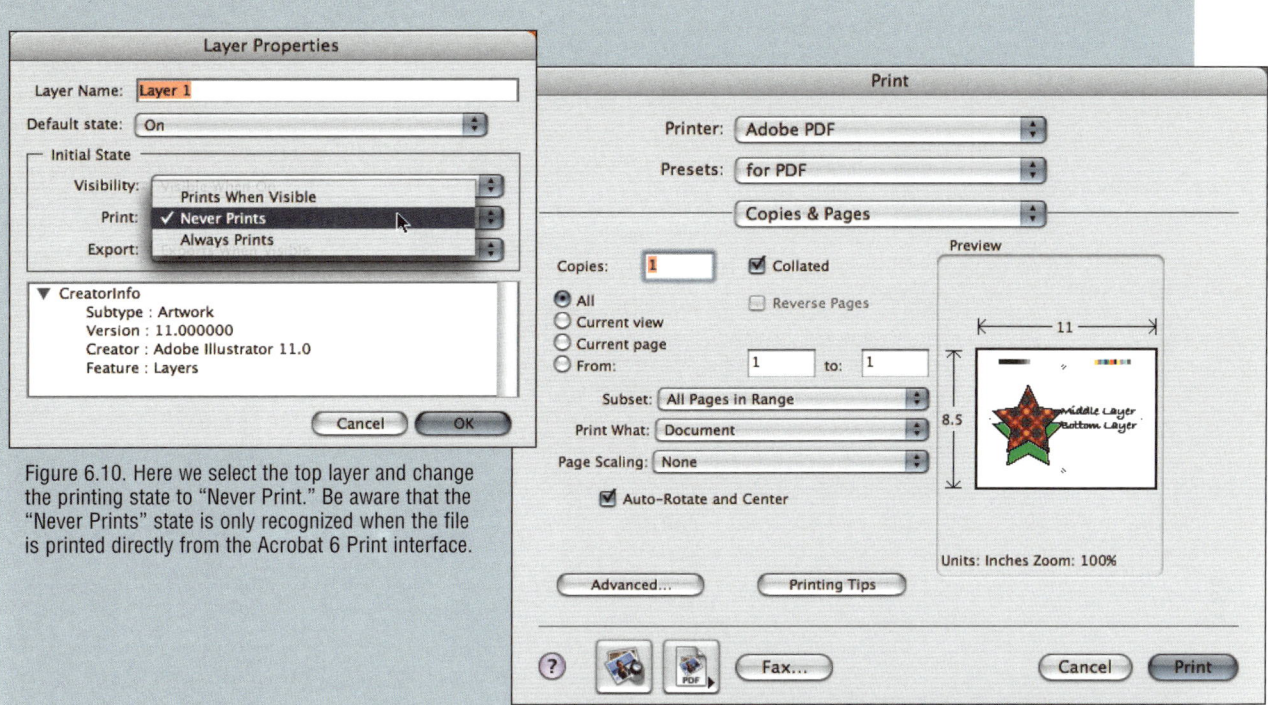

Figure 6.10. Here we select the top layer and change the printing state to "Never Print." Be aware that the "Never Prints" state is only recognized when the file is printed directly from the Acrobat 6 Print interface.

Figure 6.11. The top layer, set to "Never Print," does not appear in the Print Preview.

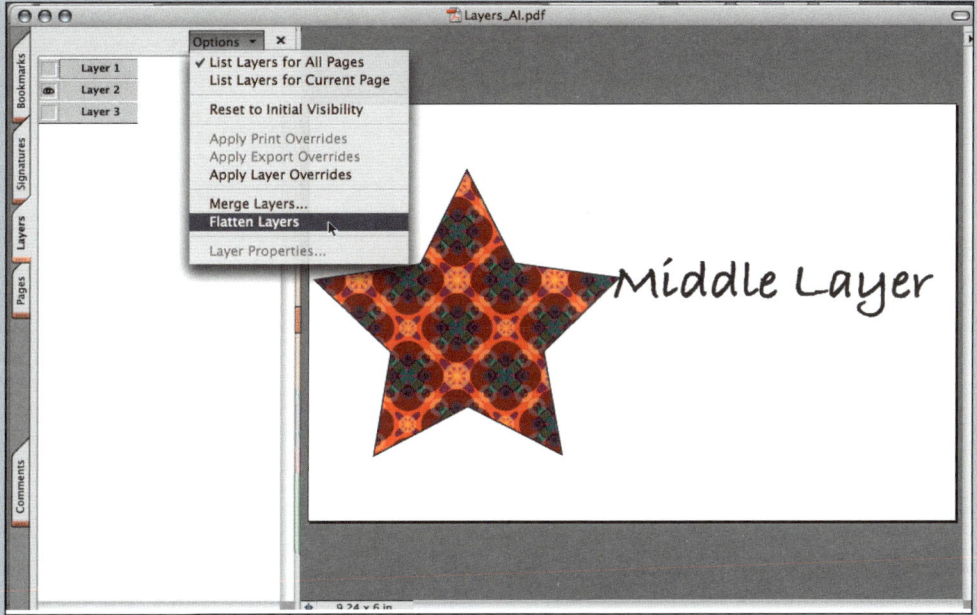

Figure 6.12. Create files for print by flattening layers and saving as a separate PDF.

in Acrobat 6 Pro, it is not honored elsewhere. In our example, we have set the top layer to "Never Print" in the Layer Properties dialog. When we print this from the Print dialog in Acrobat 6, only the middle and bottom layer show up in the preview window; the top layer is not recognized and will not print (Figure 6.11). However, when we submitted this same PDF file directly to a PDF-based prepress workflow solution, the RIP did not recognize the instructions set in the Layer Properties dialog box of Acrobat 6 Pro, and all three layers printed, on top of one another.

One way to avoid this is to create separate PDF files for each layer before printing. To do this, simply use the Layers navigation tab and make layers you do not wish to print invisible by clicking on the eye icon. Then select *Flatten Layers* from the Options pull-down (Figure 6.12). The resultant PDF file will contain only the visible layer. Make sure you "save as" the resultant PDF file and give it a new name, or the non-visible layers will be permanently lost.

DCS

DCS image files can contain more than the four process color channels and are often used to add a "touch plate" to an image. The problem with DCS images is that, while they image properly when separated from a DTP layout application, they do not traditionally work well in a composite PDF workflow. For example, when separations are printed from QuarkXPress, DCS image files come through as expected. However when a composite PDF file containing a DCS image is created from Quark, the DCS image will come through as a low-resolution image in the PDF file. What's happening is that the placeholder image in the layout is the only image that makes it into the PDF file; the high-resolution data is left behind.

There are several solutions to this problem. Total Integration offers a QuarkXTension Smart XT, which, when installed, is able to combine high-resolution four-color DCS data into a PDF file printed or exported from QuarkXPress. As of this writing, there is not a version available for the Mac OS X version of Quark 6, however. Another tool is the standalone application DCSMerger from Impressed.

A third option is to use InDesign CS for page layout—that's right, InDesign CS can merge the high-resolution data from a placed DCS image into a composite PDF file—another reason that InDesign is developing into the premier DTP tool, especially for PDF workflows.

Common Problems

Generally speaking, editing or correcting a PDF file is not always as simple as it would be using native applications. Adobe Acrobat alone is not a particularly robust PDF editing tool. However, by adding third-party plug-ins, Acrobat can be turned into a powerful PDF editor. Plug-ins such as Enfocus PitStop Professional, Quite A Box Of Tricks, and others will give you the ability to correct missing bleeds, embed fonts, change color spaces, and scale objects. This chapter takes a look at some of the most common errors found in PDF files provided for print production and offers some solutions in getting around them.

Figure 6.13. PDF page boxes consist of (A) media box, (B) bleed box, (C) trim box, and (D) art box.

Problem: Missing Bleeds

Bleed refers to an object that extends beyond the trim of a page. Oftentimes the bleed is not included with the PDF document, and this typically occurs for one of two reasons. Either the bleed was not created in the original application at all, or the bleed area was not included during the PostScript printing process.

Before we can address how bleeds are fixed in a PDF file, we must first discuss the concept of page boxes or arrays as they are defined in a PDF file. Page boxes are boundaries drawn around objects on a PDF page and around the page itself. Page boxes cannot be viewed in Acrobat without a plug-in such as Enfocus PitStop Professional. Here is a description of each of the various types of page boxes that can be a part of a PDF file, including the media box, bleed box, trim box, art box, and crop box (Figure 6.13, on previous page).

Media box. The media box is (or should be) the largest page box defined in a PDF document. The media box represents the page size selected in conjunction with a PPD, or printer description, in the print dialog box of a layout application. The media box is equivalent to the size of the actual media on which the file would be printed if it were being printed to a physical output device; think of it as virtual paper which will be printed to a virtual printer: Distiller. The media box must be large enough to encompass all the other page boxes (i.e., bleed, trim, art, and crop boxes).

Bleed box. If the document includes bleeds, the PDF document will also have a bleed box. The bleed box ensures that when a job is printed and trimmed, images and objects will be printed all the way to the page's edge.

Trim box. The trim box represents the document's final size after it has been printed and trimmed. It's usually defined by the actual document size of the native layout file.

Art box. This is the box around the contents of the pages in the document.

Crop box. PDF pages can be cropped by using a tool like the Crop tool in Acrobat. The crop box represents the size that the page is displayed in Acrobat.

When a PDF file with bleeds is created correctly, the media box has been set up to be large enough to contain the bleed area. It will be slightly larger than the trim box. When a PDF file with bleeds is set up incorrectly, the media box is exactly the same size as the trim box, leaving no margin to contain the bleed.

If you get a file with the bleed chopped off, there is a way to add it back on! Enfocus PitStop Professional provides an interface to the page boxes within a PDF document. This will allow the user to resize any of the boxes, including the media box. The following example shows how to add 1/8-in. bleeds to an 8.5×11-in. PDF using PitStop Professional.

1. Select *Window>Show PitStop Global Change.*

2. In the PitStop Global Change dialog box, select the Page tab, then select the Page Boxes tab.

3. To add bleed to the page, the media box must first be enlarged. To add 1/8-in. to all four sides of the page, be sure that the Media Box option is selected. Note the values in the Coordinates section. The lower lefthand corner of the page is coordinate 0.0. To add 1/8-in. to the media box on the left and bottom of the page, type in −0.125 to the Left and Bottom fields respectively. To add 1/8-in. to the media box on the right and top of the page, add 0.125-in. to the Right and Top values respectively. Click the Apply button.

4. To view the document with the new media box, select the View Page Boxes tool in PitStop.

Expanding the media box is the easy part. Now you have to access the objects that are intended to extend the bleed beyond the trim into the bleed area. This can be done as follows:

Select *Window> Show PitStop Global Change.*

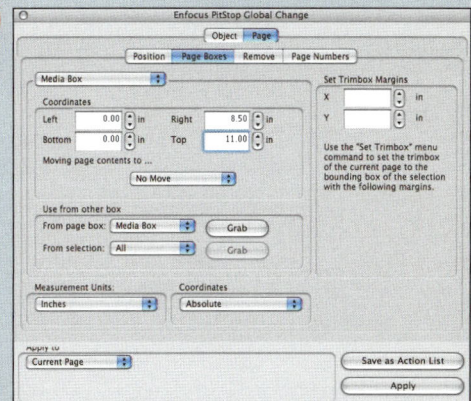

In the PitStop Global Change dialog box, select the Page tab, then select the Page Boxes tab.

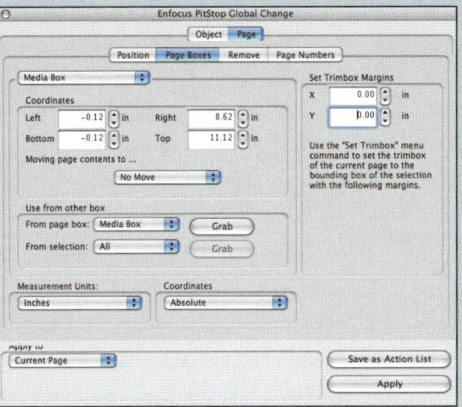

To add bleed to the page, the media box must first be enlarged. Note the values entered in the coordinates section for our example.

To view the document with the new media box, select the View Page Boxes tool in PitStop.

Problem: Missing Bleeds (continued)

1. Select the Edit Path tool in PitStop.

2. Click on the object to edit the path. The anchor points become visible but are not selected yet. Click on a specific anchor point. A selected anchor point will appear larger, indicating that it can be moved. Click on the anchor point and drag it beyond the trim into the bleed area.

3. Repeat Step 1 for all of the remaining objects that require a bleed.

4. Save the PDF.

This gets even more difficult when the object that has to fill to the bleed is a bitmap image. This will require some tricky additional steps, but it can be accomplished. By opening the image in Photoshop using the TouchUp Object tool, you can increase the canvas size of the image enough to accommodate the additional area needed for bleed. Then, you can clone additional image area along the edges of the image to create bleed pixels. (Remember, a bleed is just to ensure that no white edges of paper are showing along the trimmed edges of a printed piece. Details of what makes up the bleed are not critical, so even fairly sloppy cloning of pixel data to an image file typically will not be a problem.)

Save this image and it will be updated into the PDF document. It won't look any different than it did before the image was altered because there is a bounding box around the image object matching the original dimensions of the image. Using PitStop Professional, it is possible to view a PDF document in wireframe mode (much like an illustration application). In wireframe mode it is fairly easy to select this old bounding box and delete it (there may actually be several of them) and expose the newly enlarged image file.

In most cases, we admit, it may be easier simply to request a new PDF document or even the native file from the client. But in a pinch, this technique will work.

1

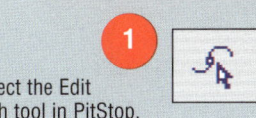

Select the Edit
Path tool in PitStop.

2

Click on the
object to edit
the path.

3

Repeat Step 1 for
all of the remaining
objects that require
a bleed.

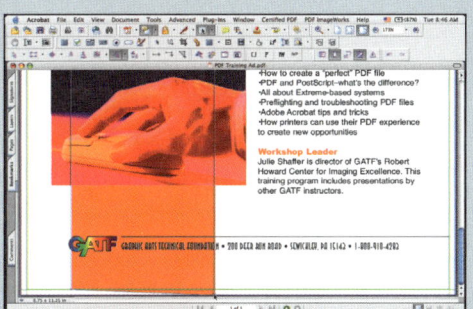

4

Save the PDF.

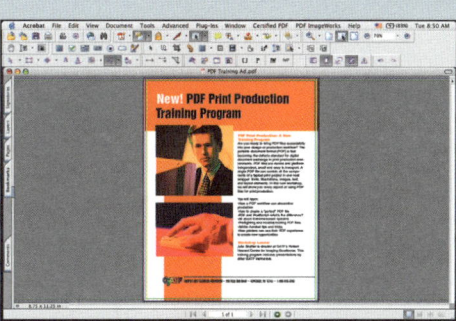

Problem: Hairline Rules

Applications that allow lines or rules to be defined as "hairline" can cause problems in PDF files. Hairlines can be interpreted by the printer driver as "the smallest possible line that you can render." This means that a hairline rule can be as small as one machine pixel wide; for a file intended for high-resolution output to a 2400-dpi imagesetter or platesetter, this will be 1/2400th of an inch wide. In other words, it will be invisible to the eye. This same rule would be much thicker when viewed on screen or imaged on a lower-resolution laser printer or proofing device. When PDF files are created via Distiller, and both the PostScript file and Distiller have been set to create a file for an output resolution of 2400 dpi, hairline rules essentially will disappear.

The following example shows how to give all hairlines in a PDF a minimum thickness (weight) using PitStop Professional.

1. Select *Window>Show PitStop Global Change*.

2. In the Enfocus PitStop Global Change dialog box, select the Object tab, then select the Prepress tab.

3. Click on the Line Weight radio button and specify a minimum line weight for the Current Page, Page Range, or Complete Document. Click *Apply* to force all hairline rules to 0.5 point.

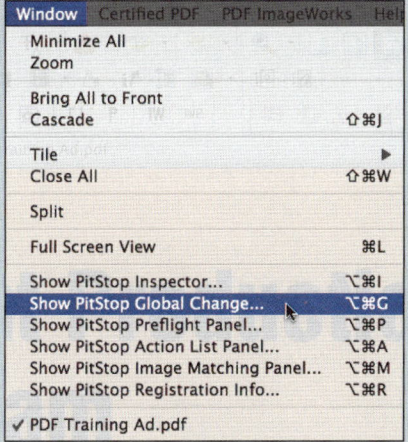

Select *Window>
Show PitStop
Global Change*.

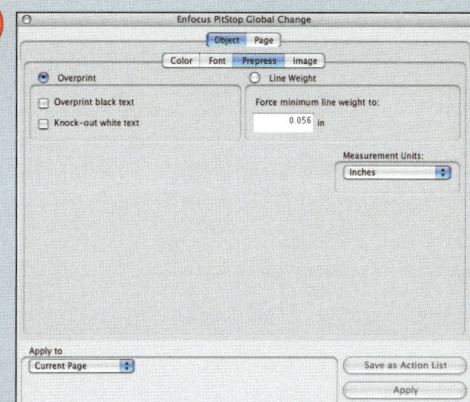

In the Enfocus
PitStop Global
Change dialog
box, select the
Object tab, then
select the
Prepress tab.

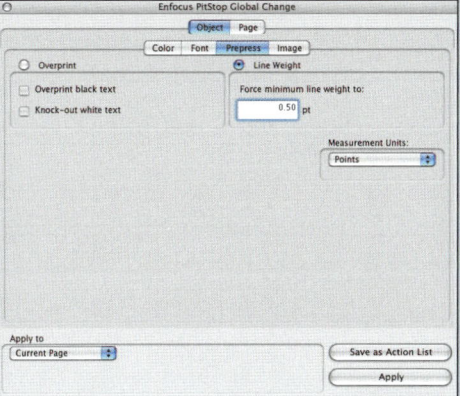

Click on the Line
Weight radio
button and specify
a minimum line
weight for the
Current Page, Page
Range, or Complete
Document. Click
Apply to force all
hairline rules to 0.5
point.

Problem: Spot Color Not Specified CMYK

Spot colors are printed with premixed inks. With spot color printing, each color is produced from its own printing plate. Spot color equivalents also may be created using CMYK screen tints. If a job is to print using CMYK inks only and the spot color is not specified as a CMYK build in the native application, it will print on its own plate when the job is output.

The following example illustrates how to convert a spot color to CMYK using Enfocus PitStop Professional.

1. Select *Window>Show PitStop Inspector.*

2. Select the Select Objects tool in PitStop.

3. Click on the spot color object on the page. Using the PitStop Inspector, note the CMYK equivalent of the selected spot color.

4. Select *Window>Show PitStop Global Change.*

5. Make sure that the spot color object is still selected. In the PitStop Global Change dialog box, make sure that the Object and Color tabs are selected.

6. In the Color tab, click the Grab Fill button in From Selection Color (in the left column). The color will reflect the spot color to be converted to CMYK. In To CMYK (in the right column), type in the CMYK equivalents from Step 3. In the lower lefthand corner of the PitStop Global Change dialog, you can choose to apply the change to the current page or complete document.

7. Click *Apply.*

8. Save the document.

Spot Color Not Specified CMYK

1

Select *Window>
Show PitStop
Inspector.*

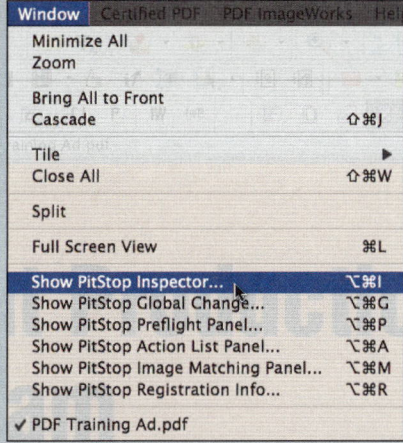

2

Select the
Select Objects
tool in PitStop.

3

Click on the spot
color object on
the page. Using
the PitStop
Inspector, note
the CMYK
equivalent of
the selected
spot color.

4

Select *Window>
Show PitStop
Global Change.*

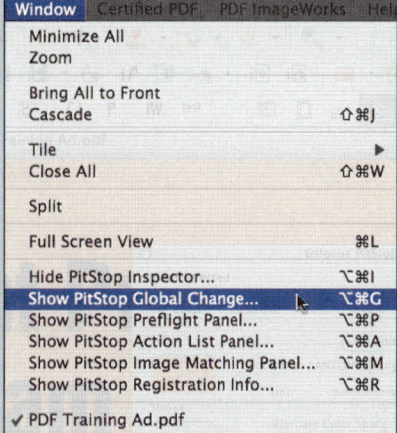

5

Make sure that the
spot color object is
still selected. In the
PitStop Global
Change dialog box,
make sure that the
Object and Color
tabs are selected.

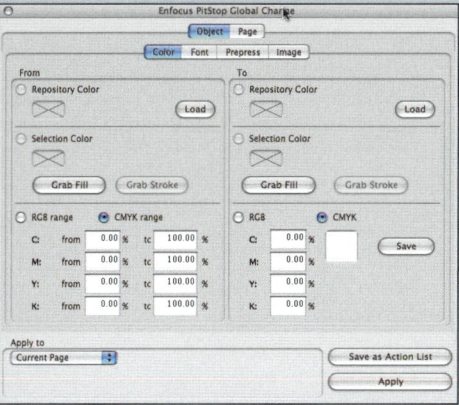

6

In the Color tab,
click the Grab Fill
button in From
Selection Color
(in the left column).
The color will reflect
the spot color to be
converted to CMYK.
In To CMYK (in the
right column), type
in the CMYK
equivalents
from Step 3.

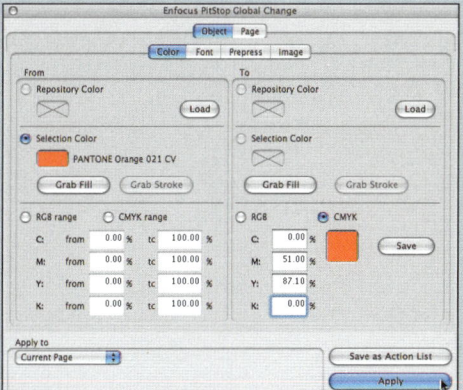

Problem: Missing Spot Color

If a PDF file is missing a spot color, you can apply a spot color using Enfocus PitStop Professional. New in PitStop Professional 6.0 is a PANTONE® spot color library. In addition, spot colors can be loaded manually into a color repository in PitStop and then used to color objects in the PDF file. Spot colors assigned in layout applications generally come through properly in resultant PDF files except in the case of most Microsoft Office products, particularly on the PC platform, where they will be converted to RGB.

1. Select *Window>Show PitStop Global Change.*

2. In the Enfocus PitStop Global Change dialog box, select the Object tab, then the Color tab.

3. Click on the Select Objects tool.

4. Click to select an object in the PDF file to be converted to a spot color. In the Enfocus PitStop Global Change dialog box, click on the From Selection Color radio button, then click *Grab*.

5. In the Enfocus PitStop Global Change dialog box, click *Load* in the To Repository Color section.

6. In the Color Picker dialog box, use the pull-down menu to select a color from the PANTONE® spot color library. Click *OK*.

7. In the Enfocus PitStop Global Change dialog box, click *Apply* to convert the selected color to spot throughout the entire PDF.

Select *Window> Show PitStop Global Change.*

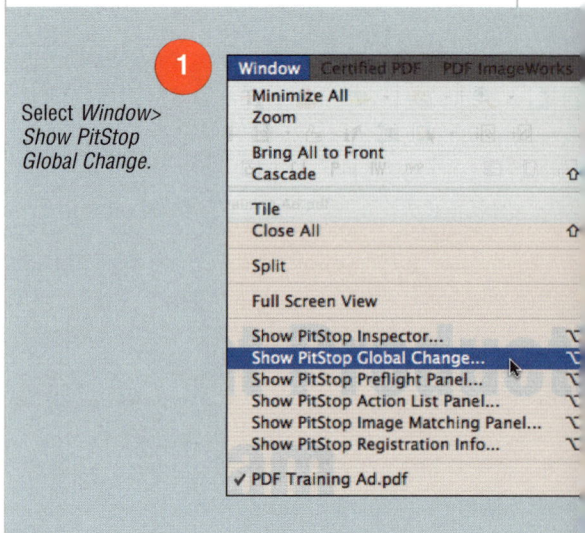

2

In the Enfocus PitStop Global Change dialog box, select the Object tab, then the Color tab.

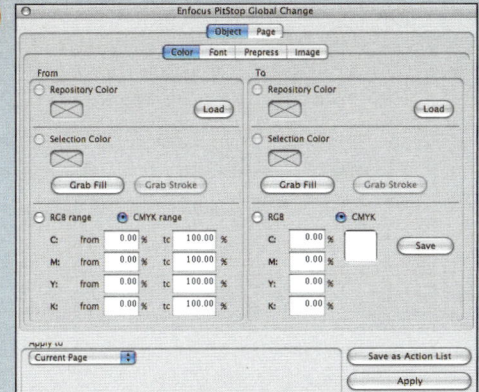

3

Click on the Select Objects tool

4

Click to select an object in the PDF file to be converted to a spot color. In the Enfocus PitStop Global Change dialog box, click on the From Selection Color radio button, then click Grab.

5

In the Enfocus PitStop Global Change dialog box, click Load in the To Repository Color section.

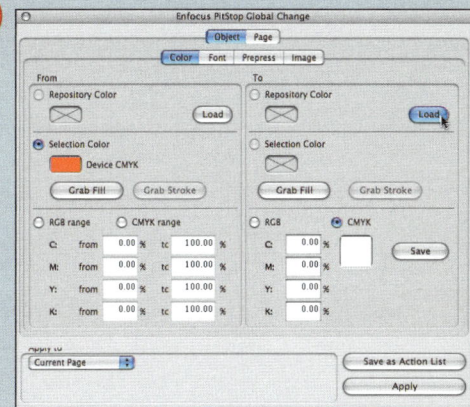

6

In the Color Picker dialog box, use the pull-down menu to select a color from the PANTONE® spot color library. Click OK.

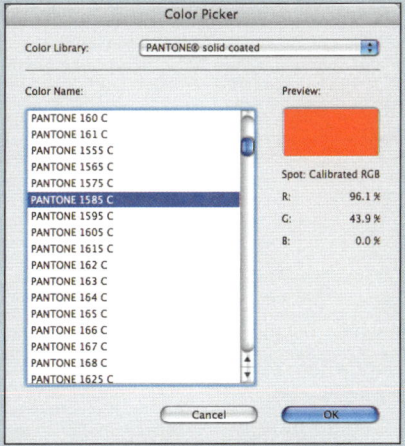

7

In the Enfocus PitStop Global Change dialog box, click Apply to convert the selected color to spot throughout the entire PDF.

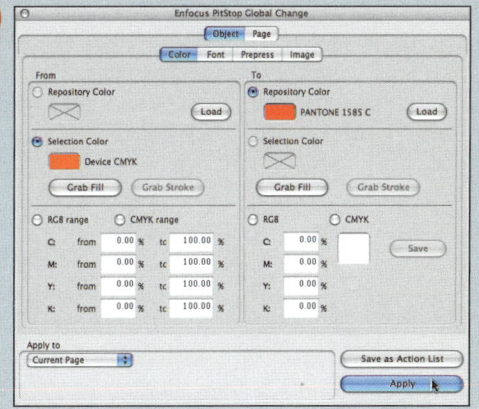

Problem: RGB Text or Graphics (When the Original Was Not RGB)

A frequently cited problem with PDF documents created for print production is that text that should be black-only ends up as RGB in the PDF file. Similarly, images that started out in the CMYK mode in the original layout are converted to the RGB color space in the PDF file. It happens with spot colors, too.

Why? The reason is that some applications (including Microsoft Office products) do not create their own PostScript on printing; rather, they depend on the driver to generate PostScript for them. The color included in files from these applications will be that of the operating system (GDI for Windows and QuickDraw for Mac OS 9.2 or earlier). The color model for GDI is RGB; hence, color output from applications that use the driver to create PostScript will be converted to the RGB color space. Applications that generate their own PostScript will not exhibit this same problem. These include Adobe Acrobat, Adobe PageMaker, Adobe Illustrator, Adobe InDesign, Adobe Photoshop, CorelDRAW, Corel Ventura Publisher, Macromedia FreeHand, and QuarkXPress.

It seems that more and more users of Microsoft Office products are attempting to use these applications for print production projects (certainly not something we recommend, but we can't deny that it is happening). PDF files created using Microsoft Office products will commonly contain RGB black text and images. Some output devices will automatically convert RGB objects to CMYK, so that in this case the black text will print on all four plates. This would make for a trapping disaster on press! The best way to handle conversion of RGB objects to the proper color space (black for text, CMYK for RGB objects) is to do so before the file hits the RIP. There are a number of ways to convert objects from one color space to another in Acrobat. The Acrobat native TouchUp Object tool can be used to open images into an image editor, or vector art and text into an illustration application, where color conversion can be done. Editing tools PitStop Pro or Quite A Box Of Tricks can be used as well. Here is an example of how RGB black text can be converted to black-only using Quite A Box Of Tricks.

1. In the Quite A Box Of Tricks Recolour Document dialog, select the Colours tab. Click the RGB Gone—All Colours to CMYK radio button. Click the Setup button.

2. In the Convert to CMYK Setup dialog, select *Convert* text and line art and *Treat R=G=B as Greyscale*. Click *OK*.

3. In the Recolour Document dialog, click *Apply*.

4. A message dialog indicating pages affected will appear.

5. Save the document.

IN THE TRENCHES

1

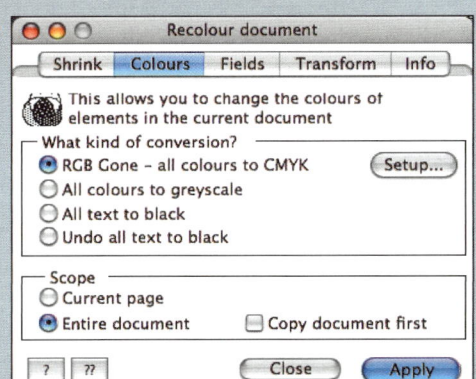

In the Quite A Box Of Tricks Recolour Document dialog, select the Colours tab. Click the RGB Gone—All Colours to CMYK radio button. Click the Setup button.

2

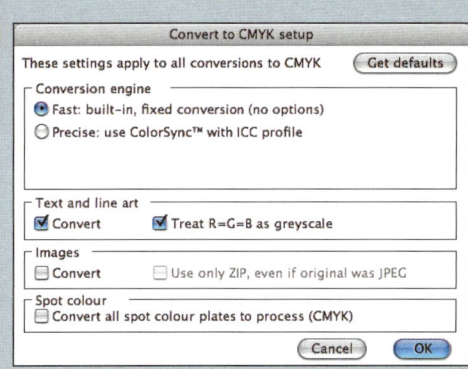

In the Convert to CMYK Setup dialog, select *Convert Text and line art* and *treat R=G=B as Greyscale*. Click *OK*.

3

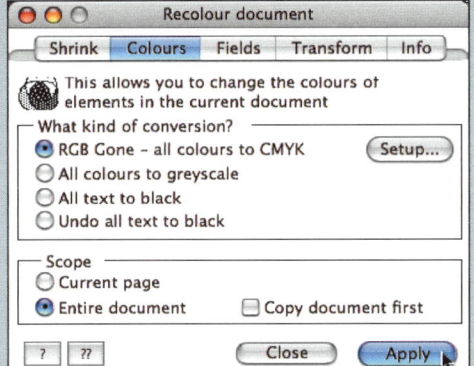

In the Recolour Document dialog, click *Apply*.

4

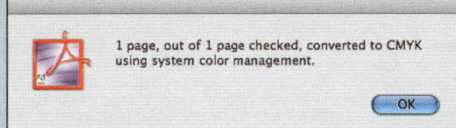

A message dialog indicating pages affected will appear.

Problem: RGB Text or Graphics (When the Original Was Not RGB —continued)

Most of the time, RGB black text that should be simply black is made up of equal amounts of red, green, and blue. The QABOT method of converting them relies on this (hence the distinction R=G=B). However, if color management was enabled within the application the PDF file was generated from, the RGB black text may come through as unequal amounts of RGB, making this QABOT method ineffective. In this case, Enfocus PitStop can be used to convert the equal RGB black into real black. Here's a simple way to do it using PitStop Global Change:

1. Using the PitStop Select Objects tool, select a text object with the unequal RGB color.

2. With the object still selected, switch to PitStop Global Change. Click the Object tab and then the Color tab.

3. On the From side, click the Grab Fill button under Selection Color. The RGB color should show up in the color preview window.

4. On the To side, click *CMYK* and key in 100% K. Click *Apply*.

5. The RGB black text will be converted to 100% black.

An alternate way to do this is to convert the color to 0% RGB instead of 100% K so that it will become R=G=B. Then run a PitStop Action or Preflight Profile that specifies RGB black be converted to gray. In this way, all RGB black or gray objects in the PDF file will be converted at the same time with the same method.

The problem of RGB black text generated from Windows applications can be prevented from happening in the first place simply by changing two default properties settings for the Distiller printer. Access Properties by right-clicking on the Distiller printer and go to the Graphics tab. Check the two boxes *Convert gray text to PostScript gray* and *Convert gray graphics to PostScript gray* and *Apply*. From this point, black text will show up as 100% gray in PDF files created via Distiller.

How about process-color images that should be CMYK but are RGB in the PDF file? Both QABOT and PitStop Pro provide easy methods to convert RGB image objects to CMYK. Both offer a means to do so with a built-in conversion method or via a user-specified ICC profile. The built-in algorithm offers the user no specific controls, and we've seen posts on any number of online forums complaining that the resultant CMYK color from PitStop Pro does not look good. Figure 6.14 shows an RGB test file and Figure 6.15 shows how it looks when converted to CMYK using the built-in PitStop algorithm. Colors tend to go very flat and muddy. Fortunately, PitStop Pro contains color management tools, so it's possible to make the conversion using an ICC profile for more acceptable results.

Figure 6.14. and 6.15. Conversion from RGB (left) to CMYK (right) using Pitstop Pro without an ICC profile.

1

Using the PitStop Select Objects tool, select a text object with the unequal RGB color.

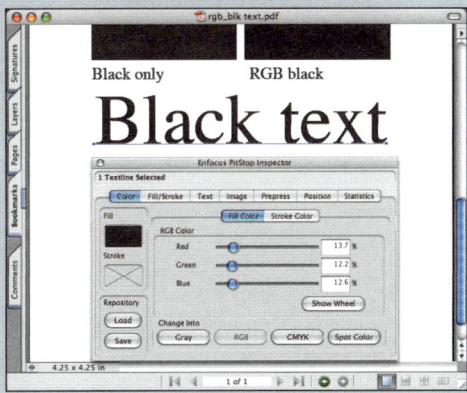

2

With the object still selected, switch to PitStop Global Change. Click the Object tab and then the Color tab.

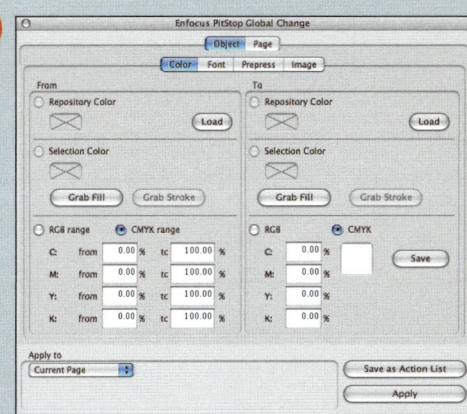

3

On the From side, click the Grab Fill button under Selection Color. The RGB color should show up in the color preview window.

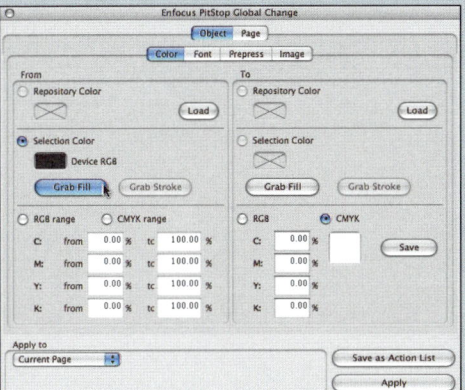

4

On the To side, click CMYK and key in 100% K. Click *Apply.*

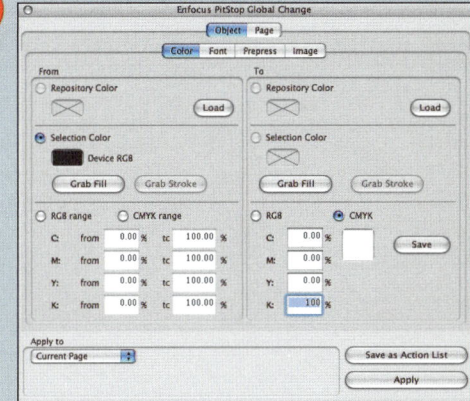

5

The RGB black text will be converted to 100% black.

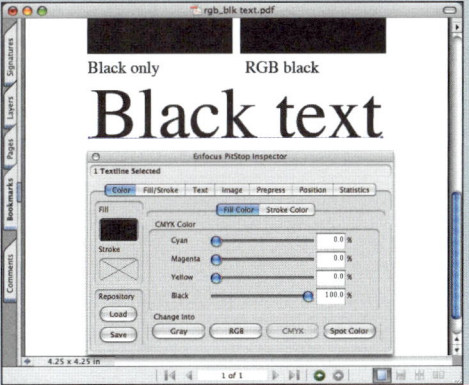

Problem: RGB Text or Graphics (When the Original Was Not RGB —continued)

Here's how to convert RGB graphics to CMYK using a specific ICC profile via Enfocus PitStop Pro's Preflight Panel.

1. To enable PitStop color management globally, access Enfocus PitStop Preferences (via *Acrobat>Preferences>Enfocus PitStop Professional)*, select the Color Management tab and check the Enable Color Management box. Select the default profiles you'd like to use for each color space. When color management is enabled in this way, the default profiles will be used for RGB to CMYK conversions with PitStop tools.

2. You can build actions to convert color from RGB to CMYK or set up a PitStop Preflight Profile to convert color using a particular profile. Access the PitStop Preflight Control Panel and create a new profile.

3. The Color Management window offers the same setup as the Color Management preferences window. Setting them here ensures that they will be used whenever this profile is run, even on another computer, so if you're building a profile to share with others, set up the default profiles to be used for color conversion, or ICC profile tagging, here.

4. In the Process Color window, check *Enable Process Color* and under Problems to Detect, check *RGB is used* and *Convert to CMYK.* You'll also want to check the options *RGB black (or gray) is used* and *Replace with real black (or gray).* This will take care of converting RGB text built of equal amounts of RGB into the gray equivalent.

5. Save the file, click the Checking tab, and *Create Report.* The preflighted file and RGB color will be converted using the profiles selected instead of the built-in algorithm.

1

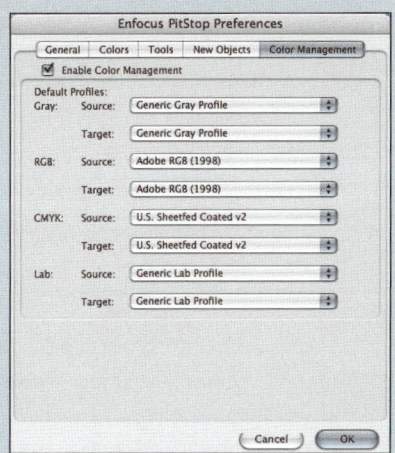

To enable PitStop color management globally, access Enfocus PitStop Preferences, select the Color Management tab, and check the Enable Color Management box.

2

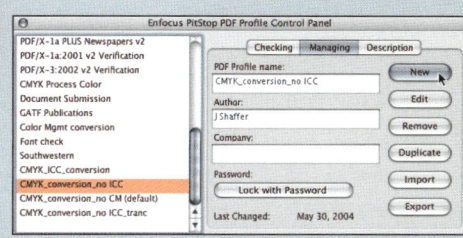

Access the PitStop Preflight Control Panel and create a new profile.

3

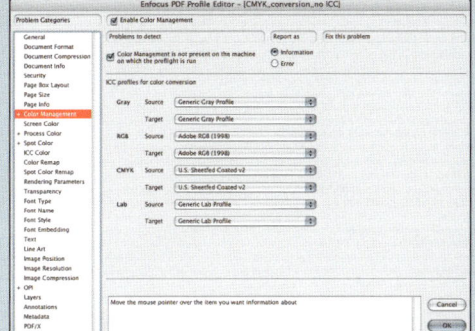

Setting color management options here ensures that the ICC profile chosen will be used whenever this PitStop profile is run, even on another computer.

4

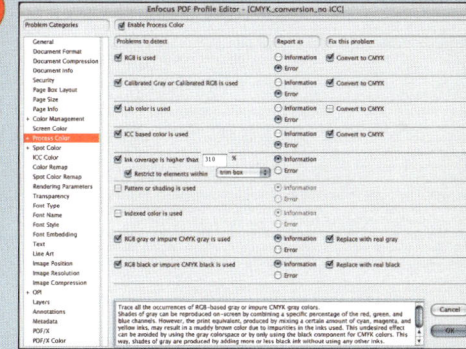

In the Process Color window, check *Enable Process Color,* and under Problems to Detect, check *RGB is used* and *Convert to CMYK.* Also, check the options *RGB black (or gray) is used* and *Replace with real black (or gray).*

5a

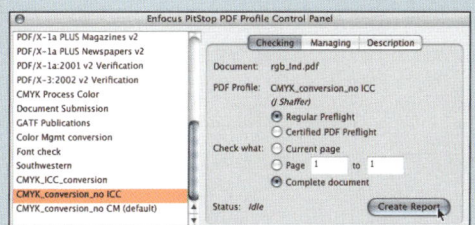

Save the file, click the Checking tab, and *Create Report.*

5b

The preflighted file and RGB color will be converted using the profiles selected instead of the built-in algorithm.

Problem: Font Not Embedded

One of the most common problems with PDF files is missing fonts. If fonts are not properly embedded in a PDF, the font will be substituted using Adobe Sans or Adobe Serif. Fonts will not be embedded in a PDF file for a variety of reasons. First, if the font was not active in the native application at the time of PostScript creation, the font will be missing from the PDF. Second, if Font Inclusion is not set to *All* in the PostScript settings dialog box, the font will be missing from the PDF. The last place for faulty font embedding can occur with improper Distiller settings. Remember, you should always choose to embed all fonts when distilling a PostScript file.

You can embed fonts using Acrobat alone or with PitStop Professional. To embed fonts with either application, you must have a copy of the font active on your system.

The following example illustrates how to embed a font using Adobe Acrobat.

1. To determine whether or not a font has been embedded in a PDF, select *File>Document Properties,* then select the Fonts option. In the Fonts Used in this Document list, determine which fonts have not been embedded in the PDF. Remember, fonts not embedded will use Adobe Sans MM or Adobe Serif MM as a substitute for the actual font (in our example, the font Helvetica Condensed is not embedded).

2. Next, activate the font(s) on your system to be embedded using Suitcase or some other font management software. Remember, when you activate a font you must quit out of Acrobat and restart in order for the font to be active in Acrobat.

3. Using the TouchUp Text tool, select the font in the PDF file that is not embedded.

4. Next, control-click and select *Properties...* from the pull-down menu. A TouchUp Properties dialog box appears.

5. In the TouchUp Properties dialog box, select the Text tab. Be sure that the font you want to embed is selected from the font pull-down menu, then click the Embed checkbox. Note that depending upon individual font licensing restrictions, the font may not be able to be embedded.

6. Now that the font has been embedded, save the PDF file.

Font Not Embedded

1

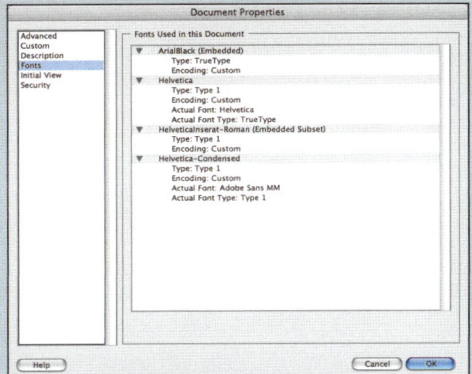

To determine whether or not a font has been embedded in a PDF, select *File>Document Properties,* then select the Fonts option.

2

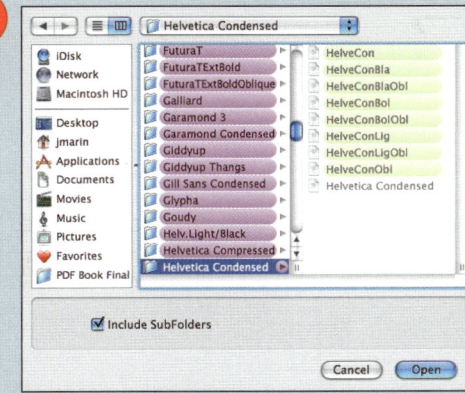

Activate the font(s) on your system to be embedded using Suitcase or some other font management software. Quit out of Acrobat and restart in order for the font to be active in Acrobat.

3

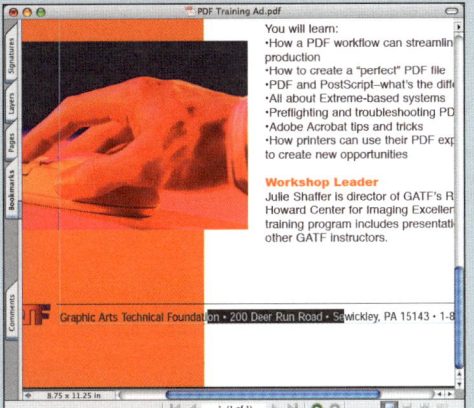

Using the TouchUp Text tool, select the font in the PDF file that is not embedded.

4

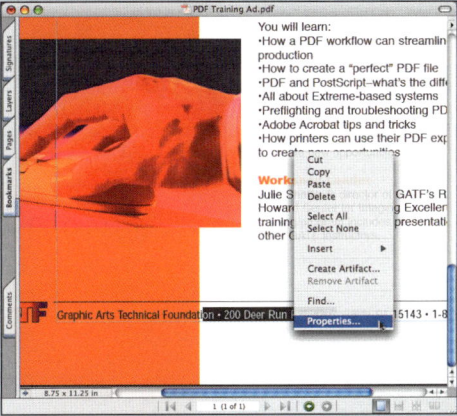

Control-click and select *Properties...* from the pull-down menu. A TouchUp Properties dialog box appears.

5

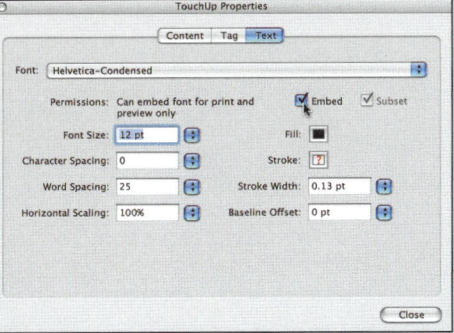

In the TouchUp Properties dialog box, select the Text tab. Be sure that the font you want to embed is selected from the font pull-down menu, then click the Embed checkbox.

Problem: Font Not Embedded (continued)

This next example illustrates how to embed a font using Enfocus PitStop Professional.

1. To determine whether a font has been embedded in a PDF, select *File>Document Properties,* then select the Fonts option. In the Fonts Used in this Document list, determine which fonts have not been embedded in the PDF. Remember, fonts not embedded will use Adobe Sans MM or Adobe Serif MM as a substitute for the actual font (in our example, the fonts HelveticaInserat-Roman and Anna are not embedded).

2. Next, activate the font(s) on your system to be embedded using Suitcase, Font Reserve, or some other font management software. Remember, when you activate a font you must quit out of Acrobat and restart in order for the font to be active in Acrobat.

3. Next, we'll create an Action List in PitStop Professional that will embed all missing fonts. Select *Window>Show PitStop Action List Panel.*

4. In the Enfocus PitStop Action List Control Panel, select the Managing tab.

5. In the Enfocus PitStop Action List Editor, click *Add.*

6. In the New Action Type dialog box, click the Selections tab and choose *Select Embedded Fonts* from the list. Click the Add button.

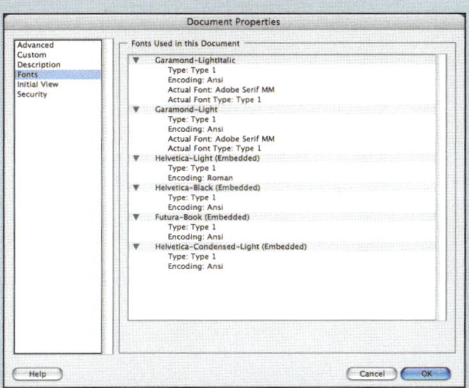

1 o determine whether a font as been embedded a PDF, select *ile>Document Properties,* then elect the Fonts ption.

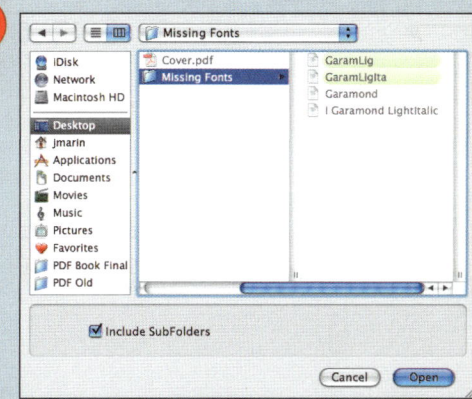

2 Activate the font(s) on your system to be embedded using Suitcase or some other font management soft-ware. Quit out of Acrobat and restart in order for the font to be active in Acrobat.

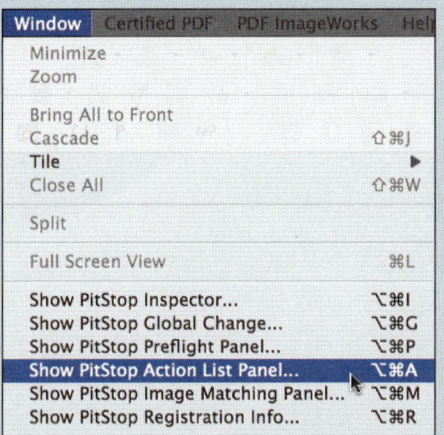

3 reate an Action ist in PitStop rofessional that ill embed all issing fonts. elect *Window> how PitStop ction List anel.*

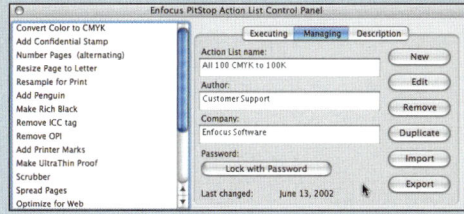

4 In the Enfocus PitStop Action List Control Panel, select the Managing tab.

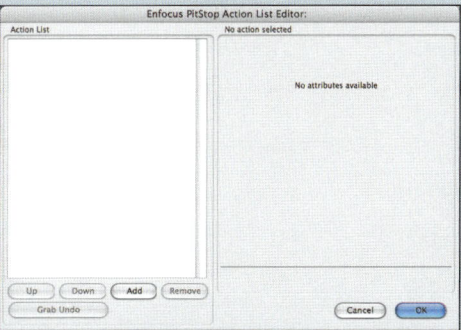

5 the Enfocus itStop Action st Editor, click *dd.*

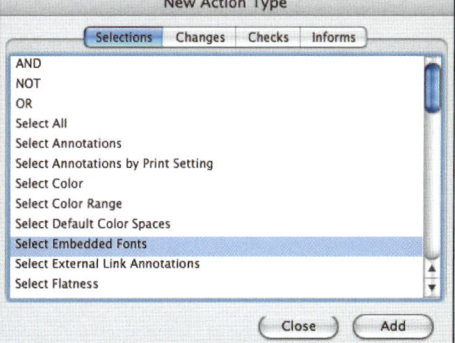

6 In the New Action Type dialog box, click the Selections tab and choose *Select Embedded Fonts* from the list. Click the Add button.

Problem: Font Not Embedded (continued)

7. In the New Action Type dialog box, click the Selections tab and choose *NOT* from the list. Click the Add button.

8. In the New Action Type dialog box, click the Changes tab and choose *Embed Font* from the list. Click the Add button. Click the Close button.

9. In the Enfocus PitStop Action List Editor, click *OK.*

10. In the Enfocus PitStop Action List Control Panel, select the Executing tab. Finally, click the Execute button to embed all missing fonts into the PDF.

The action you've just created can now be used to embed fonts into any PDF file. You can create more Action Lists of your own or download from an Action List library at www.enfocus.com.

7

In the New Action Type dialog box, click the Selections tab and choose *NOT* from the list. Click the Add button.

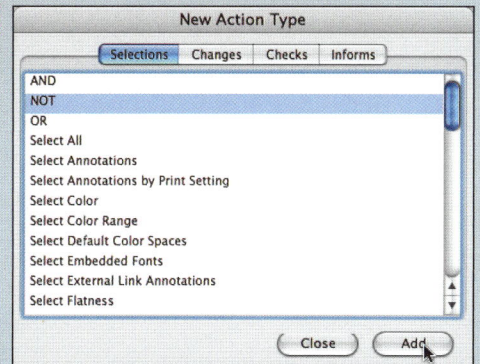

8

In the New Action Type dialog box, click the Changes tab and choose *Embed Font* from the list. Click the Add button. Click the Close button.

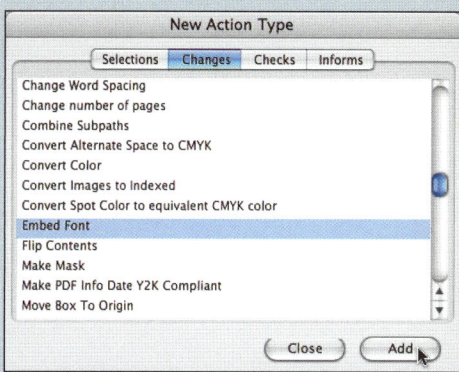

9

In the Enfocus PitStop Action List Editor, click *OK*.

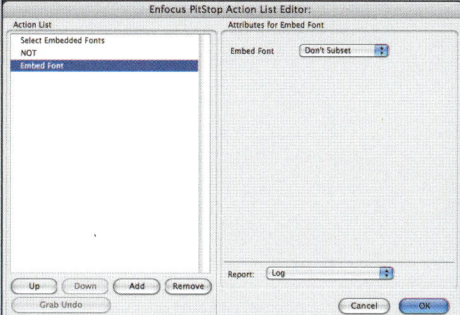

10

In the Enfocus PitStop Action List Control Panel, select the Executing tab. Click the Execute button to embed all missing fonts into the PDF.

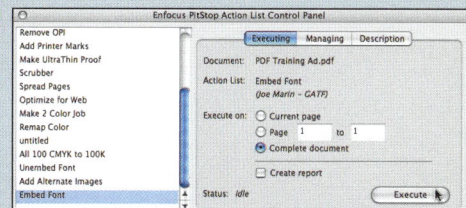

Problem: Converting an Image to a Duotone

As previously discussed, converting images from one color space to another (such as RGB to CMYK or grayscale) can be accomplished quite easily using Acrobat's TouchUp Object tool. But what if you have to convert an image to a duotone? An image can be extracted from a PDF using the TouchUp Object tool and converted to a duotone in Photoshop easily. The problem is saving the duotone back into the PDF from Photoshop...it cannot be done! The only option is to save that duotone to your hard drive as an image file.

The following example shows how to convert an image to a duotone using standard Acrobat tools.

1. Select the TouchUp Object tool. Option double-click on the image to be converted to a duotone.

2. If the image is in color, convert it to grayscale in Photoshop by selecting *Image>Mode>Grayscale*. Then convert the grayscale image to a duotone by selecting *Image>Mode>Duotone*.

3. In the Duotone Options dialog box, change *Monotone* to *Duotone* from the pull-down menu, then specify a spot color.

4. Select *File>Save As* and choose *Photoshop PDF* as the file format.

5. Using the TouchUp Object tool, click on the image in the PDF to be replaced with the duotone image.

6. Open the duotone image in Acrobat. Using the TouchUp Object tool, click on the duotone and select *Edit>Copy*.

7. Go back to the PDF file where the duotone will be placed. Select *Edit>Paste*.

8. Save the document.

1 Select the TouchUp Object tool. Option double-click on the image to be converted to a duotone.

Converting an Image to a Duotone

2

the image is
color, convert
to grayscale in
hotoshop by
electing *Image>
Mode>Grayscale*.

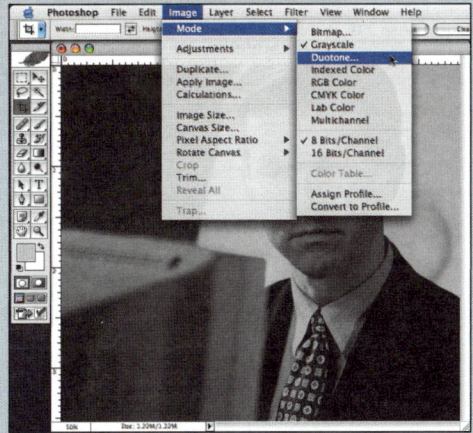

3

In the Duotone
Options dialog
box, change
Monotone to
Duotone from
the pull-down
menu, then specify
a spot color.

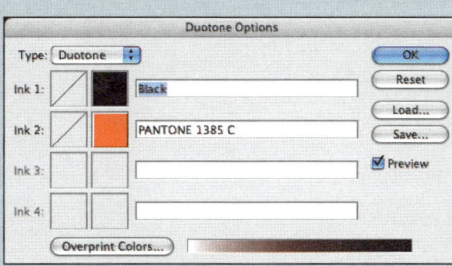

4

elect *File>Save
s* and choose
Photoshop PDF
s the file format.

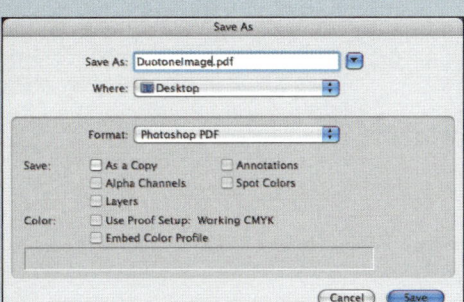

5

Using the TouchUp
Object tool, click
on the image in
the PDF to be
replaced with the
duotone image.

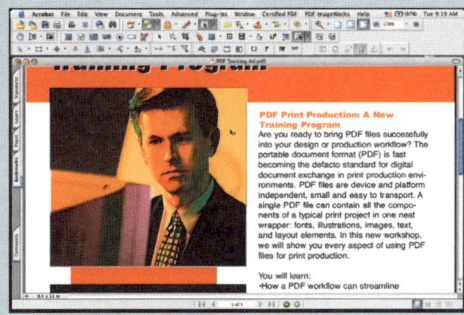

6

pen the duotone
mage in Acrobat.
sing the TouchUp
bject tool, click
n the duotone
d select *Edit>
opy*.

7

Go back to the
PDF file where
the duotone will
be placed. Select
Edit>Paste.

Problem: Change the Colors within a Duotone

It is possible to change either color that makes up a duotone image without taking the image out to Photoshop via the TouchUp Object Edit Image option—as long as you have access to Enfocus PitStop. Here's how.

1. Select the duotone image you wish to change with the PitStop Selection Tool and launch the PitStop Inspector.

2. Click the Image tab and then the Remap tab. Both colors that make up the duotone will show up in the window under Remap Spot Colors. Select the color that you wish to change.

3. Under *Remap to*, you have the option to remap the color to another one from the document or from the PitStop Color Repository. Select a color and click *Apply*.

4. The old color is replaced by the new.

1

Select the duotone image you wish to change with the PitStop Selection Tool and launch the PitStop Inspector.

2

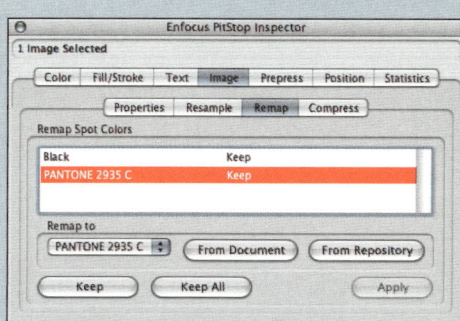

Click the Image tab and then the Remap tab. Both colors that make up the duotone will show up in the window under Remap Spot Colors. Select the color that you wish to change.

3

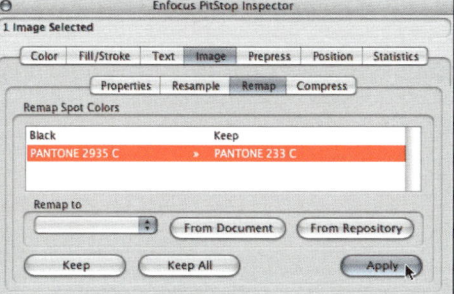

Under *Remap to,* you have the option to remap the color to another one from the document or from the PitStop Color Repository. Select color and click *Apply.*

4

The old color is replaced by the new.

Problem: Editing an Entire Paragraph I

Text does not flow in a PDF file like in other desktop publishing applications such as QuarkXPress or InDesign. Because of this, editing an entire paragraph of text in a PDF file can be a difficult task. Typically, going back to the native application to edit the paragraph and re-saving the page is the fastest method. But if you don't have access to the native application, there are a few ways to edit a paragraph in a PDF file. The most accurate method is to reset the paragraph in a page layout application, save it as a PDF, then copy and paste the new paragraph into the PDF file. In a pinch, you can also try to use Enfocus PitStop Professional's Edit Paragraph tool or Acrobat's Text Box tool.

The following example shows how to edit a paragraph of text in a PDF file using Acrobat's TouchUp Object tool.

1. In another desktop publishing application (we'll use QuarkXPress in our example), set a new paragraph of text using the correct font, size, etc. Be sure that the paragraph's box size is the same size as the paragraph being replaced in the PDF file. Save the document as a PDF.

2. Select the TouchUp Object tool.

3. Open the PDF with the new text. Click to select the text box. Select *Edit>Copy*.

4. Open the PDF where the new text is to be placed. Select *Edit>Paste*.

5. Select the TouchUp Text tool.

6. Select and delete the old text from the PDF.

7. Using the TouchUp Object tool, position the new paragraph of text on the page.

8. Save the document.

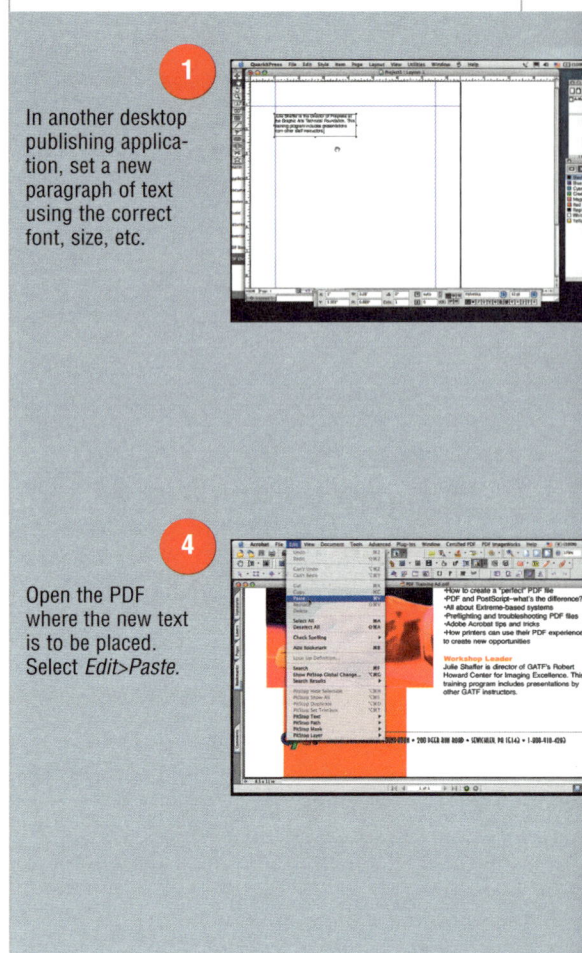

1

In another desktop publishing application, set a new paragraph of text using the correct font, size, etc.

4

Open the PDF where the new text is to be placed. Select *Edit>Paste*.

2

Select the TouchUp
Object tool.

3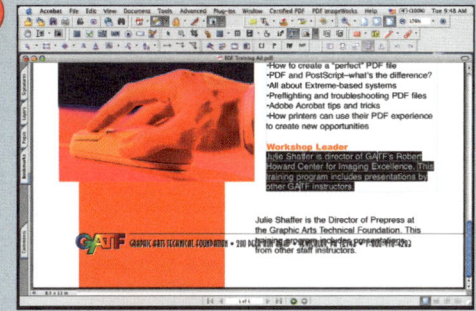

Open the PDF
with the new text.
Click to select the
text box. Select
Edit>Copy.

Julie... ...is the...Director of Prepress at
the G...chnical Foundation. This
train......ludes presentations
from......uctors.

5

Select the TouchUp
Text tool.

6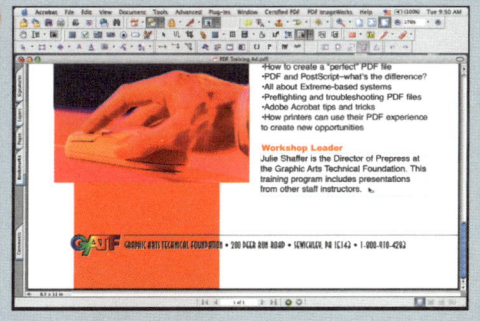

Select and delete
the old text from
the PDF.

7

Using the TouchUp
Object tool, position
the new paragraph
of text on the page.

8

Save the
document.

Problem: Editing an Entire Paragraph II

The following example illustrates editing an entire paragraph using Enfocus PitStop Professional.

1. The font you wish to edit must be installed on your computer. If you activate the font using Suitcase or some other font management software, you must quit and restart Acrobat for the font to be available.

2. Select the Edit Paragraph tool.

3. Click and drag to select the paragraph of text you wish to edit, and begin to add new text.

4. After you've finished editing the paragraph, save the document.

Editing an Entire Paragraph II

1

To edit a font, it must be installed on your computer. If you activate the font using Suitcase or some other font management software, you must quit and restart Acrobat for the font to be available.

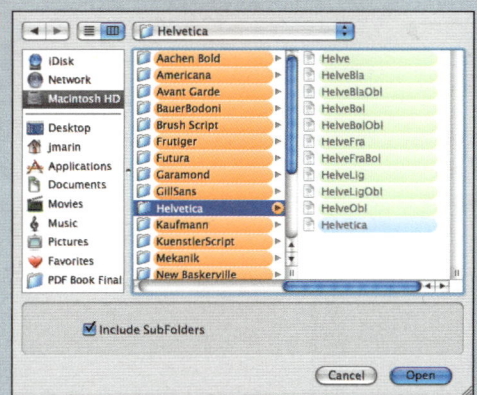

2

Select the Edit Paragraph tool.

3

Click and drag to select the paragraph of text you wish to edit, and begin to add new text.

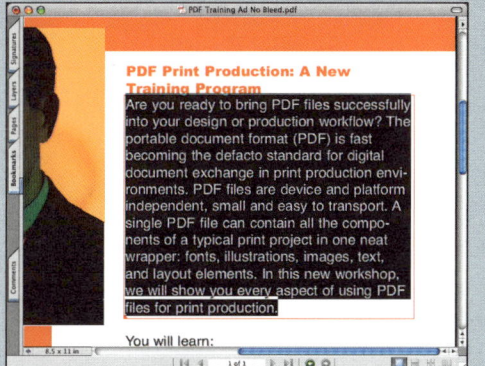

4

After you've finished editing the paragraph, save the document.

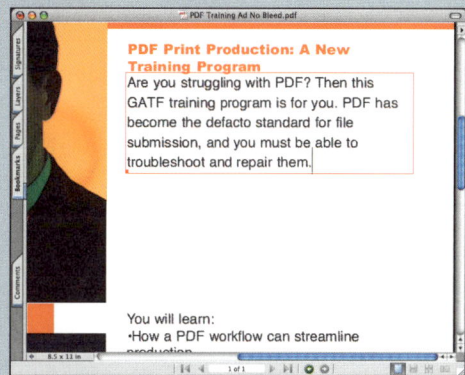

Problem: Editing an Entire Paragraph III

The following example shows how to edit a paragraph of text in a PDF file using Acrobat's Text Box tool.

1. Select the Text Box tool.

2. Draw a box on the page to the approximate size of the paragraph to be replaced.

3. In the box you've drawn, type in text for the new paragraph.

4. Select the Hand tool.

5. Select *View>Toolbars>Properties Bar.*

6. Click and drag to select all of the new text. Using the Text Box Text Properties toolbar, specify the font, size, and alignment for the text.

7. Deselect the text and click on the handles of the box containing the new text. Using the Text Box Text Properties toolbar, select an appropriate fill color for the text and box. If no line is necessary for the box, set the thickness to 0 pt.

8. Using the Hand tool, position the new paragraph over the old one.

9. Because the FreeText tool is a comment tool, you have to remember to check the Comments box in the Print dialog box.

10. Save the document.

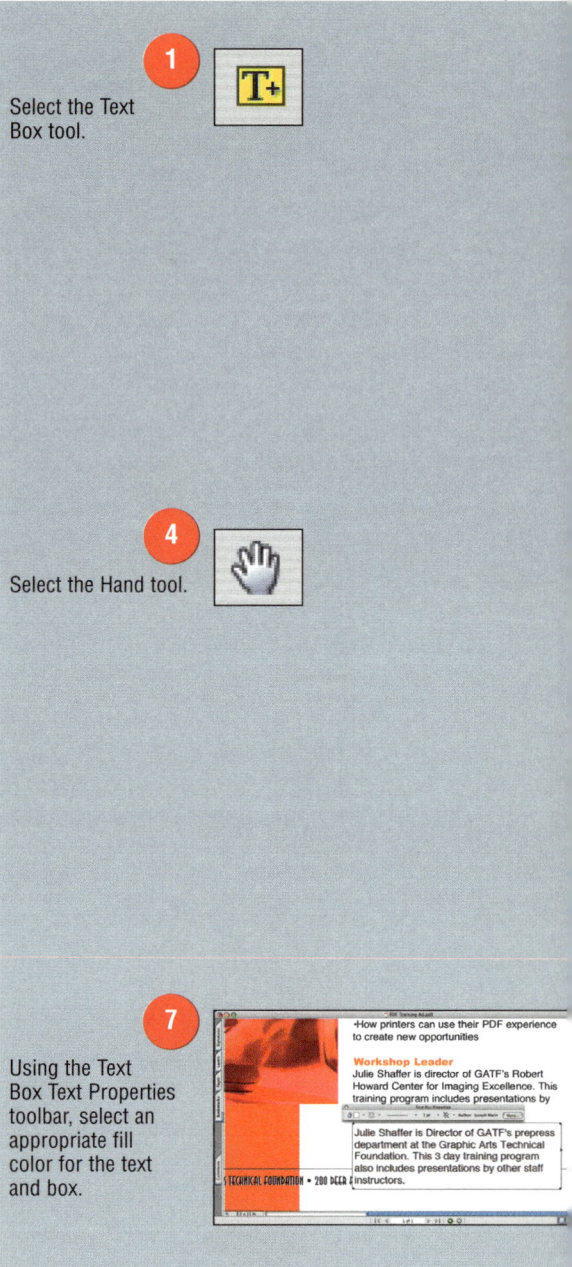

1 Select the Text Box tool.

4 Select the Hand tool.

7 Using the Text Box Text Properties toolbar, select an appropriate fill color for the text and box.

Editing an Entire Paragraph III

2

Draw a box on the page to the approximate size of the paragraph to be replaced.

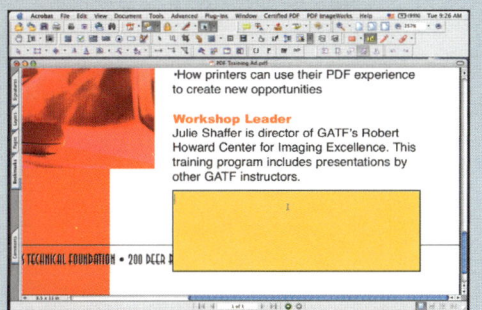

3

In the box you've drawn, type in text for the new paragraph.

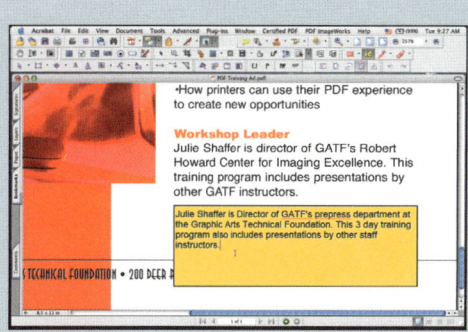

5

Select *View> Toolbars> Properties Bar.*

6

Click and drag to select all of the new text. Using the Text Box Text Properties toolbar, specify the font, size, and alignment for the text.

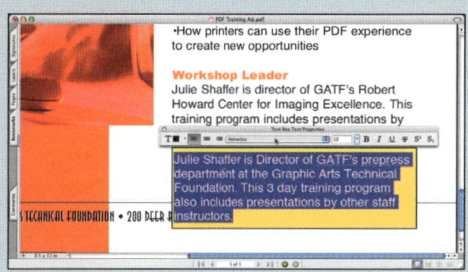

8

Using the Hand tool, position the new paragraph over the old one.

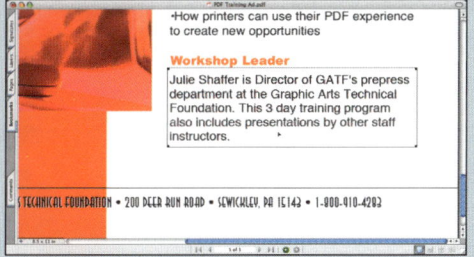

9

Because the FreeText tool is a comment tool, you have to remember to check the Comments box in the Print dialog box.

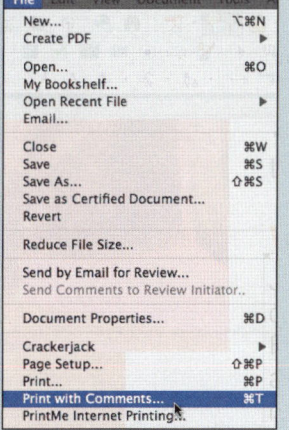

Problem: Converting Multiple PostScript Files to a Single PDF Document

What do you do if you have a lot of existing PostScript files that you'd like to convert into a single, multi-page PDF document? You could Distill each file individually and then use the Document>Insert Pages option in Acrobat to create the multi-page PDF document. This is ponderous, however, and if the individual PDF files contain embedded font subsets, the resultant combined PDF file will contain multiple copies of the same base font.

There is an easier way to combine multiple PostScript files into a single PDF document by using the Create PDF option found in Acrobat. This tool will allow you to select multiple PostScript (or other compatible) files that can be ordered, then converted to PDF via Distiller.

1. Since Distiller is used to create the PDF, the first thing to do is select the Adobe PDF Settings you wish to use to create the PDF.

2. In Acrobat, select *File>Create PDF>From Multiple Files*.

3. In the Create PDF from Multiple Documents section, click *Choose*.

4. Navigate your hard drive to the files to be converted to PDF, click on the files (hold the Shift key to select multiple files), and click *Add*.

5. In the Create Multiple Documents dialog box, you can arrange the order by clicking on the file and moving it up or down the list.

6. Click *OK* to convert the multiple files to a single PDF.

Converting Multiple PostScript Files

1

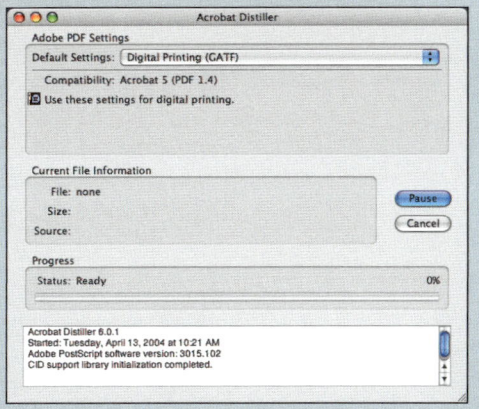

Since Distiller is used to create the PDF, the first thing to do is select the Adobe PDF Settings you wish to use to create the PDF.

2

In Acrobat, select *File>Create PDF>From Multiple Files.*

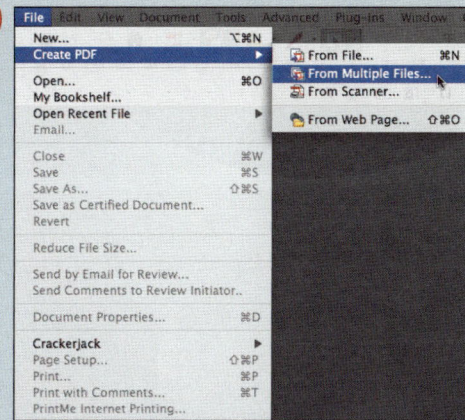

3

In the Create PDF from Multiple Documents section, click *Choose*.

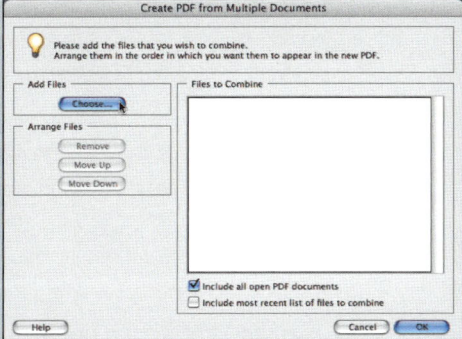

4

Navigate your hard drive to the files to be converted to PDF, click on the files (hold the Shift key to select multiple files), and click *Add*.

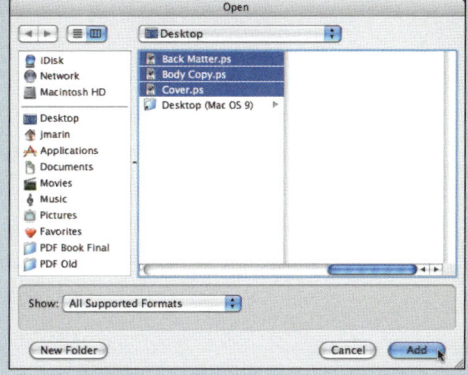

5

In the Create Multiple Documents dialog box, arrange the order by clicking on the file and moving it up or down the list.

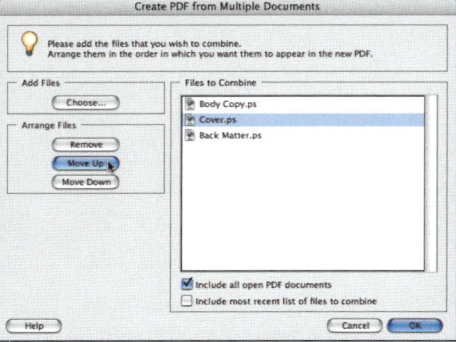

6

Click *OK* to convert the multiple files to a single PDF.

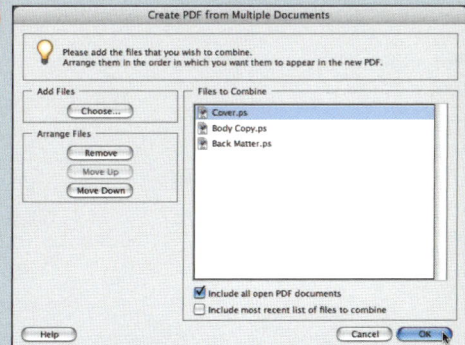

Problem: Images Draw Slowly in PDF

Have you ever noticed that PDF files that contain many large images can take a long time to render on screen? Every time you zoom in, zoom out, or go to the next page in a PDF, you're waiting, waiting, waiting, and not being very productive. Fortunately, Enfocus PitStop Professional has a feature that allows images to draw on screen much more quickly. Here's how it's done.

1. Select *Window>Show PitStop Action List Panel*.

2. In the Enfocus PitStop Action List Panel, select the Managing tab. Next, click *New*.

3. In the Enfocus PitStop Action Editor, click *Add*.

4. In the New Action Type dialog, select the Changes tab, then select *Add Alternate Images* from the list. Click *Add*.

5. In the Enfocus PitStop Action Editor, you can designate an image resolution for images to draw on screen. Keep in mind that the resolution you choose will not downsample images in the PDF file for printing, only for viewing. Click *OK*.

6. Open a PDF file that has many large image files. In the Enfocus PitStop Action List Panel, select the Executing tab. To add alternate images for faster screen drawing in a PDF, click *Execute*.

Images Draw Slowly in PDF

Select *Window>
Show PitStop
Action List Panel.*

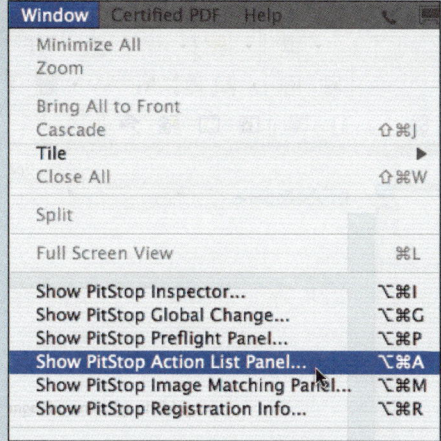

In the Enfocus
PitStop Action
List Panel, select
the Managing tab.
Next, click *New.*

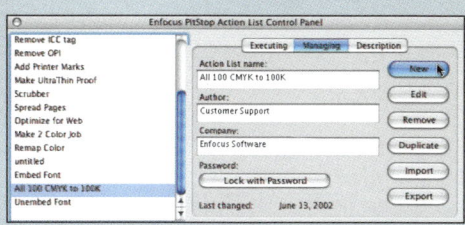

In the Enfocus
PitStop Action
Editor, click *Add.*

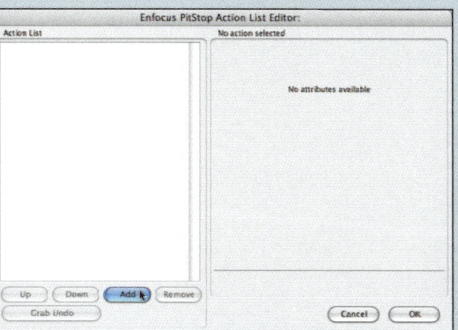

In the New
Action Type dialog,
select the Changes
tab, then select
*Add Alternate
Images* from the
list. Click *Add.*

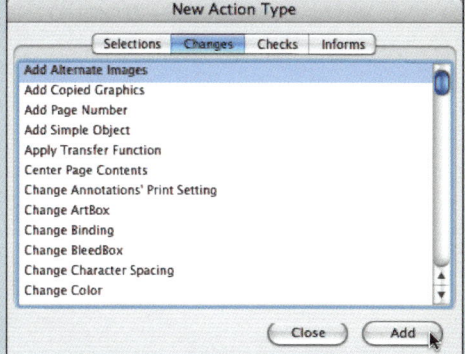

In the Enfocus
PitStop Action
Editor, designate
an image resolution
for images to draw
on screen.

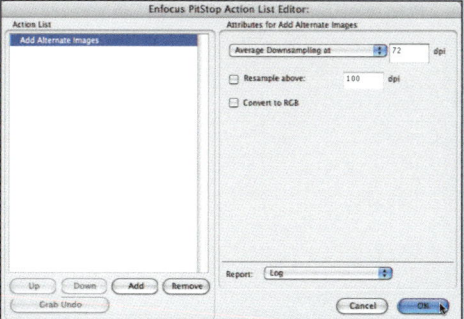

In the Enfocus
PitStop Action
List Panel, select
the Executing tab.
To add alternate
images for faster
screen drawing in
a PDF, click *Execute.*

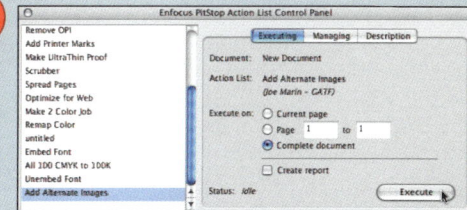

Problem: Images Draw Slowly in PDF (continued)

Now that the alternate images have been created, there is one more thing you must do in order to take advantage of them. You must set up your PitStop Professional preferences to use alternate images when they are available in the PDF.

7. Select *Acrobat>Preferences>Enfocus PitStop Professional.*

8. In the General tab, make sure that *Speedup image display using alternates (when available)* is selected. Click *OK.*

9. Zoom in and out of the PDF, notice how much more quickly the images redraw on screen. Remember, you have not made the images in the PDF file a lower resolution, only the on-screen preview of that image is lower resolution.

7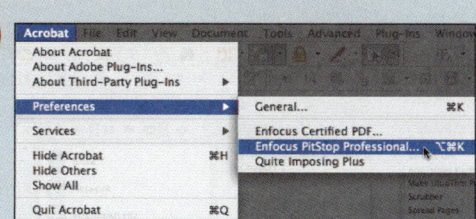

Select *Acrobat>
Preferences>
Enfocus PitStop
Professional*.

8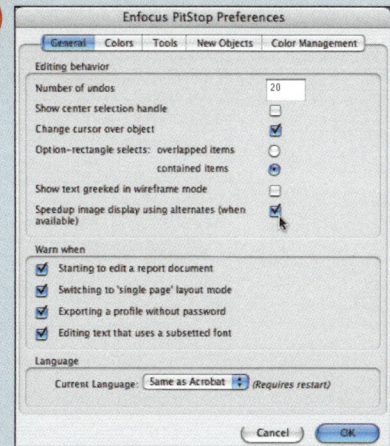

In the General
tab, make sure
that *Speedup
image display
using alternates
(when available)* is
selected. Click *OK*.

Solution: Creating a PDF/X-1a-compliant PDF File

As we discussed earlier in this book, the ISO-certified standard, PDF/X, is a way to eliminate many of the most common problems with PDF files. If a PDF file is created to meet the PDF/X-1:2001 standard, for example, needed fonts cannot be missing because in order to comply with the specification, fonts must be embedded in the file.

To make a PDF/X-compliant PDF file you can create one with Acrobat Distiller, or if you already have a PDF, you can create one using Acrobat. Acrobat's Preflight tool has a PDF/X1-a (and a PDF/X3) verification and creation profile. The verification profile can be used to determine if a PDF is PDF/X-compliant, and the creation tool allows you to create a PDF/X-compliant file from an existing PDF. Here's how to create a PDF/X1-a-compliant file:

1. Open a PDF file that you wish to save with PDF/X compliance in Acrobat. Select *Document> Preflight.*

2. In the Preflight Profiles dialog box, select *PDF/X.*

3. In the Preflight PDF/X dialog box, select *Use PDF/X1-a Specification* from the pull-down menu at the top. Next, click the Save as PDF/X1-a button.

4. Next, an ICC printer profile must be attached to the PDF. The profile you choose here will not change the color in the PDF, but a profile is required for PDF/X1-a compliance. Select a profile and click *Save.*

5. If the PDF passes the PDF/X-compliance check, you will see a dialog box with a green "passed" button. If the PDF fails to meet compliancy, you will get a dialog with a red "failed" button as in our example. Next, click the Report button to see why the PDF failed to meet compliancy.

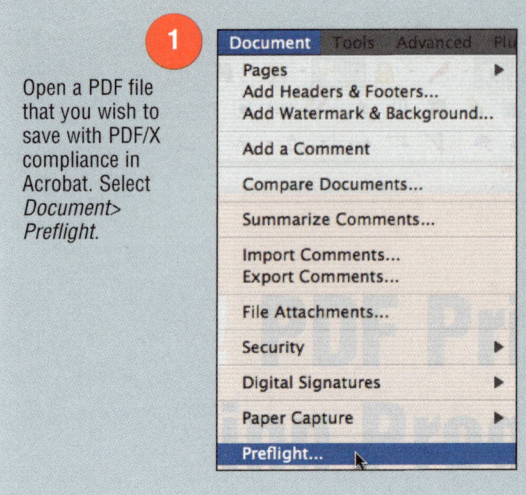

1
Open a PDF file that you wish to save with PDF/X compliance in Acrobat. Select *Document> Preflight.*

6. In the Preflight Results dialog, we can see that the PDF failed because of an RGB image. To fix this, we'll have to convert the image to CMYK and repeat steps 1 through 5.

7. Once the image has been converted to CMYK, the PDF can now be made to meet PDF/X1-a compliance.

2

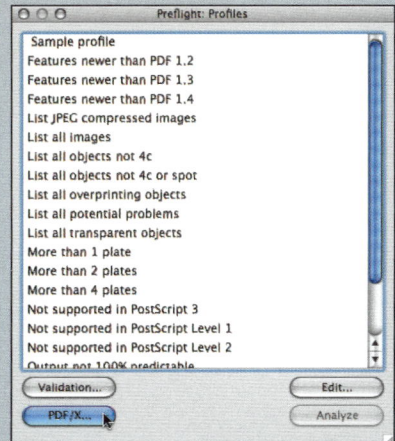

the Preflight
Profiles dialog
box, select *PDF/X.*

3

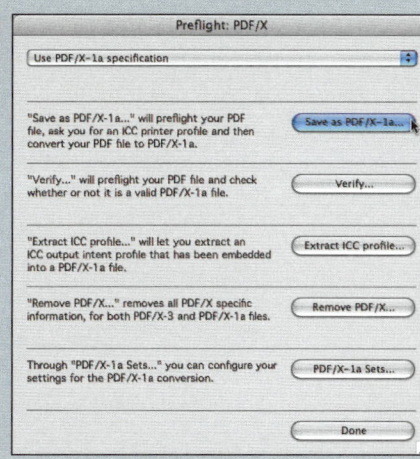

In the Preflight
PDF/X dialog box,
select *Use PDF/X1-a
Specification* from
the pull-down menu
at the top. Click the
Save as PDF/X1-a
button.

4

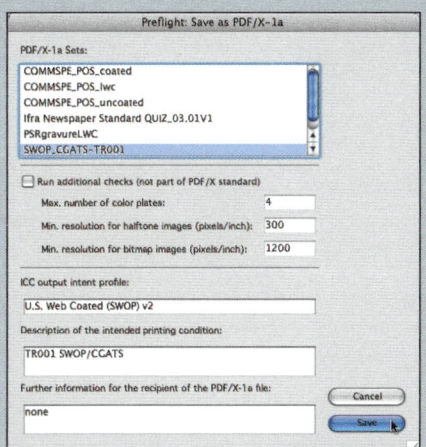

ttach an ICC
rinter profile
o the PDF.

5

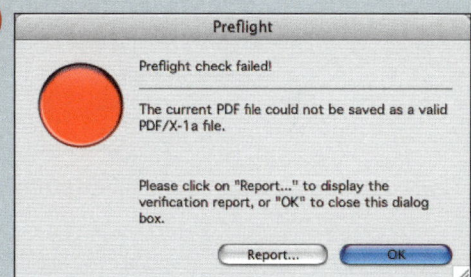

If the PDF passes
the PDF/X-
compliance check,
you will see a dialog
box with a green
"passed" button.
If the PDF fails to
meet compliancy,
you will get a dialog
with a red "failed"
button as in our
example.

6

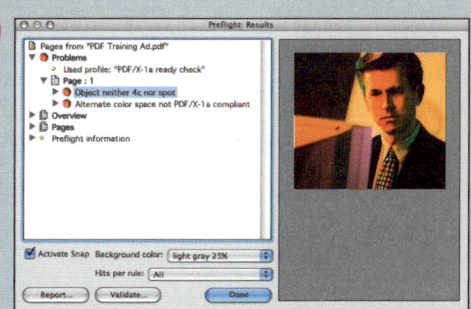

the Preflight
esults dialog,
e can see that
e PDF failed
ecause of an
GB image. To fix
is, we'll have to
onvert the image
CMYK and repeat
teps 1 through 5.

7

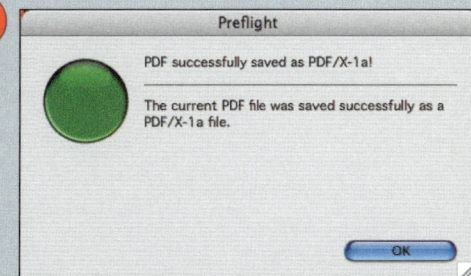

Once the image
has been converted
to CMYK, the PDF
can now be made
to meet PDF/X-1a
compliance.

Solution: Create Traps in a PDF File Using Enfocus PitStop Pro

Because PitStop offers a way to manipulate vector objects in a PDF file, it can be used to create traps for certain types of objects in a PDF file. This is somewhat akin to the way one can trap objects in Adobe Illustrator by creating a stroke to the desired trap thickness on a vector object and setting that stroke to overprint. Here is how to do this using PitStop Pro tools in Acrobat.

1. With the PitStop Select Object tool, select the object to be trapped with an overprinting stroke. This should launch the PitStop Inspector. If it doesn't, launch the Inspector.

2. Select the Fill/Stroke tab and click the On radio button for Stroke. This will create a stroke on the object.

3. The stroke will be black by default. To make it the same color as the object, click the Color tab and select the Load button to add the object's fill color to the Repository.

4. Now that the stroke has been assigned a color, select the Stroke tab again, and key in a thickness for the stroke you've created in the Weight field. Remember the stroke thickness should be twice the trap needed. Standard trapping for offset printing is 0.25 pt.

5. Select the Prepress tab. A new set of tabs will appear; select *Overprint* from this group. To the left side of the dialog box, you will see two windows showing the fill and stroke colors. Click the button beside the Stroke window and choose an Overprint Mode.

6. Make sure that Overprint Preview is on, and zoom in to take a look at the newly created trap. Traps will be part of the PDF file once it's been saved.

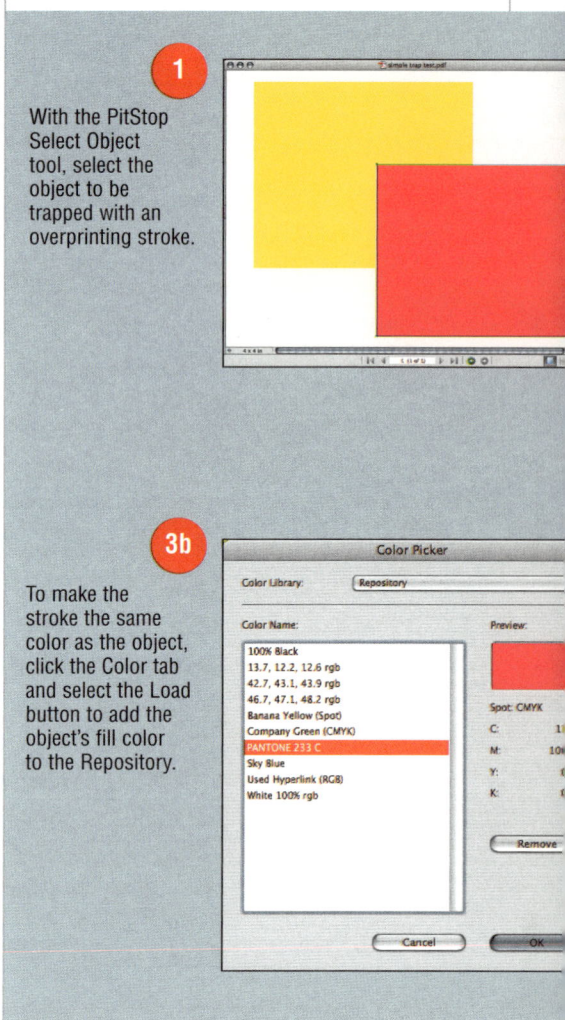

1 With the PitStop Select Object tool, select the object to be trapped with an overprinting stroke.

3b To make the stroke the same color as the object, click the Color tab and select the Load button to add the object's fill color to the Repository.

2

elect the Fill/
troke tab and
ick the On radio
utton for Stroke.

3a

The stroke will be
black by default.

3c

nce the fill color
as been added to
e repository, load
e color and assign
to the stroke.

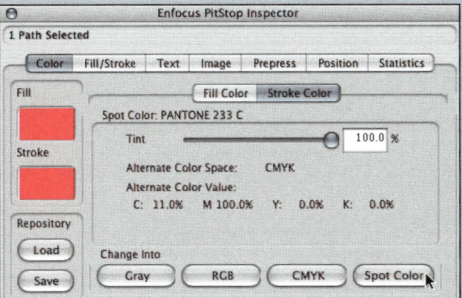

4

Now that the
stroke has been
assigned a color,
select the Stroke
tab again, and key
in a thickness for
the stroke you've
created in the
Weight field.

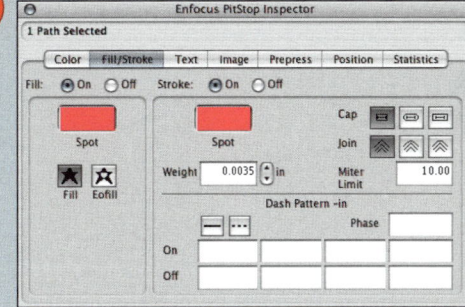

5

elect the Prepress
b, then the
verprint tab.
ick the button
eside the Stroke
indow and choose
Overprint Mode.

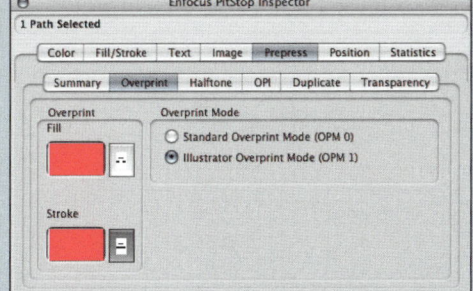

6

Make sure that
Overprint Preview
is on, and zoom in
to take a look at the
newly created trap.

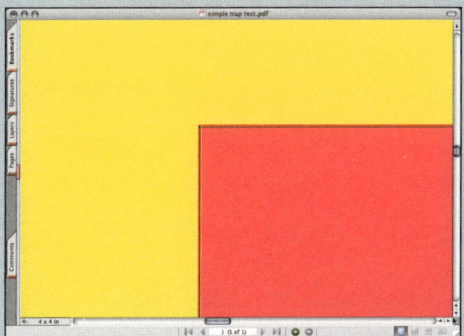

Problem: PDF File from Illustrator Is Wrong Size

We've had a number of folks write and ask us why a PDF file they received had extra white space (sometimes many inches' worth) on either side of the live copy area (Figure 6.16). Invariably, these PDF files were created from Adobe Illustrator files that contained large objects within a clipping mask. The PDF is made to the bounding box of the largest object on the page. PDF files with this problem can be cropped or resized using editing tools in Acrobat. Here's how to prevent it from happening in the first place.

1. From within Illustrator, select all objects so you can see anything that may exist outside of the live area.

2. Create a box to the size you wish the final PDF file to be. Set it to have no color or fill, and position it so that all of the objects on the document are inside of it. Align precisely, as this will be the bounding area of the final PDF file. With this box selected, choose *Crop Area>Make* from the Object menu.

3. Save the PDF file. The crop area has defined the page size, and the resultant PDF file will be the correct size.

Figure 6.16. A PDF file with way too much white space was probably created from an Adobe Illustrator file containing one or more large objects within a clipping mask.

PDF File from Illustrator Is Wrong Size

1

Illustrator, select objects so you n see anything at may exist tside of the e area.

2

Create a box to the size you wish the final PDF file to be.

3

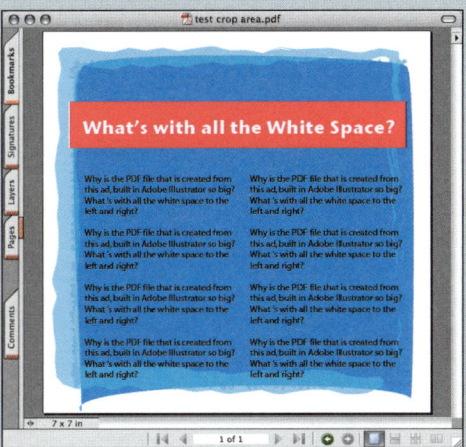

ve the PDF file. e crop area has fined the page ze, and the sultant PDF file ll be the correct ze.

Solution: Create Composite, Trapped PDF files from InDesign CS

When Adobe released InDesign CS, they really put some thought into making sure it was a great tool for print production. PDF files created with InDesign CS can be fully trapped using a trapping engine built right into the application. It will even trap placed PDF files, including PDF files that come from QuarkXPress (it will create traps based on the InDesign trapping engine, but will not retain Quark traps). This option, in addition to InDesign's ability to include high-resolution data for DCS images in composite PDF files, almost makes up for some of the production problems they introduced with other options, like transparency.

Traps will only be included in PDF files that are created by printing PostScript from the Print dialog and then submitting the PostScript file to Acrobat Distiller. It does not work for PDF files created via the Export option in InDesign. There are a few more specific caveats: placed EPS graphics will not be trapped with built-in trapping, and any text, paths, and frames created in InDesign won't trap correctly if they overlap a frame containing a placed graphic that built-in trapping won't trap. There are also some

issues with trapping of TrueType fonts. Adobe recommends that to avoid problems, you can convert TrueType fonts to outlines within InDesign. Built-in trapping is very memory-intensive, so you will need to have a lot of disk space available.

Since you may often use the same trapping for many projects, it is a good idea to create a trapping preset before trapping an individual job.

1. Choose *Window>Trap Presets* (Figure: 6.17.). Choose *New Preset* in the palette menu to create a preset, or double-click to edit an existing one.

• **Name**—Type a name for the preset. The [Default] trap preset cannot be renamed.

• **Trap Width**—Enter a width up to 4 points. A standard trap amount is 0.25 pt.

• **Trap Appearance**—Specify options for controlling join and end styles. Miter is the way the Adobe Trapping Engine has traditionally handled join areas.

• **Images**—Specify settings that determine how to trap imported bitmap images. A trap placement of center usually works well. If you have only four-color images, you may not want to select *Trap Images to*

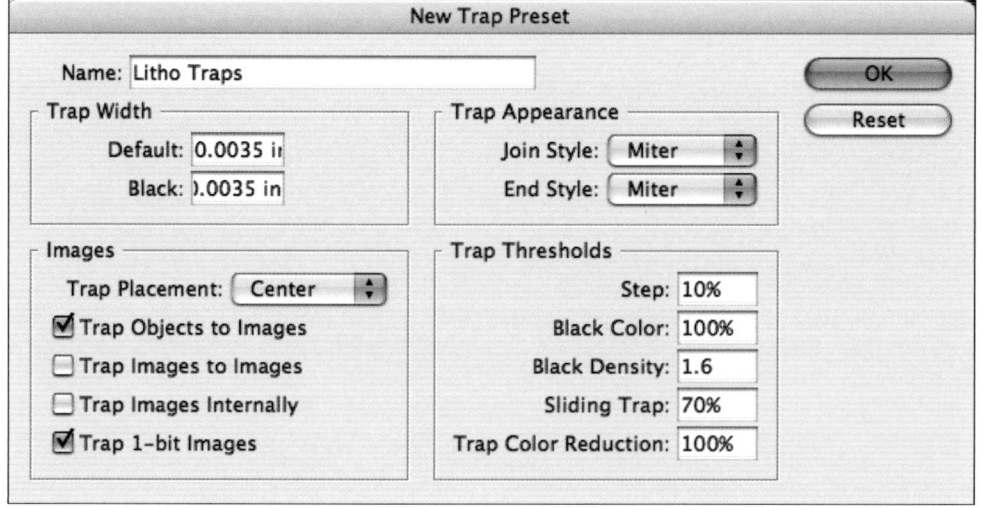

Figure 6.17. The Trap Preset window contains options required to refine how InDesign will set traps in a file.

Images. You will typically not want to choose the Trap Images Internally option.

• **Trap Thresholds**—These values determine the conditions under which trapping occurs.

- *Step* determines how different adjacent colors must be before they're trapped. The default is 10%, use a range of between 8–20% here.

- *Black Color* indicates the minimum amount of black ink required before the Black trap width setting is applied. Use no less than 70%.

- *Black Density* indicates the neutral density value at which InDesign considers an ink to be black. Typically, you will want to use the default setting of 1.6.

- *Sliding Trap* adjusts how InDesign handles trapping along gradients. At 0%, all traps default to centerline; at 100%, sliding traps are turned off, forcing one color to be spread fully into another. The default is 70%.

- *Trap Color Reduction* allows the adjustment of the color of a trap area so that it doesn't look much darker than the two colors abutting it. A value of 0% makes a trap with a neutral density equal to the neutral density of the darker color.

• Click *OK* and the new preset will appear in the Trap Presets window (Figure 6.18). To assign this preset to the job, click the arrow in the upper right corner of the presets window and select *Assign Trap Preset…*. Select the preset you've just created and make it the default preset (Figure 6.19).

To create a trapped PDF file, you will print a PostScript file from the InDesign CS dialog. Here's how:

1. Choose *File>Print.*

2. Choose *Adobe PDF* as the printer in the General window.

3. Under Setup, make sure you set the page to the appropriate size to accommodate bleed.

4. Add marks and indicate bleed amount under Marks and Bleed.

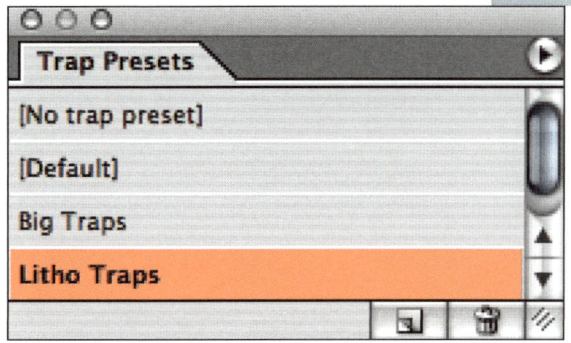

Figure 6.18. Once saved, Trap Presets are added to the list of available sets through the Trap Presets window.

Figure 6.19. Click the arrow in the upper lefthand corner of the the Trap Presets windows (see figure 6.18) and the window will display. Select the preset you want to use from the pull-down menu and click *Assign.*

5. Under Output, select *In-RIP Separations* from the Color option and *Application Built-In* from the Trapping option. You can also merge color plates or convert spot colors to process in the Inks area, and, with the Ink Manager, change the neutral density of colors to force them to trap differently than they would with the default density. This is not something you should attempt to do unless you've got some experience with file trapping.

6. Make sure fonts are included in the PostScript file and images are included with the Graphics window.

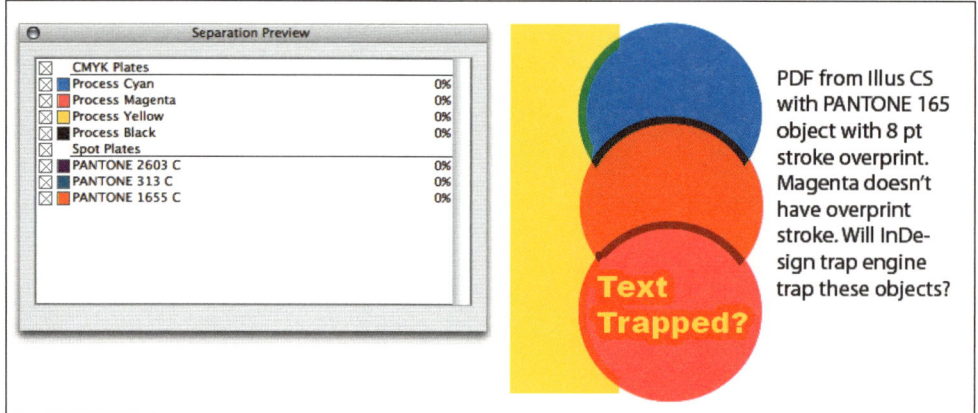

Figure 6.20. Here is a PDF file created from InDesign CS with traps. The objects that show trapping at right started as a PDF file placed as an image in InDesign CS.

7. Indicate a print profile under Color Management if you're working in a fully color-managed workflow.

8. Under Advanced, only select *OPI Image Replacement* if you're working in a picture-replacement workflow; otherwise, leave it unchecked. Since PostScript doesn't handle transparency, you will have to indicate a Transparency Flattening option.

9. Check out your summary then click the Printer button.

10. Select *Adobe PDF* as the printer and then, under Output Options, select *Save as File* and choose *PostScript*. You'll be prompted to give the .ps file a name and indicate a place to save the file. Click *Print* again.

11. Once the PostScript file is complete, convert it to PDF using Acrobat Distiller.

12. Take a look at the file in Acrobat 6. Turn on Overprint Preview; you should see the trapped areas of the file (Figure 6.20).

CHAPTER 7

PDF FORMS

Getting Started with Adobe PDF Forms

While the focus of this book is PDF for print production, that is just a small subset of what is being done with PDF files. The U.S. government is one of Adobe's largest Acrobat customers, primarily because PDF can be used as a data-gathering tool. Using Adobe Acrobat, a user can create, fill in, and submit electronic forms. A PDF form can be designed entirely from scratch, or you may take existing electronic (and even paper) documents, convert them to PDF, and add form fields. This chapter is a brief introduction to forms creation in PDF.

The examples in this chapter are provided for you to use as a hands-on introduction to the concept of Adobe PDF forms. Please visit www.gain.net/pdfguide.html to download the form example (called Form.pdf) used below. There is also a completed example of the form (called Form_Completed.pdf) available on this website.

Creating a PDF form from beginning to end requires four sequential steps:

1. Determine the type of data that you will need to collect.

2. Using page layout software, design a document that will eventually become the PDF to which form fields will be added.

3. Convert that page layout document to a PDF file.

4. Add form fields to the PDF file.

Determining the Data to Be Collected

Before designing a form, you must decide what type of data will be collected. The type of data that you

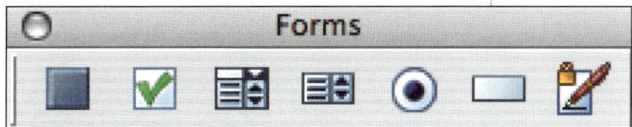

Figure 7.1. Forms toolbar.

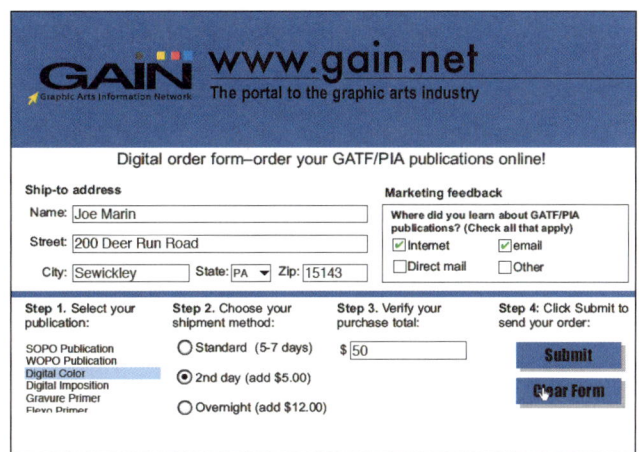

Figure 7.2. A completed PDF form.

need to collect will dictate the type of form fields that will be used in the PDF file. Acrobat has the ability to capture data using a variety of tools. To make the forms toolbar visible, select *Tools>Advanced Editing>Forms>Show Forms Toolbar* (Figure 7.1).

In our example, we will be creating a form that would allow a user to order a book through the PIA/GATF bookstore (Figure 7.2). This form contains fields for name and address, marketing feedback, a list of books, shipping options, purchase total verification, and submitting the data. To capture this information, we will be using the various tools

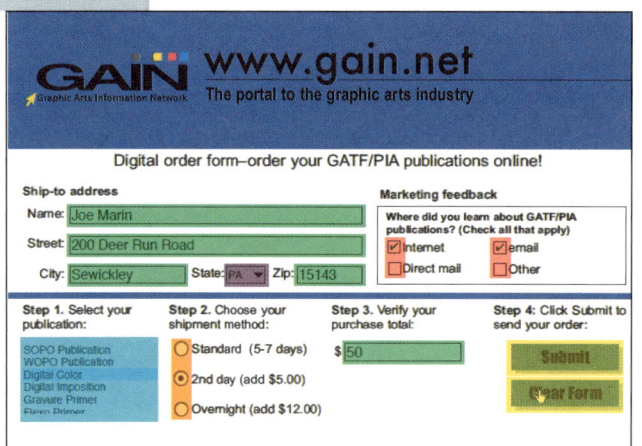

Figure 7.3. Forms key.

contained in the forms toolbar (for a key of which tools were used on the form, refer to Figure 7.3):

The Button Tool (highlighted in yellow). This tool can specify an action such as opening a file, submitting a document, or opening a URL in an Internet browser.

The Check Box Tool (highlighted in pink). This tool is used to create a list of options to choose from. A list of check boxes can be created that allows the user to select one or more options. For a list of items where only one choice can be made, use combo boxes, list boxes, or radio buttons.

The Combo Box Tool (highlighted in purple). This tool can be used to create a menu for users to choose from. Since combo boxes are pop-up style, they take up less space than list boxes.

The List Box Tool (highlighted in cyan). This tool will display an entire list of options that the user can scroll through.

The Radio Button Tool (highlighted in orange). This tool is used to create a list of choices from which the user can only select one.

The Text Field Tool (highlighted in green). This tool allows the user to fill in name, address, and phone number. You can apply a style (font, color, size, etc.) to the text fields created within the PDF.

The Digital Signature Tool. Allows the user to digitally sign PDF documents.

Design the Document

Once you've decided on the information that you want to capture, the next step is to design the document. To design a usable form, there are a few things that must be taken into consideration. Since the form is designed for on-screen access, the size and dimensions of the document should fit into a standard computer monitor orientation. Standard "paper" sizes, like 8.5×11-in. or "letter" won't work in the typical portrait position—it will require the users to scroll around to see the entire document clearly. Turned on the side, to 11 inches wide and 8.5 inches tall, does work, allowing the end user to view the entire form on screen without scrolling.

Next, select a font and font size that is legible for on-screen viewing. While serif fonts such as Times are good for print, they are not the best choice for on-screen viewing. For the main text body of the document, a sans serif font such as Helvetica or Arial will be much easier to read. In addition, the font size will have to be a bit larger than what is normally used for print. Generally speaking, 14-pt. type or larger is comfortable for on-screen viewing. In our example, QuarkXPress was used to design the document (Figure 7.4).

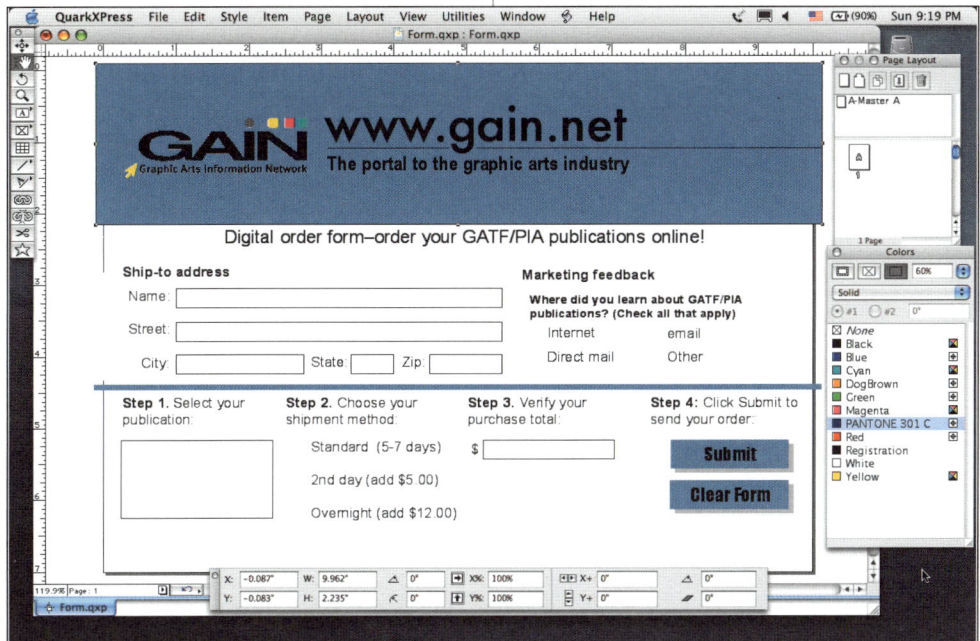

Figure 7.4. A simple form designed in QuarkXPress.

Convert the Document to PDF

If you've read this book, you should already know how to create a good PDF file. Since PDF forms are designed to be filled out electronically, you'll probably want to use PDF settings that are optimized for screen (see page 47 and 48 for screen settings). The basic rules apply: Embed all of the fonts, use JPEG compression with low to medium quality, and set the compatibility to Acrobat 4.0, since there are still many people using older versions of Acrobat and Reader.

Add Form Fields

Now that the PDF file has been created, the next step is to add the form fields. Open the Form.PDF document that you downloaded from www.gain.net/pdfguide.html to begin.

Adding Form Fields
for Name and Address

These fields will gather name, address, and ZIP code information.

1. Select the Text Field tool.

2. Click and drag a box to the approximate size of the "Name" box. A Text Field Properties dialog box appears.

3. Click the General tab and name the field "Name." Each text field you create will have a specific name.

4. Click the Appearance tab and set the Border Color and Fill Color to *No Color.* The Appearance tab also gives you the ability to specify the font, size, and color of the text that will appear within the field.

5. Repeat steps 1–4 for the "Street" and "City" boxes, giving them a unique name.

6. Select the Hand tool and try out each of the fields.

1

Select the Text Field tool.

2

Click and drag a box to the approximate size of the "Name" box.

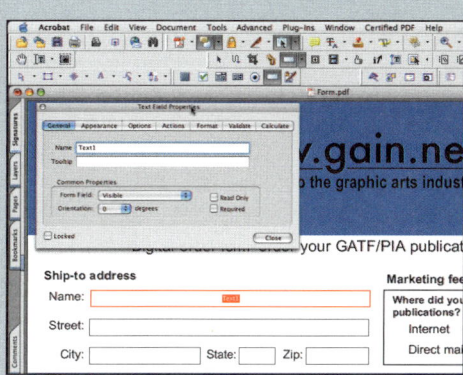

3

Click the General tab and name the field "Name."

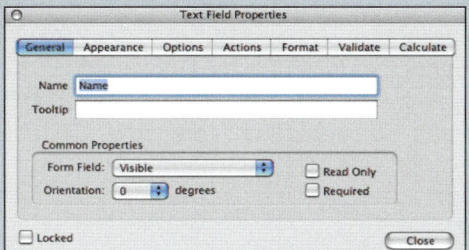

4

Click the Appearance tab and set the Border Color and Fill Color to *No Color.*

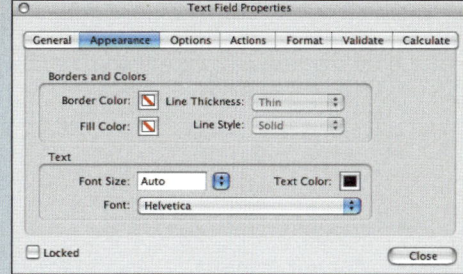

5

Repeat steps 1–4 for the "Street" and "City" boxes, giving them a unique name.

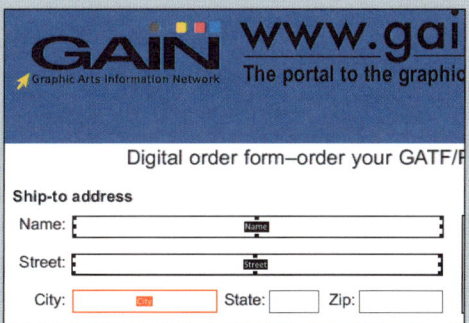

Adding a Form Field for ZIP Code

This field is similar to the name, street, and city fields. What will be different in this example is that only numeric information will be allowed in this field.

1. Select the Text Field tool.

2. Click and drag a box to the approximate size of the "Zip" box. A Text Field Properties dialog box appears.

3. Click the General tab and name the field "Zip."

4. Click the Appearance tab and set the Border Color and Fill Color to *No Color*.

5. Click the Format tab. From the Select format category pull-down menu, choose *Special*. Under Special Options, choose *Zip Code*. This specifies that this field will only contain a five-digit ZIP code. Only five numbers (and no other characters) can be entered into this field.

6. Select the Hand tool and try out the ZIP field.

1

Select the Text
Field tool.

2

Click and drag a box
to the approximate
size of the "Zip" box.

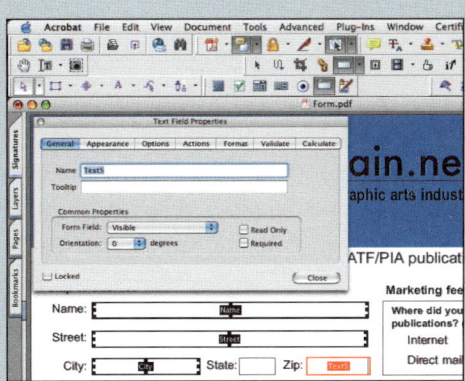

3

Click the General
Tab and name
the field "Zip."

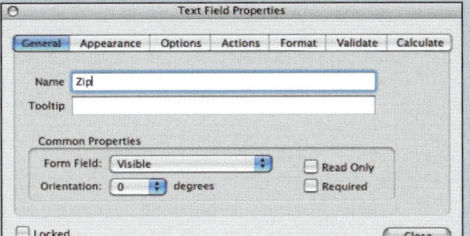

4

Click the Appearance
tab and set the
Border Color and
Fill Color to *No
Color*.

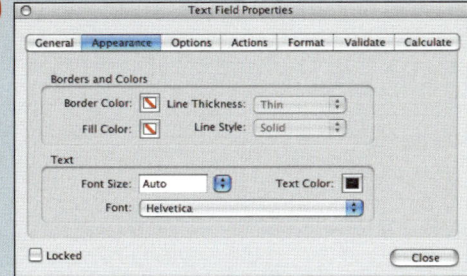

5

Click the Format
Tab. From the Select
Format category
pull-down menu,
choose *Special*.
Under Special
Options, choose
Zip Code.

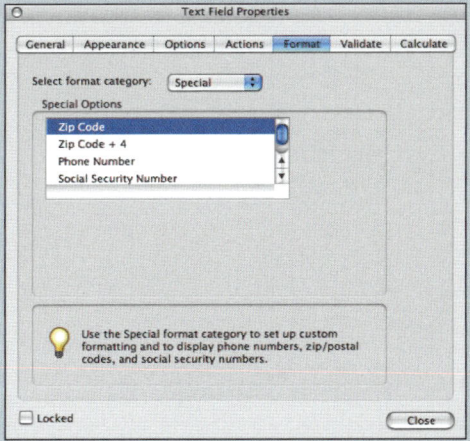

Adding a Form Field for States

For the states field, a pull-down menu of state abbreviations will be created.

1. Select the Combo Box tool.

2. Click and drag a box to the approximate size of the "State" box. A Combo Box Properties dialog box appears.

3. Click the General tab and name the field "State."

4. Click the Appearance tab and set the Border Color and Fill Color to *No Color*.

5. Click the Options tab. In the Item field, type in a state abbreviation and click *Add*. Type in a few more state abbreviations and click *Add* for each one.

6. Select the Sort Items option. Notice that the states now appear in alphabetical order.

7. Select the Hand tool and try out the state field.

Adding a Form Field for States

1

elect the
ombo Box tool.

2

Click and drag a box
to the approximate
size of the "State"
box. A Combo Box
Properties dialog
box appears.

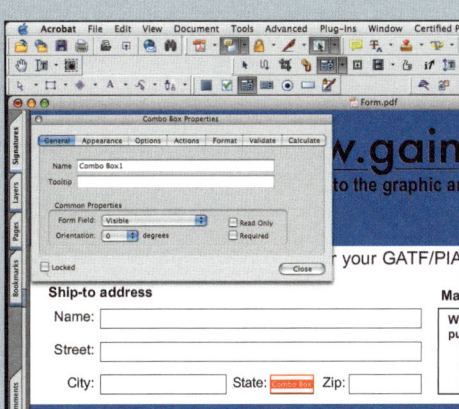

3

ick the General
b and name
e field "State."

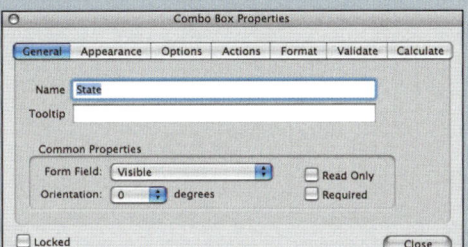

4

Click the Appearance
tab and set the
Border Color and
Fill Color to *No
Color*.

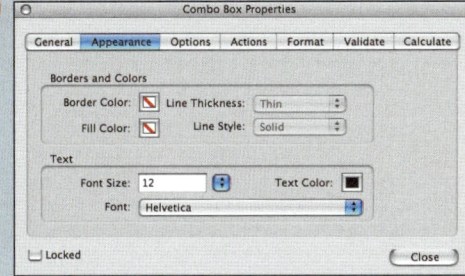

5

ick the Options
b. In the Item
eld, type in a state
breviation and
ck *Add*. Type
a few more state
breviations and
ck *Add* for each
e.

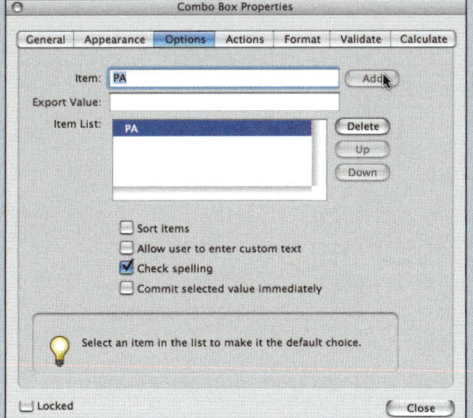

6

Select the Sort Items
option. Notice that
the states now appear
in alphabetical order.

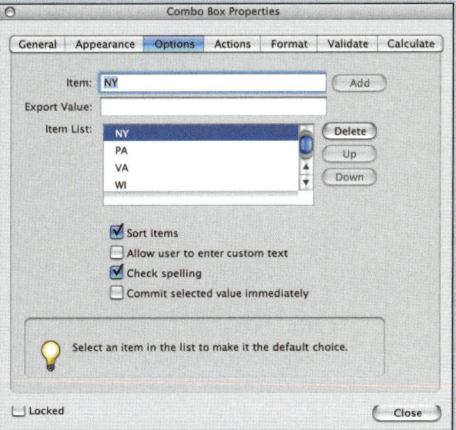

Adding Check Boxes

This section illustrates how to create check boxes for marketing information. You will be able to select one or more check boxes at the same time.

1. Select the Check Box tool.

2. Click and drag a box next to the word **Internet** (make the box about the same height as the text). A Combo Box Properties dialog box appears.

3. Click the General tab and name the field "Internet." Each check box you create will have a specific name.

4. Click the Appearance tab and set the Border Color to black, Fill Color to white, and the Text Color to green.

5. Repeat steps 1–4 for "Direct mail," "email," and "Other," giving each of them a unique name.

6. Select the Hand tool and try out each of the check boxes.

1

elect the Check
ox tool.

2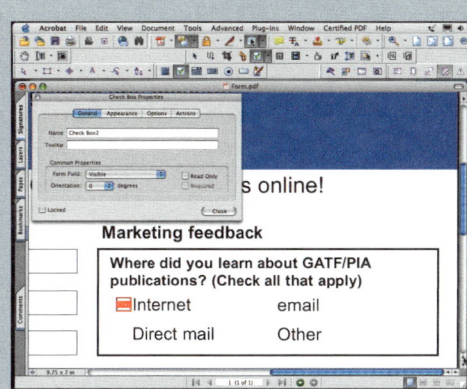

Click and drag a
box next to the
word *Internet* (make
the box about the
same height as the
text).

3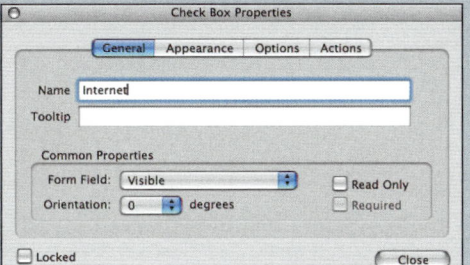

ick the General
b and name the
eld "Internet."
ch check box
u create will
ve a specific
me.

4

Click the Appearance
tab and set the
Border Color to
black, Fill Color
to white, and the
Text Color to green.

5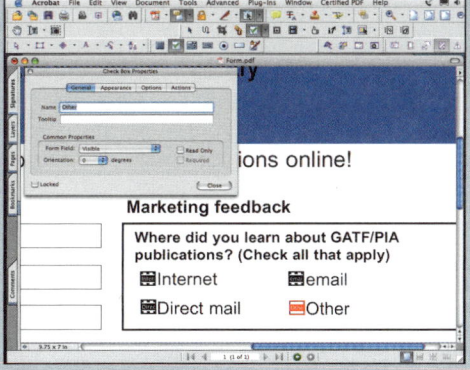

epeat steps 1–4
r "Direct mail,"
mail," and "Other,"
ving each of
em a unique
me.

Creating a List Box Field

The list box will contain a list of various publications to purchase. In addition, individual prices will be assigned to each publication.

1. Select the List Box tool.

2. Click and drag a box to the approximate size of the box below "Step 1: Select your publication." A List Box Properties dialog box appears.

3. Click the General tab and name the field "Publications."

4. Click the Appearance tab and set the Border Color and Fill Color to *No Color.*

5. Click the Options tab. In the Item field, type in the name of a book. In the Export Value field, give the book a price. Click *Add.* Type in a few more book titles and prices and click *Add* for each one.

6. Select the Sort Items option. Notice that the books in the list now appear in alphabetical order.

7. Select the Hand tool and try out the publications list field.

1

elect the List
ox tool.

2

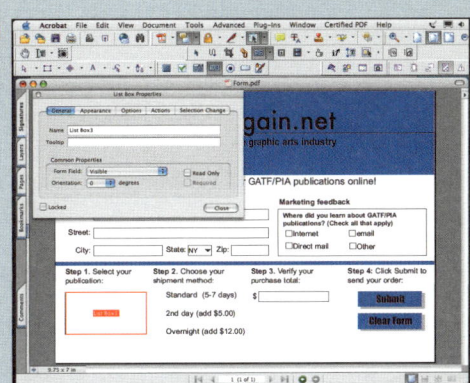

Click and drag a box
to the approximate
size of the box below
"Step 1: Select your
publication." A List
Box Properties
dialog box appears.

3

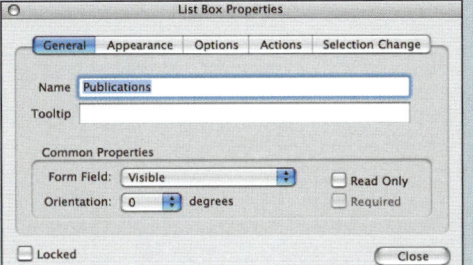

ick the General
b and name the
eld "Publications."

4

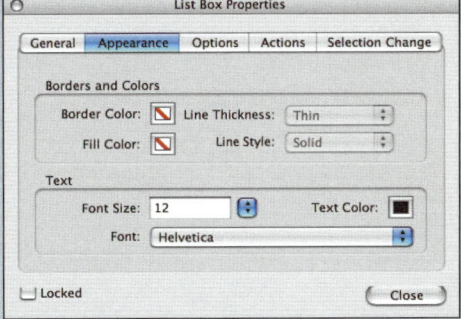

Click the Appearance
tab and set the
Border Color and
Fill Color to *No
Color.*

5

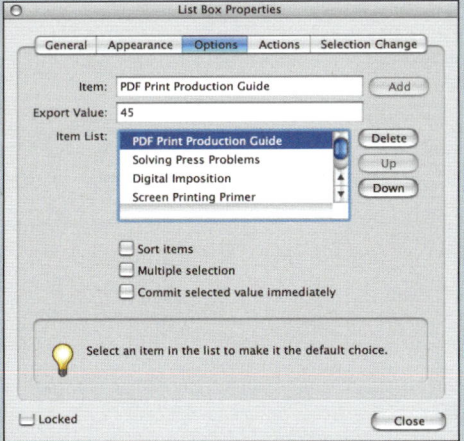

ick the Options
b. In the Item field,
pe in the name of
book. In the Export
alue field, give the
ook a price. Click
dd. Type in a few
ore book titles
d prices and click
dd for each one.

6

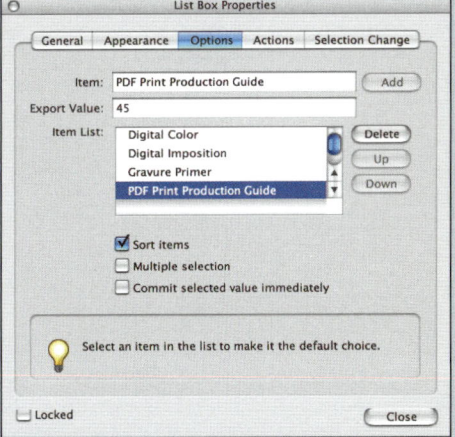

Select the Sort
Items option. Notice
that the books in the
list now appear in
alphabetical order.

Creating Radio Buttons

The radio buttons will give you choices for shipping. Unlike the checkboxes, you will only be able to select one radio button at a time. In addition, individual prices will be assigned to each method of shipment.

1. Select the Radio Button tool.

2. Click and drag a box next to the word *Standard* (make the box about the same height as the text). A Radio Button Properties dialog box appears.

3. Click the General tab and name the field "Shipping." Each additional radio button you create will have the same name. Giving each radio button the **same** name allows you to only choose one option.

4. Click the Appearance tab and set the Border Color to black, Fill Color to white, and the Text Color to black.

5. Click the Options tab and set the export value to 0 (since standard shipping is no additional charge).

6. Repeat steps 1–5 for "2nd day" and "Overnight," giving them the **same** name as the first radio button. In addition, set the export value for "2nd day" to 5 and "Overnight" to 12.

7. Select the Hand tool and try out each of the radio buttons.

1

...lect the Radio
...tton tool.

2

Click and drag a
box next to the
word *Standard*
(make the box
about the same
height as the text).

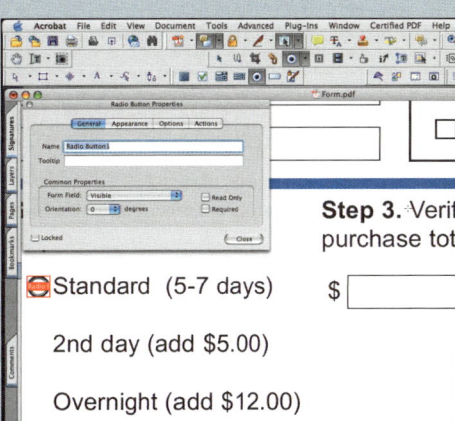

3

...ck the General
...b and name the
...ld "Shipping."
...ch additional
...dio button you
...eate will have
...e same name.

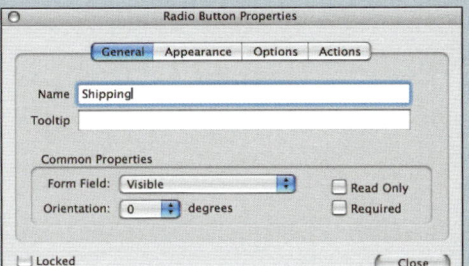

4

Click the Appearance
tab and set the
Border Color to
black, Fill Color
to white, and the
Text Color to black.

5

...ck the Options
...b and set the
...port value to 0
...nce standard
...ipping is no
...ditional charge).

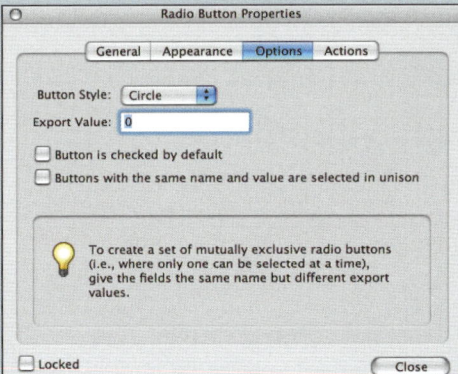

6

Repeat steps 1–5
for "2nd day" and
"Overnight," giving
them the same
name as the first
radio button. In
addition, set the
export value for
"2nd day" to 5 and
"Overnight" to 12.

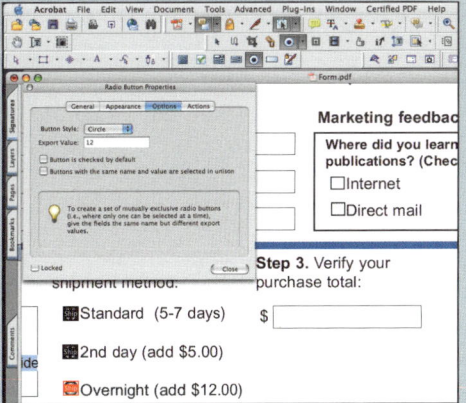

Adding a Calculation Form Field

This field is similar to the name, street, city, and ZIP fields. What will be different in this example is that the publication and shipment method choice (based on the values you assigned earlier) will be calculated in this field.

1. Select the Text Field tool.

2. Click and drag a box to the approximate size of the "purchase total" box. A Text Field Properties dialog box appears.

3. Click the General tab and name the field "Total."

4. Click the Appearance tab and set the Border Color and Fill Color to *No Color*.

5. Click the Calculate tab. Select Value is the sum (+) of the following fields. Click *Pick*.

6. In the Field Selection dialog box, choose the two fields to be added together to reflect the total cost. Place a check next to *Publications* and *Shipping*. Click *OK*.

7. Select the Hand tool. Click on various publications and shipment methods to test the total cost field you've just created.

1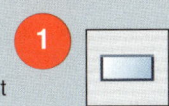

...lect the Text
...ld tool.

2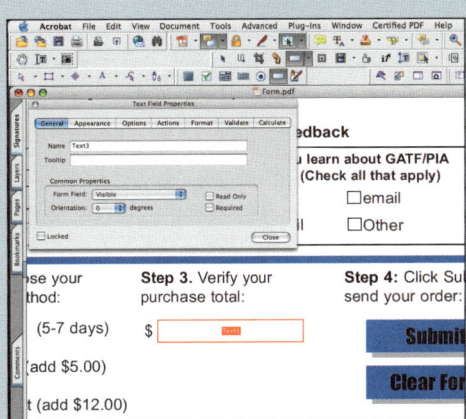

Click and drag a
box to the approxi-
mate size of the
"purchase total"
box.

3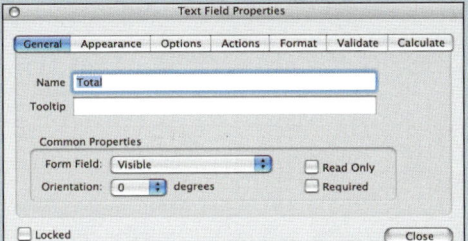

...ck the General
...b and name
...e field "Total."

4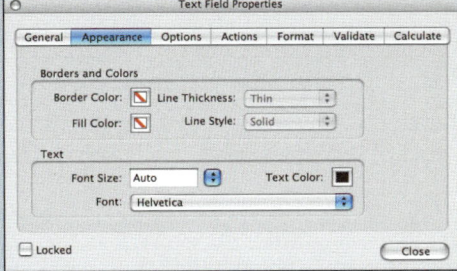

Click the Appearance
tab and set the
Border Color and
Fill Color to *No
Color*.

5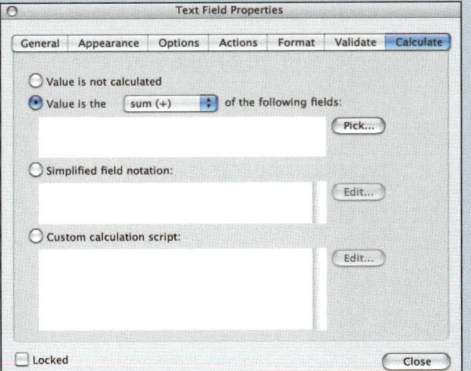

...ck the Calculate
...b. Select Value
...the sum (+) of
...e following fields.
...ck *Pick*.

6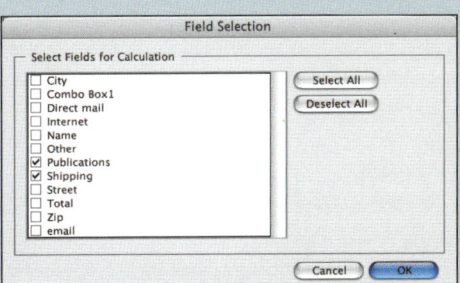

In the Field Selection
dialog box, choose
the two fields to
be added together
to reflect the total
cost. Place a check
next to *Publications*
and *Shipping*. Click
OK.

Submitting a Form

The Button tool can be used to create an action to submit the information on the form. The form data can be sent embedded within a PDF file or as data only.

1. Select the Button tool.

2. Click and drag a box over the "Submit" button. A Button Properties dialog box appears.

3. Click the General tab and name the field "Submit."

4. Click the Appearance tab and set the Border Color and Fill Color to *No Color*.

5. Click the Actions tab. In the Add an Action section, choose *Mouse Up* from the Select Trigger pull-down menu. From the Select Action pull-down menu, choose *Submit a form*. Click *Add*.

6. In the Submit Form Selections dialog box key is a destination (mailto:your email address) to send the form. The form can be sent to an email address or a URL. Next, choose *PDF The complete document*, which will email the entire PDF file along with the forms data. Click *OK*. Other export formats include:

• Form Data Format (FDF). Selecting this option will export the form data only, without the PDF file. You can import the FDF data into a blank PDF form, automatically populating the fields.

• HTML. Exports form data as HTML.

• XFDF. Exports form data as an XML file.

• PDF the complete document. Exports the entire PDF file with the forms data embedded.

7. Select the Hand tool, fill out the form, and submit the data to your email address.

1

...lect the ...tton tool.

2

Click and drag a box over the "Submit" button.

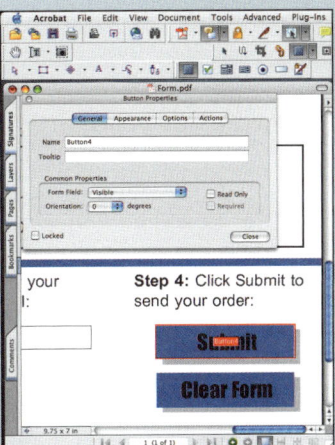

3

...ck the General ...b and name ...e field "Submit."

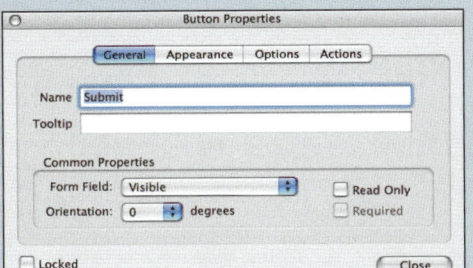

4

Click the Appearance tab and set the Border Color and Fill Color to *No Color*.

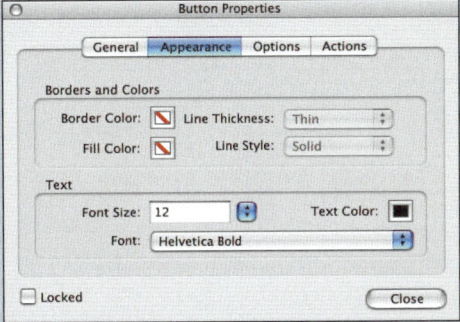

5

...ick the Actions ...b. In the Add an ...tion section, ...oose *Mouse ...p* from the Select ...igger pull-down ...enu. From the ...elect Action ...ull-down menu, ...oose *Submit a ...rm*. Click *Add*.

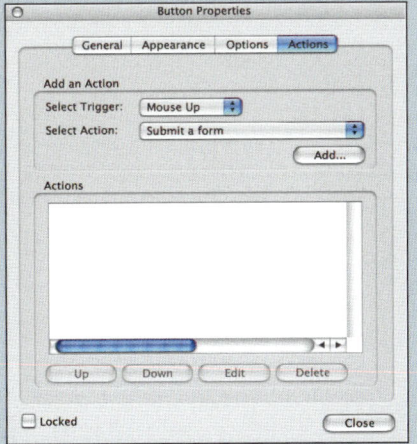

6

In the Submit Form Selections dialog box key is a destination (mailto: your email address) to send the form.

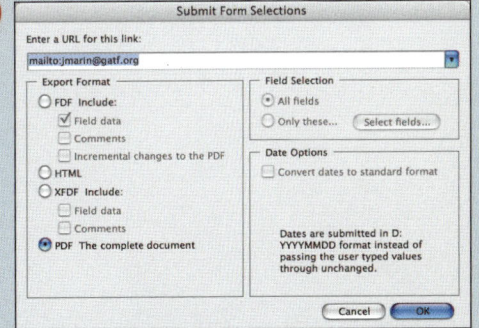

Clearing Form Data

Finally, the Button tool can be used to clear the information on the form.

1. Select the Button tool.

2. Click and drag a box over the "Clear Form" button. A Button Properties dialog box appears.

3. Click the General tab and name the field "Clear."

4. Click the Appearance tab and set the Border Color and Fill Color to *No Color.*

5. Click the Actions tab. In the Add an Action section, choose *Mouse Up* from the Select Trigger pull-down menu. From the Select Action pull-down menu, choose *Reset a form.* Click *Add.*

6. In the Clear Form Selections dialog box, click the Select All button to select all of the fields to be reset. Click *OK.*

7. Select the Hand tool, fill out the form, then reset them form by clicking on the Clear Form button.

This chapter is intended to be just a brief introduction to working with forms data in PDF. We hope you enjoyed it!

1

elect the
utton tool.

2

Click and drag a
box over the
"Clear Form"
button.

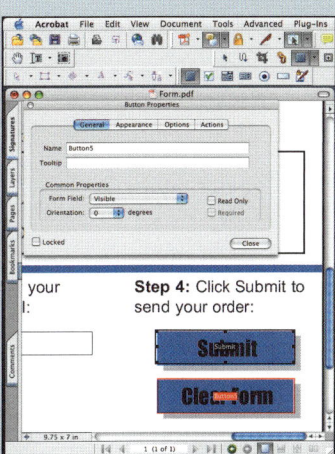

3

ick the General
b and name
e field "Clear."

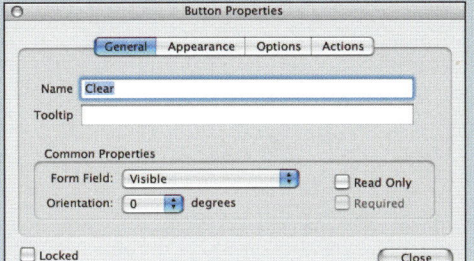

4

Click the Appearance
tab and set the
Border Color and
Fill Color to *No
Color*.

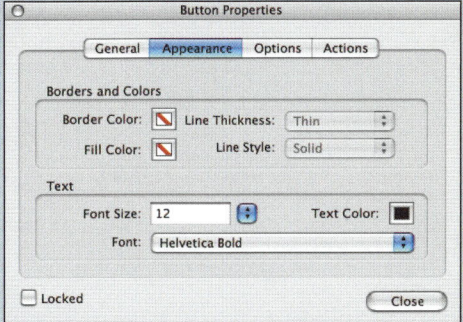

5

n the Clear Form
elections dialog
ox, click the Select
l button to select
l of the fields to
e reset. Click *OK*.

6

Select the Hand
tool, fill out the
form, then reset
the form by
clicking on the
Clear Form button.

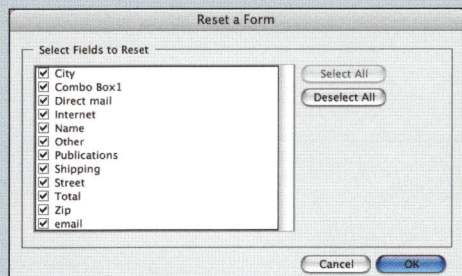

CHAPTER 8

REFERENCES

Questions and Answers

Is it possible for speech recognition programs to "strip" the text out of a PDF for display to the visually impaired?

Accessibility for visually impaired users is a key benefit of Acrobat. PDF documents can be created with a logical structure so objects like headlines, paragraphs, and images are tagged as such. Properly tagged PDF documents can be read by Microsoft Windows-based screen readers, available from companies like Freedom Scientific and GW Micro. For people who have low visual acuity, PDF documents can be displayed in high-contrast mode, by setting whatever foreground and background color the user desires in *Acrobat>Preferences>General> Accessibility*. Tagged documents can be magnified and then set to reflow so that the text fits into the display window and the user does not have to scroll back and forth to view it.

How does InDesign create PDF files?

InDesign has Distiller-like functionality built in (via the Adobe PDF Library). PDF files may be generated directly from InDesign by selecting *File>Export* and selecting *Adobe PDF* from the pull-down menu, then clicking *Save*. The next dialog box shows controls that are similar to Distiller. Set up your options under Compression, Fonts, Color Management, etc., and create the PDF.

Are Acrobat and Distiller available for both Mac and Windows platforms?

Yes, these applications are available for both Mac and Windows operating systems.

.PDF is the file extension for Windows. What is the Windows file extension for a PDF/X file?

.PDF is the proper extension for a PDF/X file. On a Mac you can specify that the Apago Checkup plug-in rename a PDF/X file with a .pdfx extension, but we think this is a bad idea, especially for cross-platform compatibility.

Does PDF/X support the use of spot colors in a document?

The PDF/X format does support/allow spot (PMS) colors.

Does a k-v pair refer to DSC-related comments?

PDF metadata, such as the information retained in a PDF file when you check *Preserve Document Information from DSC* from the Advanced Distiller Job Options, is stored in the form of key-value pairs. The information that you see in Acrobat's Document>Summary is stored as key-value pairs. So if Title is the key, the actual name or title assigned to the document is the value.

What standard methods of encryption are allowed for the PDF/X format (specifically the source code of the PDF/X file)?

Standard encryption, Acrobat's means of securing PDF documents, is restricted by the PDF/X-1 standard. By *restricted*, we mean that encryption may be employed but only if access to viewing and printing a PDF document is never denied. In the PDF/X-1a conformance level of the PDF/X standard, the use of any form of encryption is prohibited.

Does PDF support duotones?

Duotones (and other objects using DeviceN colors, such as colorized TIFF images and spot-to-spot blends) are supported by PostScript 3 RIPs. True duotones (meaning those created in Photoshop, particularly version 6) placed in layout applications that are then processed into PDF files generally survive intact (i.e., the image will survive as a two-color bitmap object and not be converted to process).

Are there PDF or PDF/X applications or plug-ins which can automatically convert or correct errors in PDF or PDF/X?

Yes, check out Enfocus's suite of PDF creation and editing tools at www.enfocus.com or Quite A Box Of Tricks at www.quite.com.

How do you specify a spot color in a PDF?

One way to specify a spot color in an existing PDF file is by using Enfocus PitStop Professional. PitStop 6.0 now has the PANTONE® library built in, or you can choose to load your own spot colors into a color repository in PitStop, then use them to color objects in the PDF file. Spot colors assigned in layout applications generally come through properly in resultant PDF files, except in the case of most Microsoft Office products, particularly on the Windows platform.

Why does PDF/X allow indexed color?

For much the same reason, we imagine, that it allows low-resolution images: because it could be a design element. While most of us in prepress, when we think of indexed color, probably think of those tiny, low-resolution GIF images downloaded from a website that occasionally pop up in the jobs our clients send us for high-resolution output, they could actually be used intentionally. We've seen indexed color images, for example, that were created to achieve a posterization effect in a bitmap image.

Can PDFs be imposed directly to imposition software?

Most imposition software applications support native PDF files. This means that PDF is not converted to PostScript at any time during the imposition process (PDF-in, PDF-out). One application that allows imposition directly in Acrobat is Quite Software's Quite Imposing.

How do you train customers who are spread across the country?

Well, that has always been a challenge, even with the submission of native files. Forums like a webinar are one way. This technology can allow the presenter to walk through applications with attendees, giving them the opportunity to actually show the customer how to set up Distiller properly, for example. Employing more strict methods of file delivery, such as the online preflighting tools offered by Markzware and Extensis, which can prohibit the transfer of files (including PDF) that do not meet the criteria of the recipient, is another. Providing them tools, like Enfocus Instant PDF, that create "certified" PDF files based on profiles set up by you, the printer/publisher, is another.

Is it possible to merge two different spot colors of different names?

If you are referring to PDF files with extra colors, such as the same Pantone color specified by two different names, plug-ins like Enfocus PitStop Professional or ARTS PDF Crackerjack offer the ability to merge different colors into one.

Is there a free application or plug-in for clients to fill out PDF forms and resend?

There are no freebies that we know of. Full Acrobat (Standard or Pro) is needed to fill out forms. If the form is served via the Web, much like an HTML form, it can be filled out if one has the Acrobat browser plug-in.

How do you explain the font issue to customers in PDF/X? Many of them don't have "legal" fonts.

Fonts in PDF files must be legally embeddable. At this point, there is no mechanism to verify that a font is, indeed, legally owned by the user, so this is really not enforceable. Newer font types, such as OpenType, can be licensed with certain restrictions, however. So, for example, they could be restricted for use to view and print only. In the future, it will likely be less possible to use pirated fonts, so the issue will eventually take care of itself.

How do you change objects in a PDF from a four-color black to black-only?

Using PitStop Professional, objects that are four-color black can be selected individually or globally in the PDF, then converted to black-only.

Doesn't the fact that all the font vendors can now keep the fonts from being embedded defeat the whole purpose of a PDF file?

We agree. Unfortunately, we are at the mercy of the companies creating the fonts.

Must you be Adobe-certified to train people on how to create PDF/X files?

No. The PDF/X specification is the result of the work of manufacturer/vendor-independent groups (CGATS, DDAP) accredited by standards bodies (ANSI, ISO) and not tied to Adobe in any way.

How are PDF files without legally embeddable fonts handled?

If the fonts aren't embedded, font substitution will occur using Adobe Sans and Serif Multiple Master fonts. If the font used is simple (something like Helvetica) then the substituted font may be acceptable. If not, it's time to ask the client to select another font that is embeddable.

Is it possible to save a PDF file backwards to an earlier version (for example 1.5 to 1.4)?

If you have a copy of Acrobat 6 Professional, it can be done. Select *Advanced>PDF Optimizer* to select compatibility (you can go all the way back to Acrobat 4), compression settings, font settings, etc., then save your PDF file to disk.

Why do grayscale images print as CMYK in a PDF file?

It depends on which application/version you are using. They work fine if saved from Photoshop version 5.5 and above, placed in the most prominent graphics applications (Quark, PageMaker, InDesign) on the Mac platform. Where you might see this happening is with grayscale images from Photoshop 5.01 or from PC-based applications, particularly Microsoft Office applications.

Is there software available to eliminate color shifting when printing PDFs to digital output devices?

Well, this question can't be answered without asking a whole bunch of other questions. When does the color "shift"? As compared to what: the original, a proof, the computer screen? Are we talking about PDF files containing DeviceCMYK images? RGB images? Both? ICC-tagged images? Is output to a desktop printer? A CTP system? An inkjet proofing system? A profiled system? Is the printing from the Acrobat application? Is the PDF file placed in a RIP hot folder in the front of an output device? We're stepping outside of a pure discussion of PDF and into the realm of color management here.

Is there a plug-in that allows you to flow variable data in a PDF file?

One tool for working with variable data in a PDF workflow is an Acrobat plug-in called pdfExpress, from Think121, Inc. Check them out at www.think121.com.

Why does color shift from RGB to CMYK?

Any time images are converted from RGB to CMYK, there will be a color shift. This is because the RGB color gamut (millions of colors) is much larger than the CMYK color gamut (thousands of colors).

With Microsoft Word not supporting spot colors, is there a way to accept a two-color PDF file from an MS Word file and get color-separated output?

If you cannot specify a spot color in the layout application, you won't be able to maintain spot colors from that application, even in placed images. Simple two-color documents, without spot-to-spot blends or complicated illustrations, can be edited using PitStop Professional in Acrobat. Otherwise, we're afraid you're out of luck.

How do you convert spot colors to process in a PDF file?

PitStop Professional offers tools which allow the conversion of spot (PMS) colors to CMYK.

Are there plug-ins that will enable one to extract embedded graphics from a PDF file?

Acrobat's built-in TouchUp Object tool will allow you to extract embedded graphics, as long as the PDF file hasn't been encrypted to disallow editing.

How can you use Photoshop DCS2 files with a PDF workflow?

If you wish to place the DCS2 file into a Quark layout and then create a PDF file, there are a couple of options. Quark XTension SmartXT will download the high-resolution data from a placed DCS image during the PostScript printing phase. Impressed offers a product, DCSMerger, which will do likewise. Preseparated DCS2 files can also be merged into a composite PDF from Acrobat using the Creo plug-in Seps2Comp.

Is there a plug-in that allows you to convert an RGB color to spot?

Yes. Enfocus PitStop Professional will allow the selection of any colored object in a PDF file. That colored object can then be assigned a spot color using the color repository.

Is PDF/X a term that GATF started or is this coming from Adobe?

PDF/X, a subset of the PDF file format, was created by independent committees (CGATS) and accredited by standards committees (ANSI, ISO). PDF/X has no connection to GATF and was not initiated by Adobe at all.

Are there rulers in Acrobat?

If you're talking about Acrobat versions 5 or older, we're afraid you're out of luck. New to Acrobat 6 is the ability to show rulers. Select *View>Rulers* to make it active.

I've been using older versions of QuarkXPress to Save Page As EPS and running the EPS through Distiller; is this OK?

Distiller is capable of producing PDF files from EPS as well as PostScript files, so if this workflow works for you, go ahead and use it.

When one is using QuarkXPress to make a PDF, can the Export as PDF... function be used to make "perfect" PDFs, or does GATF recommend the slower, more time-consuming process of printing to a PostScript file and dropping it into Distiller?

Using the Export to PDF function in Quark-XPress 6.0 is a perfectly acceptable method for creating PDF files.

Will Distiller convert RGB images to CMYK?

No. Distiller can only convert CMYK to RGB.

Can the Distiller Font Locations use the Windows System Fonts?

Yes, it can reference the Windows System Fonts directory, like any other.

If Illustrator Overprint Mode is deselected in Distiller, will overprints set in Illustrator be ignored?

Yes. The overprinting set in the illustration will not be honored.

Does Illustrator Overprint Mode affect FreeHand illustrations?

Yes. When this option is selected in Distiller, any overprints set in FreeHand will be honored.

How do you maintain QuarkXPress trapping preferences?

Quark trapping is only honored when printing separations. The only way to maintain Quark trapping is to print separations from Quark and use a tool such as Creo Seps2Comp to re-composite the PDF file.

Is it possible to edit PDF job ticket?

Yes, with workflow solutions that take advantage of job ticketing, such as Adobe Extreme-based systems, Agfa Apogee, or Creo Prinergy.

When printing out of QuarkXPress, why is there no option for 1270 dpi?

It isn't necessary to precisely match every possible resolution available on every marking engine. The idea is simply to create a PostScript file with sufficient resolution to successfully image on a particular device; 1200 dpi is sufficient in the PostScript even if you will be imaging to a 1270-dpi device, and 2400 works even with 2540 devices.

Why should we use the Acrobat Distiller PPD exclusively in the print settings? We have been using device-specific PPDs successfully.

The reason for using the Acrobat Distiller PPD is that the resulting PDF file will be device-independent. When you choose a printer-specific PPD, the PostScript and resulting PDF created is not device-specific.

Where can we get the Acrobat Distiller PPD from?

The correct Acrobat PPD can be found at www.adobe.com.

Is it better to create a PostScript file then distill or create the PDF from applications such as PageMaker?

Since creating a PDF from PageMaker actually invokes Distiller in the background, the resulting PDF file would be the same.

Is there any way to print a PDF file on a PostScript Level 1 imagesetter?

You cannot print a PDF directly to a PostScript Level 1 RIP. The PDF must first be converted back to PostScript before it can be printed. You can also print directly out of Acrobat to a PostScript device or you can Print As Image. If nothing else, printing the file as an image can work.

When using Acrobat 4.0, how can you invoke PostScript Level 3 smooth shading?

Place this line of code into the prologue.ps file: $<</IdiomRecognition\ true>>\ setuserparams.$

How extensively can you edit a PDF file? Can you add a whole paragraph?

You can edit paragraphs of text in a PDF file using Enfocus PitStop Professional. Another method is to create a new block of copy using the annotation tool Freeform Text.

What do I do when the PDF file is missing punctuation (quotations, bullets, long dashes, etc.)?

As long as the font is loaded on your system, you can make minor text edits using the TouchUp Text tool or Enfocus PitStop Professional.

How do you create a PostScript file from a PDF?

Open the PostScript file in Acrobat, then select *File>Save As,* and choose *PostScript* from the pull-down menu.

Is there a limit to how many PDFs you can create on Adobe's website for the $9.99 fee?

There is no file limit.

What is the problem with using ASCII instead of Binary?

Binary is a better format when working with bitmap images. It also creates smaller files.

Is there a maximum number of font folders Distiller can watch?

We are not sure if there is a maximum number. We have tested it to watch twenty font folders with no problems.

Is PDF/X more of a PDF preflight for customers to see the problems with their PDF before submitting it to a service provider?

It can be used that way. It is designed to be a "clean" PDF file for high-end print with no forms, no audio, etc.

I have heard a lot about JPEG2000 compression. Do you lose image quality with this type of compression?

Actually, with JPEG2000 compression you have the option of choosing lossless compression or lossy compression on images. Be aware that JPEG2000 compression is only compatible with PDF 1.5 files.

If I create a PDF file (Acrobat 4 compliant) and then I make changes and save it in Acrobat 5, will the file be converted to Acrobat 5 version?

Yes.

How long does Adobe's website take to create a PDF online?

It depends on the file size and activity on Adobe's site; it could be within minutes or hours.

Can you use the TouchUp Object tool to open an RGB image, save it in Photoshop as CMYK, and update the PDF?

Yes. This method works perfectly.

Is creating PDFs out of PageMaker a good option?

Well, if you need to get a PDF file from a PageMaker layout, sure it is! PageMaker uses Distiller in the PDF-creation process, so it generally works very well.

Is it better to use Quite Imposing and PitStop Professional together when printing and handling customer PDF files?

Enfocus PitStop has been incorporated into many high-end workflow systems, including Agfa Apogee, Creo Prinergy, and Heidelberg MetaDimension. If you're attempting to build a "homegrown" PDF workflow with a suite of Acrobat plug-ins rather than investing in a full vendor-specific workflow, these two applications are something of a de facto standard.

How compatible is PDF with OPI?

Many companies are using it quite successfully. If you'd like to ask some of them, become a member of the PDF user community via online forums. There are several good ones out there, including one hosted at www.planetpdf.com and another at www.infomania.com. General print production forums are hosted at www.printplanet.com.

Have you ever heard a PDF file having a pink cast in the final output when using the binary data format?

Are you using an ICC profile that attempts to simulate white paper on a proof? If so, this could be the cause of the background tinting.

How do you add bleeds?

If a PDF file is created without bleeds, PitStop Professional may be used to add them. First, make the media box larger, then extend the objects that bleed beyond the trim.

What are the different ways fonts can be embedded in a PDF?

Fonts may be embedded in a PDF file in one of three ways: (1) including them in the PostScript file, (2) during the PDF creation process in Distiller, (3) or embedding fonts when exporting to PDF directly from the application.

How do you fix low-resolution art in a PDF?

If the art (images) in a PDF file is low-resolution, the only way to remedy the problem is to go back and re-scan the images. Resolution cannot be added to an image.

Is there a better, faster way to create spot colors other than in QuarkXPress and PitStop Professional?

Well, spot colors can be a part of any PDF file if they've been specified in the original layout application (and you're not working with Microsoft Office products).

What is the best tool for editing PDFs?

We've mentioned some good tools, like Enfocus PitStop Professional and Quite Software's Quite A Box Of Tricks. Check out the hundreds of PDF plug-ins at www.planetpdf.com, many of which offer thirty-day evaluation trials, and judge for yourself.

What is the best way to convert a PDF into a text file that maintains indents, table alignments, centering, etc.?

Formatted text and tables can be exported from a PDF file by using third-party plug-in tools such as CZ-Pdf2Txt (Windows only). Find this plug-in at www.convertzone.com.

How do I create a PDF/X file from QuarkXPress?

PDF/X files are created using special tools that are not a part of any particular layout application. Here's one scenario: From QuarkXPress, one would Export a PDF file. Then this resultant PDF file would have to be opened into Acrobat where Apago's Checkup plug-in resides. Checkup can fix most of the minor issues that would make this PDF file non-compliant (things like setting the trapping key to *yes* or *no* instead of *unknown,* the default that Distiller sets). If Checkup gives the "thumbs up" to this file, save it, and you've got a good PDF/X-1 file. Acrobat 6 Professional also has the ability to make a PDF/X-compliant file using the preflight tool.

Many of our clients send us PDFWriter files from Microsoft products. Is there a good way to fix all of the problems?

While some of the problems associated with creating PDFs using PDFWriter cannot be fixed, like low-resolution EPS images, some PDF editing tools that can work for you are Enfocus PitStop and Quite A Box Of Tools.

What is job ticketing used for?

Job tickets are used to communicate information about the job to everyone in the workflow chain, from client to output service provider.

Is there any way to view Illustrator overprints in Acrobat?

In Distiller select *Illustrator Overprint Mode* in the Advanced tab. Then open the PDF in Acrobat and select *View>Overprint Preview.*

What are the advantages of creating a PDF in Distiller versus Acrobat?

Distiller and Acrobat are two distinct components of a PDF workflow. Distiller is used to create PDF files, Acrobat is used to view, comment on, and edit PDF files.

What is an OPI environment?

OPI stands for *open prepress interface.* Basically, you would have all of your high-resolution images on a central server while low-resolution images are placed in the page layout application. These low-resolution images are swapped for the high-resolution images during the printing process, reducing network traffic and freeing your computer up more quickly.

Are there tools to convert RGB objects in a PDF into CMYK and spot colors?

Enfocus PitStop Professional may be used to perform these functions.

Why does Acrobat 5 add so many PPDs?

It isn't Acrobat 5 that installs all of the PPDs but all of the other applications that you install on your system (such as QuarkXPress, Illustrator, etc.).

We have to use Prologue and Epilogue with our Rampage workflow to get spot colors to show up as spot colors. Is this not necessary in Acrobat 5.0?

We're sure it's necessary with Acrobat Distiller 4.05a. It depends upon whether you're manually converting PDF files to EPS in Acrobat before introducing them to Rampage or having them "normalize" in the Rampage system (which I believe still converts them to EPS, as that's the working file format of the Rampage system). Even spot-to-spot color blends work with Distiller 5, with no special intervention.

Is the Overprint Preview option available in Acrobat Reader?

No. Overprint Preview is only a function available in full Acrobat.

PDF/X-1a is for blind ad transfer. If I create a PDF/X-1a file and send it to ten printers, am I guaranteed that they will all come out the same way?

This is the world of print production—there are no guarantees! Seriously, you will certainly have a better chance of expecting the same results from all printers, but the fact is that if each of them has a different workflow system and RIP, there is a chance that they each have their system set up differently and the PDF/X-1a file could be interpreted differently. For example, one may have the RIP set to automatically convert all black text and line art to overprint, and another may not. So the same file may print differently from each of those printers.

Would you recommend subsetting fonts before RIPing a PDF?

Yes. Subsetting is not a bad thing. Subsetting renames the embedded fonts with a five-letter prefix. This ensures that the font actually used in the PDF will be printed and not those of the service provider.

Should you also use Distiller on the PC when distilling PC PostScript files? We currently distill everything on the Mac regardless of where the PostScript file was created.

Unless you are embedding fonts using Distiller and not in the PostScript file, it won't matter which platform is used to distill the file.

When using the TouchUp tool to edit an image, sometimes the image will come back into the PDF upside down, a different size, or completely out of the image bounds. Is there any way to fix the images or a workaround?

If this is an ongoing problem, try PDF Image-Works from ARTS PDF. This plug-in for Acrobat allows image editing without leaving Acrobat.

How do you repaginate Acrobat files for output to a printing press (for example, two-up or four-up)?

You can use any imposition software application that supports PDF, such as Quite Software's Quite Imposing or Creo Preps.

Why is it bad to convert TrueType to Type 1?

It is not necessarily "bad" to convert TrueType to Type 1 fonts, but you should be aware of the differences in the resultant PDF file when you do so. Mac OS PostScript printer drivers will send TrueType fonts as Type 42 if the printer has a TrueType rasterizer or as Type 1 or Type 3 if it doesn't. When you use the AdobePS printer driver and the Acrobat PPD to create PDF files and embed fonts into the PostScript stream, any TrueType fonts in the document will be converted to Type 1. A downside of this is that Type 42 (TrueType) fonts are searchable in PDF files while Type 1 or Type 3 files may not be.

How do you determine which font is corrupt and therefore hanging up Distiller?

Finding a corrupt font on a computer full of them can seem like finding a needle in a haystack, but it can be done by process of elimination. First, you have to deactivate all of the fonts on the computer other than the bare minimum fonts necessary for the system to function properly (of course, only those bare bones fonts should reside in the system fonts folder; all other fonts should be managed with font management software). Turn off all of the fonts that you can (everything except the system fonts) and then launch Distiller. If it will launch, then you know that one of the non-system fonts is the culprit. Quit out of Distiller, then activate half of your fonts (this works best if you have all fonts organized in a single location, preferably in alphabetized subfolders), everything from A to M for example, and relaunch Distiller. If it doesn't work, you know the culprit is a font in the still-open group. Quit out of Distiller and open only half of those fonts, and so on until you've uncovered the corrupt font.

Why do I sometimes get a missing font message in Distiller (usually Helvetica or Times) when those fonts are not used in my document? Often, even after I have pointed Distiller to these fonts, I still get the missing font message and have to set embedding to warn and continue.

We tried to recreate this problem in our lab but couldn't. Some thoughts: Are you using the latest version of Distiller? Are you using the AdobePS driver and Distiller PPD to create the PostScript file or some other printer description file? There will not be fonts associated with the Distiller PPD. Are you using an application with master pages that may have either of these fonts associated with it? What about Multiple Master fonts; should you subset those fonts to make the PostScript file smaller? Multiple Master fonts will always subset, regardless of how you have Distiller font options set.

Is it possible to re-encode fonts that have been embedded with different creators?

Well, you can replace one font with another in a PDF document, but once a font has been embedded with a specific encoding method, you can't re-encode it from, say, WinAnsi to MacRoman and thus change a glyph from one set to match the other. The actual glyphs would have been embedded in the PDF file by that point.

I receive PDF files that have black text specified as RGB. Is there a way to fix this?

Yes, you can use either Enfocus PitStop Professional or Quite A Box Of Tricks to convert RGB text to black only.

Can you colorize a grayscale TIFF in a PDF file with a spot color?

Yes. First, you have to open the grayscale image in Photoshop, convert it to a duotone, and save it to your hard drive as a Photoshop PDF. Next, import the duotone into the PDF file by inserting it as a page. Finally, copy and paste the duotone in place of the grayscale image in the PDF.

How do you tell the resolution (dpi) of the PDF that you received?

To determine the resolution of the PDF (meaning the resolution of all the images in the PDF), you can use the TouchUp Object tool to open an image in Photoshop and check the resolution there. A more efficient way is to use a preflighting tool such as FlightCheck or PitStop.

Why is it not a good idea to separate PDF out of Quark?

If the PDF contains spot colors, they will not be honored in the Quark document and will not separate out of Quark when you try to print the file.

What are DCS/DCS2 files?

The Desktop Color Separation (DCS) format is a version of the EPS (Encapsulated PostScript) format that allows you to save color separations of CMYK images. The DCS 2.0 format is used to export images containing spot-colored channels.

I cannot seem to insert a blank page in an Acrobat file.

That depends on what you mean by "blank page." There is no "New" option under the File menu in Acrobat to create a new blank page, unless you have PitStop Professional installed. However, if you create a PDF file from a Quark layout, for example, with nothing on the layout, then you've got a blank page that you can insert into an existing PDF document using the Insert Pages option under the Document menu in Acrobat.

How do I make a four-color-process-plus-one-spot-color PDF?

Spot colors, if they are specified properly in the original document, will carry over perfectly into a PDF file. If you are talking about already having a PDF file where you need to specify new spot colors, you can do that with PitStop.

Is it possible to maintain spot-to-process gradients in a PDF document?

Yes. PDF spec 1.3, 1.4, and 1.5 support DeviceN color spaces that will honor spot colors used in gradients, images, etc.

When printing to Distiller from Microsoft products, the black becomes RGB. This would be OK except it is not a black RGB; it becomes a dark gray RGB. Currently I use PitStop Professional to fix. Is there a shortcut?

If you're working from a PC, selecting *Convert to PSgray* under Distiller Properties will automatically convert text that should be black to 100% gray (black) and not allow it to be converted to RGB.

Does PitStop Professional work with Agfa Apogee?

Yes. As a matter of fact, PitStop is an integral part of the Apogee workflow and actually ships with the product.

When we get files created from PDFWriter or from a PDF exporter, we get a gray bounding box around all graphics. This box is only visible to our imagesetters, not our laser printers or even on the screen. At this point I have not found a way to fix this. We usually have the customers send us native files, then we have to go through proofing and sign-offs. Is there a program or a way to eliminate those bounding boxes?

Files created with PDFWriter are usually problematic in a print production workflow, and you should advise customers not to use it. You can detect and delete bounding boxes like this in Acrobat using a tool like PitStop Professional. We've also heard that this sort of thing can happen with certain rendering intents when color management is being used in Distiller.

We have one client who uses nothing but Multiple Master fonts. About half of the PDF files that they send us have bad or missing fonts/text. They only use Adobe fonts and are using Acrobat 5. They had called tech support and have gotten nowhere. Any ideas?

Multiple Master fonts are sometimes problematic in PDF files when they've been manipulated into new "instances" with ATM. Mac OS X users can't manipulate Multiple Master. Unfortunately, we don't have a solution to offer for this random problem other than to advise users to avoid manipulating MM fonts (and that's what they're intended for!).

PDF
RESOURCES

The following is a list of organizations that have something to offer PDF aficionados, especially those who are print production or creative professionals.

ARTS PDF
www.artspdf.com

A division of BinaryThing, ARTS PDF develops PDF tools for PDF separation, editing, encryption, collaboration, workflow, and on-demand publishing.

Adobe Systems Incorporated
www.adobe.com

The original creator of the Portable Document Format, you will find tons of PDF resources and products at Adobe's home website.

Agfa Corporation
www.agfa.com

Agfa created one of the first Adobe Extreme-based PDF workflow systems, Agfa Apogee. Agfa continues to support high-end print production with a cornucopia of industry products.

Apago
www.apago.com

Apago offers software solutions for PostScript, PDF, and PDF/X, including PDFmerge, PDFshrink, PDF Enhancer, Pheon, and PDF/X Checkup.

Apple
www.apple.com

Mac OS X uses PDF as its imaging model to deliver high-quality graphics within the operating system.

Callas Software
www.callassoftware.com

Callas Software's PDF workflow solutions have grown from Acrobat plug-ins pdfInspektor2 and pdfOutput Pro, to entire prepress workflows solutions, like process|prepress.

Creo Inc.
www.creo.com

Creo embraces end-to-end workflow solutions and a core product in their line is Prinergy, one of the first Adobe Extreme-based PDF workflow solutions.

DAliM Software
www.dalim.com

DAliM offers a full range of production workflow solutions, including LiTHO, SWiNG, and TWiST.

Dynagram Software
www.dynagram.com

Dynagram Software's DynaStrip supports imposition of native PDFs.

Enfocus
www.enfocus.com

Enfocus provides a full suite of PDF workflow tools, including Instant PDF, PitStop Professional, and PitStop Server.

Extensis
www.extensis.com

Extensis offers Preflight Pro, a preflighting tool which can be used to preflight PDF files.

Fuji Photo Film U.S.A., Inc.
www.fujifilm.com

FujiFilm offers CVS and CVXS, a PDF Workflow System which supports color management, imposition, proofing, and output.

Global Graphics Software Inc.
www.globalgraphics.com

Global Graphics offers a full line of print production products including Harlequin Classic RIP, Jaws PostScript Compatible Interpreter, Jaws PDF Creator™, and Jaws PDF Courier™.

Heidelberg (Heidelberger Druckmaschinen AG)
www.us.heidelberg.com

Heidelberg offers a number of PDF-related solutions, including the MetaDimension PDF workflow, and Acrobat prepress workflow plug-ins Supertrap and Supercolor.

infomania
www.infomania.com/pdf-prepress-l

An Internet mailing list created to exchange information and discuss solutions regarding PDF in prepress.

Lexigraph
www.lexigraph.com

Lexigraph pioneered the area of manufacturing PDF and variable data PDF with a line of PDF manipulation products, including pdfExpress.

Markzware
www.markzware.com

Markzware's FlightCheck preflighting software will preflight PDF and native application files.

OneVision
www.onevision.com

OneVision offers a range of workflow solutions, including Asura, Solico, and Speedflow, an all-in-one PDF workflow solution aimed at commercial printing operations.

PDFzone.com
www.pdfzone.com

This PDF portal offers PDF news reporting, interviews, and products.

PlanetPDF.com
www.planetpdf.com

The PlanetPDF.com website delivers current PDF news and tips as well as user forums and a store for hundreds of PDF-related tools and workflow solutions.

PrintPlanet
www.printplanet.com

PrintPlanet hosts well-attended eCommunities (user forums) for the graphic communications and printing industries.

PrismaTek
www.printthat.prismatek.com

PrismaTek offers PrintTHAT!, a Web-enabled PDF creation system, based on Global Graphics PDF Courier technology.

Quite Software
www.quite.com

Quite Software provides PDF editing solution with Quite A Box Of Tricks and Quite Revealing and PDF imposition with Quite Imposing.

Rampage Inc.

www.rampageinc.com

Long-time prepress workflow solution, Rampage RIPing System, offers a client-server environment and offers a unique, last-minute screening technology.

RIPit Computer Corp.

www.ripit.com

RIPit offers OpenRIP, an inexpensive RIP solution that has done very well in Seybold's PDF Shootout.

Dainippon Screen Engineering of America

www.dsea.com

Among the software solutions offered by Screen is the Trueflow Workflow Solution.

Xinet, Inc.

www.xinet.com

Xinet's FullPress 12 offers PDF creation through printer queues, in addition to client-server file sharing, print spooling, color conversion and automated output of PDF, TIFF/IT, and PostScript.

COMMON FILE EXTENSIONS

.$$$	temporary work file
.$DB	dBase temporary file
.$VM	Windows 3.x virtual memory temporary file
.??_	compressed file
.??~	compressed file
.000	double-space compressed volume file
.1ST	instruction file for running software
.386	Windows 3.x protected mode driver
.3DS	3D Studio graphics file
.3FX	Corel Chart effect file
.4SW	4Dos swapfile
.A	ADA source code
.ABK	Corel Draw automatic backup file
.ACB	associative coder data file
.ADL	adapter description library
.AFM	Adobe PostScript font support file
.AI	Adobe Illustrator file
.ALL	WordPerfect printer and font definition files
.ANN	Windows help annotation file
.ANS	ANSI graphics file
.ARC	compressed file archive
.ARJ	compressed file archive
.ART	First Publisher graphics file; CorelXara file
.ASC	ASCII text file
.ASI	Borland C Assembler include file
.ASM	assembly language source code
.ASP	Procomm communications program script file

.ATM	Adobe Type Manager data file
.AU	audio data file
.AVI	audio video interleaved file
.BAK	backup file
.BAS	BASIC program file
.BAT	batch file
.BCP	Borland C++ makefile
.BDR	Microsoft Publisher border
.BGI	Borland graphical interface device driver
.BIB	bibliography file
.BIN	binary file
.BIT	Lotus Manuscript graphics file
.BLD	saved BASIC binary file
.BMK	Windows 3.x Help bookmarks file
.BMP	bitmap graphics file
.BPT	Corel Draw bitmap fills file
.C	source code for the C programming language
.CAL	calendar file
.CAT	master catalog file for MSBACKUP in DOS 6
.CBL	Cobol source file
.CCH	Corel chart file
.CDR	Corel Draw graphics file
.CFG	configuration file
.CFL	Corel flow file
.CFN	configuration file
.CGM	computer graphics metafile
.CHK	DOS CHECKDISK command file

.CLASS	Java class file
.CLP	Windows clipboard file
.CMD	OS/2 batch file
.CMF	(1) Corel metafile; (2) creative music file
.CMV	Corel movie animation file
.CMX	Corel presentation exchange
.COB	source code for the COBOL programming language
.COD	object code file used by compilers
.COM	command file
CONFIG.SYS	ASCII file containing the system configuration commands used to boot, or start, an MS-DOS/Windows computer
.COR	Corel Draw installation backup file
.CPI	code page information file (for a foreign character set)
.CPL	Windows control panel file
.CPP	C++ file
.CPT	Corel Photopaint file
.CRD	Windows card file
.CRF	cross reference file
.CST	terminate cost file
.CSV	comma-separated value ASCII text file
.CUR	cursor file
.CUT	Halo I, II, III graphics file
.DAT	data file
.DB	(1) database file; (2) Netscape cache index file
.DB2	dBASE II file
.DB3	dBASE III file
.DB4	dBASE IV file
.DBF	dBASE or compatible database file
.DCT	dictionary file
.DEF	C definition file
.DEV	device driver file

.DHP	Dr. Halo PIC graphics format file
.DIB	device-independent bitmap graphics file
.DIC	dictionary file
.DIF	data interchange format ASCII spreadsheet file
.DIZ	shareware text file describing software; description in ZIP file
.DJP	Hewlett-Packard Deskjet printer SoftFont file
.DLL	(Windows) dynamic link library file
.DOC	(1) Microsoft Word file; (2) documentation text file
.DOT	(1) Corel Draw line-type definition file; (2) Microsoft Word template file
.DRV	hardware driver file
.DRW	Corel Draw or Micrographx graphics file
.DSW	Turbo C context file
.DVP	DESQview configuration file
.DVR	device driver file
.DWG	Autocad drawing file
.DXF	Autocad graphics file
.EMF	enhanced Windows metafile
.END	Corel Draw arrow file
.EPS	encapsulated PostScript file
.EVY	WordPerfect Envoy document
.EXE	executable file
.EXT	extension file
.FAQ	frequently asked questions file
.FIF	Fractal image format file
.FLT	Microsoft filter file
.FMT	dBASE III formatting file
.FNT	font file
.FON	font file

.FOR	FORTRAN language source code file
.FOT	TrueType scalable outline font for Windows
.FOX	FoxBASE database file
.FRM	form file
.FUL	full backup catalog file for DOS 6
.GEM	vector graphics file
.GDI	GEM metafile
.GIF	graphics interchange format file
.GRP	Windows program manager group data file
.GX1	partner graphics file
.H	C language header file
.HDX	help index file
.HLP	help file
.HPF	Hewlett-Packard printer control language Bitstream SoftFont file
.HPG	Hewlett-Packard graphics language file
.HPJ	Windows help project file
.HST	program history file
.HTM	hypertext markup (language) file
.HTML	hypertext markup language file
.HYC	hyphenation list file (WordPerfect)
.ICO	icon graphics file (Windows Program Manager)
.ID	disk identification file
.IDE	Borland C project file
.IDX	FoxBASE database index file
.IFF	Deluxe Paint II graphics file
.IMG	GEM Paint graphics file
.INC	incremental backup file (DOS 6)
.INF	information file

.INI	Windows initialization (configuration) file
.ISF	IBM image support facility file
.JDF	Job Definition Format
.JPEG	Joint Photographic Experts Group compressed graphics image file
.JPG	JPEG (Joint Photographic Experts Group) compressed graphics image file
.JP2	JPEG2000 compressed graphics image file
.KEY	keyboard macro definition file
.LBM	Deluxe Paint graphics file
.LEX	lexicon dictionary file
.LIB	computer language compiler library file
.LNK	Windows 95 Shortcut
.LRF	Microsoft C linker response file
.LST	list of files
.LTR	letter file
.LZH	compressed archived file
.MAC	(1) MacPaint graphics file; (2) macro file
.MAK	Turbo C makefile
.MAN	software program manual
.MAX	3D Studio scene file
.MDB	Microsoft Access database file
.MEU	DOS Shell menu group
.MGF	Micrografx font file
.MID	musical instrument digital interface audio file
.MIDI	musical instrument digital interface audio file

.MNU	(1) menu file; (2) mouse control file
.MOD	file to support data exchange between DOS and Windows
.MPEG	Moving Pictures Expert Group video file
.MPG	Moving Pictures Expert Group video file
.MRB	multiple-resolution bitmap (MS C)
.MSC	Microsoft C makefile
.MSG	message file
.MSP	Microsoft Windows graphics file
.MTH	derive math file
.MUS	music file
.NAM	Print Shop name file
.NCD	Norton change directory data file
.NDX	dBASE index file
.NFO	information file
.NG	Norton Guides database file
.NTX	dBASE index file
.OBD	Microsoft binder file
.OBJ	object code file
.OBT	Microsoft binder file
.OCX	object linking and embedding custom control
.OLD	backup file renamed "old"
.OVL	overlay file
.OVR	overlay file
.OPT	Quarterdeck Enhanced Memory Maker optimize support file
.P	Pascal language source code
.PAK	compressed archived file
.PAL	palette file
.PAS	PASCAL programming or source code file

.PAT	Corel Draw vector fill file
.PCC	Z-Soft graphics file
.PCD	Kodak Photo-CD graphics file
.PCH	Microsoft C precompiled header file
.PCX	PC Paintbrush graphics file
.PDF	(1) printer definition file; (2) portable document format file
.PDV	Microsoft Paintbrush device driver file
.PDX	Paradox file
.PFB	Type 1 font file
.PFM	Type 1 font metric file
.PGM	binary program file
.PGP	Pretty Good Privacy encrypted file
.PIC	graphics file
.PICT	Mac graphics file
.PIF	Windows program information file
.PIM	permanent image file
.PKG	installer script file
.PKT	Fidonet packet (Internet) file
.PLT	plotter file
.PMR	PageMaker file
.PNG	portable network graphics file
.PNM	Print Shop name file
.POG	Print Shop graphics file
.PPT	Microsoft Powerpoint file
.PRD	printer definition file
.PRG	programming source file
.PRJ	project file
.PRN	print text file
.PRS	WordPerfect printer definition file
.PRT	print file
.PS	PostScript interpreted file
.PSO	PostScript page description language printer file for Bitstream SoftFonts
.PUB	Microsoft Publisher file
.PWL	password list file (Windows 95)

.QDK	Quarterdeck Extended Memory Manager installation backup files
.QLB	Microsoft C quick library file
.QTM	QuickTime Movie file
.QTW	Apple QuickTime for Windows file
.QWK	quick reader message file
.QXP	QuarkXPress file
.RAM	real audio file
.RAR	compressed file
.REC	Windows macro recorder file
.REG	registry file
.RES	C compiled resource file
.RLE	run-length-encoded graphics file
.RPT	report file
.RSP	response file
.RTF	rich text format file
.SAM	AmiPro word processing file
.SAV	backup file
.SCR	(1) telecommunications script file; (2) screen (capture) file; (3) DOS debug script file; (4) screen saver file
.SCT	(1) Lotus Manuscript screen capture text file; (2) Scitex CT bitmap file
.SCX	RIX/EGA and ColoRix graphics file
.SDN	compressed archived file
.SDR	Printmaster name file
.SEA	self-extracting archive file
.SET	(1) MSBACKUP set; (2) setup options file
.SFL	Hewlett-Packard printer control language [4] bitmapped SoftFont file (landscape orientation)
.SFP	Hewlett-Packard printer control language [4] bitmapped SoftFont file (portrait orientation)

.SFS	SoftFont screen font file
.SHB	Corel Show background file
.SHP	Printmaster graphics file
.SHW	(1) Corel Show presentation file; (2) Harvard Graphics presentation file; (3) Word Perfect presentation file
.SIG	signature file (for Internet email)
.SIT	compressed archive file
.SK	SideKick Plus utility file
.SND	sound file
.SQL	structured query language database file
.STY	WordPerfect Style file
.SYM	symbol file
.SYS	operating system device driver file
.TC	Turbo C configuration file
.TCH	Turbo C help file
.TD	Turbo debugger configuration file
.TF	Turbo profiler configuration file
.TGA	Targa 16
.THS	WordPerfect thesaurus file
.TIF	tagged image file format (raster graphics)
.TIFF	tagged image file format (raster graphics)
.TMP	temporary file
.TPU	Turbo Pascal unit
.TST	test file
.TTF	Windows header file for a TrueType scalable outline font
.TUT	tutorial file
.TXT	text file

.UC2	(1) compressed file archive; (2) Ultracompressor II datafile
.UPD	updated history file
.UUE	UNIX-to-UNIX encoded compressed binary file; often a graphic
.VBX	Visual Basic control file
.VOC	Soundblaster audio file
.VXD	Windows virtual device driver
.WAV	Windows audio file
.WIZ	Microsoft Publisher page wizard
.WK1	LOTUS spreadsheet version 2.0 file
.WK?	Lotus spreadsheet temporary work file
.WKE	LOTUS educational worksheet file
.WKQ	QUATTRO spreadsheet file
.WKS	LOTUS spreadsheet version 1A file
.WMF	Windows metafile graphics format file
.WPG	WordPerfect graphics file version 5.0 and later
.WPK	WordPerfect keyboard macro file
.WPM	WordPerfect macro file
.WQ1	Quattro spreadsheet version 1.0 file
.WRI	Windows Write text file
.WRK	Symphony spreadsheet file
.WSD	WordStar file
.WVL	wavelet compressed bitmap
.XLS	Microsoft Excel spreadsheet file
.XLT	translation table file
.XML	extensible markup language
.XTP	Xtree overlay file
.ZIP	compressed file archive
.ZOO	compressed file archive

Glossary

Adobe Acrobat. One popular portable document file (PDF) format. Through Acrobat, users can read electronic versions of printed documents that maintain the attributes (bold and italic type and other formatting choices) assigned to a printed original. See also: *portable document format.*

aliasing. A jagged or "staircase" effect in a raster image, caused by an insufficient number of image samples.

artifact. A visible defect in an electronic image, caused by limitations in the reproduction process (hardware or software). Aliasing patterns are an example of artifacts.

ASCII. American Standard Code for Information Interchange. A standard code that uses a set of seven-bit coded characters (eight bits when the parity check is included) to facilitate information interchange without formatting codes among data processing, data communications systems, and associated equipment. The ASCII set consists of both control and graphic characters.

ASCII file. A text file containing ASCII characters only. The lowest common denominator for exchanging text among programs. Almost any word processor or desktop publishing program can read or write ASCII files. Also known as text-only files.

banding. An electronic prepress term referring to visible steps in shades of a gradient.

batch processing. Automated execution of a set of instructions on a sequence of computer files.

binary. A choice or condition with two possible values or states.

binary code. A representation of information using a sequence of zeros and ones.

binary digit (bit). The most basic unit of information in the binary numbering system. Binary information is stored as a series of zeros and ones, indicating low (off) or high (on) electrical current.

binary file. Information stored as binary digits; in other words, in machine-readable form. Images transported over the Internet are encoded as binary files.

bitmap. An image represented by an array of picture elements, each of which is encoded as one or more binary digits.

bleed. Pictures, lines, or solid colors that extend beyond the edge or edges of a page so that when margins are trimmed, the image is trimmed even with the edge of the page.

blend. Joining two colors so smoothly that there is no perceptible line at the intersection. In digital painting, the quality of the blending process is an indication of the quality of the electronic prepress system.

color bar. A device printed in a trim area of a press sheet to monitor printing variables such as trapping, ink density, dot gain, and print contrast. It usually consists of overprints of two- and three-color solids and tints; solid and tint blocks of cyan, magenta, yellow, and black; and additional aids such as resolution targets and dot gain scales. Alternative terms: *color control strip; color control bar.*

color management system. An electronic prepress tool that provides a way to correlate the color-rendering capabilities of input devices (e.g., scanners and digital cameras), color monitors, and output devices (e.g., digital color proofers, imagesetters, and color printers) to produce predictable, consistent color. Color management consists of three primary steps: (1) calibration of input devices, monitors, and output devices to known specifications, (2) characterization, which is a way of determining the color "profile" of a particular device, and (3) conversion, which performs the "color correction" function between color-imaging devices.

color separation. Using red, green, and blue filters to divide the colors of a multicolored original into the three process colors and black. The four resulting film intermediates are used to prepare the yellow, magenta, cyan, and black printing plates. Color separation is most often accomplished with an electronic color scanner, but film-contacting and process-camera methods are also employed on occasion.

color space. The three-dimensional area where three color attributes, such as hue, value, and chroma, can be depicted, calculated, and charted.

compression. Reducing the size of a file for storage purposes or to enhance the speed of data transfer by eliminating the redundancies and other unnecessary elements from the original.

continuous tone. A photographic image or art (such as a wash drawing) that has not been screened. It has infinite tone gradations between the lightest highlights and the deepest shadows.

continuous-tone gray scale. A scale of uniform tones, from white to black or transparent to opaque, without a visible texture or dot formation.

crop marks. Small lines placed in the margin or on an overlay, denoting the image areas to be reproduced.

dialog box. Window appearing on a computer screen requiring the user to provide additional information before a command can be completed or to choose among different options.

dot gain. The optical increase in the size of a halftone dot during prepress operations or the mechanical increase in halftone dot size that occurs as the image is transferred from plate to blanket to paper in lithography. Alternative terms: *dot spread; ink spread.*

duotone. A special effects technique that consists of making a two-color halftone reproduction from a single-color original. In the most common type of duotone, the two halftones are printed in two different colors—one in a color (a normal halftone negative) and the other in black (to print the lighter-than-normal shadows).

encode. To convert data to machine-readable form.

encrypt. To convert data into such a form that it cannot be read if intercepted by the wrong people. Only those who hold the key to an individualized encryption scheme can decrypt these messages.

font. A complete collection of characters in one typeface and size, including all letters, figures, symbols, and punctuation marks.

gray component replacement (GCR). In areas where yellow, cyan, and magenta overprint, the process of replacing all or a percentage of the least dominant process color, along with appropriate percentages of the other two colors to produce a gray, with an appropriate value of black. Color variation on press is less serious when GCR is used. See also: *undercolor removal.*

gray scale, continuous. A narrow continuous-tone black-and-white image on film in which the density gradually increases from zero (the transparent film base). Alternative term: *gray scale, step tablet; wedge.*

halftone. A printed reproduction of a continuous-tone image composed of dots that vary in frequency (number per square inch), size, or density, thereby producing tonal gradations. The term is also applied to the process and plates used to produce this image.

hyperlink. An emphasized word or phrase that connects related documents in a hypertext system.

imagesetter. A device used to output fully paginated text and graphic images at a high resolution onto photographic film, paper, or plates. See also: *PostScript; raster image processor; vectors.*

imposition. The process of placing graphics into predetermined positions on a press-size sheet of paper. Page layout is the process of defining where repeating elements such as headlines, text, and folios (page numbers) will appear on multiple pages throughout a document, while imposition can be thought of as defining where these completed pages will appear on much larger sheets of paper.

impression. (1) The printing pressure necessary for ink transfer. (2) A single print.

JPEG. The compression scheme based on the discrete cosine transform (DCT) lossy compression algorithm that is a de facto standard on the Internet. Named for the Joint Photographic Experts Group, which developed this compression scheme. JPEG allows the user to control the compression ratio and reproduction quality at the point of compression. It can also incorporate other algorithms, such as one-dimensional modified Huffman compression for lossless compression.

line art. Type matter and drawings that can be reproduced without the use of a halftone screen. Alternative terms: *line copy; line work; line drawing.*

lines per inch. Designates the resolution of a halftone screen. Screens with a higher number, such as 120 or 133, have a higher resolution than screens with lower numbers, such as 65 lines per inch. Alternative term: *screen ruling.*

lossless algorithm. A mathematical formula for image compression that assumes that the likely value of a pixel can be inferred from the values of surrounding pixels. Because lossless compression algorithms do not discard any of the data, the decompressed image is identical to the original.

lossy algorithm. A mathematical formula for image compression in which the data in an image that is least perceptible to the eye is removed. This improves the speed of data transfer but causes a slight degradation in the decompressed image.

misregister. Printed images that are incorrectly positioned, either in reference to each other or to the sheet's edges. See also: *register.*

moiré. An undesirable, unintended interference pattern caused by the out-of-register overlap of two or more regular patterns such as dots or lines. In process-color printing, screen angles are selected to minimize this pattern. If the angles are not correct, an objectionable effect may be produced.

network. A computer system that allows several users at remote terminals to exchange data electronically through a common central computer or with a modem over conventional telephone lines.

open prepress interface (OPI). A set of standardized protocols that allows desktop equipment to be linked with color electronic prepress systems (CEPS). High-resolution color images are stored on a central network server, and low-resolution files are used for positioning, scaling, etc. in the page layout program. At output time, the high-resolution images are swapped for the low-resolution images.

optical character readers (OCR). Equipment that scans, interprets, and converts any copy or graphic elements to a machine-readable format.

optical character recognition (OCR). A technique in which any printed, typed, or handwritten copy or graphic images are scanned by an electronic reader that converts the information into a form that can be read, interpreted, and displayed by computers.

orientation. The direction in which a page is printed, i.e., the portrait (vertical) or landscape (horizontal) mode.

original equipment manufacturer. A producer who sells goods to another company for use as components in their own equipment or for resale to end-users. An OEM may sell only to companies for resale or may also compete in the end-user marketplace.

output device. The machine that translates the electrical impulses representing data as processed by a computer into permanent results. A laser printer, imagesetter, or phototypesetter are some examples.

overprint. Solid or tint quality control image elements that are printed over or on the top of previously printed colors. Overprint patches are used to measure trapping, saturation, and overprint color densities. Like other quality control elements, overprints may be measured from a color bar in the trim of a press sheet or from the printed image itself.

page description language (PDL). In an electronic publishing system, the format by which all of the elements to be placed on the page, their x-y coordinates (respective position on the page), and the page's position within the larger document are identified in a manner that the output device can understand. Alternative terms: *page descriptor; document descriptor.* See also: *imagesetter; PostScript; raster image processor; vectors.*

page layout. A dummy indicating page size; trimmed job size; top, outside, and foot trims; untrimmed page size; and head, foot, outside, and bind margins.

pixel. Picture element. The smallest tonal element in a digital imaging or display system.

pixelization. A technique used to represent areas of complex detail as relatively large square or rectangular blocks of discrete, uniform colors or tones.

plug-in. A software utility developed to operate through another application, performing a specific task.

portable document format (PDF). A computer file format that preserves a printed or digital document's original layout, type fonts, and graphics as one unit for digital transfer and viewing. The recipient uses compatible "reader" software to access and even print the PDF file.

posterization. A special effects photographic technique that renders continuous-tone copy into an image represented by a few broad, flat, dark middletones and shadow areas. All highlight and light middletone areas are eliminated.

PostScript. Adobe Systems, Inc. tradename for a page description language that enables imagesetters and other output devices developed by different companies to interpret electronic files from any number of personal computers ("front ends") and off-the-shelf software programs.

PostScript, encapsulated. A file format used to transfer PostScript image information from one program to another.

preflighting. An orderly procedure using a checklist to verify that all components of an electronic file are present and correct prior to submitting the document for high-resolution output.

prepress. All printing operations prior to presswork, including design and layout, typesetting, graphic arts photography, image assembly, and platemaking.

printer's spread. A pair of pages in the order necessary for printing, folding, and binding to yield the desired results.

process inks. The yellow, cyan, magenta, and black colorants that, when combined in a photomechanical printing process, reproduce four-color images.

proof. A prototype of the printed job made photomechanically from plates (a press proof), photochemically from film and dyes, or digitally from electronic data (prepress proofs). Prepress proofs serve as samples for the customer and guides for the press operators. Press proofs are approved by the customer and/or plant supervisor before the actual pressrun.

proof, soft. An intangible image, such as that on a computer monitor.

raster. An image composed of a set of horizontal scan lines that are formed sequentially by writing each line following the previous line, particularly on a television screen or computer monitor. See also: *bitmap; line art; vectors.*

raster image processor (RIP). The device that interprets all of the page layout information for the marking engine of the imagesetter or platesetter. PostScript or another page description language serves as an interface between the page layout workstation and the RIP.

rasterization. The process of converting mathematical and digital information into a series of variable-density pixels.

reader's spread. A pair of pages positioned across the binding edge, or gutter, from each other after the book is assembled; e.g., pages six and seven of a book.

register. The overall agreement in the position of printing detail on a press sheet, especially the alignment of two or more overprinted colors in multicolor presswork. Register may be observed by agreement of overprinted register marks on a press sheet. In stripping, film flats are usually punched and held together with pins to ensure register. The punched holes on the film flat match those on the plate and press specified for the job. Alternative term: *registration.* See also: *misregister.*

resolution. (1) The density of dots or pixels on a page or display usually measured in dots per inch. The higher the resolution, the smoother the appearance of text or graphics. (2) The precision with which an optical, photographic, or photomechanical system can render visual image detail. Resolution is a measure of image sharpness or the performance of an optical system. It is expressed in lines per inch or millimeter.

rule. A printed line, usually specified by its arrangement and thickness or "weight," such as hairline, 2-point, 6-point, or parallel.

sampling rate. The amount, as expressed in inches or millimeters, of electronic information sampled in both scan directions.

scale. A range of values.

scaling. Process of determining the correct final size for an image that must be enlarged or reduced.

screen angle. The position of the rows of dots on halftone screens in relation to a reference grid with horizontal and vertical lines. The most dominant color screened is positioned at a 45° angle to the reference grid.

screen ruling. The number of ruled grid lines per inch on a halftone screen.

server. A device on a computer network that allows networked users (clients) access to a specific service on the network. An example is a file server, which allows the users to share data files and application software.

service provider. A business that specializes in Internet and LAN/WAN network connectivity.

Specifications for Web Offset Publications (SWOP). A set of standards for color separation films and color proofing developed for those involved in publications printing. The SWOP standards help magazine printers achieve accuracy when color separations from many different sources are printed on one sheet.

spot color. The use of one or more extra colors (in addition to cyan, magenta, yellow, and black) on a page, used for a number of purposes including highlighting specified page elements.

spread. An image that extends across two facing pages in a book or magazine, crossing over the binding. Alternative term: *crossover*.

stochastic screening. A halftoning method that creates the illusion of tones by varying the number (frequency) of micro-sized dots (spots) in a small area. Unlike conventional halftoning, the spots are not positioned in a grid-like pattern. Instead, the placement of each spot is determined as a result of a complex algorithm that statistically evaluates and distributes spots under a fixed set of parameters. With first-order stochastic screening, only the number of dots in an area varies, but with second-order stochastic screening, both the number and size vary. Alternative terms: *FM dots; FM screening*.

tagged image file format (TIFF). A file format for exchanging bitmapped images (usually scans) between applications.

trapping. How well one color overlaps another without leaving a white space between the two or generating a third color.

trim. The excess area of a printed form or page in which instructions, register marks, and quality control devices are printed. The trim is cut off before binding.

trim size. The final dimensions of a page.

TrueType. A typeface format developed by Apple Computer.

Type 1. A format for storing digital typefaces developed by Adobe Systems. The most popular typeface format for PostScript printers.

undercolor removal (UCR). A technique used to reduce the yellow, magenta, and cyan dot percentages in neutral tones by replacing them with increased amounts of black ink.

vectors. Mathematical descriptions of images and their placement. In electronic publishing, vector graphics information is transferred from a design workstation to a raster image processor (RIP) that interprets all of the page layout information for the marking engine of the imagesetter.

WYSIWYG (what-you-see-is-what-you-get). Computer screen displays that approximate the true size and true shape of typographic characters, rules, tints, and graphics.

Index

A

B

D

E

F

M

N

O

P

Q

R

About the Authors

Joseph Marin

Prior to joining PIA/GATF in June 1995, Joseph Marin was a prepress specialist for Herrmann Printing and Litho, Inc. in Pittsburgh, Pennsylvania. He holds a Bachelor of Science degree in graphic communications technology, concentrating in offset lithography, from the California University of Pennsylvania. Currently, Marin is the senior prepress technologist/instructor for the Center for Imaging Excellence (CIE), an electronic prepress training and production facility at the Graphic Arts Technical Foundation (GATF) near Pittsburgh, Pennsylvania.

Marin specializes in prepress and prepress instruction and leads several PIA/GATF training programs, including Orientation to the Graphic Arts, Computer-to-Plate and Digital Proofing, and Orientation to Desktop and Digital Prepress. He also contributes to other PIA/GATF training programs such as PDF and Digital Prepress Workflows, Sheetfed Offset Press Operating, and Web Offset Press Operating. Marin also conducts seminars at leading trade shows including Print and GraphExpo and performs technical consultations for commercial and in-plant printers.

His extensive practical knowledge of prepress issues has led Marin to be come a key developer of PIA/GATF's Imaging Skills Training Curriculum, covering the essentials of digital prepress operations. Marin has also authored articles which have appeared in *GATFWorld* and the annual *Technology Forecast*.

About the Authors

Julie Shaffer

Julie Shaffer is the director of PIA/GATF's Robert Howard Center for Imaging Excellence. She is known nationwide for her prepress expertise and often conducts seminars at industry events on the subject. Shaffer leads several PIA/GATF training programs including PDF and Digital Prepress Workflows and Preflighting and File Repair.

Shaffer's extensive prepress background has led her to perform technical consultations for commercial and in-plant printers around the country. She has also authored a research report, *The PDF Era: PDF Usage in the Real World,* and numerous articles for *GATFWorld* and other trade publications. Julie is a graduate of Point Park College with a BA in Journalism/Communications.

About PIA/GATF

The Graphic Arts Technical Foundation (GATF) and the Printing Industries of America, Inc. (PIA), along with its affiliates, deliver products and services that enhance the growth, efficiency, and profitability of its members and the industry through advocacy, education, research, and technical information.

The 1999 consolidation of PIA and GATF brought together two powerful partners: the world's largest graphic arts trade association representing an industry with more than 1 million employees and $156 billion in sales and a nonprofit, technical, scientific, and educational organization dedicated to the advancement of the graphic communications industries worldwide.

Founded in 1924, the Foundation's staff of researchers, educators, and technical specialists help members in more than 80 countries maintain their competitive edge by increasing productivity, print quality, process control, and environmental compliance and by implementing new techniques and technologies. Through conferences, Internet symposia, workshops, consulting, technical support, laboratory services, and publications, GATF strives to advance a global graphic communications community.

In continuous operation since 1887, PIA promotes programs, services, and an environment that helps its members operate profitably. Many of PIA's members are commercial printers, allied graphic arts firms such as electronic imaging companies, equipment manufacturers, and suppliers. To serve the unique needs of specific segments of the print and graphic communications industries, PIA developed special industry groups, sections, and councils. Each provides members with current information on their specific segment, helping them to meet the business challenges of a constantly changing environment. Special industry groups include the Web Offset Association (WOA), Graphic Arts Marketing Information Service (GAMIS), Label Printing Industries of America (LPIA), and Binding Industries of America International (BIA). The sections include Printing Industry Financial Executives (PIFE), Sales & Marketing Executives (S&ME), *EPS—the Digital Workflow Group* (EPS), Digital Printing Council (DPC), and the E-Business Council (EBC).

The GATF*Press* publishes books on nearly every aspect of the field; training curricula; audiovisuals (CD-ROMs and videocassettes); and research and technology reports. It also publishes *GATFWorld,* a bimonthly magazine providing articles on industry technologies, trends, and practices, and PIA's *Management Portfolio,* a bimonthly magazine that provides information on business management practices for printers; economic trends, benchmarks, and forecasts; legislative and regulatory affairs; human and industrial relations issues; sales, marketing, and customer service techniques; and management resources.

For more information about PIA/GATF special industry groups, sections, products, and services, visit www.gain.net.

GATFPress Selected Titles

- **The Basics of Print Production**
  by Mary Hardesty

- **Computer Color Graphics**
  by Harry Waldman

- **Computer-to-Plate Primer**
  by Richard M. Adams II and Frank J. Romano

- **The GATF Guide to Desktop Publishing**
  by Hal Hinderliter

- **The GATF Guide to Direct-Image Presses**
  by Richard M. Adams II and Frank J. Romano

- **The GATF Imaging Skills Training Curriculum**
  by Daniel G. Wilson, Hal Hinderliter, Joe Marin

- **Lithography Primer**
  by Daniel G. Wilson

- **Nine Steps to Effective and Efficient Press OKs**
  by Diane J. Biegert

- **On-Demand and Digital Printing Primer**
  by Howard M. Fenton

- **PrintScape: A Crash Course in Graphic Communications**
  by Daniel G. Wilson with Deanna M. Gentile and GATF Staff

- **Scanning Primer**
  by Richard M. Adams

- **Understanding Digital Imposition**
  by Hal Hinderliter

- **The Very Last Designer's Guide to Digital, On-Demand, and Variable Data Color Printing**
  by David Clark and Frank J. Romano

Colophon

The PDF Print Production Guide, Second Edition, was edited, designed, and printed at the Printing Industries of America/Graphic Arts Technical Foundation, headquartered in Sewickley, Pennsylvania. The text was created by the authors using Microsoft Word, then edited at GATF and imported into QuarkXPress 4.1 on an Apple Power Macintosh G4. Images were collected as screen captures from various software programs or were created using Adobe Illustrator 10. The primary fonts used for the interior of the book were Garamond Light Condensed, Helvetica Condensed, and Trebuchet. Pages for author approval were proofed on a Xerox Regal color copier with Splash RIP.

Upon completion of the editorial/page layout process, the illustrations were transmitted to GATF's Robert Howard Center for Imaging Excellence, where all images were adjusted for the printing parameters of GATF's in-house printing department and proofed.

The preflighted pages were printed to Agfa's Apogee production system. Agfa's Sherpa 43 was used to produce the digital imposed proofs for customer approval. Creo Preps was used to impose the pages, and then the book was output to a Creo Trendsetter 800 Quantum platesetter. The interior of the book was printed on GATF's 26×40-in., four-color Heidelberg Speedmaster Model 102-4P sheetfed perfecting press, and the cover was printed two-up on GATF's 20×28-in., six-color Komori Lithrone 28 sheetfed press with tower coater. Finally the book was sent to a trade bindery for coil binding.